D0215722

Encyclopedia of
Guerrilla Warfare

Encyclopedia of
Guerrilla Warfare

Ian F. W. Beckett

ABC-CLIO

Santa Barbara, California
Denver, Colorado
Oxford, England

Library of Congress Cataloging-in-Publication Data
Beckett, I. F. W. (Ian Frederick William)
    Encyclopedia of guerrilla warfare / Ian F. W. Beckett.
        p.   cm.
    Includes bibliographical references and index.
    Summary: An encyclopedia of articles examining guerrilla warfare
throughout the world, focusing on military tactics utilized by
minority groups within a state or indigenous population to oppose
the ruling government or foreign occupying forces.
    1. Guerrilla warfare—Encyclopedias.   [1. Guerrilla warfare—
Encyclopedias.]   I. Title.
U240.B43   1999
355.4'25—dc21   98-55119
                                                                                  CIP
                                                                                  AC

        ISBN 0-87436-929-0 (cloth)
        ISBN 157607-189-8 (pbk.)

05   04   03   02   01   00   10   9   8   7   6   5   4   3   2

ABC-CLIO, Inc.
130 Cremona Drive, P.O. Box 1911
Santa Barbara, California 93116-1911

This book is printed on acid-free paper ∞.

Manufactured in the United States of America

Contents

Preface and Acknowledgments ix

Introduction xi

List of Acronyms xix

Encyclopedia of Guerrilla Warfare

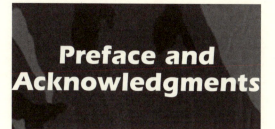

Preface and Acknowledgments

This volume is intended to be a guide to modern guerrilla and counterguerrilla warfare, covering a period beginning in the late eighteenth century and embracing the transition from guerrilla warfare to revolutionary guerrilla warfare or insurgency as well as that from counterguerrilla warfare to counterinsurgency. Here are working definitions for certain terms:

Guerrilla warfare is a set of military tactics utilized by a minority group within a state or an indigenous population in order to oppose the government or foreign occupying forces.

Partisan warfare is the use of irregular tactics by regular or organized irregular troops in support of conventional operations.

Revolutionary guerrilla warfare or *insurgency* is a campaign fought by a minority group within a state to gain political power through a combination of subversion, propaganda, and military action.

Counterguerrilla warfare and *counterinsurgency* are the actions of existing governments and their armed forces to combat guerrilla warfare and insurgency and to prevent its resurgence.

I particularly wish to thank Dr. Jaap de Moor of the University of Leiden, the Netherlands, for help with information on Klaas van der Maarten, and Dr. Tom Young of the Strategic Studies Institute of the U.S. Army War College in Carlisle, Pennsylvania, for assistance with locating information on several lesser-known Americans.

Introduction

Guerrilla warfare is almost as old as recorded time. The word *guerrilla,* literally meaning "little war," derives from activities during the Spanish national struggle against French occupying forces during the Peninsular War between 1808 and 1814. However, the first documented reference to what is recognizably guerrilla warfare occurs in the *Anastas,* a Hittite parchment dating from the fifteenth century B.C. The actual minutiae of guerrilla tactics portrayed in the writings of a leading twentieth-century theorist of revolutionary guerrilla warfare, the Chinese communist leader Mao Tse-tung, are not that different from those discussed in an ancient Chinese text dating to the fourth century B.C. and identified as the work of Sun Tzu of Ch'i. The Old Testament, which dates in part from the first century B.C., has many references to what are clear instances of guerrilla warfare, such as the revolt against the Syrians led by Judas Maccabeus between 166 and 158 B.C. in the Book of Daniel as well as the two books of the Maccabees in the *Apocrypha.* The works of classical historians such as Polybius, Frontinus, Plutarch, Appian, and Tacitus similarly catalogue a succession of guerrilla opponents encountered by the legions of imperial Rome. During the European Middle Ages, the twelfth century Welsh scholar Giraldius Cambrensis described Welsh guerrilla tactics against the English, and in the fourteenth century the constable of France, Bertrand du Guesculin, conducted a series of guerrilla raids

on the occupying English forces. Eastern Europe witnessed endemic guerrilla conflict, during the same period, between the Ottoman Turks and Balkan Christian groups like the Haiduks and the Klephs.

All these campaigns were characterized by common features that have remained constant over the centuries. Inevitably, guerrilla groups operated in difficult terrain such as mountains, deserts, and forests. Within these environments they possessed local knowledge that was often denied their opponents. Often, they enjoyed a degree of popular support from local inhabitants. They were generally more mobile than their opponents and would undertake hit-and-run raids that enabled them to damage yet also evade their opponent—and thereby prolong the struggle. On occasion, certainly, such conflict was merely brigandage, which might acquire the status of legend. However, guerrilla warfare was generally understood as the natural military recourse of indigenous groups in opposition to occupation or oppression, either where a conventional army had been defeated or had never existed. It was also clearly a strategy of the weak faced by a stronger military power.

By the eighteenth century, military theorists increasingly appreciated that even conventional armies might benefit by adopting guerrilla tactics in certain circumstances and by raising irregular units to support conventional operations. Thus irregular units, designed to operate on the flanks and in the rear of an opposing army, began to appear in several European armies. The Habsburgs of Austria, for example, recruited Magyar and Croat light infantry in the mid-eighteenth century, to which the Prussians responded with their own specially raised light troops. North America became a proving ground for English and French armies, who recruited Indians as well as colonists for woodland warfare. These irregular units, acting in concert with regular troops, were often referred to as "partisans," and this association of the partisan being a regular soldier detached in an irregular role from the main army has remained the classic characteristic of the partisan into the twentieth century.

It is significant that the first modern texts on irregular warfare appeared in the late eighteenth century as a direct result of the North American experiences of two Hessian officers serving with the British army, Johann von Ewald and Andreas Emmerich. They were followed by other theorists who derived their lessons from the French Revolutionary and Napoleonic Wars (1792–1815). In seeking to defend new liberties, the French transformed into a "nation in arms," raising large conscript armies motivated partly by patriotic nationalism as well as revolutionary zeal. However, among the defeated peoples, subjugation at the hands of the French and the experience of French ideology and reforming instincts frequently engendered a national response. Republican ideals provoked resistance even in France proper, as manifested in the popular revolt in the Vendée region in 1793.

Beyond their frontiers the French encountered what might be termed "people's wars," for example, in the Austrian Tyrol and especially in Spain. The notion of a people's war was repugnant to regimes that were restored to power following France's defeat in 1815, and military theorists in the nineteenth century preferred to contemplate only the continuation of more traditional partisan war. Indeed, even though

those on the political left such as Marx and Engels accorded some attention to the prospects of urban insurrection, even they believed there was little scope for people's war in industrialized Europe. They felt that any revolution would depend on the moral rather than the military collapse of capitalist authority at some appropriate moment. Mainstream military thought was little affected by nonconventional patterns of war. This was the case despite the fact that most European armies were increasingly fighting a succession of campaigns against a variety of irregular opponents as European colonial empires steadily expanded in Africa and Asia.

Indeed, prior to the twentieth century, few military theorists made any direct connection between guerrilla warfare and political change. Guerrilla warfare continued to be waged along traditional lines—even for much of the first half of the twentieth century. However, some groups and a handful of individuals increasingly began to harness guerrilla tactics in pursuing overtly political ends. It might be argued that among these groups the Internal Macedonian Revolutionary Organization (which fought the Ottoman Turks in Macedonia during the 1880s and 1890s) and the original Irish Republican Army (which fought during the Anglo-Irish War, 1919–1921) were true forerunners of modern revolutionary guerrillas. Three individuals can also be recognized as having a thoroughly modern understanding of the political and socioeconomic potentials of insurgency: the Ukrainian anarchist Nestor Makhno (who fought the Bolsheviks between 1919 and 1921); Thomas Edward Lawrence (the legendary Lawrence of Arabia, who played a major role in the Arab Revolt against Ottoman Turkey between 1916 and 1917); and Augusto Sandino (who waged a campaign against the Nicaraguan National Guard and its ally, the United States Marine Corps [USMC], in Nicaragua between 1927 and 1933).

During World War II, European resistance movements fighting the Germans and Southeast Asian resistance movements fighting the Japanese further fused military and political activities. This was especially so in Southeast Asia, where the Malayan Anti-People's Japanese Army in Malaya, the Hukbalahap in the Philippines, and the Vietminh in Indochina were dominated by communists. Even more influential was Mao Tse-tung, whose theories of rural revolutionary guerrilla warfare were honed against the nationalist Kuomintang (KMT) during the Chinese Civil War (1926–1949) as well as against the Japanese, who had intervened in the conflict effectively to pursue selfish ambitions to conquer China.

The fusion of the traditional guerrilla military tactic of hit-and-run with political objectives—and the addition of political, socioeconomic, and psychological measures, not least political mobilization of the population—to enhance military tactics marked the emergence of a new style of guerrilla warfare. This can be termed "revolutionary guerrilla warfare," but it is also commonly referred to as "insurgency." Mao's success in China led others to emulate his methods, not only in Southeast Asia but also in Africa and Latin America. Revolutionary guerrilla warfare or insurgency, however, should not be confused with the aforementioned people's war or, indeed, even with revolution, because it (i.e., insurgency) is invariably intended as a means by which a small minority can gain political power.

It should be emphasized that insurgency is not predestined to succeed, yet the combination of guerrilla action, propaganda, subversion, and political mobilization implicit in insurgency has been sufficiently successful so as to become the most prevalent form of conflict since 1945. In 1983, for example, a directory of guerrilla and terrorist organizations cataloged a staggering total of 569 groups that had emerged since the end of World War II. Clearly, therefore, it has been widely perceived that insurgency is an effective means either of achieving power and influence in a state or

of bringing a particular cause to the notice of the national or international community. Indeed, it has become something of a cliché that today's guerrilla is tomorrow's statesman, although someone's freedom fighter can just as equally be another's terrorist.

The variety in motivations of the guerrilla groups emerging since 1945 is enormous. Some were ideologically motivated, such as the communist Vietcong in South Vietnam between 1960 and 1965. Others were anticolonial nationalists, such as the Front de Libération Nationale (FLN) in Algeria between 1956 and 1962. Still others have managed to combine communist ideology, nationalism, and tribalism, as in the case of the three rival groups fighting the Portuguese in Angola between 1961 and 1974: Frente Nacional de Libertação de Angola (FNLA); Movimento Popular de Libertação de Angola (MPLA); and União Nacional para a Independência Total de Angola (UNITA). Some are purely tribal, like the Mau Mau in Kenya between 1952 and 1960. A group like Ethniki Organosis Kyprion Agoniston (EOKA) almost defies any categorization; it fought British authorities on Cyprus between 1955 and 1958 not for independence of the island but for enosis (union with Greece).

All these groups clearly fall within the classic tradition of rural guerrillas making use of difficult terrain to survive in the face of stronger military forces. However, in the late 1960s the focus switched from rural to urban guerrilla warfare in recognition of the changing nature of the world itself. By the mid-1960s many parts of the Third World were indeed rapidly becoming urbanized and industrialized. Accordingly, it made little sense to follow Maoist precepts for revolutionizing the rural peasantry when the majority of the world's population now lived in urban centers. The simple absence of population had doomed the so-called *foco* theory of rural revolution advocated by Che Guevara in Latin America. Guevara himself had been killed trying to implement his theories in Bolivia in 1967. Thus, revolutionary groups like the Montoneros in Argentina and the Tupamaros in Uruguay moved into the subcontinent's teeming cities, where the juxtaposition of high unemployment, high inflation, and widespread deprivation had created a situation that appeared ripe for political exploitation. New theorists like the Brazilian Carlos Marighela articulated how the media could be manipulated to serve the urban guerrilla through the use of "armed propaganda." But as the Cuban leader Fidel Castro had always insisted, the city proved the "graveyard" of the urban guerrilla. In any event, urban guerrilla warfare merely served to confuse the definition of insurgency by way of its similarity with terrorism.

Terror, of course, has always been a tactic used by guerrillas to intimidate opponents and to ensure active support (or at least acquiescence) among civilian populations. However, terrorism emerged in its own right as a separate phenomenon alongside urban guerrilla warfare in the late 1960s and early 1970s. Urban guerrilla groups like the Tupamaros clearly shared the ideology and methods of terrorist groups like the Brigate Rosse (Red Brigades) in Italy and Rote Armee Fraktion (Red Army Faction, popularly known as the Baarder-Meinhof Gang) in West Germany. Like guerrilla groups, terrorist groups could also have varied motivations. Thus, whereas the Red Brigades were ideologically motivated, the Basque group Euskadi Ta Askatasun (ETA) in Spain was clearly made of separatists. Equally, some terrorist groups were overtly sponsored by states like Iraq, Libya, Syria, and Iran as a means of pressuring Israel and Western governments supporting the continued existence of Israel. As such, terrorism was clearly a recourse of the weak, for the Israelis had comprehensively destroyed the conventional military challenge coming from its neighbor Arab states. And whereas most guerrilla groups intended to achieve political power, this was by no means true of most terrorist groups: Their premedi-

tated violence was perpetuated without constraint to influence national and international audiences and often for its own sake.

Despite the failure of urban insurgency during the 1960s and 1970s and the fact that most democratic governments found responses that were effective and acceptable to general populations, guerrilla and terrorist groups continue to flourish. Indeed, they have become increasingly sophisticated. Thus, contemporary guerrillas combine rural and urban actions but also project causes onto the international stage. In the mid-1950s Vietnamese theorists such as Vo Nguyen Giap and Truong Chinh were already adapting Maoist principles to a modern world shrinking with advances in technology and communications—and the trend has continued. In Mexico, for instance, the Zapatista Army for National Liberation not only hacked into the Mexican government's computer system but also established its own internet site on the world wide web. Potentially, continuing advances in electronics as well as development of chemical and bacteriological agents has made guerrillas and terrorists even more dangerous.

Governments habitually portray insurgents or terrorists as criminals, and the trend for these groups has been toward criminal activity. Urban guerrillas in particular often rob banks to acquire funds, and most contemporary groups are skilled in extortion and money-laundering. Indeed, there is a growing link between insurgent and terrorist groups on the one hand and organized crime on the other. This is perhaps most evident in Colombia, where Fuerzas Armadas Revolucionarias de Colombia (FARC) is closely linked to drug cartels.

In some respects, the end of the Cold War with the disintegration of the communist system in the Soviet Union between 1989 and 1991 was expected to decrease the likelihood of conflict in the modern world. Certainly, it diminished the prospect of major global conflict and removed the external stimulus to many so-called "proxy" conflicts waged by the superpowers through groups in third countries. And the Gulf War in 1991 suggested that in a "new world order" the international community acting in concert would promptly restore peace wherever it was threatened. The reality is that conflict has not ceased. Between 1990 and 1996 there were at least 98 conflicts inflicting 5.5 million deaths, but only seven of these were waged between recognized states. In other words, internal conflict and challenges to states from subnational groups have not ended, and guerrilla warfare remains a potent weapon for which armed forces must be prepared.

Traditionally, however, most soldiers have believed that they exist primarily to fight large scale conventional wars. Even in the past, this did not bear much relation to the practical experience of soldiering. The United States Army, for example, fought more that 1,000 engagements against "hostile" Native Americans in the Great Plains and the Southwest between 1866 and 1890. Yet the army continued to regard its only fixed mission—policing the always-moving American frontier—as a rather tiresome distraction from the study of "real war" in Europe. Similarly, the USMC, which had gained considerable experience in counter-guerrilla warfare during the 1920s and 1930s, had become so immersed in its amphibious role during World War II that its now celebrated *Small Wars Manual* (1935) had been completely forgotten by the time the Marines were asked to turn yet again to fighting insurgency in 1960 during the Vietnam War. Indeed, civilian advisers in the administration of Pres. John F. Kennedy (and even the chief executive himself) identified communist-inspired insurgency as the predominant threat to U.S. interests; the U.S. army in particular remained wedded to a doctrine suitable only for conventional warfare in Europe. One American general, remarking on the Vietnam War to a researcher from the Rand Corporation in 1970, said he would not permit the U.S.

army's doctrine and traditions to be destroyed "just to win this lousy war."

Similarly, modern British doctrine remains based on experiences from the World War II campaign in northwest Europe (1944–1945). Yet out of 94 separate operational commitments undertaken by the British army between 1945 and 1982, only 14 were not in some form of what might be termed "low intensity" conflict. Indeed, the British army's significant conventional experience since 1945 was 35 months during the Korean War (1950–1953), where no more than five infantry battalions were deployed at any one time; ten days at Suez in October 1956; 24 days during the land campaign in the Falkland Islands in 1982; and just 100 hours of land operations during the Gulf War in 1991.

To a large extent, institutional conservatism has guided the military view toward guerrilla warfare. However, the kind of conflict that has actually provided the staple operational fare of most modern armies is also regarded as distinctly unglamorous. Results cannot be obtained quickly in the kind of protracted, low-level conflict that has become the hallmark of guerrilla war. Success can rarely be measured in conventional military terms of decisive battles won. Military careers might not be enhanced even if success is demonstrated. Above all, what one American general described as "uncomfortable wars" confront soldiers with political and social pressures to a far greater extent than more conventional forms of conflict. Consequently, soldiers' distaste for guerrilla warfare has remained constant over centuries.

One commentator, remarking in 1763 during Pontiac's Uprising on the tasks facing the British commander in that North American conflict, said that the campaign would be tedious and far from glorious, for it would be "conducted by a spirit of murder rather than of brave and generous offence." Earlier, an American colonist had spoken, during the so-called King Philip's War (1675–1676) in New England, of the need for Europeans to adapt to local conditions and learn the "skulking way of war." Similarly, reflecting on the guerrilla war in Spain between 1808 and 1814, the Swiss military theorist Baron Henri Jomini wrote that he greatly preferred what he perceived as the more gentlemanly conventional war of the eighteenth century to "the frightful epoch when priests, women and children throughout Spain plotted the murder of isolated soldiers." The difficulty of separating insurgents from the general population is a particularly difficult one, and of course the strains of waging this kind of war can create morale problems like those in the U.S. army during Vietnam, and in some cases it will even lead to the politicization of armed forces. This was certainly the case with the Portuguese army, which overthrew its own government in 1964, and the French army, elements of which attempted a coup in Algiers in April 1961. In the latter case, greater politicization was implicit within the new counterinsurgency doctrine of *guerre révolutionnaire* (revolutionary war) adopted by the French army after its earlier defeat in Indochina.

These sentiments go far to explain why, for example, the British army has often been accused of historical amnesia regarding guerrilla war, of having to relearn the same lessons over and over. Yet in the British case—as for most other armies that confronted the new kind of insurgency after 1945—there was a residue of experience on which to draw. Lessons had been transmitted from one generation of soldiers to another, even if informally. Indeed, particular national traditions had developed in the nineteenth century that could be readily adapted to the twentieth century. The early-eighteenth-century Spanish Gen. Marquès de Santa Cruz and the mid–nineteenth-century French Gen. C. M. Roguet had commented on the techniques of counterguerrilla warfare in surprisingly modern terms.

However, modern counterguerrilla warfare and modern counterinsurgency theory is essentially a product of its late–nineteenth-century origin and rests on the experience gained in the expansion of European colonial empires. The British, for example, fought 35 major campaigns between 1872 and 1899, none in Europe. The enemies and difficulties faced in fighting were immensely varied. The lessons, however, were merely adequately analyzed and codified with the publication of Charles Callwell's *Small Wars: Their Principles and Practice* (1896). A similar study by Dutch Capt. Klaas van der Maarten, based on the campaigns in the Dutch East Indies, appeared the same year. Four years later, an article by Louis-Hubert-Gonzalve Lyautey provided a succinct summary of the pacification method known as *tache d'huile* (oil slick), pioneered by Joseph-Simon Galliéni in French Indochina and Madagascar; Lyautey himself would apply it in Morocco after 1912.

It is fair to say that these texts were essentially about colonial policing, and although guerrilla warfare itself was beginning to change during the interwar period, military authors like Sir Charles Gwynn (*Imperial Policing,* 1934) or those of the USMC's *Small Wars Manual* (1935) generally failed to notice the growing politicization of conflict. Too often (although this was not true of the civic action favored by the USMC), soldiers stressed only a military response to guerrilla warfare. Thus, modern technology such as airpower and gas had been quickly pressed into service against guerrillas. World War II naturally focused renewed attention on "real war." In fact, many armies found themselves in the business of actually promoting irregular warfare in German-occupied Europe and Japanese-occupied Southeast Asia. However, they tended to regard this as traditional partisan warfare, and there was certainly a direct revival of that tradition by the Soviet army on the Eastern Front. There was, therefore, a slowness to adapt to new challenges posed by politically inspired insurgency, especially communist-inspired insurgency, after 1945. Nonetheless, most armies had either a recognizable doctrine or at the very least established principles that could be readily adapted to changing circumstances. Campaigns like that of the British in Malaya between 1948 and 1960 became models of adaptation of older principles.

Generally speaking, armies that have succeeded against modern insurgency by developing counterinsurgency theory have been those that recognized the need for a political rather than a military response. (Indeed, four of Sir Robert Thompson's five principles of counterinsurgency are political: for government to have a clear political aim; to function within the law; to establish an overall plan whereby all political, socioeconomic, and military responses are coordinated; to give priority to the elimination of political subversion; and to secure base areas before conducting a military campaign.) Beyond recognizing the political nature of insurgency, however, there has been a second basic requirement of any successful counterinsurgency strategy, namely to coordinate the military and civil response. A third has been the need to ensure coordination of intelligence, and a fourth to separate insurgents from their base of popular support either by physical means or by a government campaign designed to win the allegiance—winning "hearts and minds" of the population, as Sir Gerald Templer, British high commissioner and director of operations in Malaya from 1952 to 1954, would put it. Physical separation was often pursued in reviving the late-nineteenth-century technique of resettling the population within protected communities. A fifth requirement for successful counterinsurgency has been the appropriate use of military force against insurgents separated from the population. And finally, long-term reform addressing the political and socioeconomic grievances that had led some to support the insurgents in the first place has been necessary in order to ensure that insurgency did not recur.

More often than not, the British were more successful than other armies in meeting the challenges they faced, but such was not always the case. Indeed, the urban environment posed more difficult problems for the British in campaigns, such as that on Cyprus between 1955 and 1959, Aden between 1963 and 1967, and Northern Ireland since 1969, precisely because of the greater proximity of the media. In fact, liberal democracies generally need to tread the thin line between imposing appropriate security measures and impinging on the democratic rights of citizens. As suggested above, urban guerrilla warfare and even terrorism have not generally proved a mortal danger to a healthy society since indiscriminate violence by urban guerrillas or terrorists tends to impel ordinary citizens toward authorities. This makes it difficult for democratic societies to eradicate the threat altogether, but violence might be reduced to what can be regarded as an acceptable level.

It remains, however, that insurgencies most likely to succeed are those that enjoy substantial external assistance, especially military assistance. This was the case with the colonial guerrillas during the American War of Independence (1775–1783), the Spanish guerrillas during the Peninsular War, the Vietminh against the French in Indochina (1946–1954), and the Vietcong against the United States in South Vietnam. As Mao Tse-tung well knew, guerrilla action alone was not likely to be enough, and at some point guerrillas needed to transform into a conventional army capable of meeting conventional enemies on the battlefield.

The continuing prevalence of insurgency has compelled contemporary armed forces to take insurgency far more seriously. However, there is still a tendency to locate insurgency within the broad spectrum of nonconventional duties required of armed forces. In the 1980s LIC (low-intensity conflict) was often used to denote a range of activities that included counterinsurgency and counterterrorism but that also might embrace peacekeeping and even humanitarian missions by armed forces. Indeed, there was much confusion of terminology during this time, in the British army and U.S. army the spectrum of nonconventional duties is now described as OOTW (operations other than war). Although that is a more sophisticated analysis, it is not necessarily more helpful or more likely to convince the majority of soldiers that insurgency is a more significant professional challenge than preparing for conventional war.

Acronyms

AAA	Alianza Anticommunista Argentine
ADSIDS	air-dropped sensors
AFPFL	Anti-Fascist People's Freedom League
AID	Agency for International Development
ALF	Arab Liberation Front
ALN	Acçâo Libertadora Nacional, or Action for National Liberation
ALN	Armée de Libération Nationale
ANAPO	National Popular Alliance
ANC	African National Congress
APRA	Alianza Popular Revolucionaria Americana
ARD	Accelerated Rural Development
ARDE	Democratic Revolutionary Alliance
ARVN	South Vietnamese army
BATT	British Army Training Team
BRIAM	British Advisory Mission to South Vietnam
BSAP	British South Africa Police
CAPs	Combined Action Platoons
CATs	Civil Action Teams
CGDK	Coalition Government of Democratic Kampuchea
CGSB	Coordinatora Guerrillera Simón Bolivár, or the Simon Bolivar Guerrilla Coordinating Board
CIA	Central Intelligence Agency
CIDG	Civilian Irregular Defense Group
Comops	combined operations headquarters
CORDS	Civil Operations and Rural Development Support
COREMO	Comite Révolucionário de Moçambique
COSVN	Central Committee
CPC	Chinese Communist Party
CPP	Communist Party of the Philippines
CPT	Thai Communist Party
CPY	Yugoslavian Communist Party
CSOC	Communist Suppression Operations Command
DA	Democratic Alliance

DGS	security police
DLF	Dhofar Liberation Front
DMZ	demilitarized zone
DPU	Dispositif de Protection Urbane
DSE	Democratic Army
DSE	Dimokratikos Stratos Ellados
DSO	Distinguished Service Order
DUP	Democratic Unionist Party
EAM	Ethnikon Apeleftherotikon Metopon
EDCOR	Economic Development Corps
EDES	National Democratic Greek League
EDSN	Ejército Defensor de la Soberania Nacional
EIC	East India Company
ELAS	Ellinikos Laikos Apeleftherotikon
ELF	Eritrean Liberation Front
ELINT	electronic intelligence
ELN	Ejército de Liberación Nacional, or the National Liberation Army
EOKA	Ethniki Organosis Kyprion Agoniston
EPL	Ejército Popular de Liberación, or the Popular Liberation Army
EPLF	Eritrean People's Liberation Front
EPR	Popular Revolutionary Army
EPRDF	Ethiopian People's Revolutionary Democracy Front
ERP	Ejército Revolucionario del Pueblo
ETA	Euskadi Ta Askatasun
EZLN	Zapatista Army for National Liberation
FALN	Fuerzas Armadas de Liberación Nacional
FAR	Fuerzas Armadas Rebeldes
FARC	Fuerzas Armadas Revolucionarias de Colombia, or the Revolutionary Armed Forces of Colombia
FBI	Federal Bureau of Investigation
FDN	Nicaraguan Democratic Forces
FIS	Front Islamique du Salut, or Islamic Salvation Front
FLING	Frente para a Libertação e Independência de Guine
FLN	Front de Libération Nationale
FLOSY	Front for the Liberation of Occupied South Yemen
FMLN	Frente Farabundo Martí de Liberación Nacional
FNLA	Frente Nacional de Libertação de Angola
FPL—FM	Fuerzas Populares de Liberación—Farabundo Martí
FRELIMO	Frente de Libertação de Moçambique
FRETILIN	Frente Revolucionária Timorense de Libertação e Independência, or Revolutionary Front for the Liberation and Independence of Timor
FUNCINPEC	National United Front for an Independent, Neutral, Peaceful, and Cooperative Cambodia
GEP	Grupos Especiais de Paraquedistas
GNA	Greek National Army

HMB	Hukbong Mapagpalaya ng Batan
ICEX	Intelligence Coordination and Exploitation Program
ICP	Indochinese Communist Party
INLA	Irish National Liberation Army
IPKF	Indian Peacekeeping Force
IRA	Irish Republican Army
IRB	Irish Republican Brotherhood
ISOC	Internal Security Operations Command
JUSMAG	Joint U.S. Military Advisory Group
JUSMAG	Joint U.S. Military Assistance Group
KDP	Kurdish Democratic Party
KKE	Kommounisitikon Komma Ellados
KMT	Nationalist Party, or Kuomintang
KNDO	Karen National Defence Organization
KNIL	Royal Dutch Indies Army or Koninklijk Nederlandsch-Indisch Leger
KPNLF	Khmer People's National Liberation Front
KPR	Kenya Police Reserve
KUFNS	Kampuchean National United Front for National Salvation
LEHI	Lehame Herut Israel (the Stern Gang)
LIC	low-intensity conflict
LLDB	Luc Luong Dac Biet
LRDG	Long Range Desert Group
LTTE	Liberation Tigers of Tamil Eelam
M-19	Movimiento 19 de Abril or 19 April Movement
MAAG	United States Military Assistance Advisory Group
MAC—V	Military Assistance Command—Vietnam
MC	Military Cross
MCP	Malayan Communist Party
MCS	Malayan Civil Service
MDRM	Mouvement Démocratique de la Rénovation Malgache
MFA	Armed Forces Movement
MIR	Movimiento de Izquierda Revolucionaria, or the Movement of the Revolutionary Left
MNLF	Moro National Liberation Front
MPAJA	Malayan People's Anti-Japanese Army
MPLA	Movimento Popular de Libertação de Angola
MR-13	Movimiento Revolucionario 13 de Noviembre, or 13 November Revolutionary Movement
MRLA	Malayan Races Liberation Army
MRTA	Movimiento Revolucionario Tupac Amarú
MTLD	Movement for the Triumph of Democratic Liberties
NAAFI	Navy, Army, and Air Force Institute
NICRA	Northern Ireland Civil Rights Association

NLF	National Liberation Front
NPA	New People's Army
NVA	North Vietnamese army
OAS	Organisation d'Armée Secrète
OAU	Organization of African Unity
OBE	Order of the British Empire
OKCHN	Pan-National Congress of the Chechen People
OKW	Oberkommando der Wehrmacht
OLAS	Organization for Latin American Solidarity
OOTW	operations other than war
PAC	Pan-Africanist Congress
PAIGC	Partido Africano da Independência de Guiné e Cabo Verde
PDRY	People's Democratic Republic of Yemen
PF	South Vietnamese Popular Forces
PFLO	Popular Front for the Liberation of Oman
PFLOAG	Popular Front for the Liberation of the Occupied Arabian Gulf
PFLP	Popular Front for the Liberation of Palestine
PIRA	Provisional IRA
PKK	Kurdistan Workers' Party
PKM	National Peasants' Union
PLA	People's Liberation Army
PLAF	People's Liberation Armed Forces
PLO	Palestine Liberation Organization
POLISARIO	Popular Front for the Liberation of Saguiet el Hamra and Rio de Oro
PRG	Provisional Revolutionary Government
PRP	People's Revolutionary Party
RAF	Royal Air Force
RENAMO	Resistançia Naçional Moçambicana
RPVs	remotely piloted vehicles
RUC	Royal Ulster Constabulary
SAF	Sultan's Armed Forces
SAP	South African Police
SAS	special administrative sections
SAS	Special Air Service
SDLP	Social Deocratic and Labour Party
SEPs	surrendered enemy personnel
SFG	Special Forces Group
SIGINT	signals intelligence
SKLP	South Korean Labor Party
SLA	Symbionese Liberation Army
SOE	Special Operations Executive
SOG	Studies and Observation Group
SS	Schutzstaffeln
SWAPO	South West Africa People's Organization

TNI   Indonesian Republican Army

UDA   Ulster Defence Association
UFF   Ulster Freedom Fighters
UNITA   União Nacional para a Independência Total de Angola
UNO   National Opposition Union, or Union Nacional de la Oposición
UNTAC   UN Transitional Authority in Cambodia
UPA   União das Populações de Angola
USAAF   United States Army Air Force
USAFFE   United States Armed Forces in the Far East
UUP   United Unionists Party
UVF   Ulster Volunteer Force

ZANLA   Zimbabwe National Liberation Army
ZANU   Zimbabwe African National Union
ZAPU   Zimbabwe African People's Union
ZIPRA   Zimbabwe People's Revolutionary Army

A

Abane, Ramdane (1920–1957)

Abane was a leading militant in the Front de Libération Nationale (FLN) who fought against the French in Algeria from 1954 until his murder by rival nationalists in 1957. Imprisoned by the French from 1950 to 1955 after his earlier involvement in the Sétif Uprising of 1945, Abane first became prominent when he went on a hunger strike in prison. After his release, Abane helped to build the FLN's organization in Algiers, but this organization was destroyed in the Battle of Algiers in 1957, and he fled to Morocco. A critic of increasing military rather than political influence within the FLN, Abane was strangled on the orders of the movement's coordinating committee on 26 December 1957.

See also: Algeria; Algiers, Battle of; Front de Libération Nationale (FLN)
Further Reading: Horne, Alistair, *A Savage War of Peace* (London, 1977).

Abd el-Kader (1808–1883)

Abd el-Kader opposed the French conquest of Algeria between 1832 and 1847. The emir (ruler) of Mascara, Abd el-Kader proved a skillful guerrilla leader, outwitting a series of French generals who could not match the mobility of his 10,000 tribesmen. However, the reorganization of French forces by Thomas-Robert Bugeaud deprived el-Kader of access to supplies and drove his followers westward. El-Kader's *smala* (mobile headquarters) was overrun by the French in May 1843, and he fled into Morocco. Attempting to return, el-Kader was defeated decisively by Bugeaud at Isly on 14 August 1844. He continued to attempt raids into French territory but was eventually compelled to surrender on 22 December 1847. After a period of detention in France, Abd el-Kader spent his remaining years in Egypt.

See also: Algeria; Bugeaud, Marshal Thomas-Robert; French army; Morocco
Further Reading: Porch, Douglas, *The Conquest of the Sahara* (Oxford, 1986).

Abd el-Krim, Mohammed ben (c. 1882–1963)

Abd el-Krim led the Rif Rebellion in Spanish Morocco from 1921 to 1926. A well-educated *caid* (Islamic judge) of one of the Berber tribes inhabiting the Rif Mountains, el-Krim initially worked for the Spanish authorities. However, opposition to Spain's exploitation of the Rif's mineral resources led to his arrest in 1917. After his release, el-Krim feared that his equal criticism of French exploitation of Morocco would lead to extradition, and he fled to the mountains. El-Krim and his younger brother then raised the Riffs in rebellion in May 1921, destroying a Spanish army at Anual. By 1924 el-Krim had proclaimed a Rif republic, but his invasion of French territory failed between April and July 1925. Subsequent joint Franco-Spanish military action led to his surrender on 27 May 1926. Exiled to Réunion, el-Krim moved to Egypt in 1947 and died there.

See also: Anual, Battle of; Morocco; Spanish army
Further Reading: Wollman, David, *Rebels in the Rif*
(London, 1969).

Aden

Aden was and remains a major port on the southern coast of the Arabian Peninsula commanding the entrance to the Red Sea. Occupied by Britain in 1839 as a coaling station on the route to India, it became the focus for a nationalist insurgency against the British between 1963 and 1967. Aden became a British Crown Colony in 1937 and, in 1963, a part of the wider Federation of South Arabia formed from the many surrounding small emirates, sheikhdoms, and sultanates formerly known as the Aden Protectorate. Britain had promised eventual independence by 1968, but Adenis did not want their independence linked to the semifeudal states of the federation. Inspired by growing Arab nationalism in the Middle East, the Marxist-dominated National Liberation Front (NLF) emerged in June 1963, followed by the rival Front for the Liberation of Occupied South Yemen (FLOSY) in May 1965. An unsuccessful grenade attack was made on the British high commissioner on 10 December 1963; that event was followed by not only escalating violence in Aden but also attacks on British forces in early 1964 by tribesmen in the outlying Radfan District of the federation.

Grenade attacks and sniping were the methods most favored by the insurgents as British casualties rose from just two in 1964 to 44 in 1967. In all, 382 people were killed in terrorist incidents between 1964 and 1967, including 57 British servicemen. The most serious incident was in Aden's Crater District on 20 June 1967 when members of the locally raised South Arabian Police and Aden Armed Police mutinied, killing 23 British servicemen. After 15 days under nationalist control, the Crater was then reoccupied by the First Battalion, Argyll, and Sutherland Highlanders led by Lt. Col.

Colin Mitchell. The greatest difficulty for the British army was the desire of the British Labour government led by Harold Wilson to leave Aden. Wilson's 22 February 1966 announcement that the British would not retain Aden as a base after federal independence undermined the federal authorities, and the British presence was condemned by the United Nations as well as many of the government's own supporters in Parliament. And even though British losses were far fewer than in the Malayan Emergency (1948–1960) or Kenyan Emergency (1952–1960), increasing media coverage of the campaign gave British casualties greater significance. British forces withdrew on 28 November 1967, transferring power to the NLF, which had won a violent internal struggle for power with FLOSY. The resulting People's Democratic Republic of Yemen then supported the insurgency in the Dhofar Province of neighboring Oman in the 1970s.

See also: British army; Dhofar; Kenyan Emergency;
Malayan Emergency; National Liberation Front (NLF)
Further Reading: Harper, Stephen, *Last Sunset* (London,
1978); Ledger, David, *Shifting Sands: The British in South
Arabia* (London, 1983).

Adowa, Battle of (1896)

Adowa (or Adua) on 1 March 1896 resulted in the complete rout of an Italian army in Abyssinia (Ethiopia). It was one of the worst disasters ever suffered by European forces fighting against indigenous opponents. Italy had attempted to match the territorial expansion of other European powers into Africa by establishing a presence in Eritrea on the coast of the Red Sea in 1885. Subsequently, the Italians believed, wrongly, that Emperor Menelik II of Abyssinia had agreed to the extension of an Italian protectorate over his territory, and war broke out in January 1895. Gen. Oreste Baratieri, advancing into Abyssinia with 17,000 Italian troops, was beset with transport and supply problems in the mountainous terrain. He also greatly underestimated the strength of Menelik's army—more than 100,000 men, many with modern firearms. Separated into four columns, Baratieri's army was overwhelmed at Adowa, suffering more than 6,300 dead, including two column commanders; 1,500 wounded, including a third column commander; and 3,900 captured, including the fourth column commander. Abyssinian losses were also heavy, but the defeat, which brought down the Italian government, compelled the Italians to confine their presence in East Africa to Eritrea for another 40 years.

See also: Eritrea; Italian army
Further Reading: Gooch, John, *Army, State, and Society in Italy, 1870–1915* (London, 1989).

Afghanistan

Afghanistan is a mountainous country in southwest Asia bordering on Pakistan, Iran, China, and former Soviet Central Asia. Its geographical location between British India and tsarist Russia made it a focus for political activity by both empires in the nineteenth century. Britain could not allow a hostile power to control Afghanistan and so threaten the security of India across India's North-West Frontier (in modern Pakistan). As a result, the British and British Indian armies fought two Anglo-Afghan wars—in 1838–1842 and 1878–1881—in an attempt to secure British influence over Afghanistan; a third war occurred in 1919 when the Afghans sought greater freedom of political action. In each case, British forces invaded Afghanistan, occupying much of the country in 1838 and in 1878. However, the Afghans rose in revolt against British occupation of the capital, Kabul, in November 1841. Forced to make a disastrous retreat back to India, almost all of the 16,000-strong British army was killed or captured. Similarly, the first phase of the Second Anglo-Afghan War resulted in the British occupation of Kabul and Kandahar, but a small British mission left in Kabul was massacred in September 1879,

necessitating reoccupation. A British force from Kandahar was then defeated at Maiwand on 27 July 1880, and Kandahar was besieged. Sir Frederick (later Lord) Roberts undertook a famous march from Kabul to relieve Kandahar in August 1880, but the British forces withdrew from Afghanistan in April 1881. British operations in Afghanistan in 1919 were largely unsuccessful; the 1921 Treaty of Kabul effectively established Afghanistan's independence from British influence.

There had also been a serious frontier clash between the Russian army and Afghan forces at Panjdeh in March 1885, but direct intervention came only in December 1979. Soviet forces came to the assistance of a Marxist government that had come to power in Kabul through a military coup in April 1978. The hostility of the revolutionary government toward the Islamic religion led to increasing opposition, whereas the ruling People's Democratic Party itself was increasingly split into rival factions known as the Khalq (People's Party) and the Parcham (Flag Party). Soviet intervention on 24–27 December 1979 installed Babrak Karmal of the Parcham Party in power. However, the Soviet presence quickly led to the emergence of the mujahideen, who waged a guerrilla war against Soviet and government forces. The Soviet army found it no easier than the British to operate against Afghan guerrillas in the mountains, even when able to deploy modern airpower and helicopters against them. The mujahideen had a safe refuge in Pakistan and received modern weapons, including Stinger antiaircraft missiles from the United States. International opposition and the rising cost of the war, including an estimated 13,000 dead, led to Soviet withdrawal in February 1989 and the fall of Kabul to the mujahideen in April 1992. However, fighting between rival groups has continued, with an extremist Islamic faction known as Taleban (Religious Students Movement) taking Kabul in September 1996.

See also: Airpower; British army; Helicopters; Mujahideen; North-West Frontier; Roberts, Field Marshal Earl (Frederick Sleigh); Russian army; Soviet army
Further Reading: Heathcote, Tony, *The Afghan Wars, 1839–1919* (London, 1980); Isby, David, *War in a Distant Country, Afghanistan: Invasion and Resistance* (London, 1989).

African National Congress (ANC)

The ANC was the principal African nationalist organization opposing apartheid (racial segregation) in South Africa. In the Afrikaans language, *apartheid* means "apartness," and it was gradually extended after 1948 by the Nationalist Party, which represented the interests of the descendants of the white Afrikaner or Boer settlers who had originally come to southern Africa from the Netherlands in the seventeenth century. The ANC originated as the South African National Native Congress in 1912, formed to resist exclusion of Africans from owning land outside native reserves. As apartheid was extended in the 1950s, the ANC first used nonviolent methods such as civil disobedience. The more militant Pan-Africanist Congress (PAC) broke away from the ANC in 1959, and a PAC demonstration at Sharpeville on 21 March 1960 resulted in the deaths of 69 Africans and the outlawing of both organizations. The ANC then created a clandestine military wing, Umkhonto we Sizwe (Spear of the Nation), led by Nelson Mandela. Its first bomb attacks were carried out in December 1961. However, most ANC leaders including Mandela were arrested, and the group was compelled to operate from outside South Africa. Attempts at infiltration through Rhodesia failed in 1967–1968, and attacks were not resumed until after the independence of Mozambique in 1974. The Nkomati Agreement reached between South Africa and Mozambique in March 1984 ended these attacks, but international pressure—rather than ANC military effectiveness against the powerful South African army—led to Mandela's release from prison in February 1990. A new South Africa emerged under his presidency in May 1994.

See also: Mozambique; Rhodesia; South African army
Further Reading: Benson, M., *Nelson Mandela: The Man and the Movement* (New York, 1986).

Airpower

Airpower is the application of the capabilities of aircraft as fighter, bomber, reconnaissance, or transport planes to warfare. Although the struggle for command of the air (air superiority) is generally associated with conventional war, airpower is equally applicable to guerrilla warfare. Indeed, the very first use of aircraft in warfare occurred in a colonial campaign when Italian aircraft dropped improvised bombs on Turkish troops in Libya in October 1911 during the Italo-Turkish War (1911–1912).

After World War I, there was a greater recognition of the potential of aircraft in colonial warfare. Britain's Royal Air Force (RAF) employed what was called "air control" and "aerial policing" against rebellious tribesmen in the Iraq Revolt, the Sudan, Somaliland, and the North-West Frontier in the 1920s. It was thought that this was far cheaper than deploying large numbers of troops on the ground, especially in more remote areas. In fact, though, using aircraft was not as cheap as anticipated since it was often very costly to maintain airfields in inhospitable desert or mountain terrains, and it became apparent that troops were still needed on the ground to occupy territory and hunt down smaller rebel bands. There were also moral reservations about what critics regarded as "frightfulness" or even "baby-bombing." Nonetheless, aircraft were increasingly used. The United States Marine Corps, for example, used aircraft in the Caribbean in the 1920s, especially in the Dominican Republic and the campaign against Augusto Sandino in Nicaragua. The Soviet army used aircraft during the Basmachi Revolt (1918–1933), and Italian aircraft were again being used in Libya in the 1920s, this time against Senussi tribesmen. Above all, the Italian army used aircraft to drop mustard gas on their opponents during the invasion of Abyssinia (Ethiopia) in 1935–1936.

The same kind of offensive role for aircraft was common after World War II. In the Greek Civil War (1946–1949), for example, American-supplied dive-bombers were used by the Greek National Army (GNA) to spearhead the attack on the mountain strongholds of the communist Democratic Army (DSE) in August 1949. However, during Fidel Castro's campaign against the Cuban government between 1956 and 1959 the forests of the Sierra Maestra Mountains were so dense and damp that bombs and even napalm dropped by the government's aircraft had little effect on Castro's guerrillas. Similarly, British bombing of the Aberdare Forest during the Kenyan Emergency (1952–1960) was so ineffective that it was abandoned.

Indeed, airpower has often been more usefully applied in guerrilla warfare in the form of providing transport. In the Malayan Emergency (1948–1960), for example, the jungle forts established by the British Special Air Service (SAS) were supplied by air; the SAS also experimented with parachute drops of patrols into the jungle canopy. It was calculated that ten minutes by air saved ten hours on foot in the jungle. Helicopters, of course, have also been used extensively in guerrilla warfare since 1945 and likewise have often been better employed in transporting troops than in taking an offensive role.

The potential disadvantages of assuming that airpower would be effective against guerrillas were perhaps best illustrated by the war in Vietnam between 1965 and 1973. Between 1965 and 1968, for example, American aircraft dropped 643,000 tons of bombs on North Vietnam and 2.2 million tons on South Vietnam without achieving military victory. The United States assumed that bombing North Vietnam would force the communist leadership into negotiations. In fact, Pres. Lyndon B. Johnson called temporary halts to the bombings between 1965 and 1968 to encourage such negotiation. However, the effectiveness of the initial bombing campaign over North Vietnam ("Operation Rolling Thunder") between March 1965 and October 1968 was limited by the decision to avoid targeting the Red River dikes, Haiphong Harbor, and the center of Hanoi for political reasons. These included the risk that Soviet supply ships might be hit in Haiphong, thereby possibly escalating the war into a wider confrontation between the United States and the Soviet Union. Moreover, the bombing of the Ho Chi Minh Trail did not halt the flow of men and equipment into South Vietnam. In any case, the North Vietnamese and Vietcong forces in the south required few supplies because, as guerrillas, they were not engaged in continuous combat. The use of American airpower did halt the large scale conventional offensive by the North Vietnamese army (NVA) in March 1972. However, it was only when Pres. Richard Nixon renewed the bombing campaign against North Vietnam between May and October 1972 ("Operation Linebacker I") and in a 12-day onslaught in December 1972 ("Operation Linebacker II") without targeting restrictions that sufficient pressure was exerted on the Hanoi leadership to negotiate seriously. In all, 170,785 tons of bombs were dropped on North Vietnam during the Linebacker operations. This led to a cease-fire agreement in January 1973 and subsequent American withdrawal from South Vietnam.

See also: Basmachi Revolt; Castro, Fidel; Cuba; Greek Civil War; Helicopters; Ho Chi Minh Trail; Iraq Revolt; Italian army; Kenyan Emergency; Malayan Emergency; Nicaragua; North-West Frontier; Sandino, Augusto César; Senussi; Somaliland; Soviet army; Special Air Service (SAS); United States Marine Corps (USMC); Vietcong; Vietnam War
Further Reading: Clodfelter, Mark, *The Limits of Air Power: The American Bombing of North Vietnam* (New York, 1989); Omissi, David, *Air Power and Colonial Control* (London, 1990); Towle, Philip, *Pilots and Rebels* (London, 1989).

Akehurst, Gen. Sir John (1930–)

Akehurst led the Dhofar Brigade of the Sultan's Armed Forces (SAF) in the last phase of the Dhofar campaign in Oman from September 1974 to December 1975. Commissioned in the British army in 1949, Akehurst twice served on the instructing staff at the army's Staff College as well as at the Royal College of Defence Studies. When Akehurst was seconded to Oman to command Dhofar Brigade, he inherited a healthy military situation. Construction of a fortified line had cut off the guerrillas of the Popular Front for the Liberation of the Occupied Arabian Gulf (PFLOAG) from their support within the neighboring People's Democratic Republic of Yemen (PDRY). Akehurst concentrated on clearing operations east of this "Hornbeam" line and had a second "Damavand" line constructed farther west. A final offensive in October 1975 drove PFLOAG back into Yemen, and Akehurst was able to announce final victory on 4 December 1975. Subsequently, Akehurst commanded a British armored division in Germany. He was also commandant of the Staff College and then commander of U.K. Land Forces, retiring in 1987.

See also: British army; Dhofar; Popular Front for the Liberation of the Occupied Arabian Gulf (PFLOAG)
Further Reading: Akehurst, John, *We Won a War* (Salisbury, 1982).

Algeria

Algeria is the second largest state in Africa (after the Sudan) in geographic size, bordering on seven other countries as well as the Mediterranean. Seized by France in 1830, Algeria provided an arena for the development of the French army's counterinsurgency techniques. In particular, the French fought against Abd el-Kader between 1832 and 1847 and against the Front de Libération Nationale (FLN) between 1956 and 1962. The latter conflict led to Algeria's independence. Since 1992 there has been increasing internal violence in Algeria orchestrated by the fundamentalist Front Islamique du Salut (FIS) or Islamic Salvation Front movement.

The initial French invasion of Algeria in June 1830 led to the rapid occupation of Algiers, but consolidation of French control proved far more difficult. Rule over Algeria by the Turkish Ottoman empire since the sixteenth century had never been readily accepted by the Arab and Berber peoples of the interior. The French were even less acceptable. Consequently, it took until 1847 for the French to defeat the followers of Abd el-Kader, and that was accomplished only after a transformation of French tactics by Thomas-Robert Bugeaud, who was appointed governor-general and commander in chief in November 1840. Bugeaud substituted "flying" columns—small and highly mobile troops—for the large and cumbersome columns previously employed by his predecessors. This allowed him to match the mobility of the tribesmen and to launch *razzia* (punishment raids) aimed at destroying the crops and seizing the livestock of the insurgents. Bugeaud also established a network of French posts throughout the country as bases for flying columns and for political officers of the Bureau Arabe (Arab Bureau), who took over local administration.

In 1848 Algeria became a part of metropolitan France. In theory, Muslims could gain French citizenship, but only if they renounced their legal rights and obligations under Muslim law. The real power in Algeria lay with French settlers and their descendants, who were variously called *colons* (colonizers) or *pieds noirs* (black feet), the latter supposedly deriving from the French army's polished boots or from the sunburned feet of settlers. By 1954 there were about 1 million *colons* in Algeria who bitterly opposed any political concessions to the 8.4 million Muslims. Growing Muslim frustration with their lack of real political influence was vividly illustrated by the May 1945 Sétif Uprising, in which 103 Europeans were killed by insurgents and possibly as many as 5,000 Muslims by French retaliation. Many of the first leaders of the FLN, which emerged in July 1954, such as

Ben Bella, had served with French forces in World War II but were horrified at the scale of French reprisals. A new uprising planned by the FLN to secure independence began on 1 November 1954.

Initially, the FLN's bombing campaign was poorly coordinated, and its fortunes were revived only by the independence of Morocco in 1956, which gave the movement safe havens across an international frontier. A more militant leadership epitomized by Ramdane Abane also emerged. However, the defeat of the FLN in the so-called Battle of Algiers between January and September 1957 forced it to switch operations to the mountainous Berber tribal areas of the Aurès and Kabylia. In fact, the French army was successful not only in dominating Algiers but also clearing the Kabylia by the end of 1959. The French were equally successful in cutting off FLN infiltration into Algeria from Morocco and Tunisia through construction of the fortified barriers of the Pedron Line and the Morice Line respectively. However, French military successes came at the price of alienating Muslim and international opinions. The new French counterinsurgency doctrine of *guerre révolutionnaire*—based on the lessons of French defeat at the hands of the Vietminh (the Viet Nam Doc Lap Dong Minh Hoi or Vietnamese Independence League) in French Indochina—combined military and political action in an attempt to separate the insurgents from the support of the population. In theory, popular support would be won by a psychological and political campaign demonstrating the value of the French presence in Algeria. The insurgents would be ruthlessly eliminated by traditional military means not unlike those favored by Bugeaud, with helicopters giving the French additional mobility.

However, in practice French soldiers frequently resorted to coercion against the population, and the Battle of Algiers was effectively won by intelligence gained through the systematic torture of those de-

tained. In addition, some French soldiers in Algeria increasingly identified with the cause of the *colons*. The army was implicated in the overthrow of the French Fourth Republic in May 1958, which brought Charles de Gaulle to the presidency of a new Fifth Republic. Soldiers expected de Gaulle to retain French control of Algeria, and when he offered self-determination to Algerians in September 1959 some began to plot against him. This politicization of the army, including the French Foreign Legion, culminated in an attempted coup against de Gaulle led by Raoul Salan and three other French generals in Algiers in April 1961. The coup soon collapsed, but those who escaped formed the Organisation d'Armée Secrète (OAS) to assassinate de Gaulle.

De Gaulle began negotiations with the FLN in April 1961, and agreement was reached in March 1962, Algeria becoming independent on 3 July 1962. The war since 1954 had cost France 35,500 dead, with a further 3,663 Europeans and more than 30,000 Algerians killed by the FLN. The French estimated that the FLN had lost at least 158,000 dead; Algerians themselves claimed the war cost 300,000 people their lives. The exploitation of oil and natural gas deposits in the Sahara initially brought independent Algeria considerable prosperity, but falling oil prices resulted in increasing economic and social difficulties in the 1980s.

In December 1991 the first round of elections to the National People's Assembly resulted in the majority of seats contested being won by the FIS, which had been formed in 1989 in the belief that Algeria should become a fully Islamic republic ruled by strict adherence to Muslim law. However, the Algerian army then canceled the second round of elections in January 1992, resulting in a continuing terrorist campaign by the FIS against the authorities. There have been an estimated 75,000 deaths since 1992.

See also: Abane, Ramdane; Abd el-Kader; Algiers, Battle of; Bugeaud, Marshal Thomas-Robert; French army; French

Foreign Legion; French Indochina; Front de Libération Nationale (FLN); *Guerre révolutionnaire;* Helicopters; Intelligence; Morice Line; Morocco; Organisation d'Armée Secrète (OAS); Politicization of armed forces; Salan, Gen. Raoul; Vietminh

Further Reading: Clayton, Anthony, *The Wars of French Decolonisation* (London, 1994); Horne, Alistair, *A Savage War of Peace* (London, 1977); Talbott, John, *The War Without a Name* (New York, 1980).

Algiers, Battle of (1957)

The so-called Battle of Algiers (January–September 1957) was an intensive struggle for control of the city's Casbah District between the French army and its nationalist opponents, the Front de Libération Nationale (FLN), during the latter's campaign for an independent Algeria. The organization of the FLN, which first rose against the French in November 1954, was at its strongest within Algiers. Indeed, while the region around Algiers was one of the FLN's

wilayas (command zones), the city itself was considered an autonomous command within. Ramdane Abane was one of the FLN leaders over the Algiers region, but operational control in Algiers itself was in the hands of Saadi Yacef. Yacef largely conducted his urban terrorist campaign from within the Casbah. This rabbit warren of streets was home to more than 80,000 Muslims, among whom the activists could easily hide. Faced with escalating violence and a threatened general strike by the Muslim population, the French resident minister, Robert Lacoste, ordered the French Tenth Colonial Parachute Division, commanded by Jacques Massu, into Algiers on 7 January 1957. The Casbah was allocated to Marcel Bigeard's Third Colonial Parachute Regiment. The general strike was broken in just two days by the French, forcing businesses to open and strikers back to work and entic-

French paratroopers under General Jacques Massu search an Arab on the outskirts of Algiers, 23 January 1957. They are looking for terrorists responsible for the deaths of six French citizens just two days before. (UPI/Corbis-Bettmann)

ing children into schools by means such as handing out sweets. Total military control was imposed by constant patrolling, house-to-house searches, and checkpoints. Massu seized the police files and instituted large-scale arrests, which enabled the French to build up a detailed intelligence picture of the FLN's organization; a system of collective responsibility was also introduced by Roger Trinquier, making designated inhabitants report on suspicious behavior in their sectors (some were even responsible for individual buildings); identity cards and a careful census extended French control.

The struggle for Algiers became regarded as something of a laboratory for the new French counterinsurgency doctrine, *guerre révolutionnaire,* by leading exponents who became involved, such as Yves Godard and Trinquier. By September 1957 the FLN organization in Algiers had been broken up, as Yacef and another leading figure, Ben M'hidi, were captured. However, the brutality used by the French led to considerable international criticism. Torture was routinely used to obtain intelligence, and at least 3,000 of the 24,000 Muslim suspects arrested during the struggle in the city disappeared altogether.

See also: Abane, Ramdane; Algeria; Bigeard, Gen. Marcel; French army; Front de Libération Nationale (FLN); Godard, Col. Yves; *Guerre révolutionnaire;* Intelligence; Massu, Gen. Jacques; Trinquier, Col. Roger
Further Reading: Horne, Alistair, *A Savage War of Peace* (London, 1977).

American Civil War (1861–1865)

The war between Northern (Union) states and Southern (Confederate) states in America witnessed many examples of guerrilla warfare between April 1861 and April 1865. Some very successful guerrilla leaders emerged from the conflict, including John Singleton Mosby (the "Grey Ghost") and John Hunt Morgan; others such as William Clarke Quantrill and "Bloody Bill" Anderson also gained considerable notoriety.

Given the much greater resources of the Union, it might have been expected that the Confederacy would resort to guerrilla warfare as a means of defending the South. However, like its Union counterpart, the Confederate military leadership instinctively opposed employing the kind of irregular tactics American soldiers had faced in the war against Mexico (1846–1848) and in the earlier conflicts with Native Americans. The Confederacy's Partisan Ranger Act of April 1862, which authorized the raising of irregular units, was repealed in February 1864 primarily as a result of pressure from Robert E. Lee and other Confederate regular officers. To regulars on both sides guerrillas were simply equated with lack of military discipline, and they feared the kind of excesses that might occur. After the defeat of the Confederate armies in April 1865, some Confederates did advocate continuing the war as a guerrilla struggle, but Lee refused to contemplate such a course.

Nonetheless, guerrillas appeared in every theater of the war. In the eastern theater, Mosby's Partisan Rangers constantly harried the Union supply lines in Virginia, especially during the Union advance down the Shenandoah Valley in 1864. Beyond the Appalachian Mountains, raids by John Hunt Morgan and other Confederates forced the Union army to deploy large numbers of troops simply to guard railway lines. The kind of excesses that regular officers most feared occurred in the Transmississippi region, particularly in Kansas and Missouri. They were epitomized by Quantrill's raid on the town of Lawrence in Kansas in August 1863, which resulted in the burning of the town and the deaths of more than 150 residents. In part, greater violence stemmed from the prewar struggle between pro- and antislavery groups seeking the admission of Kansas to the Union as a slave or free state. Pro-Confederate groups led by Quantrill and Anderson were opposed by equally brutal pro-Union groups such as Charles Jennison's "Jayhawkers" and George Hoyt's "Red Legs."

In the eastern theater, the Union responded to the guerrilla threat in April 1863 with General Order No. 100—the Lieber Code—in an attempt to define how captured guerrillas should be treated. Likewise in July 1863 the Union's General Order No. 60, issued in the western theater, imposed collective responsibility for guerrilla activity on local communities in the vicinity of attacks. In the Transmississippi region, Union Army Order Nos. 10 and 11 of August 1863 allowed forcible removal of suspected guerrilla sympathizers from western Missouri. Such measures increased the degree of bitterness and sectional violence that continued in Missouri after the war. Significantly, postwar outlaws Jesse and Frank James and the Younger brothers all rode with Quantrill during the war.

See also: American Indian Wars; United States Army
Further Reading: Jones, V. C., *Grey Ghosts and Rebel Raiders* (New York, 1956); Fellman, Michael, *Inside War: The Guerrilla Conflict in Missouri During the American Civil War* (New York, 1989).

American Indian Wars

North America, from the beginning of European settlement in the sixteenth century till the western frontier of the United States was officially declared closed in 1890, experienced a series of conflicts between Europeans and native tribes. Ultimately, European technology and infectious diseases were to overcome Native American resistance, but the consolidation of European control was by no means easy. In the case of the United States Army, for example, Arthur St. Clair suffered one of the worst defeats in American military history on the Wabash River in November 1791. Equally, George Custer's "Last Stand" on the Little Big Horn in June 1876 remains an enduring image.

The introduction into the New World of European weapons (including firearms), the horse, and diseases such as smallpox and measles (to which the native population had no immunity) enabled small numbers of Spaniards to conquer the Aztecs of Mexico between 1518 and 1521 and the Incas of Peru between 1531 and 1535. However, Spanish expansion northward proved more difficult, the Pueblos all but wiping out the Spanish presence in New Mexico in 1680 before final subjugation. On the Atlantic Coast, early English settlements at Jamestown (1607) in Virginia and Plymouth (1620) in Massachusetts survived initially only through the help of local tribes. However, cultural differences soon resulted in conflicts in which the Europeans were able to exploit intertribal rivalries. Three successive wars with the Powhatans cleared Virginia's peninsula of natives by 1646; the Pequot War (1637–1638) and King Philip's War (1675–1676) broke native resistance in New England, although at great cost to European settlers. Indeed, Native Americans increasingly acquired firearms and were far more skilled in forest warfare than were Europeans.

After 1676 tribes were largely drawn into the wider conflict between the English and the French for control of the Eastern Seaboard, the French having first settled at Quebec in Canada in 1608. Tribal groups fought for both the English and the French during the European conflicts known in North America as King William's War (1689–1697), Queen Anne's War (1701–1713), King George's War (1740–1748), and the Seven Years War (1756–1763). During the preliminaries of the latter war French and native forces inflicted a crippling defeat on English regulars and Virginia militia led by Edward Braddock on the Monongahela River in May 1755. In the event, the English took Quebec in 1759 and France ceded Canada, but the English then faced a serious native uprising (1763–1765) led by Pontiac of the Ottawas.

Other tribes remained loyal to the English, thus during the American War of Independence (1775–1783) Cherokees attacked American settlements in Kentucky, Iroquois raided into New York, and Shawnees and Delawares raided into Pennsylvania. American forces under John Sullivan retaliated by invading the Mohawk Valley, and George Rogers Clark pacified the Ohio Valley.

With American leaders still wary of English interference along the Ohio, Arthur St. Clair was ordered to punish the Miamis in 1790. The loss of almost half his 1,400-strong army on the Wabash then led to another expedition under Anthony Wayne that defeated the tribes at Fallen Timbers on 20 August 1794. Increasingly, American expansion across the Appalachians rather than English intrigue fueled Native American hostility to the United States. Nonetheless, it was during the Anglo-American War of 1812–1814 (commonly known as the War of 1812) that Shawnees, under Tecumseh, and Creeks were overcome by William Henry Harrison and Andrew Jackson respectively. Later, as U.S. president, Jackson oversaw the forcible removal of Cherokees, Choctaws, Creeks, Chickasaws, and Seminoles west across the Mississippi. The expulsions lasted throughout the 1830s.

However, resistance to these and other removals resulted in the Black Hawk War (1832) in Wisconsin and the Seminole Wars (1816–1818, 1835–1842, 1855–1858) in Florida. Thereafter, the frontier of white settlement moved inexorably westward, stimulated by such events as the California Gold Rush in 1848; conflicts inevitably occurred as tribes were encountered. The government's preferred solution was to confine tribes to reservations in areas not judged suitable for white exploitation.

The most enduring conflict was that against Lakota Sioux and their Cheyenne and Arapaho allies. In August 1854 a dispute with the Sioux over a cow stolen from a Mormon wagon train resulted in the so-called Grattan Massacre of 31 soldiers, to which the army responded by destroying a Brulé Sioux village in Nebraska in September 1855. In August 1862 Santee Sioux broke out of their reservation in Minnesota, killing large numbers of settlers. Then, in September 1864 the cycle of atrocity and counteratrocity continued, with the

Sand Creek Massacre of more than 130 Cheyenne by John Chivington. The Bozeman Trail in Wyoming came under attack by Sioux and Cheyenne, resulting in the Fetterman Massacre of 81 soldiers near Fort Phil Kearney on 21 December 1866, and a campaign by Custer and others against the Cheyenne in Kansas in 1867 was conspicuously unsuccessful. Consequently, in July 1868 a peace treaty was concluded at Fort Laramie, by which the army closed its forts on the Bozeman Trail. However, a winter campaign by Custer in Kansas, culminating in his massacring the Cheyenne village under Black Kettle on the Washita River in November 1868, effectively ended the Indian challenge on the southern Plains.

The process was assisted by the systematic destruction of the buffalo herds, which formed the very basis of the Native American way of life. The Fort Laramie Treaty had left the Indians in possession of the Black Hills of Dakota, but rumors of gold there were confirmed by an expedition led by Custer in 1874. When the Native Americans declined to surrender the hills, a major campaign was mounted. This resulted in the largest concentration of Native Americans ever assembled on the Plains, under the leadership of Sitting Bull and Crazy Horse. Custer's defeat and death followed at the Little Big Horn on 25 June 1876. Reinforcements were rushed west; Sitting Bull fled into Canada, and Crazy Horse surrendered in May 1877. Crazy Horse was killed for purportedly resisting arrest on his reservation in August 1877; Sitting Bull, who returned to the United States in 1881, was killed in December 1890 in a similar incident during the suppression of the Ghost Dance movement. The government's fear of the Ghost Dance also accounted for the massacre of 146 Indians—mostly women and children—in Big Foot's village at Wounded Knee on 29 December 1890.

There had been campaigns against other tribes. Navajos were subdued by Kit Carson in 1864 and forcibly removed to new reservations. Similarly, the attempt to remove previously peaceful Nez Percé from Oregon in 1877 led to their attempted flight under Chief Joseph toward Canada. In the southwest, Apaches proved formidable foes. George Crook defeated Western Apaches in Arizona in 1875, but Chiricahua Apaches produced talented guerrilla leaders such as Mangas Coloradas, Cochise, Victorio, and Geronimo, who did not finally surrender until September 1886. Less well known are the Modocs of northern California, whose leader, "Captain" Jack, was responsible for the death of the most senior American officer to be killed during the wars—Brig. Gen. E.R.S. Canby, murdered during negotiations with Jack in April 1873.

See also: American War of Independence; Baker, Maj. Eugene M.; Crook, Maj. Gen. George; Custer, Lt. Col. George Armstrong; Seminole Wars; United States Army
Further Reading: Steele, Ian, *Warpaths: Invasions of North America* (New York, 1994); Utley, Robert, *The Indian Frontier of the American West, 1846–1890* (Albuquerque, 1984); Utley, Robert, *Frontier Regulars* (2d ed., Bloomington, 1977).

American War of Independence (1775–1783)

It is widely recognized that the struggle of the American colonies for independence from Britain began at Lexington and Concord on 18 April 1775 in skirmishes between British regulars and American militia; that same militia also inflicted heavy losses on the British at Bunker Hill on 17 June 1775. However, the eventual American victory is usually interpreted as a result of George Washington's creation of the Continental army. The measure of the Continentals' success is adjudged to be the surrender of the British army to the Americans and their French allies at Yorktown on 18 October 1781. Yet in reality American militia and irregular units, acting as partisans in support of the Continentals, played a vitally important role in the American victory, not least by their operations in the South. In fact, a brutal guerrilla war was fought in the southern theater under talented leaders such as

Francis Marion and Thomas Sumter on the American side and Patrick Ferguson and Banastre Tarleton on the British.

The American militia was modeled on that of Britain, the colonists undertaking military training in their spare time in order to defend their communities in an emergency. The term *minutemen* derived from this practice, as these citizen-soldiers were said to be ready for service at a minute's notice. Militiamen, although often skilled marksmen, had no long-term service liability, hence Washington's preference for building a regular army. Indeed, during the American Indian Wars more permanent units had been raised among the colonists, such as the Ranger unit of Robert Rogers. The British army had even raised a regular rifle regiment, the Royal Americans, from colonists in 1755, and service in North America continued to inspire the development of light infantry tactics by Hessian officers in the British army such as Johann von Ewald and Andreas Emmerich.

However, British officers still distrusted militia, and the British were slow to recruit loyalists, often relegating loyalist units to garrison duty. Indeed, Ferguson, who was killed at King's Mountain in October 1780, and Tarleton were among the few British officers to understand the value of loyalist irregulars. As a result, through the intimidation of its very presence, the American militia was able to subdue many areas where loyalism was potentially strong. Militia was also effective in subsidiary theaters of operations. Ethan Allen's "Green Mountain Boys" from Vermont captured Fort Ticonderoga in May 1775, and George Rogers Clark cleared the Ohio Valley, capturing Vincennes in February 1779.

Yet American militia and irregulars were very effective in supporting the Continental army. During the campaign that led to the surrender of Gen. John Burgoyne's British force at Saratoga in October 1777, for example, American militia led by John Stark, who had once served with Rogers's Rangers, and Seth Warner constantly har-

American colonists and British soldiers exchange fire in this nineteenth-century woodcut showing the Battle of Lexington, the first skirmish in the American War of Independence. (Corbis-Bettmann)

ried Burgoyne's advance. Similarly, when the British switched the main focus of their operations to the Carolinas in 1780, the survival of Nathanael Greene's small army of American regulars owed much to the harassing raids of militia led by Daniel Morgan, Andrew Pickens, Francis Marion, and Thomas Sumter. North Carolina militia defeated Ferguson's South Carolina loyalists at King's Mountain, and Morgan defeated Tarleton at Cowpens in January 1781.

The struggle in the South increasingly took on the appearance of a particularly brutal civil war, and neither Greene nor his British counterpart, Charles Cornwallis, altogether understood that the outcome depended more on the result of the irregular conflict at the local level than on occasional conventional battles between opposing regulars. Greene's relationship with the irregulars and especially Sumter was often strained as a result. In fact, among leading American generals, only Charles Lee suggested an alternative guerrilla strategy to Washington's pursuit of conventional military success. Consequently, American regulars continued to ignore the contribution of the militia to their success and left themselves poorly prepared to meet the postwar challenge of warfare against Native Americans.

See also: American Indian Wars; British army; Emmerich, Col. Andreas; Ewald, Lt. Gen. Johann von; Marion, Brig. Gen. Francis; Partisans; Rogers, Maj. Robert; Sumter, Brig. Gen. Thomas; Tarleton, Gen. Sir Banastre; United States Army
Further Reading: Shy, John, *A People Numerous and Armed* (2d ed., Ann Arbor, 1990); Dederer, J. M., *Making Bricks Without Straw: Nathanael Greene's Southern Campaign and Mao Tse-tung's Mobile War* (Manhatten, 1983); Weigley, Russell, *The Partisan War* (Columbia, 1970).

Angola

Angola, on the southwestern coast of the Africa, was one of Portugal's first African colonies. And even though the Portuguese reached Angola in the late fifteenth century, they did not penetrate the interior until the late nineteenth century. There was constant warfare against the indigenous tribes, with no less than 15 major pacification campaigns in the Dembos region of northern Angola alone between 1631 and 1919.

The Portuguese claimed that it was possible for Africans to become fully assimilated Portuguese citizens. However, it was extremely difficult for Africans to achieve assimilated status, and Portuguese policy was economically and socially exploitive. Africans resented particularly the compulsory cultivation of cash crops, and in January 1961 cotton plantations in northern Angola came under attack. Further attacks in the capital, Luanda, were orchestrated by the Movimento Popular de Libertação de Angola (MPLA). By March 1961 another nationalist group, Frente Nacional de Libertação de Angola (FNLA), had begun to launch attacks into Angola from Zaire. In 1966 elements of FNLA broke away under Jonas Savimbi to form a third group, União Nacional para a Independência Total de Angola (UNITA). Each drew on a different tribal group for supporters.

FNLA claimed to have 10,000 men by 1972 but was only sporadically active in trying to infiltrate into the Dembos region from Zaire. MPLA claimed to control 50 percent of the entire country, but it is doubtful if more than a small proportion of its 3,000–5,000 men were ever permanently inside Angola. Initially, MPLA operated from the Congo People's Republic, but after 1964 its main bases were in Zambia. UNITA alone operated permanently inside Angola, but it had only about 300 men by 1970. Meanwhile, the Portuguese built up their own troop strength from 3,000 men in 1961 to 60,000 in the 1970s.

When helicopters became available in 1966, the Portuguese were able to mount large-scale operations. They derived enormous advantage from their monopoly of airpower generally, and the open nature of eastern Angola made it difficult for the guerrillas to hide. The Portuguese also introduced resettlement, moving about 1 million Angolans into *dendandas* (defended villages), where they could be prevented from supporting the guerrillas. As a result, the conflict became one of "mines versus helicopters." MPLA also attempted long-range bombardments with 122mm rockets of economic targets such as Gulf Oil's important installations in the Cabinda enclave without much success.

The Portuguese achieved a situation of stalemate in Angola by 1974. However, the political and economic costs of Portugal's wars in Africa were considerable and resulted in politicization within the Portuguese army. In April 1974 the army overthrew the Portuguese government and resolved to quit Africa. In Portuguese Guinea and Mozambique, power could be handed to a single nationalist group. This was not possible in Angola, and a civil war broke out between MPLA and an FNLA/UNITA alliance before the Portuguese left on 11 November 1975. South Africa and the United States both provided limited support for FNLA/UNITA, but the situation was transformed by the arrival of more than 50,000 Cuban troops flown to Angola in Soviet aircraft. With the United States wary of new commitments in the wake of its defeat in Vietnam, the South African army withdrew from southern Angola in March 1976.

MPLA won the civil war and FNLA dissolved, but UNITA continued to wage a guerrilla struggle against the MPLA government. In December 1988 an international agreement reached on the independence of Namibia also provided for the removal of Cuban troops from Angola by 1991. Negotiations between MPLA and UNITA resulted in a cease-fire and new elections in September 1992, which were won by MPLA. UNITA then resumed its guerrilla campaign, but pressure from the United States brought new negotiations in

October 1993. Progress toward peace continued under the supervision of the United Nations, and UNITA joined a Government of National Unity and Reconciliation in April 1997.

See also: Airpower; Frente Nacional de Libertação de Angola (FNLA); Guinea, Portuguese; Helicopters; Movimento Popular de Libertação de Angola (MPLA); Mozambique; Namibia; Neto, Dr. Agostinho Antonio; Politicization of armed forces; Portuguese army; Resettlement; Roberto, Holden; Savimbi, Jonas; South African army; União Nacional para a Independência Total de Angola (UNITA)
Further Reading: Newitt, Marlyn, *Portugal in Africa* (London, 1981).

Antonov Revolt (1920–1921)

Named after Aleksandr Antonov, a peasant or Green leader, this uprising was directed against the Bolsheviks in the Tambov Province of the Volga region at the close of the Russian Civil War (1917–1921). It was one of a number of Green uprisings resulting from the imposition of harsh economic measures by the Bolsheviks. In Tambov, food requisitioning was enforced in August 1920 when the area was suffering from a second successive harvest failure. The Bolshevik response to revolt was martial law, the burning of villages, hostage-taking, and mass deportation. Subsequently, in February 1921 the Bolsheviks made temporary political concessions, but once M. N. Tukhachevsky had reorganized the Soviet forces they went over to the offensive.

The combination of military and political activity resulted in the elimination of 37,000 insurgents between May and July 1921. Antonov himself was tracked down and killed in June 1922.

See also: Russian Civil War; Soviet army; Tukhachevsky, Marshal Mikhail Nikolaievich
Further Reading: Beckett, Ian (ed.), *The Roots of Counterinsurgency: Armies and Guerrilla Warfare, 1900–1945* (London, 1988).

Anual, Battle of (1921)

Anual on 21 July 1921 was a catastrophic defeat for the Spanish army fighting against Abd el-Krim in Spanish Morocco. Opposed to Spain's economic exploitation of the mineral resources of the Rif Mountains, el-Krim raised a revolt in May 1921. Gen. Fernandes Silvestre had 20,000 troops, but they were widely dispersed through the country and of poor quality. As a result, el-Krim was able to concentrate his own forces to overwhelm the Spanish outposts in a series of attacks on 21 July. Silvestre ordered a retreat from Anual, only to see his army panic and disintegrate in a rout. More than 12,000 Spanish were killed, including Silvestre. The political results of the disaster were to contribute to the collapse of the Spanish government in 1923. Much of Spanish Morocco fell under el-Krim's control, and it would take a combined Franco-Spanish offensive to break his power in 1926.

See also: Abd el-Krim, Mohammed ben; Spanish army
Further Reading: Wollman, David, *Rebels in the Rif* (London, 1969).

Arab Revolt, First (1916–1917)

The Arab Revolt against the Turkish Ottoman empire during World War I was encouraged by Britain. Turkey had joined the war on the side of Germany and Austria-Hungary—and against Britain, France, and Russia—in October 1914. The British persuaded Hussein, the Arab *sharif* (governor) of Mecca and his son, Faisal, to lead the Arab peoples of the Ottoman empire in revolt by promising the Arabs a future state of their own. In reality, the promises made to the Arabs were to conflict with promises the British also made to Zionists to create a Jewish homeland in Palestine— and with their own intentions to divide up the Middle East between themselves and the French!

Assisted by T. E. Lawrence (Lawrence of Arabia), the Arabs attacked Medina on 5 June 1916, opening a new front against the Turks in the Arabian Peninsula. The Arabs captured the Red Sea port of Aquaba in July 1917 and then assisted the British advance on Jerusalem in autumn 1917. The greatest significance of the revolt, however, was its role in formulating Lawrence's theories on guerrilla warfare. After the war, the British had difficulties in reconciling the contradictory promises made and faced the Iraq Revolt (1920) against their rule. As a result, the British installed Faisal as emir (ruler) of Iraq in 1921. Hussein had been made king of Arabia by the British in December 1916 but was overthrown by Ibn Saud in 1924.

See also: Iraq Revolt; Lawrence, Thomas Edward; Palestine
Further Reading: Wilson, Jeremy, *Lawrence of Arabia: The Authorised Biography* (London, 1989).

Arab Revolt, Second (1936–1939)

The Arab Revolt against British rule in Palestine between 1936 and 1939 was a legacy of the contradictory promises made to Arabs and Jews during World War I. The first Arab Revolt (1916–1917) had resulted from the Arabs' belief that participation in the war against Turkey would result in the creation of an Arab state. In the event, the British had accepted so-called mandates from the League of Nations to administer Palestine, Iraq, and Transjordan themselves. The British had also promised a Jewish homeland in Palestine during the war, and Jewish immigration thus increased steadily after 1918. If Britain halted immigration into Palestine, it would alienate the Jews, and if immigration continued it would further antagonize the Arabs.

Tension increased through the 1930s with anti-British riots by both Jews and Arabs. In April 1936 Arab attacks on Jewish settlers and a general strike called by the Arab Higher Committee heralded a more coordinated Arab response; a state of emergency was declared on 12 June 1936. The Arabs accepted the British offer of a royal commission chaired by Lord Peel to investigate their grievances. However, the partition of Palestine recommended by Peel in July 1937 was unacceptable to both Arabs and Jews and prompted a serious

resurgence of Arab unrest in the form of full-scale guerrilla warfare. British personnel came under attack, as did the oil pipeline from Iraq to the port of Haifa. Jewish settlers were protected by their own Hagana (Defense) units. A young British officer sympathetic to Zionism, Orde Wingate, helped train the Hagana, and in May 1938 he also enlisted Jews in so-called Special Night Squads to raid Arab guerrilla camps and protect the oil pipeline. By 1938 the British had also introduced a "village occupation" policy to try to isolate the Arab guerrillas from their popular support. Physical barriers were constructed around such villages, including "Tegart" blockhouses, named after their designer, Sir Charles Tegart.

By October 1938 the British had two divisions in Palestine and had brought the situation under control. This enabled a conference to be held in London in February 1939 at which the British promised eventual independence without partition and new restrictions on Jewish immigration. However, these promises were to be undermined by events in Palestine during and after World War II.

See also: Arab Revolt (1916–1917); British army; Palestine; Palmach; Wingate, Maj. Gen. Orde Charles
Further Reading: Bowden, Tom, *The Breakdown of Public Security* (London, 1977).

Argentina

The second largest country in South America (after Brazil), Argentina experienced considerable political instability in the 1970s as a result of the general growth of urban guerrilla warfare in Latin America. The failure of rural guerrilla campaigns such as that of Che Guevara in Bolivia in the late 1960s persuaded revolutionaries that urban terrorism promised more success. A combination of inflation, unemployment, and a relatively youthful age structure created conditions for dissatisfaction in the slums and shanties that often surrounded larger cities such as Buenos Aires.

In Argentina a number of groups emerged, including the Trotskyist Ejército Revolucionario del Pueblo (ERP) and the Perónist Montoneros, the latter fighting to restore the former president, Juan Perón, to power. Urban guerrilla groups hoped to provoke general state repression, which would induce a wider popular insurrection. However, as elsewhere in South America, the government reaction was so severe that it quickly destroyed the guerrillas and rendered them incapable of exploiting any popular unrest. Government-sponsored counterterror in Argentina's "dirty war" destroyed both ERP and Montoneros once the army took power in March 1976. The military surrendered power in 1984 following the disastrous attempt to seize the Falkland Islands from Britain two years earlier.

See also: Dirty war; Ejército Revolucionario del Pueblo (ERP); Guevara, Ernesto Che; Montoneros; Urban guerrilla warfare
Further Reading: Kohl, J., and J. Litt, *Urban Guerrilla Warfare in Latin America* (Cambridge, MA, 1974).

Arriaga, Gen. Kaulza Oliveira de (1915–)

Known to his troops as the "Pink Panther," Arriaga was the Portuguese commander in chief in Mozambique from 1970 to 1973, directing the war against the Frente de Libertação de Moçambique (FRELIMO). Commissioned into the Portuguese army as an engineer, Arriaga held a series of largely administrative appointments, including undersecretary and then secretary of state for aeronautics from 1955 to 1962 and chairman of the Atomic Energy Board in 1967. Promoted to full general in 1968, Arriaga was posted to Mozambique the following year to command the Portuguese ground forces.

In 1970 he became commander in chief and launched "Operation Gordian Knot" with 10,000 troops to clear FRELIMO from the northern provinces. Coupled with Arriaga's emphasis on resettlement of the African population into *aldeamentos* (strategic villages) and on winning over their hearts and minds through civic action projects, such as building hospitals and improving the quality of native cattle herds, the offensive seriously damaged the guerrilla organization. Unusually among Portuguese commanders, Arriaga also developed something of a personality cult and introduced political instruction for his own troops.

Another of his initiatives was to expand the number of African troops serving with the Portuguese. However, allegations of a Portuguese massacre of Africans at Wiriyamu surfaced in July 1973, and Arriaga was recalled to Portugal. An ultraconservative, Arriaga was outraged by the criticism of Portugal's colonial role by the former commander in chief in Portuguese Guinea, Antonio de Spinola. It was not surprising, therefore, that he was retired from the army when de Spinola became president of Portugal following a military coup in April 1974. When more radical elements ousted de Spinola in September 1974, Arriaga was arrested and remained in detention until June 1976.

See also: de Spinola, Marshal Antonio Sebastião Ribeiro; Frente de Libertação de Moçambique (FRELIMO); Guinea, Portuguese; Hearts and minds; Mozambique; Portuguese army; Resettlement
Further Reading: de Arriaga, Kaulza, *The Portuguese Answer* (London, 1973); Cann, John, *Counterinsurgency in Africa: The Portuguese Way of War, 1961–1974* (Westport, 1997).

Ashanti Wars

In the eighteenth and nineteenth centuries, the kingdom of Ashanti (or Asante) ruled over much of modern Ghana in West Africa. However, its power was to be broken in the course of three wars against the British in 1824, 1873–1874, and 1895–1896. The British had established a presence on the Gold Coast in the late seventeenth century. Initially, the British had been interested in acquiring slaves. Britain abolished the slave trade in 1807, but a trading settlement was retained at Cape Coast. Ashanti raids on the coastal tribes prompted a small

British expedition toward the Ashanti capital, Kumasi, in January 1824. However, this was overwhelmed by the Ashanti.

Commercial pressures persuaded the British to remain on the coast, and in 1872 they took over former Dutch trading settlements. The Ashanti claimed a right to the Dutch settlements and invaded the territory that acted as a buffer between their kingdom and the coast. In response, the Second Ashanti War (1873–1874) saw a British punitive expedition under Sir Garnet (later Lord) Wolseley, burning Kumasi in February 1874. Wolseley's careful preparations included issuing a pamphlet on fighting tactics, which amounted to the British army's first manual on jungle warfare. The Gold Coast became a British protectorate, and in 1890 the British sought to extend the protectorate over Ashanti in order to forestall French ambitions in the region. Consequently, in the Third Ashanti War (1895–1896), the British again took Kumasi, deposing the Ashanti king in January 1896. An unsuccessful Ashanti uprising in 1900 led to formal British annexation.

See also: British army; Colonial warfare; Wolseley, Field Marshal Viscount (Garnet Joseph)
Further Reading: Lloyd, Alan, *The Drums of Kumasi* (London, 1964).

B

Bach-Zelewski, Erich von dem (1899–1972)

Bach-Zelewski was an officer in the Nazi Schutzstaffeln (SS) who headed German antiguerrilla operations against Soviet partisans on the Eastern Front in World War II. He was also responsible for the suppression of the Warsaw Uprising in August 1944. Early German victories following the invasion of the Soviet Union in June 1941 had resulted in large numbers of Russian soldiers being cut off behind German lines. They became the nucleus of partisan groups that continued the fight against the German army.

In August 1942 rear area security behind the German front was entrusted to Himmler's SS, but the army remained responsible for security against partisans in operational areas. Now *obergruppenführer* (lieutenant general), Bach-Zelewski, a former soldier who had joined the Nazi Party in 1930, was the Higher SS and Police Leader for the rear areas of Army Group Center. In October 1942, he was appointed plenipotentiary for combating partisans for the whole of the Eastern Front, receiving the title of *chef der bandenkampfverbände* (chief of anti-bandit warfare) in 1943. However, operational command still remained in the hands of field commanders.

When the Polish Home Army rose against the Germans in Warsaw in August 1944, Bach-Zelewski was placed in command of 40,000 men to suppress the rising. In all, as many as 200,000 Poles may have

died, with the city being laid to waste and its remaining inhabitants forcibly evicted. Bach-Zelewski escaped punishment immediately after the war, appearing as a prosecution witness at the war crimes trials held in Nuremberg. However, subsequently, he was tried on various occasions; he died in prison while serving a life sentence imposed in 1962.

See also: German army; Partisans
Further Reading: von Luttichau, C. P., *Guerrilla and Counter-guerrilla Warfare in Russia During World War II* (Washington, DC, 1963).

Baker, Maj. Eugene M. (1836–1884)

An officer of the United States Army's Second Cavalry during the American Indian Wars, Baker was described as one of the "true savages" on the Great Plains for his attack on a Piegan Indian village on the Marias River in northern Montana in January 1870. Baker, who graduated from West Point in 1859, served with distinction during the American Civil War (1861–1865) and again on the Plains in 1866–1869. He was chosen to punish depredations by the Piegan, who were an offshoot of the Blackfeet tribe. Although warned by a scout that the village was that of Heavy Runner, a chief who enjoyed government protection, and not that of Mountain Chief, the real target, Baker still attacked on 23 January 1870. For the loss of one man, Baker's force killed 173 Native Americans, including 53 women and children, and captured another 140. The considerable controversy resulted in the permanent shelving of a planned transfer of control of native affairs from the Interior Department to the War Department. Although defended by his superiors, Baker did not receive further promotion, yet he continued to undertake frontier duty in Wyoming and Montana. He descended into drunkenness and died at Fort Walla Walla in the state of Washington.

See also: American Civil War; American Indian Wars; United States Army
Further Reading: Utley, Robert, *Frontier Regulars* (2d ed., Bloomington, 1977).

Basmachi Revolt (1918–1933)

Basmachi is derived from the Turkish word *basmak,* meaning "to plunder" or "to violate." It describes a widespread popular revolt against Bolshevik rule in the then Soviet Central Asia following the Russian Civil War. The center of the revolt was the Fergana Valley in Turkestan, which had a tradition of opposition to previous Russian imperial rule. Turkestan as a whole had experienced considerable economic dislocation through the collapse of the cotton market during World War I. Resentment against labor conscription had also contributed to a revolt against the imperial authorities in 1916–1917. However, communism as an ideology represented a threat both to the Islamic religion and to the traditional tribal hierarchy of the Turkic peoples such as the Uzbeks, Kazakhs, and Kirghiz.

Consequently, when the Bolsheviks dissolved the autonomous government at Kokand in Turkestan in January 1918, tribal and religious leaders raised a revolt. A former bandit from Kokand known as Irgash was recognized as the first Basmachi commander, but an Uzbek elder, Madamin Bek, proclaimed his own provisional government in the Fergana. This initial revolt was successfully suppressed by the Bolsheviks, but new centers of resistance then emerged at Bukhara and Khiva in 1920.

The emir (ruler) of Bukhara named another Uzbek, Ibrahim Bey, as Basmachi commander in chief.

At their peak in 1921, the Basmachi probably had 20,000 men, but, even though well mounted and highly mobile, they had little military training and were poorly armed. They were also divided by tribal rivalries. A brief unity was attained through the efforts of the former Turkish leader in World War I, Enver Pasha, who defected to the Basmachi after having been invited to Russia by Lenin in 1919. However, Enver was killed in August 1922, and no other Basmachi leader was as successful in uniting them. Nonetheless, they did pose a substantial threat to Bolshevik control of Turkestan and caused considerable damage by attacking cotton mills, communications, and the irrigation system. As a result, when appointed to command the Soviet army in Turkestan in 1919, M. V. Frunze initiated political concessions to divide the Basmachi from their popular support.

Concessions continued in the 1920s with the suspension of forced labor and land confiscation and the reopening of Islamic schools. However, the Bolsheviks had little intention of maintaining these concessions longer than necessary; most were reversed once the revolt had been crushed. Frunze also prepared the ground for a renewed military effort by reorganizing the Soviet forces. Large numbers of troops were eventually deployed, including newly raised Islamic units, and in the final phase of the revolt (between 1929 and 1931) S. M. Budenny used artillery and aircraft against Basmachi villages.

The Soviets also pursued the Basmachi into Afghanistan, forcing the Afghans themselves to take steps to prevent infiltration into Soviet territory. By 1929 most of the leading Basmachi had been either eliminated or driven into exile, and their numbers were reduced to no more than 1,000 or 2,000. Ibrahim Bek attempted to launch new raids from Afghanistan but was captured and executed in June 1931; the former ruler of Khiva, Dzhunaid Khan, was defeated in the Karakum Desert in October 1933.

Sporadic resistance continued through the 1930s, but the main revolt had ended. For the Soviet army, the experience of the revolt had been invaluable, and its lessons were absorbed by the principal Soviet theorist of counterinsurgency, M. N. Tukhachevsky.

See also: Afghanistan; Frunze, Mikhail Vasilyevich; Soviet army; Tukhachevsky, Marshal Mikhail Nikolaievich
Further Reading: Beckett, Ian (ed.), *The Roots of Counterinsurgency: Armies and Guerrilla Warfare, 1900–1945* (London, 1988).

Batista y Zaldivar, Fulgencio (1901–1973)

Batista was the dictator overthrown by Fidel Castro's guerrilla campaign on Cuba between 1956 and 1959. Batista joined the Cuban army in 1921 and was a leading member of the so-called Sergeant's Revolt, which overthrew the Cuban government in 1933. As the army's chief of staff after the revolt, Batista was implicated in the overthrow of two more governments before becoming president of Cuba himself between 1940 and 1944, when he stepped down. However, he again seized power in a bloodless coup in March 1952, an act that was widely welcomed.

In his first presidential term Batista had been committed to social reform, but his second term was overshadowed by his increasing corruption, and Bautista succeeded in alienating virtually all sections of Cuban society. Nevertheless, Castro's first attempt to overthrow Batista in 1953 was a failure. Castro was also fortunate to survive his landing back on Cuba in December 1956, only a few of his followers escaping with him into the hills of the Sierra Maestra. However, the unpopularity of Batista and the poor quality of his army enabled Castro's campaign to succeed. In fact, it is estimated that only about 200 government troops were killed between December 1956 and January 1959, suggesting their lack of

commitment to Batista. Batista lost the support of the United States in 1958, and he fled Havana for the Dominican Republic on 1 January 1959. Che Guevara based his *foco* theory of guerrilla warfare on Batista's defeat.

See also: Castro, Fidel; Cuba; *Foco;* Guevara, Ernesto Che
Further Reading: Thomas, Hugh, *The Cuban Revolution* (London, 1971).

Begin, Menachem (1913–1992)

Begin was the leader of the Jewish terrorist group known as Irgun Zvai Leumi that fought against the British authorities in Palestine between 1944 and 1947. He was prime minister of Israel between 1977 and 1983. A Polish Zionist, Begin fell into Soviet hands in 1939 and was deported to Siberia. However, he was then released to join a Soviet-sponsored Polish army in exile in 1941, but he escaped to Palestine in the following year.

Believing that the British had done nothing to save European Jews, he became the leader of the Irgun in 1943 and declared war on the British in February 1944. His aim was the establishment of an independent Jewish state that would embrace both Palestine and Transjordan. Calculating that the British would never contemplate outright suppression, Begin wished to raise the political and military costs of their continued presence in Palestine sufficiently to persuade the British to quit. Initially, the Irgun participated in a joint campaign with another terrorist group, the Stern Gang (or LEHI, for Lehame Herut Israel), and the forces of the Jewish Agency—later the nucleus of Israel's army—including Palmach (Shock Companies).

The Jewish Agency dissolved the partnership after the Irgun's bomb attack on the King David Hotel in Jerusalem in July 1946. Thereafter, the Irgun and LEHI continued the terrorist campaign until the British announced their surrender of the Palestine mandate in September 1947.

After Israel's independence in May 1948, Begin founded the Herut (Freedom) Party. He was a member of a national unity government from 1967 to 1970, then headed the Likud (Unity) coalition parties. He became Israeli prime minister in 1977 and jointly won the Nobel Peace Prize with Egypt's Anwar Sadat in 1978 for achieving peace talks between Israel and Egypt. He resigned as prime minister in 1983.

See also: British army; Irgun Zvai Leumi; Israeli army; Palestine; Palmach; Stern Gang
Further Reading: Begin, Menachem, *The Revolt* (London, 1951).

Bell, Gen. J. Franklin (1856–1919)

A brigadier general in the United States Army, Bell became a controversial figure as a result of his conduct of a pacification campaign against Filipino guerrillas in the Batangas Province, south of Manila on the island of Luzon, between November 1901 and May 1902. A veteran of the American Indian Wars after graduating from West Point in 1878, Bell won the Congressional Medal of Honor for gallantry during the first phase of American operations in the Philippines. Bell was then appointed provost marshal for Manila in 1900 and was promoted to brigadier general to take command of a district in northern Luzon in 1901. In November 1901 he was appointed to command the Third Separate Brigade in Batangas.

His methods were a classic example of resettlement, about 10,000 people being moved into "protective zones" in order to deny their support to the insurgents, who were fighting for Filipino independence from U.S. occupation. Outside the protective zones, Bell ordered crops, livestock, and buildings destroyed. Bell's methods and those of Brig. Gen. Jacob Smith on the island of Samar were widely criticized, and the situation in Batangas was subject to investigation by U.S. Senate hearings in February 1902. In particular, it was alleged that

Bell had depopulated the province. Indeed, Bell was compared to a Spanish general, Valeriano "Butcher" Weyler, who had suppressed the Cuban revolt against Spanish rule between 1896 and 1897.

It has emerged that the population decline in Batangas by some 90,000 people between 1896 and 1902 can be only partially attributed to Bell's resettlement policy. As one historian has commented, the key factors in the demographic disaster, which resulted from a malaria epidemic, were "mosquitoes, microparasites, and *carabos* [cattle]." Having ended resistance in Batangas by May 1902, Bell himself moved on to become head of the infantry and cavalry school at Fort Leavenworth, Kansas, in 1903. Ultimately, Bell was the United States Army's chief of staff from 1906 to 1910; he returned to the Philippines as commanding general from 1911 to 1914.

See also: American Indian Wars; Philippines; Resettlement; Smith, Brig. Gen. Jacob Hurd; United States Army; Weyler, Gen. Valeriano, Marqués de Tenerife
Further Reading: May, Glenn A., *Battle for Batangas* (New Haven, 1991).

Betancourt, Rómulo (1908–1981)

Betancourt was twice president of Venezuela and played a key role in the defeat of the insurgent group, Fuerzas Armadas de Liberación Nacional (FALN), between 1962 and 1965. Betancourt was exiled from Venezuela for his left-wing political views between 1928 and 1936 and again from 1939 to 1941. However, he returned in 1941 and founded the Acción Democrática (Democratic Action) Party. He was then provisional president of Venezuela from 1945 to 1948 before being exiled yet again after the government was overthrown by a military coup.

Returning from ten-year exile, Betancourt became president for a second time in December 1958. He became the first democratically elected Venezuelan president to complete a full term. Although radical, Betancourt was not radical enough for some elements within his own party that broke away in 1960 to form a revolutionary guerrilla group, Movimiento de Izquierda Revolucionaria (MIR) or the Movement of the Revolutionary Left. MIR adopted the *foco* method of insurgency favored by Che Guevara, relying on a small nucleus of determined revolutionaries to embarrass the security forces sufficiently to compel the government to introduce generally repressive measures. They hoped the people as a whole would rise against the government and sweep them to power.

As elsewhere, *foco* failed as a revolutionary method, and MIR was all but destroyed by 1962. Betancourt also survived two attempted military coups that same year. However, dissident military officers then joined forces with surviving MIR members to form FALN in January 1963. Betancourt was determined to preserve democracy and insisted that the security forces use the minimum force necessary to defeat the insurgents. However, he was also prepared to make a maximum display of potential force to intimidate FALN and to reassure ordinary people by such means as having troops man rooftops and dominate crossroads in the capital, Caracas. The extent of his success was illustrated in the presidential election in December 1963, in which 90 percent of those eligible voted in defiance of FALN's call for an electoral boycott. Handing the reins to his elected successor, Raúl Leoni, in 1964, Betancourt chose to go abroad again. He returned to Venezuela in 1972 but failed to win the presidential election in 1973.

See also: *Foco;* Fuerzas Armadas de Liberación Nacional (FALN); Guevara, Ernesto Che; Urban guerrilla warfare; Venezuela

Further Reading: Kohl, J., and J. Litt, *Urban Guerrilla Warfare in Latin America* (Cambridge, MA, 1974).

Bifurcation

Bifurcation means a division into two branches. In a military context it is applied to divisions that can occur within an army between regular career soldiers and conscripts. Such divisions have occurred frequently during counterinsurgency campaigning because of the particular pressures placed on members of the security forces. On the one hand, counterinsurgency duties may interfere with normal military training. An example is the experience of the British army's Sixth Airborne Division in Palestine between 1945 and 1947. The division was supposed to be Britain's immediate reserve for possible use against any Soviet aggression in Europe immediately after World War II, but its deployment in Palestine prevented it from undertaking any parachute training.

On the other hand, as the Soviet army discovered in Afghanistan after 1979, counterinsurgency campaigning can also prove a welcome opportunity to enable soldiers to encounter some form of combat in the absence of any conventional war experience. However, counterinsurgency may equally prove a considerable strain on soldiers, especially if the security forces are placed in a position where any retaliation to provocation will gift a success for their opponent's propaganda machine. The role of the French army's Tenth Colonial Parachute Division in the Battle of Algiers in 1957, for example, did little to enhance France's international reputation. An even greater danger, as suggested by the experiences of both the French army and the Portuguese army, is that soldiers become politicized, or that their morale collapses, as in the case of the United States Army in Vietnam (1965–1973). Bifurcation often lies at the root of such politicization and morale problems.

In the case of the French army, no conscripts served in French Indochina between 1945 and 1954, but French conscripts did serve in Algeria from 1955 to 1962. French regular soldiers believed that the politicians had failed them in Indochina and that the army must assume responsibility for political decisions if Algeria was to remain part of France. They assumed that the conscripts shared their ideals. In reality, however, the war in Algeria was increasingly unpopular, and elite regular units such as the French Foreign Legion did most of the fighting; conscripts were mostly confined to garrison duty. As a result, when regulars staged a military coup against Pres. Charles de Gaulle in Algiers in April 1961, de Gaulle successfully appealed to the conscripts not to be subverted by soldiers opposed to government policy. The coup collapsed within a few days.

The same kind of division occurred in the Portuguese army during its campaigns in Angola, Portuguese Guinea, and Mozambique between 1961 and 1974. Elite regular units such as paratroopers and commandos did the bulk of the fighting, but the majority of the army were conscripts, and they were mostly employed in what the Portuguese called "social promotion" (e.g., building schools and roads in an attempt to win the hearts and minds of the indigenous population). The army's expansion also led to the conscription of many university graduates for officer duty. Younger regular officers greatly resented the accelerated promotion that was offered to conscript officers in 1973 as a means of trying to persuade them to prolong their military careers. Career soldiers then formed the Armed Forces Movement (MFA) in September 1973, which was to overthrow the Portuguese government in April 1974 and bring an end to the Portuguese presence in Africa.

The case of the United States Army in Vietnam became the polar opposite of the French and Portuguese experiences. Conscripts—or "draftees," as they were known—did most of the fighting, and the regular career soldiers—"lifers"—enjoyed less exposure to combat. In 1969, for example, draftees represented 39 percent of the army personnel in Vietnam but suffered 62 percent of the casualties. This contributed to a range of other morale problems within the army. It was also alleged that draftees arrived in Vietnam under the influence of new social attitudes increasingly prevalent in the United States, such as the drug culture and hostility to the war. Even though American servicemen were influenced to some degree by domestic pressures, those pressures were not as significant as the army's internally generated policies. The latter attacked self-belief in the army's mission in Vietnam.

Nonetheless, the conclusion to be drawn from bifurcation in counterinsurgency campaigns since 1945 is clear: It is better to face the challenges of insurgency with a professional army than with a conscript army.

See also: Algeria; French army; French Foreign Legion; Hearts and minds; Politicization of armed forces; Portuguese army
Further Reading: Porch, Douglas, *The Portuguese Armed Forces and the Revolution* (London, 1977); Horne, Alistair, *A Savage War of Peace* (London, 1977).

Bigeard, Gen. Marcel (1916–)

Bigeard was the archetypal paratroop colonel in the French army's campaigns in French Indochina and Algeria in the 1950s. Indeed, he was the model for Colonel Raspeguy in two novels by Jean Lartéguy (*The Centurions* and *The Praetorians*) and one of the models for Colonel Mathieu in Gillo Pontecorvo's 1966 film *The Battle of Algiers.* He was famous for arriving to visit his units by parachute rather than by staff car, his hand to the salute as he landed. He also personally designed the distinctive "lizard" cap, the *casquette de Bigeard* worn by French paratroopers in Algeria.

As a sergeant in the French army, Bigeard was captured when France fell to the Germans in World War II but escaped and was commissioned into the Free French forces in 1943. Serving in Indochina after the war, Bigeard parachuted with his regiment into Dien Bien Phu at the start of the operation and again during its siege by the Vietminh. He was promoted to lieutenant colonel for leading a counterattack but then spent three months as a prisoner of the North Vietnamese after the fall of the base.

In 1955 he was posted to Algeria to take command of the Third Colonial Parachute

Regiment; he transformed it into one of the most professional units in the French army. Wounded in 1956, he missed the regiment's part in the Anglo-French operations at Suez but again commanded it during the Battle of Algiers between January and September 1957. Indeed, Bigeard's regiment was made responsible for the security of the notorious Casbah area of the city, where the insurgents of the Front de Libération Nationale (FLN) were at their strongest. Like many others in the French army, Bigeard's sympathies lay with the French Algerian settlers. Following the army's involvement in the settler political agitation known as Barricades Week in January 1960, he was transferred out of Algeria.

Consequently, Bigeard was not involved in the attempted military coup against the French government of Charles de Gaulle in Algiers in 1961, and he did not become drawn into the activities of the Organisation d'Armée Secrète (OAS), which subsequently tried to kill de Gaulle. Progressing to full general's rank, Bigeard was briefly made state secretary in the Ministry of Defence in 1975 by Pres. Giscard D'Estaing in an attempt to "remoralize" the French conscript army. Long retired, in 1996 he campaigned to save French parachute regiments from being disbanded in military cutbacks.

See also: Algeria; Algiers, Battle of; Dien Bien Phu, Battle of; French army; French Indochina; Front de Libération Nationale (FLN); Organisation d'Armée Secrète (OAS); Vietminh

Further Reading: Bigeard, Marcel, *Pour une parcelle de gloire* (Paris, 1975).

Boer War (1899–1902)

The Boer War in South Africa between Britain and the Afrikaner or Boer republics of the Transvaal and the Orange Free State proved a bitter and prolonged guerrilla conflict. The British reversed some of the early and unexpected defeats they suffered between October and December 1899 and forced the main Boer army to surrender at Paardeburg in Febru-

ary 1900. However, although the two Boer capitals of Bloemfontein and Pretoria fell to the British in March and June 1900 respectively, many Boers continued the war by resorting to guerrilla tactics. As a result, the war was concluded only in May 1902, after the British had deployed more than 450,000 men.

In many respects, the British should not have been caught by surprise by the Boer tactics since there had been an earlier Boer War. The Boers had "trekked" away from British rule of the Cape Colony and of Natal in the 1840s, establishing their own republics. Anxious to secure newly discovered diamond fields as well as to safeguard its own colonies, Britain annexed the bankrupt Transvaal in 1877. The Transvaal Boers rose in revolt in December 1880 and, largely through their skilled marksmanship, defeated the British army in a series of battles. As a result, the Transvaal regained its independence in March 1880. However, the discovery of gold in the Transvaal in 1886 renewed British interest and coincided with the general movement by the European colonial powers to extend their empires in the "scramble for Africa."

The British high commissioner in South Africa, Sir Alfred Milner, succeeded in his aim of drawing the Boer republics into a war with Britain in October 1899. However, the Boers quickly besieged British forces in Ladysmith, Mafeking, and Kimberley. Attempts to relieve Ladysmith and Kimberley resulted in the defeat of British forces at Colenso and Magersfontein in the so-called Black Week of December 1899. Under its new commander in chief, Lord Roberts, and his chief of staff, Lord Kitchener, and considerably reinforced, the British army then began its successful counteroffensive in February 1900.

Roberts handed over command to Kitchener in November 1900, convinced that the war was won. However, about 30,000 Boers remained in the field, and Kitchener now faced talented guerrilla leaders such as "Koos" De la Rey, Christi-

British soldiers of the Royal Munster Fusiliers shooting from behind sandbags in South Africa, ca. 1900, during the first part of the Boer War. Shortly after this and similar conflicts, the Boer army fell back on guerrilla tactics, beginning a whole new phase of the war. (Library of Congress/Corbis)

aan De Wet, Jan Smuts, and Louis Botha. The Boer commandos were highly mobile, and Kitchener was compelled to develop a sophisticated antiguerrilla strategy in response. The Boer ability to maneuver was restricted progressively by the building of lines of blockhouses and barbed-wire fences across the South African veld. Boer farms and livestock were systematically destroyed; Boer women and children were incarcerated in concentration camps to de-

prive the commandos of any possible support or supplies. The policy was similar to the resettlement or reconcentration employed by the Spanish army in its campaign on Cuba between 1896 and 1897 and by the United States Army in the Philippines between 1900 and 1902. As in the United States, resettlement was controversial, with one prominent Liberal, Henry Campbell-Bannerman, denouncing the "methods of barbarism." The British also raised new mounted units to make their own columns as mobile as those of their opponents.

The conflict became a bitter one of reprisal and counterreprisal, and when it ended in May 1902 Britain had suffered more than 22,000 dead, the majority from disease, and the Boers more than 7,000 war dead. Mismanagement in the concentration camps had resulted in between 18,000 and 28,000 civilian deaths. The peace terms were generous, and in 1907 the Transvaal and the Orange Free State regained autonomy within a British South Africa.

See also: British army; Colonial warfare; De La Rey, Gen. Jacobus Hercules; De Wet, Gen. Christiaan Rudolf; Kitchener, Field Marshal Earl (Horatio Herbert); Resettlement; Roberts, Field Marshal Earl (Frederick Sleigh); Spanish army; United States Army
Further Reading: Pakenham, Thomas, *The Boer War* (London, 1979); Warwick, Peter (ed.), *The South African War* (London, 1980); Spies, S. B., *Methods of Barbarism?* (Cape Town, 1977).

Briggs, Lt. Gen. Sir Harold Rawdon (1894–1952)

Between 1950 and 1951, Briggs was the director of operations during the Malayan Emergency (1948–1960) and the architect of the so-called Briggs Plan, which laid the foundation for eventual British success against the guerrillas of the Malayan Communist Party (MCP). Briggs was commissioned in the (British) Indian army in 1914 and, during World War I, saw service against the Germans on the Western Front in France as well as against the Turks in Mesopotamia and Palestine. He served in the Waziristan campaign on India's North-West Frontier in 1930 and during the latter stages of the Tharrawaddy Revolt in Burma (1930–1932). He commanded the Second Baluch Regiment from 1937 to 1940 and, with the outbreak of World War II, commanded the Seventh Indian Infantry Brigade in Eritrea and North Africa, winning the Distinguished Service Order (DSO). In 1942 he took command of the Fifth Indian Division in North Africa and also served with it in Iraq and Burma. He was general officer commanding in Burma

from 1946 to 1948 during its transition to independence from Britain.

In April 1950 Briggs arrived in Malaya as the first director of operations at a time when the campaign against the MCP was going badly. Briggs, of course, was familiar not only with the measures used to defeat the insurgents during the Burma Revolt but also the British army's hard-won lessons in jungle warfare against the Japanese in Burma during World War II. Briggs immediately identified the need to eliminate the MCP's political organization, known as Min Yuen, as well as to tackle the guerrillas of the party's military wing, the Malayan Races Liberation Army (MRLA). What became known as the Briggs Plan aimed to ensure that Malayan authorities had an effective overall plan for prosecuting the campaign. He also intended to win over the allegiance of that part of the Malayan population most susceptible to communist influence. These were the "squatters": ethnic Chinese communities illegally occupying government land on the fringes of the jungle.

In order to achieve coordination of government effort, Briggs constructed an elaborate committee structure with a federal war council at its head and subordinate state and district war executive committees peopled with representatives of the army, police, the civil agencies, and, later, the ethnic communities. Briggs was influenced by his experience of a less elaborate version of such a committee structure in the Burma Revolt and by advisers such as Robert Thompson. For the squatters, Briggs adopted a resettlement program, moving them into "new villages" that would eventually contain amenities such as medical facilities and schools as well as cultivation plots to which the squatters eventually got legal title.

Owners of rubber estates and tin mines were also required to regroup their labor forces in supervised camps. Briggs also extended the emergency regulations to allow detention, curfews, strict control of food passing in and out of the "new villages," identity cards, deportation, and the death penalty for some terrorist offenses. By these means, Min Yuen's organization was severely disrupted and the MRLA increasingly cut off from all means of popular support and forced back deeper into the jungle.

The MCP quickly identified the dangers posed by the Briggs Plan, and it resulted in the two most bitterly contested years by far of the Malayan Emergency. The "new villages" came under sustained attack by the MRLA, and there was a considerable increase in the level of communist terror and intimidation. However, there were already signs that the tide was turning in favor of the security forces when, in October 1951, the British high commissioner, Sir Henry Gurney, was killed in a communist ambush. In December 1951 Briggs was forced to retire from ill health, dying shortly afterward.

The almost simultaneous removal of both Gurney and Briggs was an undoubted blow, but the British government then took the decision to send out Gen. (later Field Marshal) Sir Gerald Templer as both high commissioner and director of operations. Templer himself made a considerable contribution to eventual success, but he was building upon the firm foundations of Briggs.

See also: British army; Burma; Eritrea; India; Malayan Emergency; North-West Frontier; Resettlement; Templer, Field Marshal Sir Gerald; Thompson, Sir Robert Grainger Ker

Further Reading: Short, Anthony, *The Communist Insurrection in Malaya, 1948–1960* (London, 1975); Stubbs, Richard, *Hearts and Minds in Guerrilla Warfare* (Singapore, 1989).

British army

The British army is one of the world's most experienced in colonial warfare and counterinsurgency. Its imperial role can be said to date back to the establishment of a British garrison at Tangier, Morocco, in 1661. Part of the wedding dowry of the Portuguese wife of King Charles II, Tangier remained a British possession until 1684.

Although the British army has learned through experience that political action is often more effective against anticolonial irregular forces, military action is sometimes necessary. Here a machine-gunner in the British army flies over Malaya in 1953, during the Malayan Emergency. (Hulton-Deutsch Collection/Corbis)

The "first" British empire had been established in North America, the Caribbean, and India by the mid-eighteenth century, bringing British forces into combat with a variety of indigenous irregular opponents and establishing a pattern of recruiting locally raised forces. This applied to not only the majority of the army of the East India Company (EIC) but also those units raised from the North American colonies, such as the Ranger unit of Robert Rogers. The British learned irregular and light infantry tactics in the early American Indian Wars and were confronted by such tactics again during the American War of Independence (1775–1783). Indeed, Banastre Tarleton proved a talented leader of irregulars during the latter war.

Although the British lost their North American colonies in 1783, a "second" British empire emerged in the nineteenth century with continued expansion in both Asia and Africa. Between 1837 and 1854, for example, the army fought 17 major colonial campaigns; between 1872 and 1899 there were another 35 major campaigns. These nineteenth-century campaigns included the three Ashanti Wars, seven of the nine Cape Frontier Wars, and the three Maori Wars. The variety of opponents was considerable, ranging from the highly organized native army of the Zulus in South Africa to the fanatical Dervishes of the Sudan. Varied, too, was the terrain, from the mountains of Afghanistan on India's North-West Frontier to the jungles of Burma.

The British empire reached its greatest extent after World War I. There were again frequent colonial campaigns to contend with: Ireland (1919–1921), Somaliland, the Moplah Rebellion (1921) in India, the Iraq Revolt (1920), and the Arab Revolt (1936–1939) in Palestine. In World War II, the British themselves helped to organize resistance against German occupation of Europe and Japanese occupation of Southeast Asia through the Special Operations Executive (SOE); special forces were also raised, such as the Special Air Service (SAS), for operations behind enemy lines.

In every year since 1945 except 1968, the British army has been on active service somewhere in the world. It faced the new style of revolutionary insurgency in a whole series of campaigns including Palestine (1945–1948), the Malayan Emergency (1948–1960), the Kenyan Emergency (1952–1960), Cyprus (1955–1959), the Indonesian/Malaysian Confrontation in Borneo (1962–1966), Aden (1963–1967), and the Dhofar Province of Oman (1970–1975). Since 1969 there has also been the continuing commitment to Northern Ireland.

In the course of this long record of conflict, the British army has produced talented leaders of irregular forces, such as Tarleton during the American War of Independence, T. E. Lawrence (of Arabia) during World War I, and Orde Wingate during World War II. Some of the army's commanders have also excelled in colonial or counterinsurgency campaigns, such as Lords Kitchener, Roberts, and Wolseley during the Victorian era. Since 1945, successful exponents of counterinsurgency have included Sir Gerald Templer and Sir Harold Briggs in Malaya, Sir George Erskine in Kenya, Sir John Harding in Cyprus, Sir Walter Walker in Borneo, and Sir John Akehurst in Dhofar.

Britain has also produced a number of leading theorists of counterinsurgency. Wolseley's fighting instructions for the Ashanti War in 1873 represent one of the army's first real manuals on colonial warfare. However, arguably one of the most original contributions made by any British soldier to the theory of warfare generally was Charles Callwell, whose *Small Wars: Their Principles and Practice* was published in 1896. A clear line of descent can be traced between Callwell's work and Sir Charles Gwynn's *Imperial Policing* (1934) and H. J. Simson's *British Rule and Rebellion* (1937). Similarly, Gwynn's influence is apparent in the work of post–World War II theorists such as Sir Robert Thompson and Sir Frank Kitson.

The British approach to counterinsurgency has usually stressed the rule of law and the primacy of civilian control over the military. Thus, the emphasis has been on police, with the military very much in a subordinate role, for the British have tended to understand that insurgency is a political problem and requires a political as well as a military response. This has been achieved through efforts to ensure civil-military coordination, including the coordination of intelligence. It has been the practice to attempt to separate insurgents from any popular support through physical means such as resettlement and through measures designed to win over hearts and minds.

The use of the minimum force necessary in a given situation has usually been preferred as much as a matter of choice as by necessity, as the small British regular army has often had few troops available to it. There have been failures, particularly in facing urban guerrilla warfare. Generally, however, the British army has been the most successful in waging colonial campaigns and counterinsurgency.

See also: Aden; Afghanistan; Akehurst, Gen. Sir John; American War of Independence; Arab revolt (1936–1939); Ashanti Wars; Briggs, Lt. Gen. Sir Harold Rawdon; Burma; Callwell, Maj. Gen. Sir Charles Edward; Cape Frontier Wars; Colonial warfare; Confrontation, Indonesian/Malaysian; Cyprus; Dhofar; Erskine, Gen. Sir George; Gwynn, Maj. Gen. Sir Charles William; Harding, Field Marshal Lord (Allen Francis John); Hearts and minds; India; Intelligence; Iraq Revolt; Ireland; Kenyan Emergency; Kitchener, Field Marshal Earl (Horatio Herbert); Kitson, Gen. Sir Frank Edward; Lawrence, Thomas Edward; Malayan Emergency; Maori Wars; Moplah Rebellion; Northern Ireland; North-West Frontier; Palestine; Police; Roberts, Field Marshal Earl (Frederick Sleigh); Rogers, Maj. Robert; Simson, Col. Hugh James; Somaliland; Special Air Service (SAS); Special Operations Executive (SOE); Tarleton, Gen. Sir Banastre; Templer, Field Marshal Sir Gerald; Thompson, Sir Robert Grainger Ker; Walker, Gen. Sir Walter Colyear; Wingate, Maj. Gen. Orde Charles; Wolseley, Field Marshal Viscount (Garnet Joseph)

Further Reading: Mockaitis, Thomas, *British Counterinsurgency, 1919–1960* (London, 1990); Mockaitis, Thomas, *British Counter-insurgency in the Post-imperial Era* (Manchester, 1995).

Bugeaud, Marshal Thomas-Robert (1784–1849)

As governor of French Algeria between 1840 and 1847, Bugeaud was the architect of the pacification strategy against insurgents applied by the French army throughout much of the nineteenth century. Bugeaud was a veteran of the Napoleonic Wars (1792–1815). He enlisted in the French army in 1804 and had risen to the rank of colonel by the time Napoleon was finally defeated in 1815. Bugeaud's wartime service included experience of the guerrilla conflict fought against the French during the Peninsular War (1808–1814) in Spain. He was excluded from the army of the restored French Bourbon monarchy but returned to service under the Orléanist monarchy in 1830. He served briefly in Algeria in 1836.

In November 1840 he was made governor-general of Algeria, where French control was seriously challenged by Abd el-Kader. Sensing that the French were making the same mistakes as during the Peninsular War, Bugeaud reorganized the French forces into highly mobile "flying" columns that combined infantry, cavalry, and artillery. These columns were small enough to pursue guerrillas without the need for long supply trains yet strong enough to defend themselves. A number of columns could converge in order to trap the guerrillas or undertake *razzia* (punishment raids) to destroy the crops and livestock supporting the guerrillas.

At the same time, Bugeaud progressively extended French administrative control through the officers of the Bureau Arabe (Arab Bureau). Through such means, Bugeaud had forced Abd el-Kader into Morocco by 1843. When el-Kader attempted to return, Bugeaud defeated him decisively at Isly on 14 August 1844. He was rewarded with the title of Marquis de la Piconnerie. Subsequently, Bugeaud commanded French troops in Paris during the revolution of 1848 and commanded the Army of the Alps under Emperor Napoleon III.

See also: Abd el-Kader; Algeria; French army; Pacification; Peninsular War

Further Reading: Sullivan, A. T., *Thomas-Robert Bugeaud* (Hamden, 1983).

Burma

Known to its military government since 1988 as Myanmar, Burma has experienced frequent guerrilla conflict since the British occupied it in the nineteenth century in order to safeguard the eastern frontier of British India.

There were three Anglo-Burmese Wars, in 1823–1826, 1852–1853, and 1885–1889, by which British occupation was progressively extended to the whole country. In 1823 the Burmese king pursued a territorial claim on East Bengal by invading British territory. The British retaliated by capturing Rangoon in 1824 and annexing Assam. In 1852 Burmese extortion of British merchants led to a British ultimatum and the annexation of lower Burma after Rangoon had been occupied once more. Finally, in response to further commercial disputes and to forestall possible French influence, the British occupied the remainder of the country in November 1885. However, they then faced guerrilla war in the jungle waged by so-called *dacoits* (bandits), to which they responded with summary executions. In the event, it took five years and 32,000 troops to pacify upper Burma.

In 1930–1932 the British faced a new challenge in the nationalist Tharrawaddy Revolt led by Saya San. The British response was a model of the kind of imperial policing advocated by the British theorist Sir Charles Gwynn. Good civil-military relations were established with good coordination of intelligence between police and army and systematic pacification of those areas affected by military and police units acting together. An early version of the coordinating committee structure applied during the Malayan Emergency (1948–1960) after World War II was utilized, and it is significant that the British army's first director of operations in Malaya in 1950, Sir Harold Briggs, had served in Burma during the revolt.

During World War II Burma was overrun by the Japanese (early 1942), and the British were ejected. The Japanese raised the Burma Independence Army in 1941 and gave nominal independence to Burma in August 1943. However, the British Special Operations Executive (SOE) helped organize resistance to the Japanese, especially among the Karen Hill peoples of Assam. The British reconquered Burma in 1945. Burma gained its independence from Britain in January 1948, but the hill tribes wished to remain outside the new Burmese union; the Karen Revolt began in early 1949. The new Burmese government also faced a number of other insurgencies, and order was not restored until 1955.

Burma remained unstable and experienced frequent periods of military rule after 1948, during which ethnic differences continued to create unrest. The situation was worsened by the "golden triangle" of heroin production on Burma's northeastern frontier and the resulting activities of warlords involved in the drug trade. Since 1988 Karen, Kachin, and Shan guerrillas have all reemerged in opposition to the current military government.

See also: Briggs, Lt. Gen. Sir Harold Rawdon; British army; Gwynn, Maj. Gen. Sir Charles William; India; Intelligence; Karen Revolt; Malayan Emergency; Police; Special Operations Executive (SOE); Wingate, Maj. Gen. Orde Charles

Further Reading: Smith, Martin, *Burma: Insurgency and the Politics of Ethnicity* (London, 1991); Stewart, A. T. Q., *The Pagoda War* (London, 1972); George, Bruce, *The Burma Wars, 1824–1886* (London, 1973).

Cabral, Amílcar (1921–1973)

Cabral was the founder and leader of the nationalist group Partido Africano da Independência de Guiné e Cabo Verde (PAIGC), which fought for independence from the Portuguese of the Cape Verde Islands off the western coast of Africa and the West African colony of Portuguese Guinea. Independence was achieved for the state of Guinea-Bissau in September 1974 and separately for the Cape Verde Islands in July 1975. However, Cabral himself did not live to see PAIGC's success, having been assassinated by one of his naval commanders, Inocêncio Kani, on 20 January 1973.

By birth Cabral was of Cape Verdean *mestico* (mixed race) descent and he was educated in Lisbon as an agronomist (rural economist). He worked for the colonial administration in Portuguese Guinea from 1952 to 1954 then moved to a sugar estate in Angola, where he helped found the nationalist group Movimento Popular de Libertação de Angola (MPLA). Invited to the Republic of Guinea's capital, Conakry, by Pres. Sekou Touré, Cabral then founded PAIGC in 1956. PAIGC drew many of its recruits from the Balante tribe, and PAIGC was to suffer from the uneasy relationship between the Balante and Cape Verdeans. Although the Portuguese may have been involved in Cabral's assassination, given these circumstances it was more likely due to internal divisions in PAIGC.

Nevertheless, PAIGC, which opened its campaign in January 1963, was by far the most effective of the guerrilla groups fighting the Portuguese in their African colonies, and Cabral was by far the most skillful nationalist leader. Portuguese Guinea consisted mostly of tidal inlets, rivers, and swamps, and Cabral adapted the theories of rural revolutionary guerrilla warfare associated with Mao Tse-tung, trying to establish "liberated zones" in the countryside. Indeed, Cabral claimed to control 80 percent of the country by 1971, although in reality PAIGC operated mostly from the neighboring Republic of Guinea to the south and east and, after 1967, from Senegal in the north.

By 1971 Cabral had about 6,000–7,000 men and was increasingly receiving heavy weapons from the Soviet bloc. Cabral was also able to attract international recognition for PAIGC from the Organization of African Unity (OAU). A notable success in July 1970 was Cabral's papal reception in the Vatican together with two other nationalists, Dr. Agostinho Neto of MPLA and Marcelino dos Santos of Mozambique's Frente de Libertação de Moçambique (FRELIMO). After 1968, however, the Portuguese counterinsurgency effort was much improved under the dynamic leadership of Gen. Antonio de Spinola, and the situation largely stabilized from the Portuguese point of view. Thus, while PAIGC proclaimed an "independent republic" in September 1973, it was the unexpected military coup against the Portuguese government in April 1974 and not any military success on the part of the nationalist guerrillas that precipitated Portuguese withdrawal.

After the assassination, leadership of PAIGC was assumed by Aristides Pereira, but the first president of Guinea-Bissau was Amílcar Cabral's brother, Luiz Cabral.

See also: de Spinola, Marshal Antonio Sebastião Ribeiro; Guinea, Portuguese; Mao Tse-tung; Movimento Popular de Libertação de Angola (MPLA); Neto, Dr. Agostinho Antonio; Partido Africano da Independência de Guiné e Cabo Verde (PAIGC); Portuguese army
Further Reading: Cabral, Amílcar, *Revolution in Guinea* (New York, 1969); Chabal, Patrick, *Amílcar Cabral: Revolutionary Leadership and People's War* (Cambridge, 1983); McCulloch, J., *In The Twilight of the Revolution* (London, 1983).

Callwell, Maj. Gen. Sir Charles Edward (1859–1928)

Callwell was the author of one of the most influential of all counterinsurgency manuals, *Small Wars: Their Principles and Practice,* published in 1896. Commissioned in the Royal Artillery in 1878, Callwell served in Afghanistan during the latter stages of the Second Afghan War (1878–1881) and in South Africa during the First Boer War (1880–1881). Callwell attended the British army Staff College from 1885 to 1886. An excellent linguist, he was then posted to the War Office's intelligence branch from 1887 to 1892.

During the Second Boer War (1899–1902), Callwell commanded a mobile column against Boer commandos. He returned to the War Office to work in the mobilization section but retired from the British army with the rank of colonel in 1909. Upon the outbreak of World War I in August 1914 Callwell was recalled to service with the temporary rank of major general to act as director of military operations in the War Office under Field Marshal Lord Kitchener. Kitchener's personality was dominating, and Callwell was a virtual spectator. This was certainly the case during the planning for the disastrous attempt by the British and French in 1915 to knock Ottoman Turkey out of the war. After the ini-

Charles Callwell, author of *Small Wars: Their Principles and Practice.* (From Ian Beckett [ed], *The Roots of Counter-insurgency: Armies and Guerrilla Warfare* [London, 1988], p. 14. Original from Callwell's autobiography.)

tial failure to force the passage of the Dardanelles and push allied ships through to Constantinople, British, Australian, and New Zealand troops were landed on the Gallipoli Peninsula. However, the military campaign also failed, and Callwell was replaced as director of operations in January 1916. Given the honorary rank of major general in 1916, he went on a British mission to Russia and then served for the remainder of the war in the ministry of munitions. He was knighted in 1917.

If not conspicuously successful in his military career, Callwell has a deserved reputation as an author. He wrote works of history, biography, and military and naval warfare theory as well as two volumes of autobiography, *Stray Recollections* (1923) and *Experiences of a Dug Out* (1920). His interest in colonial warfare began in the

1880s with contributions to the journal of the Royal Artillery Institution. Even though still a captain, in 1887 he won the prestigious essay competition of the Royal United Service Institution with "Lessons to Be Learned from the Campaigns in Which British Forces Have Been Employed Since the Year 1865." This became the nucleus of *Small Wars: Their Principles and Practice,* which eventually went to three editions (1896, 1899, and 1906).

Callwell's book represented an attempt at a genuine synthesis of best practice in colonial warfare. Callwell divided potential opponents into six different categories: European-trained armies such as the Sikhs, against whom the British had fought in India in the 1840s; semiorganized troops such as the Afghan army; disciplined yet primitive native armies such as the Zulus of South Africa; fanatical tribesmen such as the Dervishes of the Sudan; true guerrillas such as the Maoris of New Zealand and the *dacoits* (bandits) of Burma; and, lastly, and in a category of their own, the Boers, who differed from other guerrillas in being both white and mounted.

Callwell recognized that most colonial campaigns were as much waged against difficult terrain and climatic conditions as against actual native opponents. He cautioned against becoming involved in guerrilla warfare if at all possible, recognizing that "the crushing of a populace in arms, the stamping out of widespread disaffection by military methods, is harassing form of warfare even in a civilised country with a settled social system. In remote regions peopled by half civilised races or wholly savage tribes such campaigns are most difficult to bring to a satisfactory conclusion." Thus, Callwell recommended methods by which guerrillas could be brought to battle before being able to disperse.

Some of his suggested operational principles (such as the use of rallying squares against cavalry) would have been suicidal in contemporary European warfare, where opponents were armed with modern weapons. However, others (such as the importance of intelligence and the need to seize the initiative with boldness and vigor) were universally applicable. Callwell also identified common approaches that were emerging entirely independently among different European armies faced with similar problems, such as the resettlement of population practiced by the Spanish army on Cuba between 1895 and 1898, the British in South Africa between 1900 and 1902, and the United States Army in the Philippines between 1900 and 1902.

Each successive edition of *Small Wars* incorporated the latest lessons. For example, the 1899 edition took account of hill warfare for the first time as a result of Callwell's study of the Tirah campaign on India's North-West Frontier in 1897, and the 1906 edition included the lessons of the Second Boer War. Arguably, *Small Wars* is the single most original and distinctive contribution by any British soldier to the theory of war. Certainly, a clear connection can be traced between Callwell's basic principles and those of British theorists of counterinsurgency between the two world wars, such as Sir Charles Gwynn, as well as post-1945 theorists such as Sir Robert Thompson.

See also: Afghanistan; Boer War; British army; Burma; Colonial warfare; Gwynn, Maj. Gen. Sir Charles William; India; Intelligence; Kitchener, Field Marshal Earl (Horatio Herbert); Manuals; Maori Wars; North-West Frontier; Resettlement; Spanish army; Thompson, Sir Robert Grainger Ker; United States Army
Further Reading: Beckett, Ian (ed.), *The Roots of Counterinsurgency: Armies and Guerrilla Warfare, 1900–1945* (London, 1988).

Cambodia

Situated between Thailand on the west and Vietnam on the east, Cambodia has seen much conflict since its independence from French colonial control in 1953. Initially, events in Cambodia were somewhat in the shadow of the parallel struggle for Vietnam when a small scale communist uprising began in 1967 against the government of Prince Norodom Sihanouk. The communists were led by Pol Pot and known as the Khmer Rouge (Red Khmers), the Khmer being the people of Cambodia. Sihanouk was relatively successful in containing the communists and managed to maintain Cambodia's neutrality. This was despite Cambodian territory being used by Vietcong and North Vietnamese army (NVA) units infiltrating into South Vietnam along the Ho Chi Minh Trail.

However, Sihanouk was overthrown by his prime minister, Gen. Lon Nol, in March 1970, and he promptly formed a government-in-exile in Peking (Beijing), calling for support for the Khmer Rouge. Lon Nol, who changed the name of Cambodia to the Khmer republic, received assistance from the United States, and in April 1970 U.S. and South Vietnamese army (ARVN) forces were committed to Cambodia in an attempt to cut the Ho Chi Minh Trail. Covert American air operations over Cambodian territory had also increased since March 1969. The American and South Vietnamese intervention did relieve North Vietnamese pressure on Lon Nol's forces. However, it also had the effect of dramatically increasing support for the Khmer Rouge.

After the American withdrawal from South Vietnam in 1973, the Khmer Rouge continued to enjoy success, and on 8 April 1975 the Cambodian capital, Phnom Penh, fell to them. Sihanouk once more became head of state, although he did not return until December 1975 and was to be ousted by his Khmer Rouge partners in April 1976.

In April 1975 the Khmer Rouge announced it was unable to guarantee security or food supplies for Phnom Penh's 2.5 million inhabitants and ordered them to leave within eight days. Another 500,000 people were displaced from the countryside into "new villages." The number who died in the excesses of "Year Zero" is unknown but may well have exceeded 1.4 million. The terror in what was known, after December 1975, as Democratic Kam-

puchea also resulted in hundreds of thousands of refugees fleeing into Thailand and Vietnam. Many were ethnic Vietnamese, exacerbating the tensions that had arisen between the Khmer Rouge and the North Vietnamese communists. Clashes between North Vietnamese and Khmer Rouge forces had occurred as early as 1974, but the real crisis in relations between the two new states came when Khmer Rouge forces advanced into Vietnamese territory in both April and September 1977.

In retaliation, the Vietnamese briefly invaded Kampuchea in December 1977. In December 1978, the Vietnamese named a former Khmer Rouge officer, Heng Samrin, as head of the Kampuchean National United Front for National Salvation (KUFNS) and invaded Kampuchea once more. Phnom Penh fell to them on 7 January 1979, with Heng Samrin installed as head of state of a new People's Republic of Kampuchea. The Khmer Rouge, however, continued to wage guerrilla warfare against the Vietnamese-backed government from bases close to the Thai frontier.

The situation was further complicated by the emergence of other noncommunist forces opposed to Vietnamese control. A former Cambodian prime minister, Son Sann, founded the Khmer People's National Liberation Front (KPNLF), and Sihanouk reemerged as head of the National United Front for an Independent, Neutral, Peaceful, and Cooperative Cambodia (FUNCINPEC). In June 1983 these groups joined the Khmer Rouge in a somewhat fragile Coalition Government of Democratic Kampuchea (CGDK), with Sihanouk at its head. Vietnamese troops began to withdraw from Kampuchea in February 1989, and UN-sponsored peace negotiations resulted in all parties joining a Supreme National Council chaired by Sihanouk in September 1990.

A peace agreement was reached in October 1991, and a UN force (the UN Transitional Authority in Cambodia, or UNTAC) moved in to supervise demobilization of the rival factions. Led by Sihanouk's son, Prince Norodom Ranariddh, FUNCINPEC won new elections in May 1993; the prince became joint prime minister with Heng Samrin's successor, Hun Sen. In September 1993 Sihanouk was elected king of what was again called Cambodia. But the elections were boycotted by the Khmer Rouge, who resumed their guerrilla campaign. However, the Khmer Rouge became increasingly fragmented with large-scale defections to the government in August 1996.

This fragmentation culminated in June 1997, with Pol Pot executing his own defense minister but then being captured by his rivals and apparently sentenced to life imprisonment. At the same time, the governing coalition also fell apart, with Hun Sen staging a military coup against Ranariddh in July 1997. Under a Japanese-sponsored initiative, Ranariddh returned to Cambodia in April 1998, pending new elections to be held in July 1998. Pol Pot himself died, reportedly from a heart attack, in April 1998.

See also: Ho Chi Minh Trail; Khmer Rouge; Pol Pot; Thailand; Vietcong; Vietnam War
Further Reading: Ponchaud, Francois, *Cambodia Year Zero* (New York 1978); Jackson, K. D. (ed.), *Cambodia, 1975–1978: Rendezvous with Death* (Princeton, 1989).

Cape Frontier Wars (1779–1878)

Formerly known as the Kaffir Wars and, on occasions, as the Cape-Nguni Wars, the nine Cape Frontier Wars were conflicts fought between Europeans and the Xhosa tribe on the frontier of Cape Colony in South Africa. The first two wars (1779–1781, 1789–1793) were fought by the Dutch Afrikaner or Boer settlers; the remaining seven wars (1799–1803, 1812, 1818–1819, 1834–1835, 1846–1847, 1850–1853, and 1877–1878) were fought by the British army. The Dutch first settled the Cape of Good Hope in 1652, coming into conflict initially with the indigenous Bushmen and Hottentots.

The history of southern Africa has been characterized by great migrations of population, and the Boers came into conflict with the Xhosa, a Bantu or southern Nguni people, along the Great Fish River on the eastern border of Cape Colony in the late eighteenth century as Boers moved northward and Xhosa southward. Both groups sought more land for pasture. Britain seized the cape in 1795 when the Dutch were allies of the French during the French Revolutionary and Napoleonic Wars (1793–1815). The British returned the cape to the Dutch during the brief Peace of Amiens in 1803, but with the renewal of war they seized it again in 1806 and retained control thereafter.

For the British, the Great Fish River represented the boundary between settled European land and native land, but the pressure of population led to frequent Xhosa incursions across the river, hence the frequent renewals of conflict. The Xhosa proved skilled guerrillas in the bush covering the area, and each campaign was characterized by the desultory nature of the fighting. In response to the Xhosa threat, the British gradually extended the frontier of Cape Colony beyond the Great Fish to the Kei River. After the Sixth Cape Frontier War (1834–1835), Sir Harry Smith annexed what was known as British Kaffraria between the Great Fish and the Kei. This was soon abandoned but reannexed as a result of the Seventh Cape Frontier War (1846–1847) and incorporated into Cape Colony in 1866.

For all practical purposes, the Xhosa were destroyed as a military power by Sir George Cathcart in the Eighth Cape Frontier War (1850–1853). The final attempt of the Xhosa to resist the progressive loss of their remaining territory across the Kei in the Ninth Cape Frontier War (1877–1878) began as a result of an intertribal dispute within the Xhosa between the Mfengu clan, who had accepted British protection, and the Gcaleka clan of Chief Sarhili. The Gcalekas were quickly defeated, but the

Ngqika clan then rose in rebellion under Chief Sandile. They, too, were defeated. Sandile was killed and Sarhili surrendered after remaining at large for three years. Administration of the Transkei Territory was taken over by Cape Colony, which formally annexed it in 1885.

See also: British army; Colonial warfare
Further Reading: Smithers, A. J., *The Kaffir Wars, 1779–1877* (London, 1973); Milton, John, *The Edges of War: A History of Frontier Warfare, 1702–1878* (Cape Town, 1983).

Castro, Fidel (1926–)

Castro was the leader of the successful Cuban Revolution against the government of Fulgencio Batista between 1956 and 1959. His remarkable rural guerrilla campaign in the Sierra Maestra Mountains inspired the *foco* theory of guerrilla warfare associated with Che Guevara and Régis Debray. A former law student, Castro led an attack on the Cuban army's Moncada barracks in Santiago de Cuba, the island's second city, on 26 July 1953. Most of the insurgents, including Castro, were captured, and he was imprisoned until May 1955.

Fidel Castro and two guerrillas in the Sierra Maestra Mountains during the insurgency against the Batista regime, 1958. (Library of Congress/Corbis)

Moving to Mexico, Castro then founded the 26 July Movement. The organization planned an insurrection on Cuba in November 1956, the intention being that this would coincide with Castro landing back on the island with 81 followers (including Guevara). However, there were various delays, and by the time Castro and his men landed from the motor yacht *Granma* near Las Coloradas de Belic on 2 December 1956, the insurrection had already been crushed. On 5 December the Cuban army intercepted Castro's group, and less than two dozen escaped into the Sierra Maestras. However, Batista had so alienated Cuban society and his armed forces were so inefficient that Castro was able to survive.

Indeed, Castro never had more than 300 men and yet managed to evade 11,000 troops sent into the Sierra Maestras for one last offensive in May and June 1958. The failure of Batista's offensive enabled Castro to go over to the offensive himself, and he entered Havana in triumph on 8 January 1959.

Subsequently, Castro proved rather more radical than had been anticipated, and his relationship with the United States deteriorated rapidly. Indeed, the Kennedy administration supported the unsuccessful attempt by Cuban exiles to invade Cuba at the Bay of Pigs in April 1961. Castro proclaimed himself a communist and received the backing of the Soviet Union, leading to the confrontation known as the Cuban Missile Crisis in October 1962. Castro continued to support revolutionary movements throughout Central and Latin America in subsequent years; using Soviet transport aircraft, Cuban troops also intervened in the civil war in Angola in 1975 and in the war between Ethiopia and Somalia in 1978.

Castro is now one of the longest surviving communist leaders in the world.

See also: Angola; Batista y Zaldivar, Fulgencio; Cuba; Debray, Régis; *Foco;* Guevara, Ernesto Che
Further Reading: Szuk, Tad, *Fidel: A Critical Portrait* (New York, 1986).

Challe, Gen. Maurice (1905–1979)

Challe was appointed French commander in chief in Algeria in December 1958, the subsequent "Challe offensive" bringing the French army to the brink of military victory over the Front de Libération Nationale (FLN). However, Challe became disillusioned with the policy of self-determination for Algeria pursued by Pres. Charles de Gaulle and became one of the leaders of an unsuccessful military coup staged in Algiers in April 1961.

An air force officer, Challe was active in the resistance against German occupation of France in World War II and was awarded the Distinguished Service Order (DSO) by the British government. Subsequently, he was military envoy to Britain during the planning for the Anglo-French intervention at Suez in 1956. Challe assumed that he was intended to achieve victory over the FLN when he succeeded Raoul Salan as commander in chief in Algeria. The major series of offensives between February 1959 and March 1960 successively cleared the FLN from its former strongholds in the Kabylia, Ouarsenis, and Hodna Mountains.

Challe utilized the army's Muslim units or *harkis* to locate FLN groups, highly mobile *commandos de chasse* (pursuit commandos) to pin them down, and elite units from the Réserve Générale (General Reserve) to eliminate them. Challe planned to finish off the last FLN stronghold in the Aurès Mountains. However, he was increasingly concerned at the likelihood that de Gaulle intended to leave Algeria and abandon the *harkis* to their fate at the hands of the FLN. He offered to resign his command when Gen. Jacques Massu was recalled from Algeria in January 1960, and after de Gaulle held a referendum on self-determination Challe resigned altogether from the army in January 1961. He joined the plot against de Gaulle only in March 1961 and promptly surrendered when the coup failed rather than see French soldiers fire on their comrades. He was sentenced to 15 years in prison but was released in 1966 and granted full amnesty in 1968. Subsequently overcoming cancer, he managed a freight business in Paris.

See also: Algeria; French army; Front de Libération Nationale (FLN); Massu, Gen. Jacques; Resistance; Salan, Gen. Raoul
Further Reading: Horne, Alistair, *A Savage War of Peace* (London, 1977).

Chechens

The Chechen (or Nokhchi) are a Muslim people inhabiting an area of the northern Caucasus Mountains between the Black Sea and the Caspian Sea. The southern border of Chechnya is the frontier between the Russian Federation, of which Chechnya is part, and Georgia. The Caucasus became part of the Russian empire in the late eighteenth century, but the Chechens periodically fought against the occupying Russian army. Chechens fought for the neighboring Daghestani leader, Shamil, during his revolt against Russia between 1834 and 1859 and also supported the unsuccessful attempt to create an independent Republic of the North Caucasus during the Russian Civil War (1917–1921).

Chechen unrest continued after the consolidation of Soviet control, and the Soviets resorted to mass deportations to Siberia in both 1937 and 1944. The Chechens were not allowed to return until 1957. When the Soviet Union began to break up in 1991, power was assumed by the Pan-National Congress of the Chechen People (OKCHN) under the leadership of Dzhokhar Dudayev. Independence was declared on 2 November 1991 but never recognized by the Russian Federation, which had succeeded the Soviet Union. Opposition to

Dudayev within Chechnya resulted in sporadic violence, and the Russian Federation took the opportunity to intervene in December 1994. Russian forces took the Chechen capital, Grozny, on 8 February 1995 at great cost, and the Chechens continued to wage guerrilla warfare. Dudayev was killed in a rocket attack in April 1996 and was succeeded by Zelimkhan Yandarbiyer. A cease-fire and peace agreement was eventually brokered by Alexander Lebed in August 1996 on the basis of postponing any decision on Chechnya's independence until 2001. Elections then resulted in the victory of a moderate, Aslan Maskhadov, in January 1997, but the question of Chechnya's status within the federation clearly remains unresolved.

See also: Russian army; Russian Civil War; Shamil
Further Reading: Gall, Carlotta, and Thomas de Waal, *Chechnya: Calamity in the Caucasus* (New York, 1998).

Chin Peng (1920–)

Chin Peng was the leader of the Malayan Communist Party (MCP) during the Malayan Emergency (1948–1960). He first came to prominence during World War II as the chief liaison officer between the communist-dominated Malayan People's Anti-Japanese Army (MPAJA) and the British Force 136, which was responsible for organizing resistance to Japanese occupation of Malaya. Indeed, Chin Peng received the Order of the British Empire (OBE) for his wartime services.

MPAJA was disbanded in December 1945 in return for legal recognition of the MCP by the returning British authorities. Chin Peng became general secretary of the MCP in March 1947, when its former head was revealed as a British agent. However, the MCP's leadership was inexperienced, and a crucial mistake was made in launching "armed struggle" prematurely in 1948 without the careful political preparation required by the classic guerrilla strategy advocated by Mao Tse-tung. The MCP recognized its error in October 1951, but by then

its political organization had been irretrievably damaged by the strategy developed by Sir Harold Briggs. The communists were forced deeper into the jungle, Chin Peng himself crossing into Thailand in 1953. He negotiated with the Malayan authorities at Baling in December 1955, but no agreement was reached.

Malaya's independence from Britain in 1957 deprived the MCP of any claim to be fighting against a colonial administration, and the emergency was declared at an end in July 1960. However, remnants of the communists continued to exist along the Thai frontier, and there were occasional joint Thai-Malaysian operations against them in the 1970s and 1980s. Somewhat unexpectedly, Chin Peng, whom many thought dead, emerged from the jungle to conclude a formal peace treaty with the Malaysian government in December 1989.

See also: Briggs, Lt. Gen. Sir Harold Rawdon; British army; Malayan Emergency; Mao Tse-tung; Resistance
Further Reading: Short, Anthony, *The Communist Insurrection in Malaya, 1948–1960* (London, 1975).

Chinese Civil War (1927–1949)

The long struggle for control of China between the Chinese Communist Party (CPC) and the Nationalist Party, or Kuomintang (KMT), between 1927 and 1949, which the communists won, has particular significance as the conflict that inspired Mao Tse-tung's theories of rural revolutionary guerrilla warfare. The KMT, which proclaimed a Chinese republic on the fall of the Manchu dynasty in 1911, was itself a revolutionary socialist party modeled by its first leader, Sun Yat-sen, on the organization of the Bolsheviks in Russia. However, Sun Yat-sen did not believe that Marxism itself would work in China, even though he accepted Soviet assistance. Initially, too, the Soviets encouraged the CPC, which was founded in 1921, to work with the KMT to overcome the republic's opponents. These opponents were the many warlords whose armies still controlled much of China.

When Sun Yat-sen died in March 1925, his successor was Chiang K'ai-shek. Chiang wished to unite all China by force of arms and to inspire a kind of national renaissance that would free China of foreign influence. Chiang believed the CPC a subversive element. His suspicions were increased when the communists used the KMT's successful advance against the warlords in northern China in 1926 to establish their own organization in the countryside. In the spring of 1927, therefore, Chiang began to purge the communists from the KMT. The CPC responded with attempted urban revolts in the cities of southeastern China such as Nanchang and Canton (Guangzou) but were easily crushed. Nonetheless, sufficient communists escaped to the southern mountains on the borders between the Hunan and Kiangsi Provinces. In December 1930 Chiang ordered the first of five "encirclement and annihilation" campaigns to eliminate the communist soviets (base areas). The first three of these campaigns, in 1930 and 1931, were not conspicuously successful, but the fourth and fifth campaigns (1933 and 1934) overran the southern base areas.

Faced with annihilation, the communists began the celebrated "Long March" in October 1934. About 120,000 communists began the march, being joined by other surviving communist forces along the route to the far northwestern mountains of the Shensi Province. However, barely 20,000 reached Shensi after a journey of more than 6,000 miles. Chiang's subordinates failed to achieve the final elimination of the communists he anticipated in further operations in both 1935 and 1936. Consequently, he went to the north himself in December 1936 to take personal command, only to be arrested by some of his own officers, who demanded that he form a united front with the communists against the growing threat from Japan.

The Japanese army had invaded Manchuria in September 1931, and in July 1937 it launched a full-scale invasion of northern and central China. Chiang reluctantly accepted a united front with the CPC in September 1937, but it ended after a pitched battle in January 1941 between KMT and the CPC's Fourth Red Army. The CPC's only wartime offensive against the Japanese, the so-called Campaign of a Hundred Regiments by the Eighth Route Army between August and October 1940, was a failure, and the Japanese enjoyed some success in pacification operations against the communists. However, both the KMT and the Japanese were too occupied fighting each other to worry unduly about the CPC, and this gave the communists room to reorganize after the failures of the past.

Thus, in the Shensi Province after 1935 Mao began to emerge gradually as the leading figure in the CPC and to develop his theories of rural guerrilla warfare as a means of achieving ultimate victory. Mao always intended that the Red Army would be transformed from a guerrilla force into a conventional army capable of meeting and defeating its opponents on the battlefield. However, he recognized that this process of transformation and the careful political preparation of the Chinese people to accept communism implied a "protracted war" in which the first necessity was simply to survive.

With the surrender of Japan in August 1945, the transformation of the communist forces was greatly advanced. The People's Liberation Army (PLA) was formally established in May 1946. And even though Chiang had about 3 million men opposed to 1 million communists, the KMT had been gravely weakened by the war against the Japanese. Many of its best troops had been killed and its organization greatly reduced. While the United States continued to assist the KMT, the CPC received captured Japanese arms and equipment from the Soviets. The communists were also able to consolidate control of Manchuria, which the Soviets had overrun in August 1945 and from which Soviet forces did not withdraw until April 1946.

Chiang tried to wrest back control of Manchuria, but by September 1948 his forces had been largely isolated in the cities, which were captured one by one. The PLA then went over to the offensive in the north, defeating the KMT in a bitter, two-month battle at Hsuchow (Xuzhou), between December 1948 and January 1949, that cost the KMT an estimated 500,000 men. Mao entered Peking (Beijing) on 21 January 1949. The PLA now outnumbered Chiang's forces and crossed the Yangtze (Changjiang) River in April 1949 to take Nanking (Nanjing) and Shanghai. Chiang fled to the island of Formosa (Taiwan) in December 1949. Earlier, on 1 October 1949, Mao had proclaimed the Chinese People's Republic.

See also: Japanese army; Kuomintang (KMT); Long March; Mao Tse-tung; Pacification
Further Reading: Wilson, Dick, *China's Revolutionary War* (New York, 1991); Levine, S. I., *Anvil of Victory: The Communist Revolution in Manchuria, 1945–1948* (New York, 1987).

Civil Operations and Rural Development Support (CORDS)

CORDS was established by the United States in May 1967 as a means of coordinating the efforts of the American agencies responsible for pacification in South Vietnam. It addressed the previous lack of coordination that had seen the U.S. Information Agency, the U.S. Central Intelligence Agency (CIA), and the Agency for International Development (AID) all conducting their programs independently. Technically, all three agency heads, together with that of Military Assistance Command—Vietnam (MAC—V), reported to the U.S. ambassador in Saigon. In reality, however, successive ambassadors did not fully exercise the authority given them, and little unity of purpose was apparent.

Pres. Lyndon B. Johnson became increasingly concerned, and in February 1966 Robert Komer was appointed special assistant to the president for pacification. On 9 May 1967 Johnson then authorized the creation of Civil Operations and Revolutionary Development Support under the control of MAC—V. Its title changed to Civil

Operations and Rural Development Support in 1970. Komer became head of CORDS as deputy for pacification and ranked as an ambassador. He was succeeded by William Colby in October 1968.

CORDS became responsible for a variety of existing programs such as the former AID program *chieu hoi* (open arms), which was designed to encourage former members of the communist Vietcong to come over to the government; the former MAC—V program for management of civic action; and the former CIA program known as "revolutionary development," which established "People's Action Teams" designed to win over the hearts and minds of the South Vietnamese population on behalf of the government. Only the CIA's covert operations and AID's land reform program remained outside CORDS supervision. CORDS also undertook new initiatives such as the controversial Phoenix program designed to eliminate the Vietcong's organizational infrastructure.

The creation of CORDS did not result in greater emphasis being given to pacification since overall American strategy remained firmly based on large scale conventional military operations. Yet it could be argued that the degree of coordination achieved did improve the security situation, although this also owed much to the heavy casualties taken by the Vietcong during the Tet Offensive in early 1968. CORDS continued to exist until American withdrawal from South Vietnam in 1973.

See also: Hearts and minds; Komer, Robert William; Pacification; Phoenix program; United States Army; Vietcong; Vietnam War
Further Reading: Komer, Robert, *Bureaucracy at War* (Boulder, 1986).

Civilian Irregular Defense Group (CIDG)

The CIDG concept was devised by two Americans, David Nuttle and Gilbert Layton, as a means of winning support for the government of South Vietnam among groups traditionally hostile to the Vietnamese. The force was recruited from the Montagnard Hill tribes and other ethnic minorities in South Vietnam's Central Highlands between 1961 and 1970. Raised by the U.S. Special Forces (Green Berets) and controlled by the U.S. Central Intelligence Agency (CIA), the first CIDG was organized among Rhade tribesmen around Buon Enao in Darlac Province in December 1961. The CIDG were trained both as village militia and strike force units with 43,000 and 18,000 men being deployed in these respective roles by 1963.

Unfortunately, however, when control was passed from the CIA to Military Assistance Command—Vietnam (MAC—V), in July 1963, the "cidgees" were pressed into the more ambitious and aggressive Border Surveillance Program intended to cut off the communist Vietcong infiltration routes into the south. They were too thinly spread to achieve this, however. The role of the cidgees in purely local defense was also frustrated by the Mike (later Mobile Strike) Force units, which were similarly raised from the CIDG in 1964 and from which the self-contained "Greek alphabet" hunter-killer and intelligence-gathering teams (Delta, Omega, Sigma, and Gamma) also evolved.

When control of CIDG was increasingly vested in the South Vietnamese Special Forces, or Luc Luong Dac Biet (LLDB), mutinies occurred in CIDG camps in both 1964 and 1965. At its peak, the CIDG program involved 80,000 men, but the inability of the LLDB to work well with the cidgees resulted in CIDG's end in 1970. Remaining units were converted into South Vietnamese Border Ranger and Regional Forces battalions.

See also: Green Berets; Special Forces; Vietcong; Vietnam War
Further Reading: Krepinevich, Andrew, *The Army and Vietnam* (Baltimore, 1986).

Clausewitz, Carl von (1780–1831)

Arguably the most influential of all military theorists, Clausewitz's major work, *Vom*

Krieg (On war), was published—still uncompleted—by his widow in 1832. Clausewitz was mostly concerned with conventional warfare but did recognize the emergence of "people's war" during the French Revolutionary and Napoleonic Wars (1792–1815). Commissioned in the Prussian army at the age of 12, Clausewitz was captured by the French at Auerstadt in 1806. Released ten months later, Clausewitz became assistant to the Prussian military reformer Gerhard Scharnhorst. However, he became disillusioned by Prussia's subservience to France and joined the Russian army in 1812. He returned to the Prussian army in 1814 and in 1818 became director of the War Academy at Berlin, embarking on his principal work.

In 1831 Clausewitz was recalled to active service as chief of staff of the Prussian army, being sent to help the Russians suppress the Polish revolt, but he died of cholera. Like many of his contemporaries, Clausewitz believed guerrillas would be most successful in a partisan role, assisting conventional regular operations by acting on the flank and in the rear of an army's opponents. He addressed the issue of "The People in Arms" in chapter 26 (book six) of *On War.* He suggested that guerrilla warfare could succeed only if sustained over a long period of time in the interior of a large country with rough terrain. He also suggested that the "national character" of a people had to be suited to this particular mode of warfare.

See also: Partisans
Further Reading: von Clausewitz, Carl, *On War,* trans. Howard, Michael and Paret, Peter (Princeton, 1976); Howard, Michael, *Clausewitz* (Oxford, 1983).

Collins, Gen. Michael (1890–1922)

Collins was director of intelligence for the Irish Republican Army (IRA) during its campaign against the British authorities in Ireland between 1919 and 1921. He was one of the principal negotiators of the

Anglo-Irish Treaty of 1921, which established the Irish Free State, becoming commander in chief and then prime minister. Just ten days after becoming prime minister in August 1922, Collins was killed in an ambush by those who rejected the treaty compromise, which had left the six counties of Northern Ireland outside the new state.

Born in County Cork, Collins was a civil servant in London for ten years before returning to Ireland to participate in the Easter Rising of 1916 in Dublin. Collins was imprisoned but released in December 1916. He was one of 73 members of the nationalist political party Sinn Féin (Ourselves Alone), elected to the British Parliament in December 1918, and, as one of only 26 of these MPs not in prison, was their effective leader when they declared independence from Britain on 21 January 1919. Collins was made general of volunteers and director of intelligence in the war that now began against the British.

A certain degree of mythology has surrounded the IRA campaign, and the ruthless Collins's much vaunted intelligence network was not as efficient as depicted. Indeed, while the British army made fundamental errors, the IRA itself was under severe pressure by 1921. Collins was persuaded by Eamon de Valera to accompany Arthur Griffith to London to negotiate with the British government between October and December 1921. Collins and Griffith accepted what they regarded as the best terms possible, namely, dominion status within the British empire and the exclusion of the six counties from the Free State. Collins recognized, as he put it, that he had signed his own death warrant. The terms won narrow support from the Dáil Éireann (Irish Assembly), but de Valera and the die-hard republicans rejected them, and the Irish Civil War (1922–1923) erupted.

Griffith, who had become prime minister, died on 12 August 1922; Collins, who was both minister of defense and commander in chief, succeeded him. On 22 August 1922 the convoy carrying Collins was ambushed in West Cork, and he was killed while fighting, rifle in hand.

See also: British army; Ireland; Irish Republican Army (IRA)

Further Reading: Taylor, Rex, *Michael Collins* (London, 1970); Mackay, James, *Michael Collins: A Life* (Edinburgh, 1996).

Colombia

Like many other states in Latin America, Colombia has experienced periods of military dictatorship and also periods of guerrilla warfare. The situation was complicated by the emergence of narcotics trafficking in the 1970s and the links between organized crime and insurgency. In many respects the root of the insurgency problems lay in the period of civil war between liberal and conservative factions between 1948 and 1957 known as La Violencia (The Violence). The continuing unrest enabled the communists to establish so-called independent republics in a number of rural areas, which provided the nucleus for the subsequent guerrilla movements.

The initial insurgency in 1961–1962 was inspired by the example of Fidel Castro on Cuba and followed the *foco* theory of rural revolutionary guerrilla warfare advocated by Che Guevara. With the assistance of the United States, the Colombian army adopted "Plan Lazo," a combined program of military and civic action that contributed significantly to the eradication of the independent republics and the *foco* by the end of 1965.

However, the surviving guerrillas were brought together in 1965 in a loose coalition of three main guerrilla movements. These were the pro-Soviet Fuerzas Armadas Revolucionarias de Colombia (FARC), or the Revolutionary Armed Forces of Colombia; the pro-Cuban Ejército de Liberación Nacional (ELN), or the National Liberation Army; and the Maoist Ejército Popular de Liberación (EPL), or the Popular Liberation Army. None enjoyed particular success, but their continued existence required the Colombian armed forces to sustain the counterinsurgency effort. Moreover, a new pro-Cuban group, Movimiento 19 de Abril (19 April Movement—M–19) entered the field in 1976 following a split in the radical nationalist National Popular Alliance (ANAPO), which had failed to secure the presidency in the elections held in April 1970.

Faced with the growing power of the drug cartels, the government sought a series of cease-fires with the guerrilla groups in 1984, but those with M–19 and EPL broke down in 1985, and ELN remained distant from the process. M–19 gained considerable publicity from its seizure of diplomats in the Dominican Republic's embassy in Bogotá in 1980, leading to a 61-day siege. Similarly, it seized the supreme court building in Bogotá in November 1985, with 11 judges dying (together with more than 100 others) in the subsequent gun battle.

As the reaction to insurgency and the escalating drug conflict prompted reaction from *sicarios* (literally "scarred ones," referring to right-wing death squads), the guerrilla movements forged a new organization in 1987, the Coordinatora Guerrillera Simón Bolívar (CGSB), or the Simon Bolivar Guerrilla Coordinating Board. It took its name from the early–nineteenth-century revolutionary who won independence for Bolivia, Colombia, Ecuador, Panama, Peru, and Venezuela from the Spanish. However, M–19, led by Carlos Pizzaro Leongomez, signed a new cease-fire in March 1989. Following a peace agreement in March 1990, M–19 participated in national, provincial, and local elections.

FARC, which developed links to the drug cartels and is led by Manuel Marulanda Vélez, remains the largest guerrilla movement. It operates primarily in the southwest. ELN, which has about 5,000 guerrillas, operates in the northeastern Andean foothills and, with fewer links to the drug cartels, has concentrated on attacking the multinational oil companies operating in the Casanare region. In February 1998

the excommunicated Catholic priest who had led ELN since 1973, Manual Perez Martinez, reached an accord paving the way for negotiations with the government. However, Perez died in April 1998, and it would appear that his successor, Nicolas Rodriguez Bautista, was not committed to the negotiations.

See also: Castro, Fidel; *Foco;* Guevara, Ernesto Che
Further Reading: Oquist, Paul, *Violence, Conflict, and Politics in Colombia* (Berkeley, 1978); Eddy, Paul, Hugo Sabogal, and Sara Walden, *The Cocaine Wars* (London, 1988); Osterling, Jorge, *Democracy in Colombia: Clientelist Politics and Guerrilla Warfare* (New Brunswick, 1989).

Colonial warfare

Colonial warfare implies conflicts that occurred between European forces (or those of European descent) and indigenous native forces. However, it might also mean conflict between white and nonwhite forces (the forces deployed by white powers in colonial warfare were frequently raised locally and, therefore, only white-led). It can also imply a variety of military situations.

British military theorist Charles Callwell, writing in 1896, divided what he called "small wars" into three broad categories. These were: campaigns of conquest and annexation; pacification campaigns for the suppression of insurrection or to restore order; and punitive campaigns intended as retaliation for particular outrages, although they might also extend white control. Occasionally, colonial campaigns were also fought between great powers competing for colonies.

The armies of all the great powers engaged in colonial warfare. The British, for example, conquered Burma in three successive campaigns (1823–1826, 1851–1853, 1885–1889); the French conquered Morocco (1912–1934); and the Russian army conquered much of what became Soviet Central Asia in the late nineteenth century. Pacification campaigns included those of the Dutch army on Banten in the Dutch East Indies (1888); the German suppression of the Maji Maji Rising in German East Africa

(1905–1907); and the Portuguese suppression of revolts in Niassa in Mozambique (1906, 1908–1912, 1920). Punitive campaigns included the British invasion of Abyssinia (Ethiopia) in 1868. One contest between white powers involved the United States Army, whose successes in the Spanish-American War (1898) resulted in the actual or effective annexation of former Spanish colonies such as Cuba and the Philippines.

For European armies colonial warfare did not offer particular lessons for the type of modern conventional conflict expected in Europe. Indeed, the often easy victories against poorly armed indigenous opponents suggested that little doctrine was required, but the sheer diversity of opponents in colonial warfare also militated against its emergence. Nonetheless, some common approaches to the problems of colonial warfare did become apparent by the end of the nineteenth century, such as resettlement of indigenous populations. There was even some recognition of the need to win hearts and minds, but more often than not colonial warfare was conducted with considerable brutality.

Occasional disasters did befall colonial armies, such as the defeat of George Custer at the Little Big Horn in 1876, the destruction of the Italian army at Adowa in Abyssinia in 1896, and the destruction of the Spanish army at Anual in Spanish Morocco in 1921. Mostly, however, indigenous opponents succumbed to superior European firepower, which increasingly included the most modern technology, including airpower. European armies also successfully utilized locally raised forces, which knew the extremes of terrain and climate (and conditions were often extreme) as well as the opponents did. When revolutionary ideology was grafted to the age-old tactics of guerrilla warfare after 1945, the traditional advantages enjoyed by the armies of the colonial powers were seriously challenged.

See also: Adowa, Battle of; Anual, Battle of; British army; Burma; Callwell, Maj. Gen. Sir Charles Edward; Custer, Lt. Col. George Armstrong; Dutch army; Dutch East Indies; French army; Hearts and minds; Italian army; Maji Maji Rising; Morocco; Mozambique; Pacification; Philippines; Portuguese army; Resettlement; Russian army; Spanish army; United States Army

Further Reading: Beckett, Ian (ed.), *The Roots of Counterinsurgency: Armies and Guerrilla Warfare, 1900–1945* (London, 1988).

Confrontation, Indonesian/Malaysian (1962–1966)

The Indonesian/Malaysian Confrontation of 1962–1966 was an unsuccessful attempt by Indonesia's Pres. Kusno Sosro Sukarno to prevent the creation of a Malaysian federation that include the three northern Borneo territories of Sarawak, North Borneo (Sabah), and Brunei, which Sukarno himself wished to annex. Preparation for a Malaysian federation including Malaya and Singapore as well as the three territories began in 1961. There was general support for the federation, but it was opposed by the Sarawak United People's Party and the Brunei People's Party. On 8 December 1962 the Brunei People's Party attempted a revolt in Brunei. British troops were flown in from Singapore, and the revolt collapsed by 14 December. However, many of the rebels escaped into the jungle, and Sukarno announced that Indonesian "volunteers" would now assist them to "liberate" northern Borneo. These volunteers were drawn initially from the Sarawak United People's Party, the survivors of the Brunei revolt and Indonesian communists. The first armed group crossed the frontier on 12 April 1963. However, these early attempts at infiltration were not very successful, and the Malaysian federation duly came into being on 16 September 1963 (although without the participation of Brunei). Sukarno's response was to commit Indonesian regular troops to the campaign.

The British director of operations, Maj. Gen. Walter Walker, had previously served during the Malayan Emergency (1948–1960), and he applied much the same techniques that had worked so well in Malaya.

Walker established a fully integrated command-and-intelligence structure and also began an energetic program to win the hearts and minds of the indigenous jungle tribes. Medical and agricultural help was offered, and some troops, particularly those of the Special Air Service (SAS), lived and worked alongside villagers. About 1,500 Ibans were enlisted in a tracking unit known as the Border Scouts. As a result, the Indonesians found it increasingly difficult to secure food, intelligence, and shelter inside Malaysian territory.

Helicopters, which had not been widely available during the Malayan Emergency, also enabled Walker to establish a permanent presence in the most contested areas of the 80,000 square miles of territory he had to defend. From August 1964 onward, British and Commonwealth forces also began to mount secret counterraids ("Operation Claret") into Indonesian territory. By early 1965 the Indonesians had lost the initiative, and Sukarno's popularity waned as the Indonesian economy faltered under the strain of conflict. When Sukarno fell ill in August 1965 the Indonesian army moved to assert control, and in March 1966 it stripped Sukarno of political power. The head of the army, Gen. T.N.J. Suharto, reached an agreement with Malaysia to end the confrontation on 11 August 1966.

As there had been no formal declaration of war by either side, it was easier for the Indonesians to withdraw without losing face. Indeed, the conflict generally had been low-key, with British and Commonwealth forces suffering 59 dead and the Indonesians about 2,000 dead.

See also: British army; Hearts and minds; Helicopters; Intelligence; Malayan Emergency; Special Air Service (SAS); Walker, Gen. Sir Walter Colyear
Further Reading: James, H., and D. Small-Smith, *The Undeclared War* (London, 1971); Mackie, J. A. C., *Konfrontasi* (Oxford, 1974).

Contras

The contras (from *contrarevolucionario,* or "counterrevolutionary") were supporters of the former president of Nicaragua, Anastasio Somoza Debyle. Between 1981 and 1990 contras waged a guerrilla war against the Marxist Sandinistas, who had overthrown Somoza in July 1979. The United States feared that the Sandinistas would give material assistance to the Frente Farabundo Martí de Liberación Nacional (FMLN) guerrillas fighting against the American-backed government in El Salvador and generally incite unrest throughout Central and Latin America. Consequently, an economic embargo was imposed on Nicaragua and aid given to the emerging contras in 1981.

There were two principal groups of contras. The Democratic Revolutionary Alliance (ARDE) was based in Costa Rica to the south and first led by a former Sandinista guerrilla named Eden Pastora Gomez (Commander Zero) and later by Fernando Chamorro Rapaccioli (El Negro). The larger Nicaraguan Democratic Forces (FDN) was based in Honduras to the north and led by Enrique Bermúdez. At peak strength, the contras fielded about 15,000 guerrillas, but operations were severely curtailed by the U.S. Senate decision to suspend aid in 1984, although nonmilitary aid was resumed in 1985.

Consequently, Lt. Col. Oliver North, the National Security Council deputy director for political and military affairs under Pres. Ronald Reagan, sought to finance the contras by diverting funds obtained from illegal arms sales to Iran. The scandal that became known as Iran-Contra broke in the United States in November 1986, with North being tried and convicted on three charges in February 1989. In Nicaragua itself, peace negotiations were undertaken from 1983 onward by the so-called Contadora Group of Colombia, Mexico, Panama, and Venezuela, but the process proved tortuous and was frequently interrupted by resumed fighting. Agreement was reached in 1989 for the demobilization of the contras and the holding of new elections. In February 1990 these elections saw the defeat of the Sandinistas by a 14-party coalition called the Union Nacional de la Oposición (UNO) or the National Opposition Union, and the 8,000 remaining contras laid down their weapons under UN supervision.

See also: El Salvador; Frente Farabundo Martí de Liberación Nacional (FMLN); Nicaragua; Sandinistas
Further Reading: Robinson, William, and Kent Norsworthy, *David and Goliath: Washington's War Against Nicaragua* (London, 1987); Pardo-Maurer, R., *The Contras, 1980–1989: A Special Kind of Politics* (New York, 1990).

Cordon sanitaire

Cordon sanitaire in the context of counterinsurgency means a physical barrier erected to prevent guerrilla infiltration. In particular, the term was used during the guerrilla war against Rhodesia between 1974 and 1979. Traditionally, it has been used to denote a protective cordon of friendly states serving to keep enemies at a safe distance. For instance, the guerrillas of the African National Congress (ANC) were kept away from South Africa in the 1960s and 1970s by the protective barrier provided by territories that were actually controlled by South Africa (such as Namibia); economically dependent on South Africa (Botswana, Lesotho, Swaziland); or controlled by those sympathetic to South Africa (Rhodesia and the Portuguese colonies of Angola and Mozambique).

In Rhodesia, the system of border minefields established from May 1974 onward was described as a cordon sanitaire. Once Mozambique became both independent from Portugal and a base for the Zimbabwe African National Union (ZANU) guerrillas, 111 miles of the Rhodesian frontier with Mozambique between the Musengedzi and Mazoe Rivers were fitted with a line of two game fences enclosing minefields and an alarm system. Subsequently, the system was extended to the frontier with Zambia, from which the Zimbabwe African People's Union (ZAPU) guerrillas operated. In all, 537 miles were fortified at a cost of $2,298 Rhodesian.

However, the system lacked depth, and the mines were often exposed by heavy rainfall or set off by wildlife where fences were not sufficiently maintained. The Rhodesians did not have the manpower to patrol the fences adequately.

Thus, the Rhodesian cordon sanitaire was an impediment to infiltration, not an impassable barrier; arguably, it consumed valuable resources that might have been used more effectively elsewhere. Other physical barriers, such as the Morice Line constructed by the French in Algeria in the late 1950s, were more effective.

See also: African National Congress (ANC); Angola; Mozambique; Namibia; Rhodesia; Zimbabwe African National Union (ZANU); Zimbabwe African People's Union (ZAPU)
Further Reading: Cilliers, J. K., *Counter-insurgency in Rhodesia* (London, 1985).

Crook, Maj. Gen. George (1829–1890)

Crook was one of the most successful United States Army commanders during the American Indian Wars of the later nineteenth century. Born in Dayton, Ohio, Crook attended the U.S. Military Academy at West Point from 1848 to 1852. He served in the Pacific Northwest and during the American Civil War (1861–1865). He reached the rank of major general of volunteers but reverted to his pre-1861 rank of captain at the end of the war. He returned to the Northwest and was promoted lieutenant colonel in 1866. He commanded the Department of Columbia in 1868, but in June 1871 he was posted to command the Department of Arizona. Promoted to brigadier general in 1873, he moved to the Department of the Platte in 1875.

In an ill-fated campaign in 1876 he commanded one of three columns intended to converge upon Sioux and Cheyenne. However, on 16 June his force was checked at the Rosebud River, enabling the tribes to concentrate against Custer on the Little Big Horn. Returning to Arizona in 1882, Crook campaigned against Chiricahua Apaches under Geronimo and persuaded them to surrender. He returned to the Department of the Platte, then commanded the Division of the Missouri as a major general with headquarters at Chicago, where he died.

Crook's success against Apaches was founded on the employment of highly mobile mounted columns, using mules rather than wagons for supplies, and a more extensive use of Native American scouts than was common. Indeed, Crook generally had a better understanding of and was more sympathetic to Native Americans than most contemporaries. He was regarded as eccentric for growing a luxuriant beard, wearing unconventional civilian clothes, and riding a mule.

See also: American Civil War; American Indian Wars; Custer, Lt. Col. George Armstrong; United States Army
Further Reading: Schmitt, M. F. (ed.), *General George Crook: His Autobiography* (Norman, 1946); Hutton, Paul, *Phil Sheridan and His Army* (Lincoln, 1985).

Cuba

Cuba has twice been an influential arena in the context of guerrilla warfare. First, between 1895 and 1898 a Cuban revolt against Spanish rule saw the application of controversial methods of counterinsurgency by Gen. Valeriano "Butcher" Weyler. Second, Fidel Castro's guerrilla campaign against the government of Fulgencio Batista between 1956 and 1959 inspired the development of the *foco* theory of guerrilla warfare by Che Guevara and Régis Debray.

The Spanish had faced frequent revolts on Cuba, including one between 1868 and 1878 that had been suppressed by Martinez Campos. However, his failure to deal with a new insurrection that began in eastern Cuba in February 1895 led to the appointment of Weyler as captain-general in February 1896. What aroused controversy were the brutalities Weyler wielded to exert control over the Cuban population: extensive use of the death penalty and enforced resettlement.

Cuba came under U.S. control following the Spanish-American War (1898), and the United States Army imposed a military government on the island from 1898 until Cuban independence in May 1902. However, American military control was reimposed from 1906 to 1909 when civil war broke out; U.S. Marines were also landed to protect American commercial interests during disturbances in 1912 and between 1917 and 1919.

Castro's first attempt to overthrow the Batista government by leading an attack on the Moncada army barracks in Santiago de Cuba on 26 July 1953 failed. Castro was imprisoned but was released in May 1955. Moving to Mexico, he founded the 26 July Movement to continue opposition to Batista. Castro intended to return to Cuba on 25 November 1956 with 81 followers. His landing would coincide with an urban uprising by the 26 July Movement. However, landing was delayed until 2 December 1956, by which time the urban uprising had already been suppressed. Three days later, Batista's troops decisively routed Castro's band; fewer than two dozen, including Castro and Guevara, escaped into the Sierra Maestra Mountains. Despite the unpromising situation, Castro resolved to fight on; his small band was reinforced and supplied by the surviving underground organization of the 26 July Movement.

Bautista had alienated most sectors of Cuban society, and his poor record on human rights also resulted in the withdrawal of U.S. aid in 1958. Batista's army was also poorly trained and motivated and would often flee rather than fight. Bastista's forces had all but abandoned the Sierra Maestras to Castro by the end of 1957 and then failed to reassert control over the mountains in May 1958—despite deploying more than 11,000 men against Castro's 300 guerrillas. Seizing the initiative, Castro went on the offensive himself in August 1958, and Batista's administration quickly collapsed.

Batista fled to the Dominican Republic on 1 January 1959; Castro entered Havana on 8 January. It was a remarkable victory, but Guevara and Debray mistakenly presumed that the unique circumstances that led to Castro's success would exist as a matter of course throughout Latin America.

See also: Batista y Zaldivar, Fulgencio; Castro, Fidel; Debray, Régis; *Foco;* Guevara, Ernesto Che; United States Army; United States Marine Corps (USMC)
Further Reading: Thomas, Hugh, *The Cuban Revolution* (London, 1971).

Custer, Lt. Col. George Armstrong (1839–1876)

Custer enjoyed meteoric success during the American Civil War (1861–1865), but his defeat and death at the hands of overwhelming Sioux and Cheyenne forces on the Little Big Horn in June 1876 became one of the most notorious engagements of the American Indian Wars. Born in Ohio, Custer graduated at the bottom of his class from the U.S. Military Academy at West Point in June 1861. With service at such battles as First Manassas, Gettysburg, Yellow Tavern, and Five Forks, the flamboyant Custer became the youngest major general of volunteers in the Union army; after the war he reverted to his regular rank.

Posted to the Seventh Cavalry in 1866, Custer commanded it on occupation duties in Texas before being assigned to a campaign against Cheyenne in Kansas. In the event, Custer was court-martialed and suspended from duty for a year for brutality toward his own men. However, he was reinstated in time to take part in the campaign. On 27 November 1868 he attacked Black Kettle's village on the Washita; more than 100 Native Americans, including many women and children, were killed. The affair was also marked by the loss of 20 cavalrymen whom he had detached for independent action but failed to support.

In 1874 Custer led an expedition into the Black Hills and discovered gold. The subsequent tensions with Sioux (who regarded the Black Hills as sacred) resulted in the 1876 campaign. Custer's regiment formed one part of the main column under Alfred Terry that was intended to converge on the Indian concentration; the others were commanded by John Gibbon and George Crook. Custer was sent ahead with somewhat ambiguous orders; having been discovered by the Indians, he decided to attack at once.

At the Little Big Horn on 25 June 1876 Custer split his command as he had at the Washita and attacked. However, not only was Custer outnumbered by an unprecedented concentration of an estimated 2,000 Sioux and Cheyenne warriors; he was also outgunned by the modern repeating rifles that many warriors possessed. Custer and the 224 men under his immediate command were killed. Endlessly debated to this day, "Custer's Last Stand" had great impact at the time, as it coincided with the centennial celebration of the founding of the United States.

See also: American Civil War; American Indian Wars; Crook, Maj. Gen. George; United States Army
Further Reading: Hutton, Paul (ed.), *The Custer Reader* (Lincoln, 1992).

Cyprus

The Mediterranean island of Cyprus has a majority Greek population even though it lies closer to the coast of Turkey. Disturbances in 1931 as well as the 1955–1959 guerrilla campaign against the British colonial authorities by the movement known as Ethniki Organosis Kyprion Agoniston (EOKA) were motivated by support among the Greek Cypriot population for enosis (union with Greece). Internal communal disturbances after independence from Britain in 1960 also led to the deployment of UN forces in 1964 and, ultimately, the Turkish invasion of northern Cyprus in 1974.

Cyprus was under rule of the Turkish Ottoman empire from 1571 until 1878, when Britain occupied the island as a possible base for operations in support of the Turks during the Russo-Turkish War (1877–1878). When Turkey entered World War I against Britain in 1914, Cyprus was formally annexed by the British, and it became a

Crown Colony in 1925. Cyprus, therefore, was never part of modern Greece despite the fact that about 75 percent of the population was of Greek origin. The Greek Cypriot aim of enosis first emerged in the October 1931 disturbances. The British garrison was only 125-strong but responded to riots in Nicosia by rushing into the city in commandeered civilian vehicles. Naval parties were landed from the British Mediterranean Fleet, and troops were flown in from Egypt. The British military theorist Sir Charles Gwynn used the rapid response as a case study in his influential manual *Imperial Policing* (1934).

Enosis received new impetus in 1950 with the election of Michael Mouskos as Archbishop Makarios III. As leader of the Greek Orthodox Church on the island, Makarios organized a plebiscite that showed the majority of Greek Cypriots favoring enosis. However, having been compelled to withdraw from its bases in Palestine, Britain believed it essential to retain those on Cyprus. It was announced in July 1954, therefore, that there could be no question of any change in the island's status. George Grivas, a retired colonel in the Greek army but Cypriot-born, returned to the island in November 1954 to assume command of EOKA. In December there were demonstrations in Nicosia after the UN General Assembly denied the Greek government's request to discuss the Cyprus question.

The first bomb attacks occurred on 1 April 1955. Talks between the British, Greek, and Turkish governments failed in August 1955, and Field Marshal Sir John Harding was appointed governor to take a strong line against EOKA. Harding declared a state of emergency on 26 November 1955. EOKA, operating in the Troodos Mountains and urban centers, aimed to make the cost of continued British control of Cyprus politically unacceptable. EOKA had no more than 350 activists in its military wing, but they were supported by a far larger passive wing. The targeting by EOKA of Greek Cypriots, such as policemen working for the authorities, also intimidated the population into acquiescence.

For his part, Harding introduced the same kind of integrated command-and-intelligence structure adopted by the British during the Malayan Emergency (1948–1960); British troop strength was brought up to 20,000 men. "Operation Pepperpot" was relatively successful in clearing EOKA from the Troodos in the summer of 1956, but the need to deploy British troops to Suez in November 1956 and to Jordan in 1958 hindered the counterinsurgency campaign. Nevertheless, EOKA suffered what Grivas admitted were "hard blows" when Harding switched the focus to the towns in December 1956. The increasing pressure was a factor in EOKA eventually announcing a cease-fire on 31 December 1958. A kind of impasse had been reached, but it cost the lives of at least 90 insurgents, 104 British servicemen, 50 policemen, and 238 civilians.

All parties were now prepared to accept the compromise of independence, and Makarios, who had been deported by the British in 1956, became the first president of an independent Cyprus in August 1960. Communal riots led to the deployment of UN forces in 1964; conflict between the Greek and Turkish communities renewed in 1967. In July 1974 the military government in Greece encouraged the Greek Cypriot National Guard to launch a military coup against Makarios. Turkey, like Britain and Greece, was a coguarantor of the 1960 settlement, and it intervened and seized much of northern Cyprus. Turkish forces remain on the island, but only Turkey itself recognizes the legality of the Turkish Federated State of Cyprus that was established in 1975.

See also: British army; Ethniki Organosis Kyprion Agoniston (EOKA); Grivas, Gen. George Theodorou; Gwynn, Maj. Gen. Sir Charles William; Harding, Field Marshal Lord (Allen Francis John); Intelligence; Malayan Emergency; Manuals
Further Reading: Crawshaw, Nancy, *The Cyprus Revolt* (London, 1978); Foley, Christopher, *Island in Revolt* (London 1962).

D

Davydov, Denis Vasilevich (1784–1839)

Davydov was one of the Russian army's leading partisans during the French invasion of Russia in 1812, harrying the French in their advance to and retreat from Moscow. A former aide-de-camp to the Russian commander in chief, Prince Mikhail Kutusov, Lieutenant Colonel Davydov was given just 130 men to begin operations in the rear of the French army west of Moscow in September 1812. He became a national hero for his exploits, but there was suspicion in royal circles and he was retired in 1823 (although he later returned to the army). Davydov was a minor romantic poet, celebrating the cavalryman's life in verse. He also wrote "Essay on the Theory of Partisan Warfare" in 1821, stressing the need for surprise, mobility, and flexibility on the part of the partisan, who would best be employed in attacking an opposing army's lines of communication. His partisan creed was *ubit-da-uiti* (kill and escape).

See also: French army; Partisans; Russian army
Further Reading: Laqueur, Walter, *Guerrilla* (London, 1977).

De La Rey, Gen. Jacobus Hercules (1847–1914)

De La Rey was one of the most gifted Boer guerrilla leaders against the British forces in the latter stages of the Second Boer War (1899–1902). An intensely devout man but also extremely superstitious, De La Rey was known to his men as "Oom Koos" (Uncle Koos). During the first conventional phase of the war, De La Rey commanded the Boer forces at the Battle of Modder River in November 1899, where his entrenched forces inflicted heavy losses on Lt. Gen. Lord Methuen. After the defeat of the main Boer field army at Paardeburg in March 1900, De La Rey and Christiaan De Wet were the principal exponents of continuing the struggle as a guerrilla war. De La Rey operated in the Megaliesburg area of the western Transvaal. In March 1902 he again inflicted a humiliating defeat on Methuen at Tweebosch and captured the British general.

Though a *bittereinder* (bitter-ender) committed to carrying on the war as long as possible, De La Rey participated in the postwar reconstruction of South Africa as a member of the Transvaal legislative assembly between 1907 and 1910. He was then a member of the South African Senate from 1910 to 1914. However, De La Rey strongly opposed South Africa entering World War I in support of Britain. On 15 September 1914 De La Rey was thought to be on his way to join a new Afrikaner rising when he was shot dead trying to evade a police roadblock. The revolt, which was led by De Wet, quickly collapsed, and South African forces served alongside British in the war.

See also: Boer War; British army; De Wet, Gen. Christiaan Rudolf
Further Reading: Pakenham, Thomas, *The Boer War* (London, 1979).

de Lattre de Tassigny, Jean-Marie-Gabriel (1889–1952)

A celebrated French commander during the latter stages of World War II, de Lattre was French commander in chief in French Indochina, fighting the communist Vietminh, from December 1950 until forced to retire from ill health in December 1951. In his early military career, de Lattre served in Algeria during Abd el-Krim's Rif Revolt. By the beginning of World War II he was commanding a French infantry division and, after the fall of France to the Germans, served in the army of unoccupied Vichy France. However, when the Germans occupied the Vichy zone in November 1942, de Lattre was arrested. He escaped to North Africa in October 1943 and joined the Free French forces, leading the French First Army that landed in southern France in August 1944. He represented France at the formal surrender of the German army to the Western Allies in May 1945 and then commanded the forces of the Western European Union.

In December 1950 de Lattre went to Indochina, where French forces had performed badly. The essence of his new strategy was first to secure the Red River delta by constructing a fortified line. Inevitably this became known as the de Lattre Line. Second, de Lattre sought to combine static defense with mobile striking forces; he began to organize commando groups to perform this role. The third element of his approach was to encourage the Vietnamese to assist in their own defense. De Lattre's son was killed in action in Indochina in 1951, and he was forced to retire with advanced cancer in December 1951. His defense of the Red River delta inflicted very heavy losses on the Vietminh, but the communist military commander, Vo Nguyen Giap, did not repeat the mistake of trying to force de Lattre's fortified zone.

See also: Abd el-Krim, Mohammed ben; Algeria; French army; French Indochina; Giap, Vo Nguyen; Vietminh
Further Reading: Clayton, Anthony, *The Wars of French Decolonisation* (London, 1994).

de Paiva Couceiro, Henrique Mitchell (1861–1944)

De Paiva Couceiro was one of the most distinguished officers of the Portuguese army during the era of colonial warfare in the late nineteenth and early twentieth centuries. The principle aide of the governor of Mozambique, António Enes, de Paiva led an expedition into the Magul region in 1895. However, his main contribution to the extension of Portuguese control came as governor in Angola, where he was responsible for the construction of strategic railway lines and an attempt to create a more efficient administrative structure. Returning to Portugal in 1909, he stood by the monarchy when it was overthrown the following year and subsequently led an attempted monarchist coup against the republic in 1919. He also opposed the establishment of the Salazarist dictatorship in 1932 and went into exile in 1937. De Paiva wrote a number of works on the colonization of Portuguese Africa.

See also: Angola; Colonial warfare; Mozambique; Portuguese army
Further Reading: Newitt, Marlyn, *Portugal in Africa* (London, 1981).

de Spinola, Marshal Antonio Sebastião Ribeiro (1910–1996)

De Spinola was governor-general and commander in chief in Portuguese Guinea from 1968 to 1973. The monocled de Spinola was commissioned in the cavalry in 1933, his father being a leading economic adviser to the Portuguese dictator, Antonio de Salazar. A fine horseman, de Spinola made his reputation commanding the 345th Cavalry Group in Angola between 1961 and 1964, but he also saw service with Portuguese volunteers fighting for Franco in the Spanish Civil War and as an official observer of the German army on the Eastern Front during World War II. Successively provost-marshal, inspector of cavalry, and deputy commander of the Republican Guard after his return from Angola, de

Spinola disliked assignment to Guinea in May 1968 and agreed initially only to serve for six months to report on a war he believed unwinnable. In the event, de Spinola was not to return to Portugal until August 1973. Yet he did so as a national hero, having dramatically transformed the campaign against Amílcar Cabral's nationalist Partido Africano da Independência de Guiné e Cabo Verde (PAIGC).

Reinvigorating his forces' morale through exhaustive, almost daily visits to units, de Spinola also understood the political requirements of counterinsurgency, launching what he termed "social counterrevolution" to win over the population's hearts and minds. He extended the existing resettlement program, and his forces built schools, hospitals, water points, and houses. Efforts to combat disease and improve indigenous crops and herds were undertaken. He raised indigenous forces for the Portuguese army.

Back in Portugal, de Spinola received his country's highest decoration but declined all posts offered until he finally accepted that of deputy chief of staff in January 1974 with the rank of full general. His service in the colonies had convinced him of the need for fundamental reforms of the Salazarist system and for a federal solution to Portugal's colonial difficulties. His manifesto, set out in the 1974 book *Portugal e o Futuro* (Portugal and the future), resulted in his dismissal by Salazar's successor, Marcello Caetano, on 13 March. Three days later, there was an attempted coup against Caetano; a more successful coup surfaced on 25 April. Even though not personally involved in the coup, de Spinola was invited to negotiate for its leaders and was named head of a junta (council) for national salvation the following day.

He became provisional president of Portugal on 15 May. However, the more radical elements in the Armed Forces Movement (AFM), which had engineered the coup, were suspicious of de Spinola. Faced with increasing unrest, he resigned on 30 Sep-

tember 1974. He fled Portugal after being implicated in an attempted coup against the radicals in March 1975. Briefly imprisoned on his return from exile in 1976, de Spinola was restored to his general's rank in 1978 and became a marshal in 1981. Subsequently, de Spinola acted as military adviser to Pres. Manual Soares.

See also: Angola; Cabral, Amílcar; Guinea, Portuguese; Hearts and minds; Partido Africano da Independência de Guiné e Cabo Verde (PAIGC); Politicization of armed forces; Portuguese army; Resettlement
Further Reading: Porch, Douglas, *The Portuguese Armed Forces and the Revolution* (London, 1977); de Spinola, Antonio, *Portugal and the Future* (Johannesburg, 1974).

De Wet, Gen. Christiaan Rudolf (1854–1922)

With "Koos" De La Rey, De Wet was one of the leading Boer guerrilla commanders fighting the British in the latter stages of the Second Boer War (1899–1902). Indeed, after the surrender of the main Boer field army at Paardeburg in March 1900, it was De La Rey and De Wet who principally advocated continuing the struggle through guerrilla warfare. De Wet had also fought the British in the First Boer War (1880–1881), seeing action at the Battle of Laing's Nek. After Paardeburg, De Wet became commandant-general of the forces of the Orange Free State and, subsequently, its acting president.

Operating mostly in the Free State, De Wet had a major success even before the start of the guerrilla phase of the war in crippling the British advance by stampeding the oxen of its wagon train at Waterval Drift in February 1900; he scored another notable victory at Tweefontein in December 1901. Perhaps his greatest success, however, was to invade Cape Colony in February 1901 and then successfully evade no less than 15 British columns sent to trap him. After the war, De Wet was minister of agriculture in the Free State from 1907 to 1910, but he was far from reconciled to British rule. In 1914 he was a founder of the National Party and led an attempted uprising in September 1914. De Wet was captured in December 1914 and sentenced to six years imprisonment, but he was released after a year.

See also: Boer War; British army; De La Rey, Gen. Jacobus Hercules
Further Reading: Pakenham, Thomas, *The Boer War* (London, 1979).

Debray, Régis (1941–)

Debray was a French Marxist philosopher who with Che Guevara developed a new theory of rural revolutionary guerrilla warfare known as *foco. Foco* was based on the experience of Fidel Castro's successful campaign against the government of Fulgencio Batista on Cuba between 1956 and 1959. In reality, Castro's success owed much to the support he received throughout his campaign from the urban-based 26 July Movement, which Castro himself had founded. The general unpopularity of Batista also contributed substantially to the rapid collapse of his administration.

However, in analyzing the Cuban experience, Guevara and Debray overlooked the significance of urban action. They equally rejected the emphasis in prevailing rural guerrilla warfare theory—most notably that of Mao Tse-tung—on the necessity for a prolonged period of political preparation of a population prior to the commencement of insurgency. As a result, other Latin American rural insurgencies modeled on Castro's campaign—as in Colombia (1961), Guatemala (1962), Ecuador (1962), and Peru (1963)—failed. The process culminated in Guevara's ill-fated attempt to carry revolution to Bolivia in November 1966.

Debray had visited Cuba in 1961 and became professor of history of philosophy at the University of Havana in 1966. He accompanied Guevara's group to Bolivia as a journalist. However, he was captured in April 1967, and Guevara himself was killed in October 1967. Debray was sentenced to 30 years in prison but was released after three years and returned to France. His the-

oretical publications, *Revolution in the Revolution* (1967), *Strategy for Revolution* (1973), and *The Revolution on Trial* (1978), as well as his account of Bolivia, *Ché's Guerrilla War* (1975), suggest Debray learned little from the abject failure of *foco.* Debray reemerged in France as a somewhat unlikely foreign policy adviser to Pres. François Mitterand between 1981 and 1986. Subsequently, he returned to the study of philosophy, expounding a new theory he called "mediology."

See also: Batista y Zaldivar, Fulgencio; Castro, Fidel; Cuba; *Foco;* Guatemala; Guevara, Ernesto Che; Mao Tse-tung; Peru
Further Reading: Debray, R., *Strategy for Revolution* (Harmondsworth, 1973).

Decker, Gen. Carl von (1784–1844)

Decker wrote about the experience of partisan warfare after the French Revolutionary and Napoleonic Wars (1792–1815). His book, *Der Kleine Krieg im Geiste der neueren Kriegsführung* (The small war in the spirit of the new conduct of warfare), was published in Berlin in 1822. Decker, who regarded partisans as requiring special qualities, stressed the need for mobility and for cultivating good relations with the local population. As in the work of his Russian contemporary, Denis Davydov, Decker emphasized the vulnerability of an enemy's line of communications to partisan attack. Subsequently, in 1844, he also wrote a book on the early operations of the French army in Algeria, *Algerien und die Kriegsführung* (Algeria and the conduct of warfare). He predicted that the French would be unsuccessful, but that was before Thomas-Robert Bugeaud transformed French tactics.

See also: Algeria; Bugeaud, Marshal Thomas-Robert; Davydov, Denis Vasilevich; Partisans
Further Reading: Laqueur, Walter, *Guerrilla* (London, 1977).

Dhofar

Dhofar is the mountainous southern province of the sultanate of Oman, itself situated in the southeastern part of the Arabian Peninsula. Dhofar was under attack from Marxist insurgents between 1964 and 1975, but assistance from the British army led to the comprehensive defeat of the guerrillas in a model counterinsurgency campaign.

Dhofar was geographically isolated from the rest of Oman, and opposition had grown to the rule of Sultan Said bin Taimur, who had prevented any social, economic, and political development. With help from the British Special Air Service (SAS), an earlier revolt on the Jebel Akhdar (Green Mountain) in northern Oman had been put down in 1957–1959. However, Sheikh Mussalim bin Nufl then founded the Dhofar Liberation Front (DLF), which began sabotage operations in the province in December 1962 followed by more ambitious guerrilla operations in 1964. Neither the DLF nor the Sultan's Armed Forces (SAF) were sufficiently strong to achieve military success, and the revolt appeared to have died out by 1967.

However, in November 1967 Britain withdrew from Aden, and the new Marxist government of the People's Democratic Republic of Yemen (PDRY) offered its full support to the DLF. The DLF now received Soviet and Chinese weapons, and in August 1968 the nationalist followers of Mussalim were ousted by Marxist hard-liners led by Muhammad Ahmad al-Ghassani. DLF was transformed into the Popular Front for the Liberation of the Occupied Arabian Gulf (PFLOAG). The strategic significance of Oman for both the West and the Soviet bloc lay in its command of the Strait of Hormuz, as it overlooked the route tankers navigated in carrying oil from the Persian Gulf to open sea.

In response to the increased threat, the SAF was modernized, but Sultan Said still refused to offer any concessions to the mountain peoples of Dhofar. These people were known collectively as *jebalis* after the Jebel Plateau, which dominated the interior of the province. As a result, government influence was restricted to the towns of the narrow coastal plain by early 1970. PFLOAG had about 2,000 core activists by this time and about 4,000 part-time militia. At that point, Said's son, Qaboos bin Said, mounted a near-bloodless coup on 23 July 1970 and deposed his father. Qaboos, who had been trained at Britain's Royal Military Academy at Sandhurst, immediately launched a major program of modernization. He also called for more British assistance. Even though the SAF itself was expanded to about 9,600 Omani and Baluchi troops (the latter recruited from Pakistan), the British sent about 500 personnel on secondment or contract, of whom 35 were killed. Later, in 1973, the shah of Iran sent the 2,500-strong Iranian Imperial Battle Group to assist Qaboos, and the Jordanians sent a special forces battalion in 1975.

An essential feature of the new counterinsurgency strategy was the promotion of social and economic development in Dhofar, with the campaign being directed by the Dhofar Development Committee and military operations being followed up by Civil Action Teams (CATs). It was realized that the *jebalis* were a nomadic people who would not readily accept resettlement, and therefore it became the practice to sink wells as a natural focus for population in an arid country. Efforts were also made to develop cattle breeding since cattle were the most prized possession of the *jebalis*. PFLOAG itself made the mistake of trying to impose Marxism by suppressing both the tribal structure of the *jebalis* and their Islamic religion. As a result, defections from PFLOAG began to occur, a group of 24 former DLF fighters being the first to do so in September 1970. These dissidents became the nucleus of the *firqat*, groups of former guerrillas prepared to fight erstwhile colleagues. Former guerrillas had been formed into similar pseudoforces in other campaigns, such as the countergangs during the Kenyan Emergency (1952–1960). Eventually, more than 3,000 men were enlisted into the *firqat*. The organization of the *firqat* and that of the CATs were the responsibility of the SAS, whose officers had also advised Qaboos on the overall strategy to be adopted.

The first part of the military solution to the insurgent threat posed by PFLOAG was to establish a permanent SAF presence on the Jebel; this was achieved at Medinat Al Haq (known as "White City") in October 1971. The second requirement was to interdict the supply route into Dhofar from the PDRY. In April 1972 an SAF battalion was dropped by helicopter atop the cliffs at Sarfait in western Dhofar (under which the supply route passed); but the cliffs proved too sheer to allow for easy interdiction. However, in December 1973 the Iranians established a number of fortified positions in the center of the Jebel, which enabled the construction of the Hornbeam Line in early 1974, followed by the Damavand Line farther west. With infiltration rendered much more difficult, the SAF was able to concentrate on clearing remaining PFLOAG groups to the east of the lines. It intended to construct a third line even closer to the PDRY frontier.

The intended diversions around Sarfait were so successful in October 1975 that the plan was changed in favor of a concerted drive by Brig. Gen. John Akehurst's Dhofar Brigade to the frontier together with air strikes on artillery positions inside the PDRY. The war was declared officially at an end with the capture of the last guerrilla position inside Dhofar at Dhalqut on 2 December 1975. The reform program continued after the end of the war with the result that the *jebalis* have a strong vested interest in preserving the status quo. Thus, in a troubled part of the world, Oman has remained stable.

See also: Akehurst, Gen. Sir John; British army; *Firqat;* Popular Front for the Liberation of the Occupied Arabian Gulf (PFLOAG); Pseudoforces; Special Air Service (SAS)
Further Reading: Beckett, Ian, and John Pimlott (eds.), *Armed Forces and Modern Counter-insurgency* (London, 1985); Akehurst, John, *We Won a War* (Salisbury, 1982).

Dien Bien Phu, Battle of (1953–1954)

Dien Bien Phu was the climactic battle between the French army and the Vietminh in the struggle for French Indochina between 1946 and 1954. French defeat led to withdrawal from Indochina and, as a result of the Geneva Agreement (1954), to the independence of Laos and Cambodia and to the division of Vietnam into two separate states. The intention of the French commander in chief, Lt. Gen. Henri Navarre, in "Operation Castor" was to drop parachute troops into the Nam Yum River valley of Dien Bien Phu, which lay on the frontier between Laos and northern Vietnam, about 170 miles west of Hanoi. Navarre wished to interdict the Vietminh supply lines into northern Laos.

Laos had been given autonomy by the French, and Navarre wished to demonstrate French commitment to the Laotian government. At the same time, a garrison at

French defenders of Dien Bien Phu in a trench as they plan a gallant, though hopeless, counterattack against the communist Vietminh in late March 1954. (UPI/Corbis-Bettmann)

Dien Bien Phu would assist the Meo peoples in resisting the communists and help reestablish French control over the region's opium crop, from which the Vietminh derived considerable financial benefit. Establishing a "mooring-point" in communist-controlled territory would also force the Vietminh commander, Vo Nguyen Giap, to commit his forces to attacking the French fortified positions. The first French unit, led by Col. Marcel Bigeard, dropped on Dien Bien Phu on 20 November 1953.

The difficulty with Dien Bien Phu was that it was dominated by surrounding hills and so isolated that it could only be supplied by air. It was assumed that the Vietminh would not be able to bring artillery and antiaircraft batteries into the area. In the event, this assumption was proved tragically wrong, for Giap was able to concentrate more than 37,000 men and more than 300 heavy guns against the French.

There was some confusion in the French command as to what precise function Dien Bien Phu was intended to fulfill. As the Vietminh buildup became apparent, Navarre chose to reinforce the garrison rather than withdraw it in order to take on Giap. The French eventually committed about 10,800 men to the defense of Dien Bien Phu under the command of Col. Christian de la Croix de Castries. The defense rested on nine strongpoints nicknamed Anne-Marie, Béatrice, Claudine, Dominique, Elaine, Françoise, Gabrielle, Huguette, and Isabelle. The communist offensive began on 13 March 1954, with Béatrice and Gabrielle falling within the first two days. Vietminh antiaircraft fire increasingly closed the base to supply, and reinforcement though Bigeard's regiment was successfully dropped back into Dien Bien Phu. With the Vietminh anxious to ensure success before the scheduled opening of the negotiations at Geneva, Giap committed his forces to massive wave assaults against the strongpoints. After 55 days, the surviving French surrendered on 7 May 1954. The French had lost almost 2,000 dead, the Vietminh an estimated 8,000 dead and 15,000 wounded. The Geneva conference opened the following day.

See also: Bigeard, Gen. Marcel; Cambodia; French army; French Indochina; Giap, Vo Nguyen; Laos; Navarre, Gen. Henri-Eugène; Vietminh
Further Reading: Fall, Bernard, *Hell in a Very Small Place* (London, 1966).

Dirty war (1976–1977)

Guerra sucia (dirty war) was the term used to describe the suppression of insurgency in Argentina between 1976 and 1977. After a military coup against the government of Maria Estela "Isabelita" Perón in March 1976, the government of Gen. Jorge Videla moved to eliminate left-wing groups such as Montoneros and Ejército Revolucionario del Pueblo (ERP), which had been waging a campaign of urban guerrilla warfare in Buenos Aires and other cities.

The military response was essentially one of maximum force and institutionalized counterterror. The guerrillas seem to have assumed that direct military involvement in the campaign against them would merely result in more street battles rather than the absolute repression that ensued. As in Guatemala, the armed forces were assisted by right-wing death squads such as Alianza Anticommunista Argentine (AAA) or the Argentine Anticommunist Alliance, which often included off-duty policemen. Little pretence was made at legality, with units such as GT33 attached to the Navy Engineering School alone being responsible for an estimated 3,000 deaths. By the end of 1977, perhaps 15,000 individuals had "disappeared."

Amid increasing economic problems, Videla resigned in March 1981, and in turn his successor, Roberto Viola, was replaced by Leopoldo Galtieri in December 1981. It was Galtieri's disastrous attempt to take the Falkland Islands from Britain in April 1982 that led to the collapse of military government. The democratic administration that emerged after elections in October

1983 tried many who were involved in the dirty war.

See also: Argentina; Ejército Revolucionario del Pueblo (ERP); Guatemala; Montoneros; Urban guerrilla warfare
Further Reading: Gillespie, R., *Soldiers of Peron* (Oxford, 1982); Taylor, Diana, *Disappearing Acts* (Durham, 1997).

Dutch army

In the seventeenth century the Dutch first penetrated into the interior of what became the Dutch East Indies and, subsequently, Indonesia. However, it was not until the beginning of the twentieth century that the Indonesian archipelago was fully pacified by the Koninklijke Landmacht (Royal Dutch Army) and the Royal Dutch Indies Army or Koninklijk Nederlandsch-Indisch Leger (KNIL). New insurgency then occurred in the Dutch East Indies between 1947 and 1949, which led to the independence of Indonesia.

The Dutch had little regard for the military capabilities of their indigenous opponents, and traditionally they operated with large columns. However, the Dutch East Indies varied greatly in climate and terrain, and on occasion Dutch soldiers displayed considerable tactical initiative. During a campaign on Java between 1825 and 1830, for example, Gen. M. H. de Kock developed a technique similar to that associated with the French general, Joseph-Simon Galliéni. De Kock established a network of small outposts from which small but highly mobile columns moved into the interior. The outposts themselves also became foci for population, enabling the Dutch to extend facilities to the people and to attempt to win over their hearts and minds.

In 1896 a three-volume manual, *De Indische Oorlogen* (The Indonesian wars), was published by Capt. Klaas van der Maaten. It has been favorably compared to the work of the British military theorist Charles Callwell for its insights into colonial warfare. Unfortunately, its lessons were ignored by the authors of the revised 1947 edition of *Voorschrift voor de Politiek-poli-tionele Taak van het Leger* (VPTL, or Precepts for the politico-policing task of the army). This was primarily based on the lessons of the last phase (1903–1910) of the running war fought against the sultanate of Atjeh (Aceh) in northern Sumatra when intensive and offensive patrolling sufficed to hunt down the last remnants of Acehnese resistance.

However, the Indonesian nationalists encountered in 1947 were far better armed and organized than the Acehnese. The Dutch also consistently underestimated Indonesian military leaders such as Abdul Haris Nasution. The Dutch did attempt to improve their reaction time in response to guerrilla incidents but never enjoyed sufficient popular support to defeat the nationalists. Increasingly, too, there were acts of brutality by Dutch troops, which were eventually investigated by the Dutch government in 1968. As with other colonial armies, the Dutch recruited indigenous troops. In 1905, for example, there were 15,000 Dutch regulars in the Indies together with 26,000 locally raised troops, the majority being Javanese or Ambonese. Increasingly, much of the routine policing was undertaken by the Korps Maréchaussée, an armed native police formed in 1890 and led by Dutch officers.

See also: Callwell, Maj. Gen. Sir Charles Edward; Colonial warfare; Dutch East Indies; Galliéni, Marshal Joseph-Simon; Hearts and minds; Maaten, Maj. Gen. Klaas van der; Manuals; Nasution, Gen. Abdul Haris
Further Reading: de Moor, J. A., and H. L. Wesseling (eds.), *Imperialism and War: Essays on Colonial War in Asia and Africa* (Leiden, 1989).

Dutch East Indies

The pacification of the Dutch East Indies by the Royal Dutch Army involved almost continuous campaigning throughout the Indonesian archipelago from the seventeenth century to the final campaign for independence waged by Indonesian nationalists between 1947 and 1949. Perhaps this is not surprising given that Indonesia consists of more than 13,000 separate islands. In northern Sumatra, for example, it took from 1873 to 1912 to pacify the sultanate of Atjeh (Aceh) at a cost of more than 2,000 Dutch dead. Southern Sumatra was not pacified until 1907. Similarly, the final campaign against the states of Bugis and Makasarese on South Sulawesi took place only in 1905–1906 and on Bali in 1906. As late as 1927 there was a communist-inspired revolt in west Java.

The crisis of the Dutch colonial empire came in World War II with the Netherlands itself occupied by the Germans in May 1940 and the Japanese then overrunning the Dutch East Indies, which surrendered on 9 March 1942. Upon the Japanese occupation of much of Southeast Asia, they stimulated indigenous nationalism by granting nominal independence to states such as Burma and the Philippines. In the Dutch East Indies, the Japanese permitted the nationalists Mohammad Hatta and Kusno Sosro Sukarno to establish the Putera (Center of Power) organization in March 1943, although they subsequently disbanded it. Near the end of the war, the Japanese promised full independence to Indonesia but were forced to surrender on 15 August 1945 following the dropping of the atomic bombs upon Hiroshima and Nagasaki.

With the Allies unable to organize an immediate return to occupied countries, the Indonesian nationalists seized the opportunity to declare their own independence on 17 August 1945. The first Allied troops to land on Java on 29 September 1945 were British. The British intention was to evacuate former internees and prisoners of war of the Japanese. However, the nationalists believed the British intended to facilitate the return of the Dutch, and fighting erupted at Surabaya in October; a British brigadier was killed while trying to calm an Indonesian crowd.

The British, whose last forces left Indonesia in November 1946, urged the Dutch to negotiate. The Dutch did indeed open negotiations but would not concede total independence. The Dutch presented the nationalists with an ultimatum in May 1947, demanding that Dutch sovereignty be recognized until February 1949. There was no response. On 20 June 1947, therefore, the Dutch, who had built up their forces to about 100,000, launched what they termed a "police action" in Java, Sumatra, and Madura. They achieved some success, but pressure from the United States and the UN led to further negotiations on a form of federalism. However, the Indonesians did not believe that this was acceptable, and so fighting continued, the Indonesian Republican Army (TNI) having about 175,000 men.

A second Dutch "police action" opened on 18 December 1948, with the Dutch seizing the nationalist capital, Djakarta, in eastern Java and capturing Sukarno and much of the nationalist leadership. There was savage fighting on South Sulawesi, where a Dutch captain, Raymond "Turk" Westerling, earned a particular reputation for brutality. The United States threatened the Dutch with economic sanctions on 7 December 1948, leading to a final round of negotiations and independence for Indonesia on 27 December 1949.

See also: Dutch army; Nasution, Gen. Abdul Haris
Further Reading: Holland, Robert (ed.), *Emergencies and Disorder in the European Empires after 1945* (London, 1994).

East Timor

East Timor is a former Portuguese colony in the East Indies that was invaded by Indonesia in December 1975, resulting in a continuing guerrilla war. After the Portuguese army seized power in Portugal in April 1974, fighting broke out on East Timor between rival nationalist groups. When the Portuguese finally withdrew in August 1975, the group that had won the power struggle was Frente Revolucionária Timorense de Libertação e Independência (FRETILIN), or the Revolutionary Front for the Liberation and Independence of Timor. FRETILIN declared East Timor's independence on 28 November 1975, but it was not recognized by either Portugal or Indonesia.

West Timor became part of Indonesia when the Dutch quit the Dutch East Indies in 1949. Although Indonesia had earlier failed to annex northern Borneo in the Indonesian-Malaysian Confrontation (1962–1966), the Indonesians now had similar ambitions for East Timor. On 7 December 1975, therefore, Indonesian "volunteers" invaded East Timor, and on 14 August 1976 it was announced that East Timor was to be absorbed into Indonesia. A savage guerrilla conflict has been waged ever since, costing an estimated 60,000 lives by the end of 1979. As FRETILIN was dominated by communists, Australia recognized Indonesian sovereignty in 1978 as preferable to an independent communist state. However, most members of the UN condemn continued Indonesian occupation, with Indonesian forces frequently accused of violating human rights.

See also: Confrontation, Indonesian/Malayasian; Dutch East Indies; Portuguese army
Further Reading: Budiarjo, C., and L. S. Liong, *The War Against East Timor* (London, 1984).

Ejército Revolucionario del Pueblo (ERP)

ERP or the People's Revolutionary Army was one of a number of groups waging urban guerrilla warfare in Argentina in the 1970s. It was founded in 1970 at the same time as the Montoneros. However, whereas Montoneros wished to see the return to power of former Pres. Juan Perón, ERP was filled with Trotskyist social revolutionaries. Perón did return to power in September 1973 after an 18-year exile; after his death in July 1974 the government was led by his widow, Isabel. The Perónists were far less radical than the guerrilla groups had hoped, and even Montoneros turned against Isabel Perón. Violence increased to such an extent that the army seized power in March 1976. Gen. Jorge Videla then launched the so-called dirty war against the guerrillas. Within two years, unrestrained counterterror by the security forces and right-wing death squads had destroyed ERP.

See also: Argentina; Dirty war; Montoneros; Urban guerrilla warfare
Further Reading: Kohl, J., and J. Litt, *Urban Guerrilla Warfare in Latin America* (Cambridge, MA, 1974).

El Salvador

The Central American state of El Salvador was the scene of escalating violence through the 1970s, culminating in the creation of a common front, Frente Farabundo Martí de Liberación Nacional (FMLN), uniting a number of left-wing guerrilla groups opposed to the government in 1980. FMLN then continued to wage its campaign until 1992.

El Salvador is the most densely populated state in Central America. Pressure of population was responsible for increasing economic difficulties. After a succession of military governments, pressure from the United States brought the more moderate José Napoleón Duarte to the presidency in 1980. Duarte appeared unable to control right-wing death squads responsible for the murder of Archbishop Oscar Romero in March 1980 and three American nuns the following December. Moreover, in new elections in March 1982, Duarte was re-

placed as president by the right-wing Arena Party's Roberto D'Aubuisson, who was thought to be closely involved with the death squads. The United States intervened to compel D'Aubuisson to step down after only a week, but death-squad murders were still running at a rate of 1,200 per week by the end of 1982.

Despite assistance from American advisers and American promotion of a hearts-and-minds campaign, the security forces appeared unable to suppress the insurgency. Duarte returned to power in 1984 and began negotiations with FMLN, but they failed to halt the fighting. Arena, now led by Alfredo Cristiani Buchard, won the 1989 elections. Cristiani, too, attempted negotiations. However, fighting continued as before, with a major FMLN offensive in November 1989 forcing the government to impose a state of siege in the capital, San Salvador. By 1990 an estimated 75,000 people had been killed in El Salvador. Peace

A group of El Salvadoran soldiers poses beside graffiti of their political group, the FMLN, in 1983. (Owen Franken/Corbis)

accords were finally signed between FMLN and the government in 1992.

See also: Frente Farabundo Martí de Liberación Nacional (FMLN)

Further Reading: Byrne, Hugh, *El Salvador's Civil War: A Study of Revolution* (Boulder, 1996).

Ellinikos Laikos Apeleftherotikon (ELAS)

ELAS or the National Liberation Army was the military wing of the communist-dominated Ethnikon Apeleftherotikon Metopon (EAM) or National Liberation Front during the Greek Civil War (1946–1949). ELAS had emerged during World War II in opposition to German occupation of Greece in April 1941. However, the communists were bitter rivals of the promonarchist National Democratic Greek League (EDES), and there was open fighting between EDES and ELAS as early as 1943.

When the Germans evacuated Greece in October 1944, ELAS attempted to seize Athens. British forces moved into Greece in support of the exiled Greek national government and expelled ELAS from Athens in street fighting between December 1944 and January 1945. Under the terms of a cease-fire agreement, ELAS was supposed to be disbanded but reemerged as Dimokratikos Stratos Ellados (DSE), or the Democratic Army of Greece, in December 1946 under the leadership of Markos Vaphiadis. Operating from the Grammos and Vitsi Mountains, DSE had a peak strength of 25,000 men. However, the communist political leadership under Nikos Zachariadis made the mistake of committing DSE to a conventional offensive in December 1947 in order to try to declare a provisional government in a "liberated zone."

Vaphiadis still advocated guerrilla tactics, but he was ousted in January 1949 by Zachariadis, who insisted on static defense of mountain strongholds. Yugoslavia's suspension of aid to DSE in 1948 and the Greek government's enforced resettlement of the mountain population had already effectively isolated DSE. Spearheaded by dive-bombers, the Greek National Army (GNA) launched an offensive in August 1949 that cleared the mountains. DSE announced a final cease-fire on 16 October 1949.

See also: Greek Civil War

Further Reading: Close, David H., *The Greek Civil War* (New York, 1993).

Emmerich, Col. Andreas (1737–1809)

Emmerich was a Hessian officer in the British army during the American War of Independence (1775–1783), the British hiring troops from German states such as Hesse for service in North America. Like fellow Hessian Johann von Ewald, Emmerich recognized the value of irregular warfare. In 1789 he published in London *The Partisan in War or the Use of a Corps of Light Troops for an Army,* which drew on his American experience. It was subsequently translated into his native German and published in 1791 in Dresden as *Der Parteigänger im Krieg oder der Nutzen eines Corps leichter Truppen für eine Armee.*

Like his contemporaries, Emmerich interpreted partisan warfare mainly as an activity carried out by regular troops detached from the main body of an army and operating on the flanks or in the rear of an opposing army. Consequently, partisans were largely seen by Emmerich as being composed of light infantry and light cavalry. However, Emmerich also recognized the need to gain the support of the local population when acting behind enemy lines, stressing the importance of intelligence. In retirement, Emmerich participated in the unsuccessful Marburg insurrection against the French in 1809 and was executed.

See also: American War of Independence; British army; Ewald, Lt. Gen. Johann von; Partisans

Further Reading: Laqueur, Walter, *Guerrilla* (London, 1977).

Eritrea

The former Italian colony of Eritrea was occupied by Britain during World War II, but with UN agreement it passed to Ethiopian control in September 1952. Without possession of Eritrea, Ethiopia would have no access to the sea. Accordingly, despite previous assurances given about autonomy, Ethiopia annexed Eritrea in November 1962.

The Eritrean Liberation Front (ELF) had already been formed by exiled Eritreans in 1961, but its guerrilla operations against Ethiopian forces were largely unsuccessful. In 1970 Marxist elements of the ELF broke away to form the Eritrean People's Liberation Front (EPLF). For a brief period there was hope that Marxist army officers, who overthrew Emperor Haile Selassie in September 1974, might grant real autonomy to their fellow Marxists in Eritrea. Indeed, Gen. Aman Andom, who became head of state, was an Eritrean. However, autonomy was not forthcoming, and when Andom was killed in February 1977 Mengistu Haile Mariam seized power.

Mengistu had no intention of relinquishing control of Eritrea, but EPLF strength had grown from about 2,500 in 1974 to 43,000 by 1977. Thus, even with assistance after 1977 from the Soviet Union and Cubans, who helped in training, the Ethiopian army could not destroy EPLF. Nonetheless, the war was increasingly bitter, and the Eritreans claimed that nerve gas was used against them.

Certainly, Mengistu exploited the drought that left more than 1 million dead in the region between 1983 and 1985 by trying to ensure that humanitarian supplies did not reach Eritrea. A massive population relocation program was also instituted in the guise of moving people to more fertile areas. Soviet support for Mengistu lessened after 1985, and EPLF was able to steadily increase its control in Eritrea. In 1988 EPLF, now shorn of much of its earlier Marxist ideology and led by Isaias Afewerki, seized the main Ethiopian base at Afabet and joined forces with the Ethiopian People's Revolutionary Democracy Front (EPRDF). Three years later EPLF finally succeeded in clearing Eritrea of Ethiopian troops; EPRDF successes caused Mengistu to flee the country in May 1991. Following a UN-sponsored referendum in April 1993, Eritrea received its independence on 24 May 1993.

Further Reading: Pool, D., *Eritrea: Africa's Longest War* (London, 1982); Sherman, Richard, *Eritrea: The Unfinished Revolution* (New York, 1980).

Erskine, Gen. Sir George (1899–1965)

Erskine was the British commander in chief in East Africa from June 1953 to May 1956 during the Kenyan Emergency. Erskine served in both world wars, commanding the Seventh Armoured Division in the Western Desert (in Egypt, actually a part of the greater Libyan Desert) before being controversially sacked in 1944 for failing to break out from the Normandy bridgehead. Nevertheless, after World War II, he commanded British forces in Hong Kong and was director-general of the Territorial Army and general officer commanding, Eastern Command, before taking up his African appointment.

The bluff Erskine was ideally suited to raising morale in Kenya, where the security forces lacked offensive spirit in face of the Mau Mau insurgency. He sought similar proconsular powers to those enjoyed in the Malayan Emergency (1948–1960) by Sir Gerald Templer but had to settle for operational control over the forces engaged (although he had authority to declare martial law should he deem it necessary). Erskine was determined to release the army from static guard duties and to go over to the offensive. He broke Mau Mau's political organization in Nairobi in "Operation Anvil" in 1954 and launched large scale sweeping operations against Mau Mau gangs in forested areas like the Aberdares.

Erskine understood the need to avoid indiscriminate retaliation against the African population as a whole. Thus, he deprecated any indiscipline on the part of the police and locally raised forces. Erskine also encouraged the use of the indigenous Kikuyu Home Guard under proper supervision and of the "countergangs," pseudoforces of former guerrillas willing to act against their erstwhile colleagues. After his Kenyan tour, Erskine went back to Southern Command in Britain and was lieutenant-governor and commander in chief on Jersey from 1958 until his retirement in 1963.

See also: British army; Kenyan Emergency; Malayan Emergency; Mau Mau; Police; Pseudoforces; Templer, Field Marshal Sir Gerald
Further Reading: Clayton, Anthony, *Counter-insurgency in Kenya* (Manhattan, 1984).

Ethniki Organosis Kyprion Agoniston (EOKA)

EOKA or the National Organization of Cypriot Fighters was the nationalist guerrilla group that fought against the British on Cyprus between 1954 and 1959. EOKA was led by George Grivas, a Cypriot-born retired colonel in the Greek army who proved a master of guerrilla warfare. EOKA's aim was not independence for Cyprus but enosis (union with Greece).

At its peak, EOKA had only 350 activists, divided into seven groups of no more than 15 individuals operating in the Troodos Mountains and about 50 groups of no more than five or six individuals operating in cities such as Nicosia. Grivas kept EOKA small because he insisted on maintaining absolute security within his organization. However, EOKA also had a passive wing of about 750 supporters that included women and children. Often, women and children would be used to shadow targets for assassination. They were also used to carry the weapons used in attacks on British servicemen and Cypriot police, especially Greek Cypriot police.

EOKA also specialized in bomb attacks, exploding 1,782 bombs during the course of its campaign, which began in April 1955. However, because Cyprus was effectively isolated from any possibility of external assistance, EOKA's bombs were often home-made, and 2,976 failed to explode. One of the latter was placed under the bed of the British governor, Field Marshal Sir John Harding. In 1956 Harding's "Operation Pepperpot" inflicted heavy losses on EOKA's organization in the Troodos. EOKA's effectiveness was further reduced when all Greek civilian workers were excluded from British bases in October 1958 after a bomb was exploded in the British Navy, Army, and Air Force Institute (NAAFI) in Nicosia. A kind of stalemate had been achieved between the British and EOKA by the time Grivas announced a cease-fire in December 1958.

In all, 104 British servicemen, 51 policemen, and 238 civilians had been killed together with an estimated 90 members of EOKA. The independence of Cyprus in August 1960 was in many respects a defeat for the aims of EOKA, and in 1971 Grivas returned to the island to form EOKA-B, this time waging a campaign against his former ally, President Makarios. Grivas died in early 1974, but members of EOKA-B together with the Greek Cypriot National Guard participated in an attempted coup against Makarios in July 1974. However, the coup attempt resulted in a Turkish invasion and the occupation of northern Cyprus, which continues to this day.

See also: British army; Cyprus; Grivas, Gen. George Theodorou; Harding, Field Marshal Lord (Allen Francis John)
Further Reading: Crawshaw, Nancy, *The Cyprus Revolt* (London, 1978).

Ewald, Lt. Gen. Johann von (1744–1813)

Ewald was a Hessian officer who fought for the British army during the American War of Independence (1775–1783). He joined the Danish army in 1788 and rose to the rank of lieutenant general in Danish service. The British hired troops from German states such as Hesse for service in North America. Like fellow Hessian Andreas Emmerich, Ewald wrote about his North American experiences but also drew on the Seven Years War (1756–1763) in his analysis of partisan warfare. His principle work was *Abhandlungen über den kleinen Krieg* (Treatise on the small war), published in Kassel in 1790.

Ewald's views were similar to those of Emmerich, and although his own work was cited by other theorists such as Carl von Clausewitz, it was Emmerich whom Ewald regarded as "the first partisan of our age."

See also: American War of Independence; British army; Emmerich, Col. Andreas; Partisans
Further Reading: Laqueur, Walter, *Guerrilla* (London, 1977).

Fire force

The fire force concept was developed by government security forces in Rhodesia between 1972 and 1979 as a means of offsetting a lack of manpower by concentrating firepower and mobility. The Rhodesians simply did not have enough men to mount offensive operations against guerrilla forces because large numbers were deployed to guard vital installations against attacks. "Vertical envelopment" of guerrilla forces by fire forces appeared to be a partial solution by maximizing available resources.

When a group of guerrillas from either the Zimbabwe African People's Union (ZAPU) or the Zimbabwe African National Union (ZANU) were located, a light aircraft such as a Cessna Lynx would attack the group with fragmentation and concussion bombs or napalm. Four French-built Alouette helicopters would then be deployed, each carrying four or five men to act as "beaters." Their task was to drive the guerrillas back into the path of 15 or 16 paratroopers dropped at very low level from a Dakota C-47 transport aircraft.

Four of fire forces were available, two manned by men from the Rhodesian Light Infantry and two by the Rhodesian African Rifles. By 1979 the fire forces were said to be responsible for three-quarters of all casualties inflicted on guerrillas inside Rhodesia. However, the increasing escalation of the war after 1974 meant that reaction time became greater and greater as a result of the sheer number of demands being made on the fire forces. There was also a certain amount of resentment on the part of those who tracked the guerrillas on the ground, as fire forces often got credit (and the "reward" in terms of kills) for others' labors.

See also: Helicopters; Rhodesia; Zimbabwe African National Union (ZANU); Zimbabwe African People's Union (ZAPU)

Further Reading: Cilliers, J. K., *Counter-insurgency in Rhodesia* (London, 1985).

Firqat

Firqat is the Arabic word for "a force." It was used to describe the pseudoforces of former guerrillas raised by the British Special Air Service (SAS) for service against their erstwhile insurgent colleagues in the Dhofar campaign in Oman between 1970 and 1975. The nucleus of the first *firqat*, named Firqat Salahadin, was a group of 24 men led by Salim Mubarak, who in September 1970 deserted the guerrilla organization known as the Popular Front for the Liberation of the Occupied Arabian Gulf (PFLOAG).

Mubarak and his followers were veterans of the original antigovernment guerrillas, the Dhofar Liberation Front (DLF). They had surrendered because, as a Marxist organization, PFLOAG tried to suppress both the Islamic religion and the tribal structure of the Jebali people, who inhabited the Jebel Plateau in the mountainous Dhofar Province of Oman. More than 1,000 individuals deserted PFLOAG by

January 1975, and these surrendered enemy personnel (SEPs) made up 80 percent of the 1,600 men eventually organized into 21 different *firqats.* Initially, the *firqat* had been multitribal, but following a mutiny in the Firqat Salahadin in April 1971 it was thought wiser to keep different tribal groups apart. The *firqat* were quite volatile and prone to indiscipline: In October 1971, for example, three out of five *firqats* deployed for "Operation Jaguar" refused to fight because it was Ramadan (the sacred Islamic observance). However, they proved a highly effective local defense force that increasingly prevented PFLOAG from operating on the Jebel.

See also: British army; Dhofar; Popular Front for the Liberation of the Occupied Arabian Gulf (PFLOAG); Pseudoforces; Special Air Service (SAS)
Further Reading: Jeapes, Tony, *SAS Secret War* (London, 1996).

Foco

Foco (Spanish: "focus") is the theory of revolutionary rural guerrilla warfare devised in the early 1960s by Che Guevara and Régis Debray. Guevara and Debray based their theory on the success enjoyed by Fidel Castro in Cuba between 1956 and 1959 (Guevara fought with Castro). Castro landed on Cuba in December 1956 with 81 men with the intention of assisting a planned urban insurrection in the towns of eastern Cuba against the Cuban dictator, Fulgencio Batista. In the event, Castro's landing was delayed, and the insurrection was suppressed before Castro even arrived. Three days later Castro's group ran into the Cuban army, and less than two dozen men (including Castro and Guevara) escaped into the Sierra Maestra Mountains. Thereafter, Castro never built up his force beyond about 300 men, yet he was able to overcome a Cuban army of 30,000 troops and to overthrow Batista in January 1959. In fact, Castro's victory was entirely fortuitous, for Batista's regime had been hopelessly corrupt, unpopular, and inefficient. The Cuban army thus contrived to lose a

war having apparently suffered only 200 dead in three years. Batista also lost the support of the United States through his poor human rights record.

Thus, based on Castro's success against a regime ripe for defeat, Guevara and Debray developed a model for revolution that they believed could be reproduced as a matter of course throughout Latin America, if not the Third World. Whereas the classic theorist of rural revolutionary guerrilla warfare, Mao Tse-tung, had stressed the need for an organization of parallel political and military structures, Guevara and Debray argued that the guerrillas themselves would be a revolutionary fusion of political and military authority. Mao had emphasized cultivating popular support through a lengthy period of political preparation. Guevara and Debray assumed, because of Castro's easy victory, that objective conditions favorable to revolution would exist automatically where there was but a minimum level of discontent with a government.

Accordingly, under the model, through military action alone a small and dedicated band of guerrillas would provide the focus for revolution. Progressively larger numbers of sympathizers would then support the guerrillas as their decisive military action exposed the brutal and corrupt nature of the government. In frustration at being unable to crush the guerrillas, the authorities would be forced into overreaction against the population as a whole. Thus, the guerrilla *foco* would prove a catalyst for a wider insurrection, which would topple the regime.

Guevara and Debray not only assumed that the Cuban experience could be reproduced at will elsewhere; they failed to assess correctly why Castro had succeeded. They failed to recognize the weakness of the Batista regime and the manifest incompetence of the Cuban army. And in emphasizing the need for rural guerrilla action, they did not acknowledge the considerable support Castro had derived from the underground organization, the 26 July Movement, in Cuban towns. Without this, Castro could not have survived in the Sierra Maestras. Indeed, Debray made a positive virtue out of keeping the guerrillas isolated from the population.

Through its reduced emphasis on lengthy political preparation, *foco* appeared a convenient shortcut to revolution and proved very attractive to emerging revolutionary groups in Latin America inspired by Castro's example. However, the particular circumstances of Cuba in the late 1950s simply did not exist everywhere else. For one thing, the majority of the Latin American population was no longer rural; for another the United States, alarmed by Castro's success, poured military and economic aid into states threatened by guerrillas. Thus, *foco* groups failed in Colombia (1961), Guatemala (1962), Ecuador (1962), and Peru (1963). The greatest failure of all was that in Bolivia (1966–1967), where Debray was captured and Guevara killed. The failure of *foco* led to the development of urban guerrilla warfare in Latin America in the late 1960s.

See also: Batista y Zaldivar, Fulgencio; Castro, Fidel; Cuba; Debray, Régis; Guatemala; Guevara, Ernesto Che; Mao Tse-tung; Peru
Further Reading: Anderson, Jon Lee, *Che Guevara: A Revolutionary Life* (New York, 1997).

Francs-tireurs

Francs-tireurs (literally, "French marksmen") refers to the irregular groups that harassed the German army during the latter stages of the Franco-Prussian War (1870–1871), after the rapid defeat of the main French army. The war having begun on 19 July 1870, the initial German victory over the French armies had been accomplished in little more than two months, with Emperor Napoleon III captured at Sedan on 2 September and Paris besieged on 19 September. However, on 29 September 1870 the new French Government of National Defence resolved to continue the war by resorting to guerrilla tactics. About

57,000 men enlisted in what were officially known as the *corps francs* before enlistment was suspended on 14 January 1871, when priority was accorded to raising a new French field army.

The *francs-tireurs* were poorly armed and badly led; their greatest impact was in tying down about 120,000 German soldiers on guard duty along lines of communication. They also induced a fear of a wider people's conflict in the German military and political leadership, which encouraged the Germans to end the war as quickly as possible by a bombardment of Paris. The German reaction to guerrillas was certainly severe, with collective punishments imposed on local communities and captured *francs-tireurs* being shot out of hand.

See also: German army
Further Reading: Howard, Michael, *The Franco-Prussian War* (London, 1961).

French army

There is an understandable tendency to associate the French army's experience with guerrillas mainly with nineteenth-century colonial warfare in North Africa and French Indochina or, after World War II, with campaigns in Indochina and Algeria. However, it is sometimes forgotten that the French also experienced the very conflict from which the word *guerrilla* (literally: "little war") derived, namely, the Peninsular War in Spain between 1808 and 1814. Indeed, the French fought a whole series of campaigns during the French Revolutionary and Napoleonic Wars (1792–1815) against irregular opponents; these included the Vendéan Revolt (1793–1796) in France proper, the insurrection on Haiti (1791–1802) led by Toussaint L'Ouverture, and the Tyrolean Revolt (1809) led by Andreas Hofer. Napoleon's ultimately disastrous invasion of Russia in 1812 was also noted for the enemy's effective use of partisan warfare against the French.

By exporting the French Revolution overseas upon its soldiers' bayonets in the

1790s, the French republic stimulated nationalism among defeated peoples. Spain was a case in point, as Napoleon had deposed the Spanish royal family in May 1808 and placed his own brother, Joseph, on the Spanish throne. The abdication of the Spanish king led to a spontaneous national uprising in Madrid and the provinces. French response to such nationalist opposition and, in the case of Vendée (a French department), to royalist opposition to the republic was often brutal. However, Louis-Gabriel Suchet was more successful in eastern Spain by combining political with military responses.

French officers who had served in Spain, such as Thomas-Robert Bugeaud, or who analyzed the campaigns in the Vendée, like C. M. Roguet, also recognized the errors of the French approach. Thus, in the 1820s and 1830s, when the French army saw service in a number of minor European conflicts, French soldiers began to appreciate the benefits of attempting to win the hearts and minds of the population. The combination of highly mobile columns undertaking *razzia* (punishment raids) and the steady extension of French military administration by the Bureau Arabe (Arab Bureau) was most successfully applied in Algeria after Bugeaud became governor-general in 1840. Bugeaud defeated the guerrillas of Abd el-Kader at Islay in 1844, and Abd el-Kader himself surrendered to Bugeaud's successor in December 1847.

Bugeaud's methods were then applied in French West Africa in the 1850s by soldiers such as Louis Faidherbe, who had served in Algeria. French flying columns were also employed by F. A. Bazaine during the ill-fated expedition to Mexico in the 1860s. Joseph-Simon Galliéni equally applied Bugeaud's military methods in the French Sudan in the 1880s, but Galliéni adapted and refined Bugeaud's approach in French Indochina and then Madagascar in the 1890s. Essentially, Galliéni placed even more emphasis upon political action, his system becoming known as *tache d'huile*

(oil slick, the analogy being that of French control spreading gradually into the interior as oil spreads upon water).

Galliéni's leading disciple was Louis-Hubert-Gonzalve Lyautey, who followed Galliéni to both Indochina and Madagascar before himself extending French control as resident-general of Morocco between 1912 and 1925. Lyautey also had to contend with the extension into French territory of the insurgency begun in Spanish Morocco by Abd el-Krim in 1921. In fact, the conquest of Morocco was not concluded until 1934, and the French also faced an insurrection in the Levant between 1925 and 1927.

The problem with *tache d'huile* was that, for all the apparent emphasis upon a political response to insurgency, the extension of French administration was accomplished at the expense of indigenous culture. However, as with other European imperial powers, the French were able to raise large numbers of troops from indigenous peoples. In the French case, the results were colorful, with such troops as Spahis and Zouaves (in Africa) as well as the French Foreign Legion. The kind of opposition the French had faced prior to World War II was largely tribal and lacking any coherent appeal to wider nationalism. The Vietminh, whom the French were to face in Indochina between 1946 and 1954, not only possessed a strong political organization but also were able to appeal beyond their communist ideology to Vietnamese nationalism. The French response in Indochina as epitomized by soldiers such as Jean de Lattre de Tassigny and Raoul Salan was almost exclusively military, with the establishment of fortified posts and lines designed to dominate an area and draw the Vietminh into open battle on French terms. The disadvantages of this strategy were well illustrated by the siege of Dien Bien Phu; its fall to the Vietminh in May 1954 brought final defeat in Indochina.

The scale of this jarring defeat led to a major transformation in French counterinsurgency doctrine, with younger officers such as Charles Lacheroy, Yves Godard, and Roger Trinquier developing *guerre révolutionnaire* (revolutionary war). The new doctrine was applied to the war in Algeria between 1954 and 1962. It identified modern insurgency as a combination of partisan warfare and psychological warfare and saw a solution in isolating insurgents from the population by such means as resettlement and the erection of physical barriers such as fortified lines. The purely military aspects of *guerre révolutionnaire* as illustrated by Maurice Challe's offensive in Algeria in 1958 were not very different from *tache d'huile*, with mobile columns conducting *ratissage* (sweeps) from a network of small posts known as *quadrillage* (quartering).

However, *guerre révolutionnaire* also implied a concerted political response to break the political organization of the Front de Libération Nationale (FLN). Unfortunately, as in the Battle of Algiers (1957), the destruction of FLN's organization was accomplished largely through systematic torture of suspects by the units commanded by Jacques Massu and Marcel Bigeard. Moreover, *guerre révolutionnaire* went beyond *tache d'huile* in emphasizing that France itself should be equal to the task of combating revolutionary insurgency. In the process, the French army became subject to politicization, culminating in an attempt by Salan, Challe, and others to stage a military coup in Algiers in April 1961. However, a split or bifurcation had also occurred within the army between regular soldiers committed to retaining a French Algeria and the majority of conscripts, who had no such commitment.

Since 1962 French forces have been used extensively as intervention forces in former French colonies, as in the Central African Empire/Republic (1979) and Chad (1969, 1978, and 1983). However, French counterinsurgency practice is no longer as doctrinaire as it was during the late nineteenth century and 1950s.

See also: Abd el-Kader; Abd el-Krim, Mohammed ben; Algeria; Algiers, Battle of; Bifurcation; Bigeard, Gen.

Marcel; Bugeaud, Marshal Thomas-Robert; Challe, Gen. Maurice; Colonial warfare; de Lattre de Tassigny, Jean-Marie-Gabriel; Dien Bien Phu, Battle of; French Foreign Legion; French Indochina; Galliéni, Marshal Joseph-Simon; *Guerre révolutionnaire;* Hofer, Andreas; Lyautey, Marshal Louis-Hubert-Gonzalve; Madagascar; Massu, Gen. Jacques; Mexico; Morocco; Organisation d'Armée Secrète (OAS); Partisans; Peninsular War; Politicization of armed forces; Roguet, Gen. C. M.; Salan, Gen. Raoul; Suchet, Marshal Louis-Gabriel, Duc d'Albufera; *Tache d'huile;* Toussaint L'Ouverture, Pierre François Dominique; Vendéan Revolt; Vietminh

Further Reading: Clayton, Anthony, *The Wars of French Decolonisation* (London, 1994); Porch, Douglas, *The Conquest of the Sahara* (Oxford, 1986); Porch, Douglas, *The Conquest of Morocco* (London, 1982).

French Foreign Legion

The French Foreign Legion, created in March 1831, is one of the most celebrated formations of the French army. Its particular association with the French presence in North Africa has been celebrated in innumerable novels and feature films. Originally, the Legion was raised as a means of finding employment for the many refugees who fled into France as a result of the wave of revolutions across Europe in 1830. It was moved to the new French possession of Algeria in November 1831, although it was then loaned to the Spanish monarchy from 1835 to 1839 for service in Spain against the Carlist pretenders to the Spanish throne. Reformed in Algeria, the Legion played a leading role in Thomas-Robert Bugeaud's campaigns against Abd el-Kader in the 1840s from its famous base at Sidi-bel-Abbès, which remained Legion headquarters until 1962. Legionnaires also fought in the Crimean War (1854–1856) and the Franco-Austrian War (1859).

One of the Legion's most famous exploits occurred during the French expedition to Mexico (1861–1867) in support of Emperor Maximilian. The one-armed Capt. Jean Danjou and 65 officers and men were cut off at Camerone (El Camarón) on 30 April 1863 by a greatly superior force of Mexicans and fought until only four Legionnaires remained alive. Thereafter, Danjou's wooden hand became an object of veneration in an annual memorial ceremony.

Apart from the Legion's service in the extension of French control over Algeria, Legionnaires also played a prominent role in the conquest of French Indochina, the conquest of the West African state of Dahomey in 1892, and the expedition on Madagascar in 1895. Legionnaires saw service in both world wars, during the Rif Revolt of Abd el-Krim in Morocco in the interwar years, and then in France's two major post-1945 campaigns (Indochina, 1946–1954, and Algeria, 1955–1962). Legion parachute units were among the defenders of Dien Bien Phu in Indochina in 1954 and the Tenth Colonial Parachute Division deployed in the Battle of Algiers in 1957.

Like other regular components of the French army, the Legion was disillusioned by the willingness of the government of Charles de Gaulle to abandon French Algeria. Consequently, the Legion's First Parachute Regiment participated in the attempted coup against de Gaulle in Algiers in April 1961 and was disbanded when the coup failed. Nevertheless, the Legion remains an integral part of the French army, although it is now based in southern France and on Corsica. Indeed, it has often spearheaded French intervention operations in former French colonies; it was also committed to the rescue of Europeans in the Shaba Province of Zaire during disturbances in 1978. Its most recent active employment was in the Gulf War (1991).

See also: Abd el-Kader; Abd el-Krim, Mohammed ben; Algeria; Algiers, Battle of; Bugeaud, Marshal Thomas-Robert; Dien Bien Phu, Battle of; French army; French Indochina; Madagascar; Mexico
Further Reading: Porch, Douglas, *The French Foreign Legion* (New York, 1991).

French Indochina

French Indochina comprised Cambodia, Laos, and the three territories that make up modern Vietnam—Cochin China, Annam, and Tonkin. It proved something of a laboratory for French counterinsurgency doctrine in the late nineteenth century. Equally, the defeat of the French army in Indochina by the communist Vietminh between 1946 and 1954 then led to a radical transformation of that doctrine.

France first occupied eastern Cochin China in 1862 and extended a protectorate over Cambodia the following year. The remainder of Cochin China was taken in 1867, and Annam and Tonkin were occupied in 1883. Laos became a French protectorate in 1893. However, the pacification of Tonkin in particular proved protracted, with the defeat of Gen. François-Marie-Casimir de Négrier at Lang Son in March 1885 bringing down the French government. It was in Tonkin, therefore, between 1892 and 1896 that Joseph-Simon Galliéni perfected the pacification doctrine known as *tache d'huile* (oil slick, the analogy being that of oil slowly spreading on water). Thus, initial French military action would be followed by military administration. This would spread French control into the interior, thereby drawing the population into contact with French cultural influences.

Even though *tache d'huile* was sufficient as a means of suppressing tribal opposition, after World War II it was to prove no match for the disciplined organization of the Vietminh, which could also appeal to Vietnamese nationalism. The Vietminh came into existence as an anti-Japanese coalition in May 1941 after the fall of France to Germany had seriously weakened the ability of French colonial authorities to resist Japanese pressure. Ultimately, in March 1945, the Japanese seized control of French Indochina, but Japan's sudden surrender that August enabled the Vietminh to seize Hanoi. The Vietminh leader, Ho Chi Minh, proclaimed an independent Democratic Republic of Vietnam on 2 September 1945. British troops did not arrive in Saigon until 11 September, and French troops did not effectively replace the British until May 1946.

Initially, the French attempted negotiations with the Vietminh but were prepared to offer only limited self-government. Negotiations failed, and fighting broke out in November 1946. The French reoccupied Hanoi and were convinced that they had destroyed the Vietminh. For the next three years, therefore, the French acted primarily on the defensive without realizing that the Vietminh had withdrawn into the northeast region known as the Viet Bac to regroup. Modeling their strategy on the theory of rural revolutionary warfare advocated by Mao Tse-tung, the Vietminh was able to consolidate support among the peasantry until ready to launch a major offensive in 1950. By this time, too, it had received heavy weapons from China following Mao's victory in the Chinese Civil War (1927–1949).

French outposts were surprised and overwhelmed. However, the military leader of the Vietminh, Vo Nguyen Giap, then miscalculated, launching an all-out assault on the Red River delta in order to seize Hanoi. In December 1950 a new French commander in chief, Jean de Lattre de Tassigny, consolidated French strength around Hanoi in a fortified zone known as the De Lattre Line. Giap's forces were badly mauled, suffering an estimated 12,000 casualties between January and June 1951. De Lattre established a new position at Hoa Binh some 25 miles outside the delta fortified zone, but his successor, Raoul Salan, was compelled to abandon it in early 1952. Another French advance beyond the delta line in October 1952 ("Operation Lorraine"), which was intended to capture Vietminh supply dumps along the Clear River, also became untenable.

By mid-1953 the French were bottled up once more around Hanoi and on the Laotian Plain of Jars, to which Salan had been forced to commit forces after a Vietminh invasion of northern Laos. The only apparent French option was to induce the Vietminh to attack in the open, where French firepower could be brought to bear. Salan's successor, Henri Navarre, selected the valley of Dien Bien Phu astride the Vietminh

infiltration route into Laos as the place to draw out Giap. French paratroops dropped into Dien Bien Phu on 20 November 1953, the assumption being that the Vietminh could not bring heavy weapons across the mountains and that the garrison could be supplied by air. In reality, Vietminh forces holding the high ground used artillery and antiaircraft to close the airstrips, and one by one the French outposts were overwhelmed in mass assaults. After a 55-day siege, the last of the French defenders surrendered on 7 May 1954.

An international conference scheduled to begin at Geneva on 8 May 1954 was a motivating factor for both sides in their determination to achieve victory at Dien Bien Phu. To bring about a favorable peace settlement, the Vietminh was able to exploit the demoralization of the French troops in addition to the unpopularity of the war in the French homeland. On 21 July 1954 France signed the Geneva agreement, by which it agreed to withdraw from Indochina. Geneva confirmed the independence of Laos and Cambodia in October and November 1953 respectively, and it was agreed that Vietnam should be divided along the 17th parallel pending future elections to unite north and south under a mutually acceptable leader. In the course of the conflict the French lost about 77,000 dead and 40,000 prisoners, of whom 29,000 were never repatriated. The Vietminh had an estimated 200,000 casualties.

For the French army the defeat was bitter, leading to its distrust of French politicians. As a result, the new counterinsurgency doctrine, *guerre révolutionnaire*—which emerged in the French army as a result of its study of the lessons of Indochina—would lead to increasing politicization of the army when confronted by a new insurgency in Algeria between 1954 and 1962.

See also: Cambodia; de Lattre de Tassigny, Jean-Marie-Gabriel; Dien Bien Phu, Battle of; French army; French Foreign Legion; Galliéni, Joseph-Simon; Giap, Vo Nguyen;

Guerre révolutionnaire; Ho Chi Minh; Laos; Mao Tse-tung; Navarre, Gen. Henri-Eugène; Pacification; Salan, Gen. Raoul; *Tache d'huile;* Vietminh
Further Reading: Dalloz, Jacques, *The War in Indochina* (Savage, MD, 1990).

Frente de Libertação de Moçambique (FRELIMO)

FRELIMO, or the Front for the Liberation of Mozambique, was the principal nationalist guerrilla movement fighting against the Portuguese in Mozambique from 1964 to 1974. FRELIMO was founded in 1962 from a number of earlier groups and was led initially by an American-trained anthropologist, Dr. Eduardo Mondlane. After Mondlane was killed by a bomb concealed in a book in February 1969, the movement was led by a former male nurse, Samora Machel.

Its first attack across the Rovuma River into the Cabo Delgado region of northern Mozambique from Tanzania occurred on 25 September 1964. The difficulty for FRELIMO was that its natural constituency of support was among the Makonde people of the Mueda Plateau. However, the Makonde represented less than 3 percent of the total population, and in order to reach Makonde territory FRELIMO had to pass through the tribal territory of the Macua. The Macua were largely Muslim and traditional enemies of the Makonde. FRELIMO found it equally difficult to extend operations into the Niassa region in 1967 through the hostility of the Yao and Nyanja peoples. FRELIMO, which had about 8,000 men by 1967, relied mostly on mines; the new Portuguese commander in chief, Kaulza de Arriaga, responded with an energetic road-tarring program.

However, FRELIMO proved more effective when it switched bases to Zambia in 1968 and infiltrated the Tete region, where the Portuguese were constructing the important Cabora Bassa Dam. Initially, the Portuguese were surprised, and although they successfully defended the dam against guerrilla attack FRELIMO began to infil-

trate farther south and east from Tete at the end of 1972, reaching the Zambezia region by early 1974. However, a kind of stalemate had been achieved when in September 1974 (following the military coup in Portugal in April 1974), agreement was reached with FRELIMO for independence in June 1975.

See also: Arriaga, Gen. Kaulza Oliveira de; Machel, Samora Moïses; Mondlane, Dr. Eduardo; Mozambique; Portuguese army
Further Reading: Henricksen, T. H., *Revolution and Counter-revolution: Mozambique's War for Independence* (Westport, 1983).

Frente Farabundo Martí de Liberación Nacional (FMLN)

FMLN, or the Farabundo Martí National Liberation Front, was the coalition of revolutionary guerrilla groups formed in El Salvador in 1980 that fought against the government until a cease-fire in 1992. It was named after Farabundo Martí, a communist leader who fought with Augusto Sandino against the United States Marine Corps in Nicaragua in the 1920s and was executed following the failure of a communist revolt in El Salvador in 1932. The nucleus of the FMLN was the earlier Fuerzas Populares de Liberación—Farabundo Martí (FPL—FM), which had begun to resist the military-dominated right-wing government of El Salvador in 1970.

See also: El Salvador; Martí, Farabundo; Nicaragua; Sandino, Augusto César
Further Reading: Byrne, Hugh, *El Salvador's Civil War: A Study of Revolution* (Boulder, 1996).

Frente Nacional de Libertação de Angola (FNLA)

FNLA, or the Angolan National Liberation Front, fought against the Portuguese in Angola from 1961 to 1974 but lost the subsequent civil war between rival nationalist groups in 1974–1975. Originally known as União das Populações de Angola (UPA), FNLA launched its first attacks into Angola in March 1961 from the newly independent Congo (renamed Zaire in 1965).

Indeed, its support was primarily among the Bakongo tribe, which lived on both sides of the Angola-Congo frontier. FNLA's leader, Holden Roberto, was brother-in-law to Zaire's Pres. Mobutu Sese Seko. FNLA took its new name in March 1962 and established a government-in-exile in 1963, which was recognized by the Organization of African Unity (OAU). FNLA claimed about 10,000 men by 1972, but it is unlikely if it ever had more than 6,000, and it was only sporadically active in the northern Dembos region after the initial rising had been contained.

Roberto's "foreign minister," Jonas Savimbi, broke away to form his own movement, União Nacional para a Independência Total de Angola (UNITA), in 1964, and FNLA lost the support of the OAU in 1968. Roberto was forced back on the support of Mobutu, although the United States also seems to have channeled some assistance to FNLA. FNLA and UNITA joined together to fight the Marxist-dominated Movimento Popular de Libertação de Angola (MPLA) even before the Portuguese left Angola in November 1975. With Soviet and Cuban assistance, MPLA defeated its rivals; FNLA had dissolved by early 1976.

See also: Angola; Movimento Popular de Libertação de Angola (MPLA); Portuguese army; Roberto, Holden; Savimbi, Jonas; União Nacional para a Independência Total de Angola (UNITA)

Further Reading: Bender, G. J., *Angola under the Portuguese* (London, 1978).

Front de Libération Nationale (FLN)

The FLN or National Liberation Front was the nationalist movement that fought successfully for the independence of Algeria between 1954 and 1962. The FLN formally came into existence in October 1954, having originated in July 1954 as a clandestine faction of the militant Movement for the Triumph of Democratic Liberties (MTLD). Its organization was based on what its leaders knew of the communist Vietminh in French Indochina, with Algeria divided into six *wilayas* (command zones). However, the collective leadership was divided between Arabs and Berbers, and divisions occurred within the exiled leadership (based first in Egypt and later in Tunisia as well as among the *wilayas*). In December 1957, for example, Ramdane Abane, a leading member of the Algiers *wilaya*, was murdered by three other *wilaya* chiefs. Similarly, four commanders of the FLN's military wing, Armée de Libération Nationale (ALN), were executed in 1958 for plotting against the movement's new provisional government. Hard-liners generally emerged to control the provisional government, notably Houari Boumedienne, who was to overthrow independent Algeria's first president, Ben Bella, in 1965.

The FLN was strongest in Algiers and in the mountainous Berber areas of the Aurès and Kabylia. Initially, it had as few as 400 activists; the organization was easily broken up by the French army. The FLN campaign was revived only by Morocco's independence from France in 1956 and, especially, that of Tunisia. This gave the FLN safe havens across international frontiers, and a new, more militant leadership opened a campaign of urban terrorism in Algiers. However, defeat in the Battle of Algiers between January and September 1957 and the French construction of the Morice Line along the Tunisian frontier made it difficult for the FLN to supply its forces inside Algeria. An estimated 20,000 ALN men were confined to Tunisia, with only about 8,000 activists (at most) inside Algeria proper. The FLN was driven from the Kabylia by the end of 1959. Nevertheless, the FLN was successful in internationalizing the conflict, gaining recognition from the Nonaligned Movement in 1955 and the UN in 1960. Moreover, the brutal methods of the French alienated moderate Muslim opinion in Algeria and contributed to the growing unpopularity of the conflict in France.

Pres. Charles de Gaulle began negotiations with the FLN in April 1961, and agreement was reached in March 1962. Formal independence came on 3 July 1962. The FLN (which itself lost at least 158,000) had killed more than 39,000 European settlers and members of the security forces in addition to more than 35,000 indigenous inhabitants. It remained the controlling party in Algeria until December 1991, when it lost the first round of national elections to Islamic fundamentalists; it was turned out of office when the Algerian army seized power.

See also: Abane, Ramdane; Algeria; Algiers, Battle of; French army; Morice Line

Further Reading: Horne, Alistair, *A Savage War of Peace* (London, 1977).

Frunze, Mikhail Vasilyevich (1885–1925)

Frunze briefly commanded the Soviet army's Turkestan Front during the early stages of the Basmachi Revolt (1918–1933). Frunze had been born in the Central Asian city of Bishpek (now Frunze) and was familiar with the Islamic religion and the local languages. When he arrived in Turkestan in February 1920, Frunze recognized the social and economic grievances underlying the revolt. As a result, he initiated temporary political concessions, such as allowing the reopening of Muslim courts and schools, as a means of undermining popular support for the insurgents. Although Frunze left Turkestan in September 1920, these policies continued, and the concept of extending such temporary concessions—which were withdrawn once insurgency was suppressed—remained integral to Soviet counterinsurgency.

In the strategic debate that took place within the Soviet army after the end of the Russian Civil War (1917–1921), Frunze demanded a more overtly offensive role for the army and acknowledged the value of partisan warfare. In 1923 he succeeded

Leon Trotsky as commissar for war but died as a result of an operation ordered by the Communist Party.

See also: Basmachi Revolt; Russian Civil War; Soviet army

Further Reading: Jacobs, W. D., *Frunze: The Soviet Clausewitz* (The Hague, 1969).

Fuerzas Armadas de Liberación Nacional (FALN)

FALN or the Armed Forces of National Liberation was an early exponent of urban guerrilla warfare in Venezuela between 1963 and 1965. It was led by Douglas Bravo and was formed in January 1963 from a union of dissident military officers and members of another guerrilla group, Movimiento de Izquierda Revolucionaria (MIR), or the Movement of the Revolutionary Left. MIR had been a *foco* group, following the theories of rural revolutionary warfare advocated by Che Guevara.

In some respects, there is a similarity between *foco* and urban guerrilla warfare in that the principal aim in both is to provoke repression by the armed forces in order to discredit the system as a whole in the eyes of the people. However, the Venezuelan president, Rómulo Betancourt, was determined to preserve democracy, and an attack by FALN on an excursion train in September 1963 enabled him to introduce emergency legislation. Since FALN had overstepped the indistinct line between public sympathy and public opposition by its attack on innocent civilians, the legislation was acceptable to the majority of the population. As early as December 1963 FALN's call for a boycott of presidential elections proved a complete failure. FALN fragmented soon afterward.

See also: Betancourt, Rómulo; *Foco;* Guevara, Ernesto Che; Urban guerrilla warfare; Venezuela

Further Reading: Kohl, J., and J. Litt, *Urban Guerrilla Warfare in Latin America* (Cambridge, MA, 1974).

G

Galliéni, Marshal Joseph-Simon (1849–1916)

One of the leading figures in the French army during the late nineteenth and early twentieth centuries, Galliéni was the architect of the counterinsurgency doctrine known as *tache d'huile* (oil slick). He was also one of the saviors of France during the opening campaign of World War I.

Having served during the Franco-Prussian War (1870–1971), Galliéni made his reputation in colonial warfare, although early in his career he found himself detained for five months by the ruler of the West African state of Niger. After serving as governor of French Sudan, Galliéni moved to French Indochina in 1892. His methods were built on those of Thomas-Robert Bugeaud in Algeria (the analogy of *tache d'huile* is of oil slowly spreading over water). Firm military action by the French would be followed by economic and administrative reconstruction of state by French military administrators working where possible through traditional local rulers. This policy was intended to win the hearts and minds of an indigenous population and encourage the spread of French influence into the interior. Following his success in Indochina, Galliéni became governor-general of Madagascar in 1896. He gradually extended French control throughout the island, the last resistance being overcome at Farafangane in 1905. Louis-Hubert-Gonzalve Lyautey would continue Galliéni's methods in Morocco.

Marshal Joseph-Simon Galliéni, ca. 1900
(UPI/Corbis-Bettmann)

Galliéni was considered for the post of chief of staff to the French army in 1911 but was thought too old. However, in 1914 he was recalled to service as military governor of Paris and played a crucial role in the Battle of the Marne, which forced the Germans to retreat from the French capital. Galliéni became minister of war in October 1915, but he failed in his efforts to exert influence over the commander in chief, Joseph Joffre, and resigned in March 1916. Galliéni died a few weeks later. He was posthumously elevated to the rank of marshal in 1921.

See also: Algeria; Bugeaud, Marshal Thomas-Robert; French army; French Indochina; Lyautey, Marshal Louis-Hubert-Gonzalve; Madagascar; Morocco; *Tache d'huile*
Further Reading: Paret, Peter (ed.), *Makers of Modern Strategy* (Princeton, 1986).

Garibaldi, Giuseppe (1807–1882)

Garibaldi earned a reputation as a skilled exponent of guerrilla warfare in Latin America in the 1830s and 1840s and, subsequently, played a leading role in the movement for Italian unification. Born in the then Italian possession of Nice, Garibaldi became a seaman like his father. He was serving in the navy of the Italian state of Piedmont when he came under the influence of the Italian revolutionary Giuseppe Mazzini. Garibaldi helped to foment a rebellion in Piedmont in 1834 but was forced to flee when it collapsed. Garibaldi then spent 12 years in the service of the Republic of Rio Grande in revolt against Brazil, leading an Italian legion that fought for Uruguay against Argentina. In 1848 Garibaldi returned to Italy to lead a volunteer army against Austrian rule but was defeated at Vicenza. A year later he attempted, unsuccessfully, to defend Rome against French troops sent to support the Pope against a popular revolt in the Papal States. However, in May 1860 Garibaldi landed on Sicily with 1,000 of his "Red Shirts," overcoming the vastly superior army of the king of Naples within just three months. Garibaldi landed on the mainland and marched on to Naples, handing the city and kingdom over to King Victor Emmanuel of Sardinia, who was to become king of Italy in March 1861.

Rome and the Papal States were not part of the new Italy, and Garibaldi failed to seize the city on two occasions—in 1862 and 1867. However, Rome was eventually incorporated in the new state in 1870. Garibaldi last took the field in France against the German army in the Franco-Prussian War (1870–1871).

See also: German army
Further Reading: Ridley, Jasper, *Garibaldi* (New York, 1976).

German army

The German army is not often considered in the context of colonial warfare. In reality, even though imperial Germany came late to overseas imperialism in the nineteenth century, there were frequent campaigns in German East Africa and German South West Africa (later Namibia). Moreover, the German army had experienced the guerrilla warfare carried out against it by French *francs-tireurs* (literally, "French marksmen") in the Franco-Prussian War (1870–1871). During World War I, one German soldier, Paul von Lettow-Vorbeck, proved himself a skilled practitioner of guerrilla warfare against Allied forces in German East Africa. In World War II, the German army was faced with resistance in occupied Europe after 1940 as well as from partisans in both Russia and Yugoslavia. Throughout these varied experiences of irregular warfare, however, the German army's approach tended toward the use of maximum military force.

In many respects, the Franco-Prussian War had the most profound influence on the German approach to guerrillas. Having defeated the main French field army in barely three months, the Germans were unprepared for the spontaneous response to the French government's call for *francs-tireurs* to continue the war. Almost a quarter of the German army was tied down guarding lines of communication as a result, and the Germans reacted with reprisals. Indeed, at the Hague conferences on the laws of war prior to World War I, German delegations insisted on what they termed the "rights of invaders" to summarily execute irregulars.

Much the same approach was evident in the German colonies. In the Herero Revolt

(1904–1906) in German South West Africa, for example, Gen. Lothar von Trotha instituted a policy of *schrecklichkeit* (dreadfulness) in October 1904 by which Herero fighting men were to be shot out of hand and women, children, and the elderly to be driven into the desert to die of starvation. The Herero population declined by an estimated 65,000 as a result. A similar scorched-earth policy was adopted in German East Africa during the Maji Maji Rising (1905–1907). As with other colonial powers, the Germans employed locally raised forces, and native *askaris* provided von Lettow-Vorbeck with the bulk of his small force in defying overwhelming Allied strength in a series of brilliant guerrilla campaigns in German East Africa between 1914 and 1918. Lettow-Vorbeck surrendered only after he had learned that Germany itself had capitulated in November 1918. Other German soldiers also participated in the sporadic violence that accompanied German defeat, enlisting in the irregular *frei korps* (free corps), which fought against internal and external enemies of the state.

During World War II, the German army faced differing problems once it successfully conquered much of Europe between 1939 and 1941. German occupation policy was extremely varied, and more often than not there were many different authorities involved in meeting resistance. In France, for example, internal security was shared between the army; six different police agencies; the military espionage and counterespionage service known as the Abwehr; and various French collaborationist forces. Even in German-occupied Russia after 1941 the Germans were able to raise a variety of indigenous auxiliaries such as the Hiwi (after *Hilsfwillige,* or "willing helpers"). Soviet subjects also joined the Waffen-SS, whose order of battle included a division raised from Croatian Muslims.

The emphasis on locally raised units indicates that Germany successfully met much of the resistance activity by an extension of something akin to routine policing. Certainly, the Germans were adept at manipulating collaborators, local sympathizers, and criminals. Where more organized military resistance was attempted (as in the case of the French *maquis* in the Massif Central in early 1944 or in the rising of the Polish Home Army in Warsaw in August 1944), German military response was swift and brutal. Equally, reprisals were implicit in decrees such as that of Oberkommando der Wehrmacht (OKW), or Armed Forces High Command, in December 1941, whereby ten civilians would be shot for any soldier killed by the resistance, and the Nacht und Neberlas (Night and Fog) decree of the same month. An estimated 20,000 hostages were shot in reprisal for the deaths of German soldiers in Yugoslavia alone between September 1941 and February 1942.

A different problem was posed by the kind of partisan warfare encountered in the Soviet Union and in Yugoslavia. It is now apparent that the German army was deeply implicated in the excesses that marked the extension of Nazi racial policies over Eastern Europe. At the same time, however, the army did develop adequate military responses to partisan warfare. In November 1941 guidelines were issued by a Major Stephanus that, although emphasizing the value of reprisals, pointed to the need for accurate intelligence and careful coordination of operations against partisans. Highly mobile Jagdkommandos (hunter-killer groups) were organized in most operational areas on the Eastern Front by mid-1942. In August 1942 the SS was tasked with security in rear areas behind the front line, with Erich von dem Bach-Zelewski created plenipotentiary for combating partisans in October 1942 and subsequently Chef der Bandenkampfverbände (chief of antibandit warfare) in early 1943. However, the army retained operational control, and eventually OKW produced the manual known as *Warfare Against Bands* in May 1944.

Not unlike conventional operations by the German army, in antipartisan warfare the emphasis was on encirclement of partisans, followed by concerted drives to split them into ever smaller groups. Indeed, attempts at encirclement characterized the seven consecutive offensives launched against partisans in Yugoslavia between September 1941 and August 1944. In many respects, the Germans had adapted effective military solutions to the challenge of the partisan—but too late in the war, as illustrated by the last German offensive in Yugoslavia (May–August 1944). The Germans came close to victory, but operations were abandoned to rush troops to the Eastern Front. Moreover, the continuing emphasis upon *abschreckung* (counterterror) always undermined any appeal German rule might conceivably have had for the population of occupied Europe.

See also: Bach-Zelewski, Erich von dem; Colonial warfare; *Francs-tireurs;* Herero Revolt; Lettow-Vorbeck, Maj. Gen. Paul Emil von; Maji Maji Rising; Manuals; Namibia; Partisans; Resistance; Trotha, Gen. Lothar von; Yugoslavia
Further Reading: Beckett, Ian (ed.), *The Roots of Counterinsurgency: Armies and Guerrilla Warfare, 1900–1945* (London, 1988); von Luttichau, C. P., *Guerrilla and Counterguerrilla Warfare in Russia During World War II* (Washington, DC, 1963); Kennedy, R. M., *German Antiguerrilla Operations in the Balkans, 1941–1945* (Washington, DC, 1954).

Giap, Vo Nguyen (1912–)

Giap was the Vietnamese military strategist responsible for the Vietminh victory over the French army between 1946 and 1954 in addition to the North Vietnamese victory over South Vietnam between 1959 and 1975. He was also responsible, with Truong Chinh, for refining the rural revolutionary warfare theories of Mao Tse-tung so they might be adapted to changing, post-1945 international circumstances.

Giap was born in An-Xa in the Quang-Bing Province of French Indochina, just north of the 17th parallel. Initially employed by an electric power company, Giap became active in nationalist politics as a youth. In 1933 he began studying law at Hanoi University and subsequently taught history in a private school. However, after attempting to organize student strikes, in 1939 he fled to China, where he met Ho Chi Minh. In his absence, Giap's wife was arrested by the French and died in prison. In May 1941 he became one of the founders of the Vietminh and in December 1944 formed the nucleus of the Vietminh's regular forces (Chu Luc), which would eventually become the North Vietnamese army (NVA).

When Ho Chi Minh proclaimed Vietnam's independence from the French in September 1945, Giap was made commander in chief and minister of the interior. Giap proved himself a master of the art of logistics in the subsequent war with the French. But whereas Mao had been careful during the Chinese Civil War (1927–1949) to avoid committing his guerrillas prematurely to conventional offensives, Giap was apt to press for a decisive engagement too

Master strategist Vo Nguyen Giap (left) stands with Ho Chi Minh after becoming commander in chief and minister of the interior when Ho Chi Minh proclaimed Vietnam's independence, September 1945. (AP/Wide World Photos)

early. Thus, his conventional-style assaults on French fortifications in the Red River delta in 1951 resulted in the estimated loss of one-third of his forces and compelled Giap to revert to guerrilla warfare. Similarly, Giap was quite prepared to launch massive human-wave assaults on French defenders at Dien Bien Phu in 1954 in order to obtain a decisive result and strengthen Ho Chi Minh's bargaining position before the upcoming Geneva conference on the future of Indochina.

Indeed, the awareness that Giap and Truong Chinh possessed as to how conflicts could be internationalized and revolutionary causes projected onto the global stage was their predominant contribution to the redefining of Maoist theories of guerrilla warfare in a modern age of mass communications. Giap's views on guerrilla warfare were published in *People's War, People's Army* (1961).

With the partition of Vietnam in 1954 Giap became commander in chief and minister of defense of North Vietnam and a member of the politburo. Initially, Giap's approach to the post-1959 attempt to subvert South Vietnam was essentially this simple: the North Vietnamese–supported Vietcong would undertake guerrilla warfare using supplies and reinforcements sent south along the Ho Chi Minh Trail. However, as Giap explained in *Big Victory, Great Task* (1967), the commitment of U.S. ground forces to the defense of South Vietnam in March 1965 and the formidable array of modern technology and firepower available to the Americans persuaded Giap of the need to change to a "regular force strategy." Others, such as Truong Chinh and the NVA's first commander in the south, Nguyen Chi Thanh, appear to have stressed continued political subversion, yet the NVA was increasingly committed to the war in the south.

Certainly, from the first clash between the NVA and U.S. forces, in the Ia Drang Valley in early 1965, to the fighting around Dak To in November 1967, the NVA appears to have experimented with tactics. Giap suggested that two methods were involved. The "coordinated fighting method" employed large numbers of men in assaults on selected targets of relative importance, whereas the "independent fighting method" involved a series of "gnat-swarm" attacks designed to have cumulative impact on the opponent's morale. Used alternatively, the methods could be combined into a general offensive to offset American technological superiority.

As a Maoist, Giap was quite prepared to prolong the war until the United States lost its resolve, and the Hanoi leadership as a whole was determined to pay any price to achieve its aim of conquering the south. However, Giap was always enamored of using the effect of the "bloody blow" to break an opponent's will and the use of massed conventional force as a shortcut to victory. Therefore, in January 1968 he made the mistake, as in 1951, of mounting the large-scale Tet Offensive against South Vietnam. Tet exposed the NVA and the Vietcong to the full weight of American firepower and was a military disaster for the communists, ending the Vietcong as an effective fighting force. Fortuitously for Giap, the impact of the Tet Offensive on U.S. public opinion contributed to its becoming a political success (from the North Vietnamese perspective, that is). Giap attempted another major conventional offensive in March 1972, what amounted to an all-out NVA invasion of the south. Although the South Vietnamese army (ARVN) was hard-pressed to hold the offensive, American airpower inflicted massive losses on the NVA and succeeded in blunting the threat by June 1972.

The collapse of the spring 1972 offensive appears to have been a major factor in Giap being increasingly eclipsed in influence by his military protégé, Van Tien Dung. It was Dung who directed the final NVA offensive against South Vietnam in 1975, although, significantly, American airpower was no longer available to the

ARVN. Giap remained minister of defense and also became deputy prime minister in the unified Vietnamese state. However, ironically, when war broke out between Vietnam and Cambodia in 1977–1978, Giap's advocacy of guerrilla rather than conventional strategy against the Khmer Rouge led to his 1980 removal as minister of defense. He was replaced by Dung, although he remained as a member of the politburo until 1981. His memoirs, *Unforgettable Days,* appeared in 1978.

See also: Airpower; Cambodia; Dien Bien Phu, Battle of; French army; French Indochina; Ho Chi Minh; Ho Chi Minh Trail; Khmer Rouge; Mao Tse-tung; Tet Offensive; Truong Chinh; United States Army; Vietcong; Vietminh; Vietnam War
Further Reading: O'Neill, Robert, *General Giap: Politician and Strategist* (New York, 1969); C. B. Currey, *Victory at Any Cost* (New York, 1997).

Godard, Col. Yves (1911–1975)

Godard was a leading practitioner of *guerre révolutionnaire,* the French army's counterinsurgency doctrine used against the Front de Libération Nationale (FLN) in Algeria between 1956 and 1962. He then became a leading member of the Organisation d'Armée Secrète (OAS), which tried to assassinate Pres. Charles de Gaulle. Taken prisoner by the Germans in World War II, Godard eventually escaped from a camp in Poland and made his way back to France, joining the French resistance. In 1948 he commanded a battalion in French Indochina and participated in the unsuccessful attempts to relieve the French garrison at Dien Bien Phu in 1954.

In 1956 he became chief of staff to Gen. Jacques Massu's Tenth Colonial Parachute Division in Algeria. In the Battle of Algiers in 1957, Godard was responsible for building up a detailed intelligence picture of the FLN's order of battle, known as the *organigramme.* Removed from Algeria by de Gaulle after the army's involvement with white settler groups in the so-called Barricades Week in January 1960, Godard was

refused appointment as military attaché to Poland. Godard then joined the military coup against de Gaulle in Algiers in April 1961, going underground when it collapsed.

Sentenced to death in absentia, Godard helped create the OAS and became chief of its "general staff." Godard eventually settled in Belgium and declined to return to France even after receiving amnesty. He ran a small factory, and he had completed the first volume of a planned three-volume account of the campaign in Algeria when he died.

See also: Algeria; Algiers, battle of; French army; French Indochina; Front de Libération Nationale (FLN); *Guerre révolutionnaire;* Massu, Gen. Jacques; Organisation d'Armée Secrète (OAS)
Further Reading: Horne, Alistair, *A Savage War of Peace* (London: 1977).

Greek Civil War (1946–1949)

The Greek Civil War was the first post–World War II example of security forces in Europe being confronted with a politically motivated insurgency. Open conflict broke out in Greece in October 1943 between two different groups fighting against German occupation. These groups were the centrist and right-wing supporters of the Greek government-in-exile and the left-wing Ethnikon Apeleftherotikon Metopon (EAM), or National Liberation Front. The military wing of EAM was known as Ellinikos Laikos Apeleftherotikon (ELAS), and EAM and ELAS were both effectively instruments of the Kommounisitikon Komma Ellados (KKE), or Greek Communist Party. The initial conflict was indecisive, but by the time the Germans withdrew from Greece in October 1944, EAM was clearly the stronger of the two groups.

British units moved into Greece to reestablish the authority of the Greek government, but ELAS launched an offensive to seize control of Athens in December 1944. The British brought in reinforcements, and the communists accepted a cease-fire in January 1945. Under the so-called Varkiza Agreement in February

1945, ELAS was formally disbanded in return for amnesty, a plebiscite on the future of Greece, and a general election. In the event, the communists boycotted the March 1946 election, claiming that other promises had not been fulfilled.

Increasingly, ELAS elements took to the northern mountains adjacent to the Yugoslav and Albanian frontiers. Under the leadership of Markos Vaphiadis, they adopted the title of Dimokratikos Stratos Ellados (DSE), or Democratic Army of Greece, in December 1946. DSE soon had about 25,000 men, and it enjoyed a residue of support from ELAS's wartime reputation as a broad based nationalist movement. Supplies were also readily available from neighboring communist states. However, there was disagreement over strategy, especially when KKE political leadership under Nikos Zachariadis was forced out of Athens in October 1947 and joined DSE in the mountains. Zachariadis wanted to establish a "liberated" zone and committed DES to a conventional offensive to seize Konitsa as a seat of government in December 1947. Such a conventional role was well beyond DSE's capabilities, and it was driven from many of its mountain strongholds throughout the summer of 1948.

Advised by a British military mission, the Greek National Army (GNA) also undermined DSE's infrastructure by relocating populations away from vulnerable areas and instituting a program of civic action to win over hearts and minds. Not heeding the lessons, Zachariadis ousted Vaphiadis, who advocated a return to guerrilla warfare, in January 1949. Bulgaria and Albania were increasingly wary of supporting the failing insurgency in Greece, and Yugoslavia's leader, Tito, withdrew DSE support due to his own quarrel with the Soviet Union. In these circumstances, a conventional positional strategy was a fundamental mistake, but Zachariadis concentrated his remaining forces behind fixed defenses in the Grammos and Vitsi Mountains. In August and September 1949,

these last strongholds were overwhelmed by the GNA, whose attacks were spearheaded by American-supplied dive-bombers used as flying artillery. On 16 October 1949 DSE declared a cease-fire.

See also: Ellinikos Laikos Apeleftherotikon (ELAS); Hearts and minds; Tito, Marshal Josip Broz
Further Reading: Close, David H., *The Greek Civil War* (New York, 1993).

Green Berets

The Green Berets are the United States Army's special forces. Originally raised by Lt. Col. Robert Frederick in 1942 for sabotage operations in German-occupied Norway, six battalions were eventually deployed during World War II. The special forces were revived in June 1952 but enjoyed little favor until they received the enthusiastic backing of Pres. John F. Kennedy in 1961. Indeed, it was Kennedy who officially authorized the wearing of the distinctive green beret, although it had first been worn in 1956. Personnel from the First Special Forces Group (SFG) had been training the South Vietnamese army (ARVN) since June 1957, and teams from the Seventh SFG were deployed to South Vietnam in May 1960.

Between September 1961 and March 1964 the Third, Fifth, Sixth, and Eighth SFGs were raised, with the Third earmarked for operations in Africa, the Sixth for the Middle East, and the Eighth for Latin America. In October 1964 the Fifth SFG was deployed to Vietnam to assume control of all special forces operations. The initial responsibility of the Green Berets in Vietnam was to organize the Civilian Irregular Defense Group (CIDG) among the Montagnard tribesmen of the Central Highlands, the first of which had been raised in December 1961. Responsibility for the CIDG passed to the South Vietnamese in 1964, but the tribesmen's hostility toward the South Vietnamese meant that the Green Berets never entirely escaped involvement with the "cidgees." Indeed, final withdrawal of the

Green Berets from South Vietnam did not occur until 3 March 1971, well after the 1969 policy of "Vietnamization."

The Green Berets were also closely involved with the strike force elements that evolved from the CIDG in 1964, including the joint reconnaissance and hunter-killer "Greek alphabet" teams and the quick-reaction "Mike Force." Under the auspices of the Studies and Observation Group (SOG), the Greek alphabet teams (e.g., Delta, Omega, Sigma, Gamma) undertook crossborder operations, including the attempted rescue of American prisoners of war at Son Tay in North Vietnam in November 1970. In addition, the Green Berets trained the South Vietnamese Regional Forces and the so-called Apache Force, which helped orientate new American arrivals in the country.

Eight members of the Fifth SFG won the Congressional Medal of Honor for service in Vietnam. Elsewhere, members of the Eighth SFG were present when the Bolivian army's ranger battalion, which they had trained, tracked down and killed Che Guevara in October 1967. Apart from the role in counterinsurgency, the Green Berets were also employed in covert support of conventional operations in Vietnam, and they continue to fulfill that role. There are now three regular SFGs—the Fifth, Seventh, and Tenth—of battalion size under control of the Special Operations Command with headquarters in Tampa, Florida.

See also: Civilian Irregular Defense Group (CIDG); Guatemala; Guevara, Ernesto Che; Special Forces; United States Army; Vietnam War
Further Reading: Krepinevich, Andrew, *The Army and Vietnam* (Baltimore, 1986); Blaufarb, D. S., *The Counterinsurgency Era* (New York, 1977).

Grivas, Gen. George Theodorou (1898–1974)

Grivas was the military leader of Ethniki Organosis Kyprion Agoniston (EOKA), which fought against the British authorities on Cyprus between 1955 and 1959. Grivas was also a precursor of and a model for many advocates of urban guerrilla warfare in the late 1960s. Although Cypriot-born, Grivas made his career in the Greek regular army, reaching the rank of colonel. Dedicated to the cause of enosis (union of Cyprus with Greece), Grivas returned to the island as early as 1951 to carry out initial planning for the military campaign he believed was needed to achieve his objective.

Grivas understood well that the British, who had controlled Cyprus since 1878, could not be defeated in a conventional conflict. Accordingly, he hoped that guerrilla warfare would raise the political costs of continued British presence to an unacceptable level. Grivas again returned to Cyprus in November 1954 to organize EOKA for the coming campaign, using the pseudonym "Dighenis" from a figure of Greek mythology.

EOKA was deliberately small, with no more than 350 activists divided into rural and urban service groups. However, there were also about 750 active supporters, including women and children, who could be used to collect information, shadow targets for assassination, conceal weapons, and lead demonstrations designed to lure members of security forces into sniper range. Greek Cypriot police were to be specially targeted, the intent being to intimidate Greek Cypriots who did not support enosis. Homemade bombs were also a favored weapon, EOKA successfully exploding 1,782 during the course of the campaign that began on 1 April 1955 (2,976 bombs were defused or failed to detonate).

Despite having a £1,000 price placed on his head, Grivas remained on Cyprus throughout the conflict, the British having declared a state of emergency on 26 November 1955. However, the British were able to clear the rural EOKA groups from the Troodos Mountains during the course of 1956 despite the need to detach units for the Anglo-French invasion of Egypt in November. Grivas also admitted that EOKA

George Grivas, leader of the Ethniki Organosis Kyprion Agoniston (EOKA), poses in uniform for his followers on Cyprus. This photograph of the almost legendary leader was seized from a Cyprus rebel who was captured by British forces in 1956. (UPI/Corbis-Bettmann)

suffered "hard blows" when the focus of British operations shifted to the urban centers such as Nicosia between December 1956 and March 1957. Indeed, Grivas made an offer to suspend guerrilla activities in re-

turn for Archbishop Makarios's release from detention. Makarios was the political leader of the movement for enosis whom the British had deported to the Seychelles in March 1956.

Although negotiations began between Makarios and the British, Greek, and Turkish governments, the insurgency on Cyprus resumed. In another blow to EOKA, all Greek civilian employees were dismissed from British base areas after a bomb attack on the British Navy, Army, and Air Force Institute (NAAFI) in Nicosia in October 1958. In effect, a kind of military stalemate had developed; Grivas announced a cease-fire on 31 December 1958. A compromise agreement was reached on independence for Cyprus in February 1959. The state of emergency was lifted in December 1959, and formal independence came in August 1960.

Makarios became the first president of an independent Cyprus, but that was not the objective Grivas had targeted. Grivas returned to Greece and was promoted to full general in the Greek army. In 1964 he went back to Cyprus once more to command the Greek Cypriot National Guard but was recalled by the new Greek military government in 1967 amid intercommunal disturbances sparked off by the national guard's attack on Turkish Cypriot villages. With the connivance of the Greek military government, he returned to Cyprus in 1971 to organize a new guerrilla group known as EOKA-B, this time to campaign against Makarios.

Grivas died shortly before a coup against Makarios by elements of EOKA-B and the national guard, which resulted in Turkish military intervention in July 1974 and a partition of Cyprus that endures today. In many respects, Grivas was a right-wing figure rather than a revolutionary, and his account of his campaign, *Guerrilla Warfare* (1964), was actually intended as a primer for Western governments facing communist insurgency. However, the use of terror tactics by Grivas, whether by bomb or assassination, and the emphasis on small units and youthful participation were ideally suited for imitation by urban guerrilla groups that began to emerge in the 1960s. Thus, Grivas became an inspiration not for

Western governments but for the left-wing revolutionaries he despised.

See also: British army; Cyprus; Ethniki Organosis Kyprion Agoniston (EOKA); Police; Urban guerrilla warfare
Further Reading: Grivas, George, *Guerrilla Warfare* (London, 1964); Foley, Christopher (ed.), *The Memoirs of General Grivas* (London, 1964).

Guatemala

In the early 1960s, the Central American state of Guatemala became one of the first places to experience the *foco* theory of rural revolutionary warfare developed by Che Guevara and Régis Debray. Like other *focos*, that in Guatemala ultimately failed, for it was impossible to reproduce the circumstances that had led to Fidel Castro's victory on Cuba between 1956 and 1959. Guevara and Debray had mistakenly assumed that revolutionary potential existed as a matter of course throughout Latin America. In fact, however, Batista's Cuban regime enjoyed little domestic support and collapsed outright when challenged by a force of barely 300 guerrillas.

In Guatemala, the *foco* originated among dissident army officers who had failed to overthrow the military government of Gen. Ydígoras Fuentes on 13 November 1960. Fleeing to the Izabal Mountains, the survivors of the coup attempt formed Movimiento Revolucionario 13 de Noviembre (13 November Revolutionary Movement, or MR-13). However, as elsewhere in Latin America at this time, the guerrillas, who began operations in 1962, did not enjoy popular support among the rural peasantry—but then again, Guevara had insisted that the mere existence of guerrillas was sufficient to begin a process of revolutionary insurrection. Even when MR-13 joined with Guatemalan communists and others to form Fuerzas Armadas Rebeldes (FAR) or Rebel Armed Forces, the movement was unsuccessful, and there were damaging internal divisions within.

A measure of the failure of rural revolution was the attempt to switch guerrilla

Soldiers of Guatemala's elite Kabil are extra alert because of reports of heightened guerrilla activity as they guard a work force of civilians laboring on a dirt road near the Pan American Highway on the eve of the March 7 general elections, 1982. (UPI/Corbis-Bettmann)

operations to urban areas in 1967. By this time the Guatemalan armed forces had the assistance of an estimated 1,000 U.S. Green Berets (28 U.S. servicemen were killed in Guatemala between 1966 and 1968). Substantial U.S. economic aid also enabled Guatemala to mount a credible civic action program to win the hearts and minds of the rural population. Indeed, Col. Carlos Araña Osorio launched a model civic action effort in Zacapa Province in 1967, with the Guatemalan army building schools, hospitals, and roads. However, Araña was linked with right-wing death squads and irregular militias raised by landowners; as many as 10,000 people may have been killed by security forces between 1967 and 1968.

Even though such pressure led to the neutralization of the guerrilla threat by the end of the 1960s, it did not entirely eliminate it; there has been endemic, low-level violence in Guatemala ever since.

See also: Castro, Fidel; Cuba; Debray, Régis; *Foco;* Green Berets; Hearts and minds
Further Reading: O'Neill, Bard, W. R. Heaton, and D. J. Alberts (eds.), *Insurgency in the Modern World* (Boulder, 1980); Gott, Richard, *Guerrilla Movements in Latin America* (2d ed., Harmondsworth, 1973).

Guerre révolutionnaire

Guerre révolutionnaire (revolutionary warfare) is the counterinsurgency doctrine that the French army developed after its defeat by the Vietminh in French Indochina in 1954. It was applied to the conflict against the Front de Libération Nationale (FLN) in Algeria between 1956 and 1962. Although militarily credible, *guerre révolutionnaire* had weaknesses as a political response to the threat of politically motivated insurgency. Ultimately, it led to the politicization of the French army and an attempt by some of its practitioners to overthrow the French government of Pres. Charles de Gaulle.

In some respects, *guerre révolutionnaire* was a natural development from the concept of *tache d'huile* (oil slick), the basis of the French approach to colonial warfare from the late nineteenth century onward. It was recognized that the Vietminh had established a highly integrated and structured organization and had employed a potent mix of political, military, and psychological means to infiltrate the Vietnamese population and establish an effective alternative system of authority to the French colonial government. As expressed by one of the new French theorists, Georges Bonnet, the methods of the Vietminh had been a matter of "partisan (guerrilla) warfare + psychological warfare = revolutionary warfare."

The weaknesses of the Vietminh method (in turn modeled on that of Mao Tse-tung) appeared to be the insurgents' vulnerability during the initial phase of conflict. Therefore, the moment security forces should strike was before insurgents had the opportunity to establish deep-rooted support among the population, when they were likely to be dependent on supplies brought in from neighboring states. Advocates of *guerre révolutionnaire* like Bonnet, Charles Lacheroy, Yves Godard, and Roger Trinquier believed the security forces must effect an early separation of population from insurgents through extensive resettlement of the population and the construction of physical barriers along international frontiers. Once under French control, the population could be subjected to civic action programs, and, if necessary, to military coercion in order to contain or prevent support for insurgents.

In fact, many French officers interpreted *guerre révolutionnaire* as a genuine social revolution to win the hearts and minds of the population, and some critics even accused Godard and Gen. Jacques Massu of practicing rural socialism in Algeria. However, it should be emphasized that the military campaign would be waged by military *and* psychological means without restraint. Thus, what advocates of the new doctrine termed "construction" would be closely linked to "destruction."

As in the case of *tache d'huile,* French culture exclusively was being offered to the population; the actual military methods employed in Algeria were also familiar. Thus, the military offensive conducted by Gen. Maurice Challe in 1959 was based on a refined version of traditional *quadrillage* (quartering), with a checkerboard of French outposts being backed by mobile operations in the form of large-scale sweeps. The latter were often spearheaded by French-led Muslim units, or *harkis.* But *guerre révolutionnaire* also resembled *tache d'huile* in its political implications. One of the leading proponents of *tache d'huile,* Louis-Hubert-Gonzalve Lyautey, had suggested in 1900 that the army might be required to regenerate French society itself. *Guerre révolutionnaire* also carried an implicit political message, through the army's involvement in a psychological response to insurgency.

In Algeria, psychological warfare was conducted by the Psychological Action and Information Service, better known as the Fifth Bureau and headed by Lacheroy. Lacheroy and fellow exponents of *guerre révolutionnaire* believed that, after the perceived failures of successive French governments to support the army's campaign in Indochina, it was vital that this failure of support should not recur. Indeed, it was the absolute duty of government and people to support the army so that revolutionary insurgency would be opposed by equal ideological strength and purpose on the part of the authorities confronted with it. There was a stabbed-in-the-back feeling within some elements after the loss in Indochina, but even so, young zealots among the French officers were equally suspicious of military seniors.

It was also implicit in the understanding of politically motivated insurgency that it would always serve communist interests and that avowedly nationalist movements were mere dupes for communists. In reality, although certainly socialist and anti-imperialist, the FLN was not a communist group even if it received assistance from the Soviet bloc. Moreover, the French zeal in breaking the FLN's organization, as illustrated in the Battle of Algiers in 1957, alienated moderate Muslim opinion. The advocates of *guerre révolutionnaire* were particularly prominent in the struggle for control of the city, Godard being responsible for constructing the detailed intelligence picture of the FLN's order of battle and Trinquier for the division of Algiers into sectors, subsectors, blocks, and buildings with each of these being assigned to a senior inhabitant to report on suspicious behavior.

It was not lost on many Arabs and Berbers that the personnel of the Fifth Bureau's special administrative sections (SAS) and urban administrative sections (SAU) committed to winning hearts and minds through civic action programs were often the same people who tortured FLN suspects.

Guerre révolutionnaire was certainly successful in bringing the French army a high degree of military success in Algeria by the end of 1959, yet it did not win the political struggle. Moreover, many French soldiers were increasingly disillusioned by de Gaulle's willingness to surrender sovereignty over Algeria, even though it had been regarded as part of France itself since 1848. Military sympathy for the white settlers or *colons* had been evident as early as 1958 when, for all intents and purposes, the army had brought down the French Fourth Republic and engineered de Gaulle's return to power because it believed him ready to stand by a French Algeria.

After the so-called Barricades Week in January 1960, de Gaulle removed a number of leading soldiers from Algeria, and the Fifth Bureau was disbanded in February 1960. The divisions and bifurcation within the army between regulars, who advocated *guerre révolutionnaire,* and conscripts, who had no wish to preserve French Algeria,

also became increasingly acute. Finally, four French generals including Challe and Raoul Salan staged a coup against de Gaulle in Algiers in April 1961. It collapsed after six days, but a number of those prominent in *guerre révolutionnaire* and the coup, including Godard and Lacheroy, escaped. They then founded Organisation d'Armée Secrète (OAS) to assassinate de Gaulle. Thus, *guerre révolutionnaire* ultimately led exponents to take up arms against their own government.

See also: Algeria; Algiers, Battle of; Bifurcation; Challe, Gen. Maurice; French army; French Indochina; Front de Libération Nationale (FLN); Godard, Col. Yves; Hearts and minds; Lyautey, Marshal Louis-Hubert-Gonzalve; Mao Tse-tung; Massu, Gen. Jacques; Organisation d'Armée Secrète (OAS); Politicization of armed forces; Resettlement; Salan, Gen. Raoul; *Tache d'huile;* Trinquier, Col. Roger; Vietminh

Further Reading: Paret, Peter, *French Revolutionary Warfare from Indochina to Algeria* (London, 1964); Heggoy, A. A., *Insurgency and Counter-insurgency in Algeria* (Bloomington, 1972); Trinquier, Roger, *Modern Warfare: A French View of Counterinsurgency* (New York, 1963).

Guevara, Ernesto Che (1928–1967)

Guevara has become a revolutionary icon of the twentieth century, the poster of him wearing a beret adorned by a star being almost universally familiar. Subject of the Hollywood feature film *Ché* (1969), Guevara also appears improbably as a character in the film musical *Evita.* Yet for all the posthumous cult status enjoyed by Guevara, his own revolutionary career was ultimately a failure. His theory of revolutionary guerrilla warfare, *foco,* was entirely discredited when he was killed in Bolivia in 1967.

Guevara was born in Rosario, Argentina, and began training as a doctor at the University of Buenos Aires in 1947. His own health was poor due to chronic asthma. He spent his vacations working as a male nurse on merchant ships and in 1950 unsuccessfully tried his hand at marketing an insecticide. He then traveled through Latin America, and he was in Guatemala in

Ernesto Che Guevara speaks at the Inter-American Economic and Social Conference of "an ingenious and macabre [U.S.] plot" involving an attempt to assassinate Fidel Castro's brother, Raul, and "provoke armed aggression," 8 August 1961. (UPI/Corbis-Bettmann)

1954, when the U.S. Central Intelligence Agency (CIA) engineered the overthrow of the left-wing government of Jacobo Arbenz Guzmán. This American involvement appears to have confirmed Guevara's revolutionary instincts, and after moving to Mexico he came into contact with Cuban exiles led by Fidel Castro. At this time he gained the nickname "Ché" (Spanish: "buddy" or "chum") for the frequency he used the word in conversation. He legally adopted Che (with an *e*, not an *é*) as an additional Christian name in 1959.

In November 1956 Guevara was one of the 81 men to accompany Castro in his attempt to overthrow Cuba's dictator, Fulgencio Batista. For the next two years Guevara fought in the remarkable campaign that saw Castro triumph in January 1959. Indeed, Guevara led one of the guerrilla columns in Castro's final advance on Havana and entered the capital six days before Castro himself. Guevara became minister

of industry and remained in the Cuban government until 1965. He then began to travel until arriving in Bolivia in disguise in November 1966, intending to prove the value of *foco* after a series of failures by groups utilizing his methods elsewhere in Latin America.

Foco was developed by Guevara in collaboration with Frenchman Régis Debray, a professor of the history of philosophy at the University of Havana. Overestimating the ease of Castro's success, Guevara and Debray believed revolution on the Cuban model could be reproduced as a matter of course throughout Latin America, if not the Third World. In contrast to Mao Tse-tung's classic theory of rural guerrilla warfare, which stressed the importance of parallel but separate military and political organizations, Guevara and Debray argued that guerrillas themselves could be a revolutionary fusion of political and military authority. Instead of sticking to Mao's prolonged, careful political preparation of a population, they assumed that a modicum of discontent with government would be sufficient to create objective conditions favorable to revolution. Thus, by military action alone, a small group of dedicated revolutionaries would provide the *foco* (focus) for revolution. Decisive action on the part of guerrillas would in and of itself expose the corrupt and brutal natures of authorities, who would be forced to overreact against the population when it proved impossible to eliminate the highly mobile guerrillas. The *foco* would thus become the catalyst for a wider popular insurrection.

The problem with the theory, however, was that it failed to account for the special circumstances leading to Castro's success: Batista's regime was corrupt and inefficient, and it had alienated virtually all sections of Cuban society; the Cuban army was badly led and poorly motivated; Batista had lost the support of the United States as a result of his lamentable human rights record. In addition, Guevara and Debray ignored the considerable assistance Castro's guerrillas received from the urban-based 26 July Movement; without it Castro could not have survived. Indeed, Guevara and Debray made a virtue out of keeping the *foco* distinct from the population.

Since the special circumstances of Cuba did not exist as a matter of course elsewhere, *focos* attempted in Colombia (1961), Guatemala (1962), Ecuador (1962), and Peru (1963) all failed. An additional factor in these failures was Castro's conversion to communism, which brought about renewed U.S. involvement throughout Latin America to prevent the spread of communism "in its own backyard." The Kennedy administration, in response to the Soviet Union's declared support for "wars of national liberation," extended considerable military and economic support to governments in Latin America thought to be at particular risk. Moreover, Bolivia had enjoyed a measure of land reform in the 1950s, which was sufficient to deprive any

foco of even that minimal level of discontent required by Guevara and Debray. Bolivia's Communist Party did not find Guevara's emphasis on military control of the revolution congenial, and its leadership gave him no support.

Since this was to be a rural campaign, Guevara ignored the radical tin-mining community. The local natives of the remote Nancahuazú region, where he chose to begin his campaign, also regarded his small band of assorted followers—Cubans, Peruvians, Bolivians, and one East German woman—as aliens, especially because none of them spoke the native language. The terrain was not conducive to mobility, and Guevara's group spent much time lost in the jungle. Indeed, the Bolivian authorities were not able to confirm a guerrilla presence until March 1967, and that prompted an immediate request for assistance to the United States.

U.S. Green Berets began training a new ranger battalion for the Bolivian army in June 1967; it was deployed by September. Guevara's band was broken up, and on 8 October 1967 Guevara's own group was surrounded at the village of La Higuera. Wounded and captured, Guevara was executed and his body publicly displayed in the nearby town of Valle Grande. It was once thought that the body had been thrown from a helicopter into the jungle, but in July 1997 it was identified in a grave underneath an airstrip in Valle Grande and taken to Cuba for reburial.

With the final failure of *foco*, a new generation of Latin American revolutionaries shifted emphasis from the countryside to the towns. Urban guerrilla warfare began developing in the late 1960s.

See also: Argentina; Batista y Zaldivar, Fulgencio; Castro, Fidel; Cuba; Debray, Régis; *Foco;* Green Berets; Guatemala; Mao Tse-tung; Peru; Urban guerrilla warfare
Further Reading: Anderson, Jon Lee, *Che Guevara: A Revolutionary Life* (New York, 1997); Guevara, Che, *Reminiscences of the Cuban Revolutionary War* (London, 1968); James, D. (ed.), *The Complete Bolivian Diaries of Che Guevara and Other Captured Documents* (London, 1968); Gerassi, John (ed.), *Venceremos!: The Speeches and Writings of Che Guevara* (London, 1968).

Guillén, Abraham (1912–)

Guillén, a Spaniard who fought in the Spanish Civil War (1936–1939), became one of the first theorists of urban guerrilla warfare. He was an early influence on the Tupamaros in Uruguay in the late 1960s. Influenced by Marxism as well as anarchism, Guillén settled in Uruguay after some years in Argentina. He understood the revolutionary potential of cities such as Montevideo, where the social, economic, and political grievances of the urban underclass could be readily exploited. He also recognized the contribution that youth, especially radical students, might make to a revolution. Yet like another theorist of urban guerrilla warfare, Carlos Marighela, Guillén did not resolve the contradiction of how a small revolutionary elite, cloaked in the anonymity of the city and operating mostly at night, would be able to build mass popular support.

Guillén welcomed the advent of the Tupamaros but increasingly believed that they had developed an overelaborate infrastructure. He also felt that their use of "people's prisons" sent out the wrong kind of message to the population as a whole. Indeed, Guillén abhorred unnecessary violence. Guillén remains a prolific author and, having returned to Spain, currently teaches at the Autonomous University of Madrid.

See also: Argentina; Marighela, Carlos; Spanish Civil War; Tupamaros; Urban guerrilla warfare
Further Reading: Hughes, D. C. (ed.), *The Philosophy of the Urban Guerrilla: The Revolutionary Writings of Abraham Guillén* (New York, 1973).

Guinea, Portuguese

The smallest of the Portuguese possessions in Africa, Guinea attracted neither investment nor settlement, and in any case almost 40 percent of its total area was either uninhabited or underwater. Yet the Portuguese army faced the most sophisticated of its nationalist opponents in Guinea in the form of the Partido Africano da Independência

de Guiné e Cabo Verde (PAIGC), led by Amílcar Cabral. The 1,875 white Portuguese casualties suffered between 1963 and 1974 were proportionally higher than those suffered in Angola or Mozambique. The Portuguese also admitted that 15 percent of Guinea was under PAIGC control by the end of 1963; PAIGC claimed 80 percent control by 1971.

Even though Guinea proper was of little importance, it was administratively linked to the Cape Verde Islands, which were of considerable strategic significance for the West's control of Atlantic trade routes. Thus, holding Guinea became symbolic of Portugal's determination to remain in Africa. The Portuguese had an advantage over the tribal nature of PAIGC, whose revolutionary ideology did not appeal to more hierarchical groups like the Muslim Fula. Approximately half of the 30,000 men eventually deployed in Guinea by the Portuguese were Africans.

Initially, only two infantry companies were in the colony when PAIGC launched its campaign in January 1963, and the initiative was surrendered to the insurgents. However, Portugal's commander from 1964 to 1968, Arnaldo Schultz, founded a resettlement program that his successor, Antonio de Spinola, was able to build. De Spinola also enjoyed full civil and military powers denied Schultz. De Spinola not only restored Portuguese morale; under the slogan Guiné Melhor (Better Guinea) he claimed his hearts-and-minds program was winning back 3,000 refugees a year from neighboring states. Isolated garrisons were withdrawn and helicopters used to give greater mobility to counterinfiltration. The Portuguese felt unable to engage in hot pursuit across adjacent international frontiers but were involved in an abortive landing by armed exiles in the Republic of Guinea in 1970 and may have been implicated in Cabral's assassination in 1973.

From a situation where the war was being lost, de Spinola achieved a stalemate by 1973, although at great financial cost to Portugal (perhaps 196.8 million escudos by 1973). Fighting, however, subsided after the April 1974 military coup in Portugal, and negotiations with PAIGC led to Portuguese withdrawal. The Republic of Guinea-Bissau became independent on 10 September 1974.

See also: Angola; Cabral, Amílcar; de Spinola, Marshal Antonio Sebastião Ribeiro; Hearts and minds; Helicopters; Hot pursuit; Mozambique; Partido Africano da Independência de Guiné e Cabo Verde (PAIGC); Portuguese army; Resettlement
Further Reading: Beckett, Ian, and John Pimlott (eds.), *Armed Forces and Modern Counter-insurgency* (London, 1985); Cann, John, *Counterinsurgency in Africa: The Portuguese Way of War, 1961–1974* (Westport, 1997).

Guzmán Reynoso, Prof. Abimael (1935–)

Guzmán is the leader of Sendero Luminoso (Shining Path), the guerrilla group he founded in Peru in 1980 that enjoyed some success until his arrest in 1992. Guzmán was professor of philosophy at the National University of San Cristóbal de Huamanga at Ayacucho in mountainous southeastern Peru but was able to draw support for Sendero Luminoso from the Quechua natives of the region. Indeed, Guzmán rejected what had become the usual pattern of urban guerrilla warfare in Latin America by reverting to Mao Tse-tung's theories of rural revolutionary warfare, although Sendero Luminoso represents rather a provincial urban insurgency. Therefore, after a period of political preparation, Sendero Luminoso launched its military campaign in 1982. By 1992 about 23,000 people had died in the conflict, which had gradually spread outward from the Ayacucho region. It forced Pres. Alberto Keinya Fujimori to take dictatorial powers in April 1992, but the enhanced counterinsurgency effort was rewarded by Guzmán's arrest on 12 September 1992. Guzmán was sentenced to life in prison by a military court. In January 1994 Sendero Luminoso fragmented after Guzmán offered permanent peace terms from his prison cell.

See also: Mao Tse-tung; Peru; Sendero Luminoso; Urban guerrilla warfare
Further Reading: Palmer, David Scott (ed.), *The Shining Path of Peru* (London, 1992).

Gwynn, Maj. Gen. Sir Charles William (1870–1963)

Gwynn was the author of the British army's seminal work *Imperial Policing* (1934), the principles he advocated remaining integral to the British approach to counterinsurgency. Son of the Regius Professor of Divinity at Trinity College, Dublin, Gwynn was commissioned in the Royal Engineers in 1889. He served on the Sofa expedition in Sierra Leone in 1893–1894, for which he received the Distinguished Service Order (DSO). He was on the teaching staff at the Royal Military College, Duntroon, in Australia from 1911 to 1914, and by the end of World War I he had reached the rank of brevet colonel. He received promotion to major general in 1925 and was commandant of the Staff College from 1926 to 1930, being knighted upon his retirement from the army in 1931.

Imperial Policing was a product of Gwynn's work at the Staff College. Based on a number of case studies, such as Amritsar, India, in 1919, the Moplah Rebellion (1921), and the revolt on Cyprus in 1931, Gwynn laid down four principles of counterinsurgency. These were: the need for civil primacy over the military effort; the need for the use of minimum force; the need for firm and timely action to ensure that the political situation did not get out of hand; and the need for coordination of the civil and military effort. Gwynn's principles clearly reflected the realities of the situations that had confronted the British in colonial warfare since 1919 in the context of the limitations of the army's constitutional position.

He recognized that the weapon of propaganda invariably lay in the hands of the insurgent, but he ignored the politically motivated insurgency in Ireland between 1919 and 1921. Gwynn's book became the standard text at the Staff College; his principles were reflected in the official manual issued in 1934, *Notes on Imperial Policing.*

See also: British army; Colonial warfare; Cyprus; India; Ireland; Manuals; Moplah Rebellion; Simson, Col. Hugh James

Further Reading: Beckett, Ian (ed.), *The Roots of Counterinsurgency: Armies and Guerrilla Warfare, 1900–1945* (London, 1988); Mockaitis, Thomas, *British Counterinsurgency, 1919–1960* (London, 1990).

Hamlet Evaluation System (HES)

The U.S.-initiated HES was part of the new emphasis on pacification illustrated by the establishment of Robert Komer's Civil Operations and Rural Development Support (CORDS) organization in South Vietnam in 1967. The strategic hamlets resettlement program had begun in March 1962, but it was marked by haste in construction as compared to the more careful and measured resettlement program effected by the British during the Malayan Emergency (1948–1960). Whereas the British had constructed only 509 hamlets with a population of approximately 500,000 in 12 years, the United States constructed some 7,200 strategic hamlets with a total population of 8.7 million by July 1963.

The HES, which would embrace 12,750 strategic hamlets and 200 villages spread across 244 districts and 44 provinces in South Vietnam, was intended to provide a practical means of assessing progress toward winning the hearts and minds of the South Vietnamese. From June 1967 to December 1969, results were tabulated on the basis of subjective A-E ratings by district senior advisers. Advisers utilized 37 multiple-choice questions per hamlet per month to evaluate such aspects as attempted Vietcong subversion, economic development, and education and welfare provision. From January 1970 onward, objective reports by advisers were converted to the A-E rating system through a mathematical technique known as Bayesian probability analysis. These reports were based on 21 monthly and 56 quarterly hamlet questionnaires and four monthly and 58 quarterly village questionnaires. This new means of calculating progress emphasized verifiable facts, and the standard countrywide rating criteria introduced at the same time also improved upon the variety of criteria previously used by different advisers at different times. Unfortunately, the desire for statistical scorecards tended to result in the HES becoming to pacification what the notorious body count came to represent for the United States Army.

Indeed, hamlets could be rated as satisfactory without being secure from communist infiltration, and even after 1970 there were not noticeable differences in the interpretation of results. Thus, by 1971 some 97 percent of the population was considered secure or relatively secure. There were clear improvements in 1969 and 1970, but other data (such as public opinion surveys) suggested that the residents of strategic hamlets felt far less secure than the HES might imply. In fact, there was no fundamental change in political attitudes among the rural population toward the Saigon government. The population might prefer rule from Saigon to rule from Hanoi, but the pacification program as a whole came too late to change grudging preference into wholehearted support.

See also: Civil Operations and Rural Development Support (CORDS); Hearts and minds; Komer, Robert

William; Malayan Emergency; Pacification; Resettlement; Strategic hamlets; United States Army; Vietcong; Vietnam War
Further Reading: Bergerud, Eric, *The Dynamics of Defeat* (Boulder, 1991).

See also: British army; Cyprus; Ethniki Organosis Kyprion Agoniston (EOKA); Malayan Emergency; Templer, Field Marshal Sir Gerald
Further Reading: Carver, Michael, *Harding of Petherton* (London, 1978).

Harding, Field Marshal Lord (Allen Francis John) (1896–1989)

John Harding was British governor-general of Cyprus from 1955 to 1957 at the height of the insurgency by Ethniki Organosis Kyprion Agoniston (EOKA). Born at Petherton in Somerset, Harding served in World War I before receiving a regular commission in the Somerset Light Infantry in 1920. He was a lieutenant colonel at the outbreak of World War II. His wartime promotion was rapid, and as lieutenant general he was chief of staff to the supreme Allied commander in the Mediterranean, Sir Harold Alexander. Indeed, Harding rather than Alexander came up with the idea—never executed—of a rapid advance from northern Italy to forestall the Soviet army from reaching Vienna.

Harding was knighted in 1944. Promoted to full general in 1949 and to field marshal in 1953, Harding was chief of the imperial general staff from 1952 to 1955. In September 1955 Harding was sent to Cyprus as governor-general and director of operations, a dual role similar to that enjoyed by Sir Gerald Templer during the Malayan Emergency (1948–1960). Harding followed the Malayan model in establishing coordinated command of the civil and military efforts and, following his proclamation of a state of emergency in November 1955, intensified the campaign against EOKA. Harding also deported the political leader of the Greek Cypriots, Archbishop Makarios, to detention in the Seychelles in March 1956.

By the time Harding left Cyprus in November 1957, EOKA had suffered serious damage, and Harding himself had escaped assassination when a bomb was discovered under his bed. He was raised to the peerage as Lord Harding of Petherton in 1958.

Hearts and minds

The phrase *winning hearts and minds* was coined by Sir Gerald Templer during the Malayan Emergency (1948–1960). It was intended to describe the need to isolate insurgents from any popular support by not only providing the population with security from intimidation but also giving the population positive reasons to support the authorities. Thus, winning hearts and minds implies both a physical and psychological separation of the population from the insurgents.

This idea lies at the very heart of pacification and should be regarded as the very essence of counterinsurgency. Indeed, Templer remarked on one occasion that "the shooting side of the business is only 25 percent of the trouble and the other 75 percent lies in getting the people of this country behind us."

Winning hearts and minds may take many forms. In Malaya, for example, physical separation of insurgents from population was accomplished through a resettlement program. However, resettlement and the physical control imposed upon that section of the Malayan population most susceptible to communist influence—the so-called squatters, ethnic Chinese illegally occupying government land on the jungle fringes—was only a means to an end. Gradually, therefore, amenities such as water, light, clinics, schools, and cultivation plots were made available behind the barbed wire of the "new villages" in Malaya. In December 1951 the squatters received permanent legal title to the land they now occupied, and in May 1952 village councils were introduced.

Templer emphasized a traditional rather than paramilitary role for police and involved villagers in their own defense by establishing a compulsory home guard in July 1951. In the Philippines there was a similar response to the threat posed by the communist Hukbalahap between 1946 and 1955 through the establishment, by Ramon Magsaysay, of the Economic Development Corps (EDCOR). EDCOR relocated only 5,200 people, perhaps only 20 percent of whom were former Huks. However, what was significant about EDCOR was the symbolism of establishing land-hungry peasants on new and relatively spacious farms.

In South Vietnam, too, between 1965 and 1973 the U.S. Green Berets and U.S. Marines were actively involved in winning hearts and minds. The Green Berets established the Civilian Irregular Defense Group (CIDG) program among the Montagnard tribesmen of the Central Highlands in order to cultivate their support for the government in Saigon. Within their tactical area of responsibility, the Marines began so-called county fair operations in late 1965, which combined screening the population in cordon-and-search operations with entertainment and medical treatment in a domestic American "county fair" atmosphere. More than 46,000 people were screened in 1966, and an estimated 20,000 of them received some form of medical assistance.

Unfortunately, the commitment of the U.S. army to pacification generally was less impressive. To give an example, what was described as "short-duration, high-impact pacification" during "Operation Thayer II" and "Operation Pershing" between February and April 1967 consisted primarily of daily visits to and band concerts in refugee camps effectively created by earlier operations. Simultaneously, more than 12,000 people were forcibly removed from their homes by the same operations.

Compared with the American experience in Vietnam, the British in Malaya had the considerable advantage of being able to grant the country independence in 1957. This robbed the Malayan Communist Party (MCP) of much of its political legitimacy as an allegedly nationalist organization. The United States, of course, had less opportunity to control the political agenda in South Vietnam. Equally, in declining to concede the principle of self-government the French (in French Indochina and Algeria in the 1950s) and the Portuguese (in Angola, Mozambique, and Portuguese Guinea in the 1960s) handed a ready weapon to their guerrilla opponents. In turn, this immediately undermined their efforts at winning support for the status quo. In the same way, resettlement in Rhodesia between 1972 and 1979 was largely punitive. Moreover, rather than attempting to provide rural Africans with more facilities, there was a tendency in Rhodesia to concentrate on broadening the representation of the African in government. This meant little to the average African, and the collective fines and punishments frequently imposed on the population more than outweighed the benefits on offer.

In short, if winning hearts and minds is to be successful, it is necessary to demonstrate tangible proof of genuine government concern for the social and economic grievances underlying support for insurgency. Reforms put into place under pressure of emergency must also be seen to endure long enough to ensure there is no return of insurgency in the long term.

See also: Algeria; Angola; British army; Civilian Irregular Defense Group (CIDG); French army; French Indochina; Green Berets; Guinea, Portuguese; Hukbalahap; Magsaysay, Ramon; Malayan Emergency; Pacification; Philippines; Portuguese army; Resettlement; Rhodesia; Templer, Field Marshal Sir Gerald; United States Marine Corps (USMC); Vietnam War

Further Reading: Carruthers, Susan, *Winning Hearts and Minds* (London, 1995); Stubbs, Richard, *Hearts and Minds in Guerrilla Warfare* (Singapore, 1989).

Helicopters

Since their introduction to counterinsurgency campaigns in the 1950s, helicopters have proved an invaluable extension of the

Playing an important role in military confrontations since the Malayan Emergency (1948–1960), helicopters were counted on to give these soldiers the advantage of surprise when they attacked a Vietcong stronghold in June 1965. The communist guerrillas had been warned, though, and contact was minimal. (UPI/Corbis-Bettmann)

airpower available to security forces. The helicopter offers not only transport capability but also a means of harnessing firepower and mobility.

As early as June 1932 the U.S. Marines experimented unsuccessfully with an autogiro—the precursor of modern fixed wing rotary aircraft—as a means of lifting heavy loads in Nicaragua during the campaign against Augusto Sandino. However, the logistic potential of the modern helicopter was quickly realized. During the Malayan Emergency (1948–1960), for example, it was estimated that ten minutes' flight time in a helicopter was the equivalent of ten hours' marching through the jungle. During the campaign, more than 5,000 casualties were evacuated by helicopter, more than 2.5 million pounds of freight carried, and more than 110,000 troops transported.

The helicopter was equally valuable as a transport during the Indonesian/Malaysian Confrontation (1962–1966) and in the war

in South Vietnam between 1965 and 1973. Task Force Remagen, for example, which was drawn from the First Brigade of the U.S. Fifth Infantry (Mechanized) Division, was successfully maintained in the mountainous demilitarized zone (DMZ) for the 47 days of "Operation Montana Mauler" from March to April 1969 by heavy Chinook CH-47 cargo helicopters. The Chinooks had specially designed cargo slings to eliminate their need to land (helicopters are adversely affected if there is an absence of reasonably flat and firm landing zones and by altitude).

Similarly, in Britain's Dhofar campaign in Oman between 1970 and 1975, payload depended upon temperature, and crews faced difficulties with sand ingestion, corrosion, crosswinds, and monsoon clouds. The four Wessex HC-2 helicopters of No. 74 Squadron, Royal Air Force, deployed in Dhofar between April and November 1974, logged 1,487 flying hours in carrying

2,750 short tons of freight, 15,000 passengers, and 41 casualty evacuations.

The offensive capability of the helicopter has also been well proven. In Rhodesia between 1972 and 1979 helicopters were an essential element in the fire force concept, which enabled the Rhodesians to offset their lack of manpower by mobility and firepower. In the case of the United States Army, the Eleventh Air Assault Division (Test) was established in February 1964. It resulted from the support for what was called "airmobility" on the part of a service committee known as the Howze Board. The division, with more than 400 helicopters and fixed-wing aircraft, was activated for service in June 1965 as the First Air Cavalry Division (Mobile). It saw its first action in the Ia Drang Valley in October and November 1965. At peak, the Americans had more than 5,000 helicopters deployed in South Vietnam. Sooner or later, however, troops had to land and fight on the ground. Once on the ground, American troops often proved reluctant to move beyond the "umbilical cord" of the landing zone and were content to dig in and await fire support while the Vietcong or North Vietnamese army (NVA) troops slipped away.

Helicopter losses in combat were heavy, although not as heavy as expected. The continuing vulnerability of the helicopter is illustrated by the experience of the Soviet army in Afghanistan between 1979 and 1989. Rather as the ubiquitous Bell AH-1 Huey Cobra gunship became almost a symbol of the Americans in South Vietnam, so the Mi–24 Hind gunship became a familiar image of the Soviet presence in Afghanistan. However, the helicopter was far less visible once the Afghan mujahideen took delivery of U.S.-supplied Stinger antiaircraft missiles in 1986–1987.

See also: Afghanistan; Airpower; Confrontation, Indonesian/Malaysian; Dhofar; Fire force; Malayan Emergency; Mujahideen; Nicaragua; Rhodesia; Sandino, Augusto César; Soviet army; United States Army; United States Marine Corps (USMC); Vietcong; Vietnam War

Further Reading: Towle, Philip, *Pilots and Rebels* (London, 1989).

Herero Revolt (1904–1906)

The German army's approach to the Herero Revolt in German South West Africa (later Namibia) was symptomatic of its tendency toward the use of maximum force when faced with insurgency. It is estimated that the Herero population declined by more than 60,000 during the revolt, which was a response to increasing German exploitation of the colony's resources.

Initially, the small German garrison of fewer than 800 men commanded by Maj. Theodor Leutwin was hard-pressed by the outbreak of revolt in January 1904. However, reinforcements were soon to bring the German forces to more than 7,000 men, and in June 1904 command was assumed by the ruthless Gen. Lothar von Trotha. When the leader of the Herero, Samuel Maherero, made the error of trying to hold a defended position at Watersberg on 11 August 1904 with 6,000 fighting men and 40,000 noncombatants, von Trotha was able to bring his superior firepower to bear. As von Trotha intended, the Herero were forced into retreating into the Omaheke Desert. In October 1904 he instituted the policy of *schrecklichkeit* (dreadfulness), by which all captured men were executed and women, children, and the aged driven further into the desert to starve.

Von Trotha's policy aroused some opposition in Germany, and the harshness of German colonial policy also led to the revolt of the Hottentot or Nama people in the south of the colony in 1905. Led by Hendrik Witbooie, the Hottentot proved more effective guerrillas than did the Herero, and, failing to suppress them, von Trotha was removed in October 1905. However, Witbooie was mortally wounded during a raid that same month. Von Trotha's successor, Gen. Berthold von Deimling, who arrived in June 1906, established more mobile German columns and also systematically deprived the Hottentot of their important livestock. By December 1906, when the last Hottentot guerrillas surrendered, the Germans had more than 15,000 men.

In the course of the conflict, the Germans suffered about 2,500 casualties from battle or disease, but the costs to the Herero and the Hottentot were far greater. Apart from the devastation wrought on the Herero, which had been some 80,000 strong before the revolt, the smaller Hottentot population had been reduced from about 20,000 to less than 10,000.

See also: Colonial warfare; German army; Namibia; Trotha, Gen. Lothar von
Further Reading: Bridgeman, J. M., *The Revolt of the Hereros* (Los Angeles, 1981).

Hilsman, Roger (1919–)

As director of the bureau of intelligence and research in the U.S. State Department, Hilsman was one of the architects of the strategic hamlets program in South Vietnam in 1962. A 1943 graduate of the U.S. Military Academy at West Point, Hilsman had served with Merrill's Marauders, irregulars organized by the Office of Strategic Services (OSS) to operate behind Japanese lines in Burma during World War II. He retired from the United States Army in 1953.

Hilsman became one of several civilian counterinsurgency experts in the Kennedy administration, although his influence over policy was comparatively smaller. Basing his ideas mostly on those of the British counterinsurgency theorist Robert Thompson, Hilsman submitted a paper entitled "A Strategic Concept for South Vietnam" on 2 February 1962. Like Thompson, Hilsman saw the need for an essentially political solution to insurgency in South Vietnam and emphasized the importance of civic action to win the hearts and minds of the population. He placed even greater emphasis on resettlement than did Thompson, yet Hilsman saw strategic hamlets as a symbol of civic action rather than an end in themselves.

In the event, the strategic hamlet program was expanded by South Vietnam's Pres. Ngo Dinh Diem well beyond what Hilsman or Thompson had envisaged. Subsequently, Hilsman supported U.S. involvement in removing Diem from office in November 1963. Kennedy was assassinated that month. Now assistant secretary of state for Far Eastern affairs, Hilsman was one of many Kennedy appointees removed from office by Pres. Lyndon B. Johnson.

See also: Burma; Hearts and minds; Office of Strategic Services (OSS); Resettlement; Strategic hamlets; Thompson, Sir Robert Grainger Ker; United States Army; Vietnam War
Further Reading: Hilsman, Roger, *To Move a Nation* (New York, 1967); Hilsman, Roger, *American Guerrilla: My War Behind Japanese Lines* (New York, 1990).

Ho Chi Minh (1890–1969)

Ho Chi Minh was president of communist North Vietnam from 1954 until his death, having founded the Vietminh in 1941 and led it to victory in French Indochina between 1946 and 1954. Ho Chi Minh (He Who Enlightens) was the second pseudonym chosen by Ho, who had originally adopted the name Nguyen Ai Quoc (Nguyen the Patriot). His actual name was Nguyen That Thanh. Ho was born in Kimlien in Annam, French Indochina, but left for Europe in 1911 as a ship's cook. Arriving in Paris in 1917, Ho became familiar with the ideas of socialism and Marxism and was one of the founders of the French Communist Party in 1920. He was in Moscow in 1923. While in Moscow, Ho contributed the only chapter on guerrilla warfare in a Soviet guide to insurrection published in 1928.

Returning to Indochina, he led the Revolutionary League of the Youth of Vietnam, which in turn formed the basis of the Indochinese Communist Party (ICP) in 1929. However, Ho was forced to flee from French authorities in 1932 and returned to Moscow before establishing himself in China in 1938. Japan's effective domination of French Indochina after the 1940 fall of

France to Germany led Ho to return to French Indochina in January 1941. Establishing himself at Pac Bo in the Cao Bang Province of Tonkin, Ho founded the Viet Nam Doc Lap Dong Minh Hoi (Vietminh), or Vietnamese Independence League, in May 1941. Ostensibly, it was a broadly based nationalist coalition against the Japanese, but in reality it was dominated by the ICP. Ho himself returned to China but was held in detention for more than a year by the Chinese nationalist Kuomintang (KMT), who released him in 1944.

Following the pattern set by Chinese communist leader Mao Tse-tung, the Vietminh spent much of World War II consolidating support among the population. The Vietminh also benefited from the assistance of the Western Allies, particularly the U.S. Office of Strategic Services (OSS). At the same time, the influence of the French authorities was steadily declining, as they came under pressure from the Japanese. In March 1945 the Japanese formally occupied French Indochina, eliminating most of the French administration and garrison. Ho and the Vietminh were thus well placed to fill the power vacuum when the Japanese suddenly surrendered on 15 August 1945 following the detonation of atomic bombs at Hiroshima and Nagasaki.

Accordingly, Ho proclaimed an independent Democratic Republic of Vietnam in Hanoi, the Tonkin capital, on 2 September 1945. The Allies were too short on shipping capacity to be able to respond immediately to the collapse of Japanese administration in Southeast Asia, and it was not until 11 September that British Indian troops reached Saigon, the capital of the southern region known as Cochin China. KMT forces also reached Hanoi. However, while the British acted to restore French control in the south and engaged in fighting with Vietminh supporters, the KMT blocked any immediate French return to Hanoi and turned a mostly blind eye to the Vietminh securing the weapons of the disarmed Japanese. The KMT withdrew during the course of 1946 as their renewed conflict against the communists in the Chinese Civil War (1927–1949) intensified.

Ho was ruthlessly single-minded, and whereas the French were prepared to offer some form of autonomy within a French union, he held out for full independence. Thus, although Ho accepted the limited autonomy offered him in January 1946 and allowed the French to return to Hanoi that March, the protracted negotiations grew increasingly more bitter. In November 1946 a clash between French and Vietminh forces in Haiphong rapidly escalated into full-scale battle. The conflict with the French lasted for the next eight years; Ho left its conduct to his military commander, Vo Nguyen Giap. His own role was primarily in manipulating the Vietminh's appeal to nationalists in a way that the French could not hope to match. By 1952, the Vietminh had more than 110,000 regular troops backed by perhaps 195,000 regional forces or militia.

The final defeat of the French army at Dien Bien Phu in May 1954 coincided with the opening of a scheduled international conference at Geneva to discuss Indochina and other issues. As part of the agreement, signed on 21 July 1954, the French withdrew from Indochina. Independence was granted to Laos and Cambodia, whereas Vietnam (Annam, Tonkin, and Cochin China) was to be divided along the line of the 17th parallel pending elections to be held in 1956 to reunite north and south under a mutually acceptable administration. North of the parallel (where most of the population was located), Ho would govern the Democratic Republic of North Vietnam. The United States, which had belatedly supported the French war effort without losing its general dislike of French colonialism, had not signed the Geneva accords, and the Americans opposed elections they suspected Ho would win. In any case, Ngo Dinh Diem, who quickly gained control of the Republic of South Vietnam, did not feel bound by the Geneva agreement. Thus, elections never took place, and the temporary division along the 17th parallel became a de facto partition of Vietnam.

Still committed to unifying Vietnam under communist control at any cost, Ho began supporting the southern National Liberation Front (Vietcong) in 1957. The Vietcong mostly consisted of Vietminh veterans who had remained in the south after partition. Ho and his colleagues on North Vietnam's politburo endorsed the Vietcong's aim of overthrowing South Vietnam in May 1959 and officially recognized the Vietcong in 1960. Increasingly, the Vietcong was supplemented by recruits and by North Vietnamese army (NVA) troops infiltrated south by means of the Ho Chi Minh Trail, which passed through Laos and Cambodia. The extension of the Americans' effort to sustain South Vietnam with the commitment of U.S. ground forces in 1965 forced Giap to reconsider his military strategy, but neither Giap nor Ho wavered in their determination. Indeed, the basic American attrition strategy, which assumed that North Vietnam would reach a point where the number of casualties was no longer acceptable, underestimated the willingness of Hanoi to accept any and all losses necessary to subjugate South Vietnam.

Giap remounted a large scale conventional assault, again prematurely, with the Tet Offensive in early 1968. Its political impact in the United States outweighed the considerable military defeat the communists actually suffered as a result of Tet. Thus, even though Ho died on 3 September 1969 before his dream was realized, the long negotiating process already begun at Paris would lead to the Americans' withdrawal in January 1973. That withdrawal doomed South Vietnam to final collapse in April 1975.

See also: Cambodia; Chinese Civil War; Dien Bien Phu; French army; French Indochina; Giap, Vo Nguyen; Ho Chi Minh Trail; Kuomintang (KMT); Laos; Mao Tse-tung; Office of Strategic Services (OSS); Tet Offensive; Vietcong; Vietminh; Vietnam War

Further Reading: Duiker, W. J., *The Communist Road to Power in Vietnam* (Boulder, 1981); Tønnesson, Stein, *The Vietnamese Revolution of 1945* (Oslo, 1991); Lacoutre, Jean, *Ho Chi Minh* (New York, 1968).

Ho Chi Minh Trail

The Ho Chi Minh Trail is probably the most famous logistic system in military history. Begun in July 1959, it was a complex series of routes through Laos and Cambodia that enabled the North Vietnamese to ferry reinforcements and supplies to the Vietcong and regular troops throughout the war in South Vietnam until the final communist victory in 1975.

The original trail, constructed by North Vietnamese army (NVA) construction unit Group 559, remained a single track until as late as 1964. However, between 1965 and 1971 it was increasingly expanded until it embraced more than 8,000 miles of roads through mountain and jungle, with a labor force of 50,000 men and a 25,000-strong garrison. It defended against American airpower with more than 1,000 antiaircraft guns. The trail complex included pipelines, barracks, and underground storage and repair facilities. About 20–35 percent of all supplies sent down the trail were lost, the greatest proportion due to U.S. airstrikes assisted by air-dropped sensors (ADSIDS), electronic monitoring devices. In all, the Americans dropped more than 2.2 million tons of bombs over the trail; 15 percent of all American aircraft lost between 1965 and 1973 resulted from these operations.

Yet communist supplies were being transported at the astounding rate of 10,000 tons per week on average by 1970. During one day in December 1970 Americans estimated that 15,000 vehicles were on the trail. Consequently, the momentum of communist operations was easily sustained. In addition, the infiltration of troops into South Vietnam increased from about 5,000 per year in 1960 to an estimated 90,000 in 1966. And whereas it had taken up to three months to traverse the trail in the early 1960s, the journey time to the south from the port of Haiphong, where Soviet supplies were landing in North Vietnam, had been cut to a mere ten days by 1975. Thus, U.S.-inflicted losses must be analyzed in this context.

Moreover, since Laos and Cambodia were theoretically neutral states, the United States could not interdict with ground troops in any serious way. Therefore, transportation was only briefly interrupted as a result of the limited American–South Vietnamese incursion into Cambodia in April 1970 and the South Vietnamese incursion into Laos in February 1971. The Americans were able to close the coastal route into the south by 1968; the so-called Sihanouk Trail into the Mekong Delta from Cambodia was also closed to the communists thanks to Gen. Lon Nol's government in Cambodia in March 1970.

Without the Ho Chi Minh Trail, the communists could not have achieved their ultimate victory.

See also: Airpower; Cambodia; Laos; Vietnam War
Further Reading: Karnow, Stanley, *Vietnam: A History* (New York, 1983).

Hofer, Andreas (1767–1810)

Hofer was the leader of the Tyrolean Revolt (1809) against the French during the French Revolutionary and Napoleonic Wars (1792–1815). Hofer was a wine merchant and innkeeper. He was a member of the revolutionary diet (assembly) in 1789 that demanded reforms of Austrian policy toward the Tyrol.

Staunch Catholics, the Tyroleans in particular opposed the dissolution of lay monasteries as well as the imposition of new taxes. And though the Austrian reforms were modified, the Tyrol passed to the control of Bavaria after the Austrian defeat by the French at Austerlitz. The Bavarians in turn attempted to impose new taxes and conscription and also suppressed the assembly. Consequently, in April 1809 Hofer and Josef Speckbacher raised the Tyrol. Hofer defeated the Bavarians at

Berg in August, but the French themselves then assumed control of the Tyrol. Hofer was betrayed to the French and executed at Mantua in February 1810. The Tyrol was restored to Austria in 1814.

See also: French army; Tyrolean Revolt
Further Reading: Eyck, F. G., *Loyal Rebels: Andreas Hofer and the Tyrolean Uprising of 1809* (New York, 1986).

Hot pursuit

The phrase *hot pursuit* describes the crossing of international frontiers by security forces in pursuit of guerrillas who are using another state as a refuge. The most successful guerrilla groups since 1945 have been those with access to such refuge in a nearby host state. The existence of the frontier poses a particular difficulty for the security forces because crossing it may have wide-ranging international political implications.

The United States was extremely wary of overtly violating the neutrality of Cambodia and Laos during the war in Vietnam between 1965 and 1973, although the North Vietnamese had no reservations about using the Ho Chi Minh Trail, which wended through both countries, to supply forces in South Vietnam. Consequently, American operations in and over Cambodia and Laos were for the most part covert. Similarly, when faced with the incursions of Indonesian forces into northern Borneo during the undeclared war known as the Indonesian/Malaysian Confrontation (1962–1966), British and Commonwealth forces undertook only covert counterincursions into Indonesian territory. And during the concluding phase of the Dhofar campaign in Oman in 1975, when artillery positions located inside the People's Democratic Republic of Yemen (PDRY) were supporting guerrillas of the Popular Front for the Liberation of the Occupied Arabian Gulf (PFLOAG), the Omani government chose not to inform the British government in advance of its intention to launch air strikes inside Yemen, fearing the British would veto the operations on political grounds.

Other states faced with insurgency have not shown the same restraint in crossing frontiers and have been prepared to take the political risks of undertaking not only hot pursuit operations but also preemptive strikes against guerrilla concentrations in host states. In the case of the war in Rhodesia between 1972 and 1979, Rhodesian security forces frequently launched raids into neighboring Mozambique: After independence in 1974 Mozambique had become a refuge for guerrillas of the Zimbabwe African National Union (ZANU). Raids were designed to put pressure on the guerrillas as well as their hosts. In September 1979, for example, "Operation Miracle" was designed to pressure ZANU during forthcoming negotiations in London, whereas attacks on economic targets during the conference were intended to influence the Mozambicans. The raids intensified with the approach of the rainy season in November in order to hit guerrilla concentrations that would infiltrate Rhodesia by making use of climatic conditions unfavorable to Rhodesian aircraft.

Using the example of the Israeli army, which favored hot pursuit of Arab guerrillas, the South African army also routinely pursued South West Africa People's Organization (SWAPO) guerrillas into Botswana, Zambia, and Angola during the late 1970s, soon extending hot pursuit into preemptive raids on SWAPO bases in Angola. As in Rhodesia, such raids were undertaken to preempt SWAPO offensives and to weaken SWAPO militarily at times when political negotiations looked likely. Such raids were continued into the 1980s. "Operation Protea"—carried out in Angola over 13 days in August and September 1981—resulted in the elimination of more than 1,000 SWAPO, Cuban, and Angolan troops and the seizure of supplies and weapons with a collective value of $200 million Rhodesian (£120 million).

See also: Angola; Cambodia; Confrontation, Indonesian/Malaysian; Dhofar; Ho Chi Minh Trail; Israeli army; Laos; Mozambique; Popular Front for the Liberation of the Occupied Arabian Gulf (PFLOAG); Rhodesia; South African army; South West African People's Organization (SWAPO); Vietnam War; Zimbabwe African National Union (ZANU)
Further Reading: Cilliers, J. K., *Counter-insurgency in Rhodesia* (London, 1985).

Hukbalahap

Hukbalahap was the communist-dominated movement that waged an insurgency against the newly independent government in the Philippines from 1946 until 1954. Originally formed in March 1942 as the Hukbo ng Bayan laban sa Hapon (Hukbalahap or Huks), or People's Anti-Japanese Army, the movement was an alliance of communist leaders in Manila and peasant unions of the central Luzon Plain. The Huks grew to perhaps 12,000 men, fighting the Japanese with the assistance of the United States Armed Forces in the Far East (USAFFE), which also raised its own guerrilla forces. However, population growth and progressive subdivision of land in central Luzon meant that the communist leadership was able to exploit longstanding peasant grievances in the immediate post–World War II period when former landlords emerged after the Japanese defeat to reclaim lands at a time of agricultural depression.

Former Huks formed a National Peasants' Union (PKM) and, upon the approach of formal independence from the United States, joined other groups in a loose political coalition known as the Democratic Alliance (DA) to contest the April 1946 elections. The DA won all the central Luzon congressional seats, but the government debarred them in May on the grounds of alleged electoral fraud, and when negotiations broke down the Huks took to the mountains as the Hukbong Mapagpalaya ng Batan (HMB), or People's Liberation Army, under their wartime leader, Luis Taruc.

It was never a purely communist uprising, although the peasants had far more

Philippines president Manuel Roxas, the strongarm leader who alienated the peasants, unwittingly lending strength to the Hukbalahap movement. (UPI/Corbis-Bettmann)

limited aims than the communist leadership (with whom Taruc also eventually broke). Following the rural guerrilla theories of Mao Tse-tung, the HMB attempted to create base areas in "Huklandia" such as that at Mount Arayat and to launch hit-and-run attacks on government positions. In reality, the Huks had little popular support outside the Laguna and Batangas Provinces of Luzon to the immediate south of Manila, but Pres. Manuel Roxas resorted to the so-called mailed-fist strategy.

This strategy of coercion and use of maximum force alienated the population as a whole since police and army units tended to treat every civilian as a suspect and used excessive violence. The government was also incapable of recognizing the need for land reform or for political concessions likely to undermine the insurgency. President Roxas's successor, Elpidio Quirino, attempted negotiations in June 1948, but they failed. However, in September 1950 Quirino appointed a former USAFFE guerrilla, Ramon Magsaysay, as secretary for national defense. Magsaysay launched a hearts-and-minds program to win popular support for the government. It included the creation of the Economic Development Corps (EDCOR) to build new rural facilities and a small scale but well publicized resettlement scheme to relocate former Huks and their families on Mindanao. The despised police were integrated into the army and with the assistance of the Joint U.S. Military Advisory Group (JUSMAG), the army itself was organized into small, self-sufficient battalion combat teams. One of Magsaysay's key advisers was the American air force officer and counterinsurgency expert, Edward Lansdale.

The Huks were forced to the defensive. By 1954 a total of 9,695 had been killed, 1,635 wounded, and 4,269 captured, including much of the communist politburo seized in Manila in October 1950. Even more significant, no less than 15,866 Huks had surrendered, including Taruc himself in May 1954. Magsaysay went on to become president of the Philippines in November 1953, and by the time of his death in a March 1957 air crash the Huks had been broken. A brief revival between 1965 and 1970 led by Taruc's nephew made very little impact.

See also: Hearts and minds; Lansdale, Maj. Gen. Edward Geary; Magsaysay, Ramon; Mao Tse-tung; Philippines; Resettlement; Taruc, Luis

Further Reading: Kerkvliet, B. J., *The Huk Rebellion* (Berkeley, 1977); Kessler, R. J., *Rebellion and Repression in the Philippines* (New Haven, 1989); Valeriano, N. D., and C. T. R. Bohannan, *Counterguerrilla Operations: The Philippines Experience* (New York, 1962); Greenberg, L. M., *The Hukbalahap Insurrection* (Washington, DC, 1987).

India

India's security was a constant source of concern during two centuries of British occupation, from the effective consolidation of British power in Bengal in the mid–eighteenth century to the independence and partition of the subcontinent in 1947. However, the partition between India and Pakistan in turn led to conflict, and modern India faces insurgency in the disputed region of Kashmir as well as in the Punjab and Assam. Indian support for the government of Sri Lanka (formerly Ceylon) has also led to terrorism in India itself.

The British conquest of India through the agency of the East India Company (EIC) was not complete until the 1840s, when the Sikh kingdom of the Punjab was annexed. The majority of the campaigns fought by British and locally raised EIC forces were against native armies that were modeled on European lines, but the extension of their influence in 1849 gave British India a contiguous frontier with Afghanistan. Just as the security of the eastern frontier resulted in three wars and the eventual conquest of Burma (1823–1824, 1852–1853, 1885–1889), there were three British invasions of Afghanistan (1838–1842, 1878–1881, 1919). Moreover, there was a constant threat on the mountainous North-West Frontier from tribes fiercely resistant to British and Afghan authorities alike. Between 1852 and 1908 alone there were 25 major and innumerable minor expeditions on the North-West Frontier. In India

proper, the revolt of EIC troops in the Indian Mutiny (1857–1858) resulted in direct British rule.

Although modern Indian nationalism, which emerged in the 1880s, is popularly associated with nonviolence and civil disobedience, it frequently embraced violence. There was limited terrorism in Bengal from 1906 to 1917 and then more widespread civil disturbances in 1919, one consequence being the incident at Amritsar in the Punjab on 13 April 1919, when troops under the command of Brig. Gen. Reginald Dyer opened fire on a demonstration, killing about 380 people. There was a second terrorist campaign in Bengal from 1923 to 1927 and then a third (and far more violent) campaign from 1930 to 1934. This necessitated the deployment of large numbers of troops on internal security duties; the subsequent disturbances associated with the "Quit India" movement from 1942 to 1943 also required a substantial deployment at a time when India was threatened with Japanese invasion. Ironically, the Moplah Rebellion (1921) in southern India, arguably the gravest internal threat since 1857, was not linked to nationalism but to particular local ethnic tensions.

Ethnic tension lay at the heart of the partition of the subcontinent between India and Pakistan in 1947 and two Indo-Pakistani wars (1965 and 1971). The disputed territory of Kashmir, seized by the Indian army in 1947, was fought over in both wars and remains a source of tension between the two states. In addition, Kashmiri separatists have been increasingly active in the 1980s and 1990s, frequently publicizing their cause by detaining Western tourists. Division of the Punjab between India and Pakistan in 1947 has equally resulted in conflict, and Sikh separatists supporting the establishment of "Khalistan" emerged in the early 1980s. Indian troops forcibly expelled Sikh extremists from the sacred Sikh Golden Temple in Amritsar in June 1984, killing more than 600.

Amid escalating communal violence, the Indian prime minister, Indira Gandhi, was assassinated by a Sikh bodyguard in October 1984. Sikh militants were again expelled from the Golden Temple in 1988. Indira Gandhi was succeeded as prime minister by her son, Rajiv Gandhi. Having lost office, he, too, was later assassinated by a suicide bomber while electioneering in May 1991. However, Rajiv Gandhi's assassin was a member of the Tamil Tigers, who opposed India's intervention in Sri Lanka between 1987 and 1990 as well as its continuing support for the Sri Lankan government. India has also faced sporadic guerrilla opposition to its control of Assam on the eastern frontier.

See also: Afghanistan; British army; Burma; Moplah Rebellion; North-West Frontier; Tamils
Further Reading: Nevill, H. L., *North-West Frontier* (2d ed., London, 1992); Townshend, Charles, *Britain's Civil Wars* (London, 1986).

Intelligence

Accurate intelligence is vital to security forces facing the threat of insurgency, for political and military responses can be made only on the basis of sufficient knowledge. Intelligence itself may be divided into three categories: background, operational, and criminal. *Background intelligence* enables the security forces to understand political and socioeconomic situations; *operational* or *"contact" intelligence* enables security forces to generate contacts with insurgents in the field; *criminal intelligence,* in contrast, is primarily of interest to the police, although insurgency in itself may encourage greater criminality.

The means by which any intelligence is collected will vary. Background intelligence may be gleaned from open sources such as census material and official statistics or an insurgent group's own publications and propaganda. Other "overt" intelligence will come from the presence of troops or police on the ground through their observation or operations. "Covert" or confidential intelligence can be collected though paid informers such as the "super grasses" used in Northern Ireland since 1969 or the kind of confidential questionnaires the British issued to villagers during the Malayan Emergency (1948–1960). Interrogation of prisoners and deserters is also characterized as a confidential source. However, as in the French army's conduct of the Battle of Algiers in 1957, in which a detailed order of battle, or *organigramme,* of the opposing Front de Libération Nationale (FLN) was constructed by Col. Yves Godard, interrogation may involve systematic torture.

Covert intelligence may also result from clandestine operations involving surveillance by human or technological means. The pseudoforces recruited from former insurgents such as the countergangs in the Kenyan Emergency (1952–1960) and the *firqat* in the Dhofar campaign in Oman in the 1970s were very effective in guiding the security forces in operations against their erstwhile colleagues. Increasingly, however, surveillance has been carried out by technology. Whereas in Malaya the security forces often relied on intercepting the Malayan Communist Party's (MCP) human couriers, the United States Army in Vietnam between 1965 and 1973 had access to satellite information, high-flying "spy" aircraft such as the U-2, air-dropped sensors (ADSIDS) such as those dropped along the Ho Chi Minh Trail to detect movement, remotely piloted vehicles (RPVs), and both electronic intelligence (ELINT) and signals intelligence (SIG-

INT). Indeed, it was estimated that 80 percent of the intelligence available to American forces was derived from electronic sources.

One of the difficulties facing the American forces in Vietnam was that there was almost too much intelligence available. The intelligence center in Saigon under Military Assistance Command—Vietnam (MAC—V) was receiving 3 million pages of captured enemy documents every month by 1968. Computers, automatic data processing, and systems analysis were all available to try to make sense of this extraordinary amount of information, but there were inevitable delays in assessment and dissemination. Much of the resulting product tended to be made available as rather vague "trends" analysis.

The American experience in Vietnam also demonstrated the importance of avoiding proliferation of intelligence-collecting agencies. In contrast, the British in practice usually have attempted to ensure coordination of intelligence in order to avoid duplication of efforts. The classic example: Malaya, where one of the key elements of the new counterinsurgency plan drawn up by Sir Harold Briggs in 1950 was coordination of intelligence within an elaborate committee structure. The logical solution was the appointment of a single organization or individual capable of coordinating all efforts, and in 1952 a single director of intelligence was appointed.

Yet even the British have had difficulties in collecting intelligence in many campaigns since 1945. Usually, the British relied on the police and especially the plainclothes criminal intelligence unit known as Special Branch to collect intelligence, but police are often the first targets for insurgent attack. This was the case in Palestine between 1945 and 1948 and on Cyprus between 1955 and 1959. In such circumstances, soldiers became involved in trying to rebuild an intelligence organization but often differed from the police in pursuing contact intelligence to the detriment of the political and criminal intelligence (in which the police were interested).

And if special forces are deployed with both intelligence and operational functions, there are sometimes additional problems in coordination. In Northern Ireland since 1969, for example, the "cover" of the Special Air Service (SAS) has sometimes been "blown" by members of security forces who were unaware of their presence. These problems in ensuring intelligence coordination in Northern Ireland and elsewhere prompted Sir Frank Kitson's controversial suggestion (see his 1971 *Low-Intensity Operations*) that soldiers rather than police should always be placed in control of intelligence in British counterinsurgency operations.

See also: Algiers, Battle of; Briggs, Lt. Gen. Sir Harold Rawdon; British army; Cyprus; Dhofar; *Firqat;* French army; Godard, Col. Yves; Ho Chi Minh Trail; Kenyan Emergency; Kitson, Gen. Sir Frank Edward; Malayan Emergency; Northern Ireland; Palestine; Police; Pseudoforces; Special Air Service (SAS); Special Forces; Vietnam War
Further Reading: Andrew, Christopher, and David Dilks (eds.), *The Missing Dimension* (London, 1984).

Internal Macedonian Revolutionary Organization (IMRO)

IMRO, which existed from the 1890s until the 1930s, was one of the true precursors of modern insurgent groups in terms of political organization and objectives. Initially, IMRO fought for the independence of Macedonia from the Ottoman Turkish empire. After some years of successful guerrilla activity, IMRO had effectively established what could be called a "liberated zone" in the Macedonian countryside. However, an ill-advised attempt to instigate a widespread revolt against the Turks failed in August 1903, and IMRO was forced to revert to low level guerrilla attacks, usually from bases in Bulgaria. The movement became increasingly fragmented after World War I and collapsed when the Bulgarians withdrew support in 1934.
Further Reading: Laqueur, Walter, *Guerrilla* (London, 1977).

Iraq Revolt (1920)

The Iraq Revolt resulted in the British army's largest military campaign between the world wars and required four British divisions to suppress it. Britain received the mandate for the administration of Mesopotamia, former Ottoman Turkish territory, from the League of Nations following World War I. However, the mandate conflicted with British and French promises of self-determination made to the Arabs during the Arab Revolt (1916–1917). When it became apparent that these promises would not be kept, a rising began in the north of the mandate territory in June 1920 and spread rapidly.

Reinforcements, including aircraft and armored cars, were hurried to Iraq, bringing the British strength to more than 29,000 men. By October 1920 the revolt had collapsed. Yet the British transferred effective control of Iraq to Feisal, son of the former *sharif* (governor) of Mecca, Hussein, whom the British had already installed as king of Arabia.

See also: Arab Revolt (1916–1917); British army
Further Reading: Jeffery, Keith, *The British Army and the Crisis of Empire, 1918–1922* (Manchester, 1984).

Ireland

The history of Ireland is characterized by episodes of great violence, which have continued to influence events to the present day. Anglo-Normans first attempted to conquer Ireland in the twelfth century. However, it was not until the beginning of the seventeenth century that the English controlled much more than the "Pale," or territory around Dublin, following the suppression of rebellion in Ulster and its settlement by largely Scottish Protestant Presbyterians after 1608. A major uprising in Ireland in 1641 had a significant impact on the declining relations between Crown and Parliament in England. Having suffered the depredations of Oliver Cromwell in the 1650s, Ireland was then caught in the struggle for the Protestant succession in England between the Catholic king, James

II, and Protestant William of Orange. The fate of both England and Ireland was settled by William's victory at the Battle of the Boyne in July 1690.

The next major Irish rebellion, in 1798, resulted in the passing of the Act of Union, which united Ireland with Britain and abolished a separate parliament in Dublin. The revolutionary tradition was revived by the attempted rising of the Young Ireland movement in 1848 and the formation of the Irish Republican Brotherhood (IRB), later known as the Fenians, in 1855. However, a Fenian rising also failed in 1867, as did their attempted invasion of Canada from the United States.

The granting of home rule might conceivably have arrested much of the continuing unrest, but it was bitterly opposed by Ulster Protestants fearful of being ruled by a Catholic-dominated administration in Dublin. By the outbreak of World War I, Ireland had become an armed camp, as both the Protestant Ulster Volunteer Force (UVF) and the nationalist Irish Volunteers prepared to contest Ireland's future with home rule finally poised to pass. However, the outbreak of World War I postponed the intended legislation, and the UVF and many Irish Volunteers enlisted. During Easter 1916 a hard-line group of Irish Volunteers staged a rising in Dublin. It was suppressed after a week of bitter fighting, yet the Easter Rising and subsequent executions of leading rebels transformed the political situation in Ireland.

In 1918 a new political expression of nationalism, Sinn Féin (Ourselves Alone), won 73 parliamentary seats at Westminster. The new MPs declined to take the seats; led by Michael Collins, the 26 not already in prison proclaimed Ireland's independence on 21 January 1919. In the resulting Anglo-Irish War (1919–1921), nationalists increasingly called themselves the Irish Republican Army (IRA). The first priority of the IRA was to obtain weapons by attacking police "barracks." After new emergency legislation in August 1920, the number of

British troops take refuge behind a mobile barricade composed of household furniture on a street in central Dublin during the Easter Rising, 11 May 1916. (UPI/Corbis-Bettmann)

IRA men on the run increased, and the republicans formed "flying columns" in some areas. Attempts at larger-scale operations were less successful, and by 1921 the IRA was under severe pressure to negotiate. At the same time, the British government was equally ready to talk.

The British army's role had not been properly defined, and it suffered from lack of intelligence; the IRA's own intelligence organization (headed by Collins) was not as professional as sometimes suggested. The British response to chronic manpower shortages was to raise additional police from demobilized former officers and former servicemen in the notorious form, respectively, of the Auxiliary Division, Royal Irish Constabulary, and the "Black and Tans." Negotiations opened in June 1921, the resulting Anglo-Irish Treaty excluding the six counties of Ulster, now to be known as Northern Ireland, from the new Irish Free State. This solution was unacceptable to diehard republicans like Eamon de Valera, and thus the Irish Civil War (1922–1923) broke out in the Free State.

Collins, who was prepared to accept partition and had become prime minister of the Free State, was ambushed and killed in August 1922. Ireland was still nominally a British dominion, but de Valera, who formed a new political party known as Fianna Fail (Soldiers of Destiny) in 1927 and won political power in the 1932 elections, adopted a republican constitution in 1937. However, the Irish Free State did not become the Republic of Ireland, or Eire, until 1949.

See also: British army; Collins, Gen. Michael; Intelligence; Irish Republican Army (IRA); Northern Ireland; Police
Further Reading: Townshend, Charles, *Political Violence in Ireland: Government and Resistance since 1848* (Oxford, 1983); Townshend, Charles, *The British Campaign in Ireland, 1919–1921* (Oxford, 1975).

Irgun Zvai Leumi

Irgun or National Military Organization was the principal Jewish insurgent group fighting the British in Palestine from 1944 to 1948. Formed in 1937 as the military arm of the New Zionist Organization, Irgun was originally intended to retaliate for attacks on Jewish settlements during the Arab Re-

volt (1936–1939). However, the British authorities were not prepared to tolerate Jewish retaliation, and Irgun killed its first policeman in May 1939.

Nevertheless, at the outbreak of World War II Irgun declared a truce, although some hard-liners regarded Britain as a greater enemy than Hitler's Germany, and

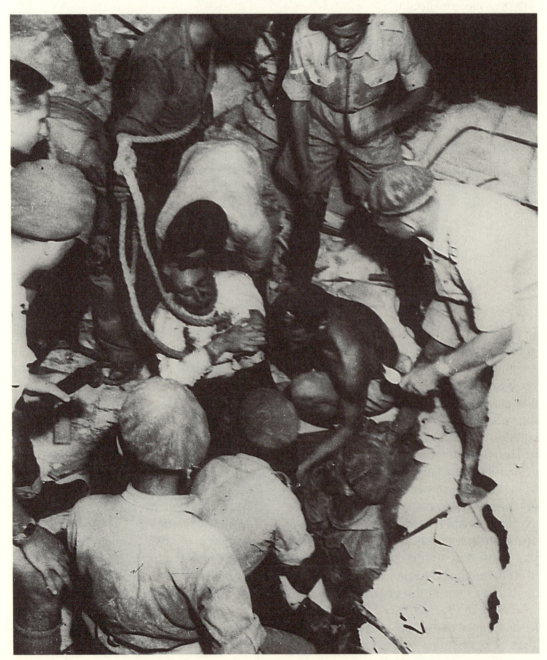

British soldiers and Palestine police help the injured assistant secretary to the Palestine government, D. C. Thompson, after the Irgun bombing of the King David Hotel in 1946. (UPI/Corbis-Bettmann)

they broke from the Irgun in 1940 to form the Stern Gang (or LEHI, for Lehame Herut Israel). Subsequently, Irgun, too, renounced its truce, with Menachem Begin's emergence as leader. Terrorist activities were not welcomed by the Jewish Agency in Palestine, whose own forces, Hagana (Defense) and Palmach (Shock Companies), took action against LEHI as well as Irgun. But at the end of war in Europe the Jewish Agency lost patience with the British government's failure to raise the quotas for Jewish immigration into Palestine; it joined LEHI and Irgun to form Tenuat Hameri (United Resistance Movement). The joint military campaign opened on 31 October 1945.

Alarmed at the bombing of the King David Hotel in Jerusalem in July 1946, however, the Jewish Agency dissolved the partnership. Irgun had about 1,500 activists and favored the use of road mines or bombs. One of its more spectacular attacks was its launching of a 600-pound barrel bomb down a ramp from a lorry into the Haifa police headquarters in September 1947. Specific British measures brought retaliation. In the most notorious incident, two British sergeants were kidnapped in July 1947 after death sentences were passed on three terrorists. Following the executions of the latter, the booby-trapped bodies of the sergeants were found hanging from a tree near Nathanya.

Irgun was also highly effective in its propaganda, receiving considerable assistance from its front organization in the United States, the American League for Free Palestine. Arguably, Irgun and LEHI were the most effective insurgent groups the British ever faced; the British announced the surrender of the Palestine mandate in September 1947 and withdrew in May 1948. Begin was Israeli prime minister from 1977 to 1983 and was succeeded by a former leader of LEHI, Yitzak Shamir.

See also: Arab Revolt (1936–1939); Begin, Menachem; British army; Palestine; Palmach; Stern Gang
Further Reading: Charters, David, *The British Army and Jewish Insurgency in Palestine, 1945–1947* (London, 1989);

Clarke, T., *By Blood and Fire* (New York, 1981); Hoffman, Bruce, *The Failure of British Military Strategy in Palestine, 1939–1947* (Tel Aviv, 1983).

Irish Republican Army (IRA)

The IRA is the principal Irish insurgent group associated with the political objective of a united Ireland and with the "troubles" that have affected Northern Ireland since 1969. However, the original movement split in 1969 into the Official IRA and the Provisional IRA (PIRA), and it is PIRA that has sustained the terrorist campaign since the Officials declared a ceasefire in 1972.

The IRA emerged from the Anglo-Irish War (1919–1921). The original IRA's campaign against the British between 1919 and 1921 was not as successful as sometimes suggested, and both sides were more than ready to negotiate after two years of bitter struggle. Although not recognized as such at the time, it was the British army's first experience in facing such a modern, politically motivated insurgency. Indeed, the British Special Operations Executive (SOE), intended to undertake sabotage in German-occupied Europe in World War II, was consciously modeled on the IRA's organization.

The Anglo-Irish Treaty (1921) partitioned Ireland by excluding the six counties of Ulster from the new Irish Free State. Some IRA leaders, such as Michael Collins, were prepared to accept the terms on offer; others led by Eamon de Valera were not. Consequently, the Irish Civil War (1922–1923) followed, whereby the IRA came to represent diehard republicans. Ultimately, although the Free State continued to make claim to Northern Ireland, the IRA was declared illegal in the south in 1936.

During World War II there was a limited and unsuccessful IRA bombing campaign in Britain and again in Northern Ireland between 1956 and 1962. Ironically, the beginnings of the "troubles" in Northern Ireland in 1969 caught the IRA by surprise. Stung by accusations that they had left the Catholic population of Ulster undefended, militants in the IRA's "Belfast Brigade" broke away from the largely Marxist, southern-based leadership to form PIRA in September 1969. In turn, the Irish Republican Socialist Party and its military wing, the Irish National Liberation Army (INLA), would break away from the Officials in 1974.

Following the introduction of internment in 1971, which allowed for imprisonment without trial of suspected terrorists, and a greater British military presence in Northern Ireland, PIRA extended its bombing campaign to the British mainland in 1974. This recognized the greater propaganda value of "spectaculars" (dramatic attacks) on the mainland, such as the Grand Hotel bombing in Brighton in October 1984 and the Baltic Exchange bombing in London in April 1992. PIRA, which has perhaps 600 activists but several thousand active supporters and an even larger body of passive supporters among Northern Ireland's Catholics, has maintained links with other terrorist groups. It has successfully extorted funds in both Northern Ireland and Eire, in addition to drawing upon financial assistance from sympathizers in the United States. In 1977 PIRA was reorganized by its then chief of staff, Gerry Adams, into a tighter cellular structure, and through its political arm, Sinn Féin (Ourselves Alone), it moved to challenge the constitutional Social Democratic and Labour Party (SDLP) for the nationalist vote.

The dual military-political strategy was articulated in November 1981 as one of "a ballot paper in one hand and an Armalite rifle in the other." Thus, there have been periodic PIRA cease-fires (as between December 1974 and November 1975, September 1994 to February 1996, and since July 1997) amid the tortuous search for a political solution acceptable to both communities in Northern Ireland. As a result of the PIRA cease-fire, Sinn Féin joined talks that led to a new power-sharing agreement in April 1998. However, this led to a split among republicans, with a new dissident group calling itself the "Real IRA" carrying out a bombing atrocity at Omagh in August 1998 in which 28 people were killed. INLA then declared a cease-fire while London and Dublin spoke of new antiterrorist legislation. The power-sharing executive including Sinn Féin was due to begin work in September 1998. As of February 1997, the "troubles" had resulted in 3,211 deaths in Northern Ireland.

See also: British army; Collins, Gen. Michael; Ireland; Northern Ireland; Special Operations Executive (SOE)
Further Reading: Coogan, Tim Pat, *The IRA: A History* (11th ed., London, 1998); Bell, J. Bowyer, *The Irish Troubles: A Generation of Violence, 1969–1992* (New York, 1993); Taylor, Peter, *Provos* (London, 1997).

Israeli army

The origin of the Israeli army, which is part of the Israeli Defense Force (IDF), lies in the forces raised by the Jewish Agency in Palestine for the protection of Jewish settlements. Israel's independence in 1948 was immediately threatened by its Arab neighbors, and the Israelis have fought three major wars (1948–1949, 1967, and 1973) to preserve that independence. In addition, Israeli forces have had to defend both territory and citizens against frequent guerrilla/terrorist attacks, as in the so-called War of Attrition with Egypt (1969–1970) and in the "security zone" Israel has maintained since intervening in southern Lebanon in 1982.

The military arm of the Jewish Agency was Hagana (Defense), formed in January 1920. Primarily a militia, Hagana had a small field force element. During the Arab Revolt (1936–1939), the unorthodox British soldier Orde Wingate formed the Special Night Squads (SNSs) to help defend oil installations against Arab sabotage; the SNSs became the predecessors of Palmach (Shock Companies). These were offered to the British by the Jewish Agency in 1941 to fight the Vichy French forces in Syria. Between December 1945 and July 1946 Hagana and Palmach briefly participated with the two terrorist groups, Irgun and LEHI (the Stern Gang), in the insurgent campaign against the British.

Despite military successes that have often provided buffer zones between the Israeli heartland and neighboring Arab states, Israel has remained vulnerable to infiltration. Indeed, occupation of Arab territory as a more defendable perimeter has presented its own security problems, as it invariably means extending control over the Arab population. Israeli battlefield prowess also stimulated the growth of the Palestine Liberation Organization (PLO) in the 1960s, thereby increasing the terrorist threat. Consequently, the Israelis have always taken a robust attitude toward terrorist attack.

In keeping with its offensive military doctrine, Israeli responses take the form of instant retaliation through hot pursuit, airstrikes, artillery bombardment, and reprisal commando raids. Unit 101, for example, was formed in August 1953 specifically to undertake retaliatory commando raids and carried out its first attack on the Jordanian village of Qibya in October, dynamiting 45 houses. Moreover, Israel will accept the risks of targeting host states (its response to the murder of three Israelis on Cyprus being an air attack on PLO headquarters in Tunis in October 1985). The Israelis have also targeted specific individuals such as the spiritual head of the Islamic fundamentalist Hizbulla, Hussein Abbas Musawi, who was assassinated in February 1992. Israeli incursions into Lebanon in 1978 and 1982 might also be regarded as very large scale retaliatory operations following Arab terrorist incidents.

In the Occupied Territories after 1967, the Israelis installed fixed defenses against infiltration backed by roving patrols. They undertook a census of the Arab population and imposed "preventative detentions"— curfews, deportations, and collective fines—

as they felt necessary. The Israeli approach tends to be heavy-handed, as in the West Bank and Gaza during the widespread Palestinian disturbances known as the intifada (literally, "shuddering") between December 1987 and September 1993 (when Palestinian authority was established under peace accords with the PLO). Much the same pattern has been evident in Lebanon. There is, however, little concept of a hearts-and-minds approach, although the Israelis have attempted to win the support of the Christian Maronite community in Lebanon with a civic aid program and have equipped the Maronite militia known as the South Lebanon Army.

See also: Arab Revolt (1936–1939); Hearts and minds; Hot pursuit; Irgun Zvai Leumi; Palestine; Palmach; Stern Gang; Wingate, Maj. Gen. Orde Charles
Further Reading: Katz, S. M., *Israeli Special Forces* (Osceola, 1993); O'Neill, Bard, *Armed Struggle in Palestine* (Boulder, 1978); Charters, David, and Maurice Tugwell (eds.), *Armies in Low-intensity Conflict* (London, 1989).

Italian army

The Italian army had little success in colonial warfare, although ironically it was innovative in its approach. Italy established a presence at Massawa on the coast of the Red Sea in what would become Eritrea in 1885 as part of the Italian attempt to rival the colonial expansion of other European powers. However, the attempt to extend Italian influence into neighboring Abyssinia (Ethiopia) resulted in the disaster at Adowa (Adua) in March 1896, the greatest defeat sustained by any European army in colonial warfare in the nineteenth century.

The next Italian colonial venture was a war against the Ottoman Turkish empire fought in Libya (1911–1912). In overcoming Turkish resistance, the Italians were the first army to employ armored cars and the first to use airpower, an Italian aircraft dropping a hand grenade on Libyan irregulars on 1 November 1911. Even though the Turks ceded Libya to the Italians, the campaign against the Senussi tribe continued well into the 1920s. Again, the Italians employed armored cars and aircraft, which dropped bombs as well as mustard gas. The Italians also poisoned wells and confined at least 12,000 nomads in detention camps. The resistance of the Senussi finally ended in 1931.

Four years later, Italy's fascist leader, Benito Mussolini, revived the attempt to add Abyssinia to the Italian empire. About 110,000 Italian troops invaded Abyssinia in October 1935. The Italian offensive toward the capital, Addis Ababa, was assisted by sealing off a corridor of advance with air-dropped mustard gas. Addis Ababa fell in May 1936 and the Abyssinian emperor, Haile Selassie, fled. Detention camps were once more established, and the nature of Italian counterinsurgency was yet again illustrated by the deaths of an estimated 30,000 people, a reprisal for the attempted assassination of the Italian commander in chief, Rodolfo Graziani, in February 1937.

Italy's African colonies fell to the Allies during World War II. Haile Selassie was also returned to his throne thanks to a five-month campaign by British forces between January and May 1941 in which British officers, including Orde Wingate, raised Abyssinian irregular units to harass the Italians. The Italian invasions of Albania in April 1939 and Greece in October 1940 and Italian participation in the German invasion of Yugoslavia in April 1941 also made the Italian army face the challenge of partisan warfare. Again it was not conspicuously successful, and Italy's sudden surrender to the Allies in September 1943 presented the German army in Yugoslavia with particular difficulties.

See also: Adowa, Battle of; Airpower; Colonial warfare; Eritrea; Partisans; Senussi; Wingate, Maj. Gen. Orde Charles; Yugoslavia
Further Reading: Whittam, John, *The Politics of the Italian Army* (Hamden, 1977); Gooch, John, *Army, State, and Society in Italy, 1870–1915* (London, 1989).

Japanese army

Having invaded Manchuria in 1931, the Japanese attempted to conquer the remainder of China beginning in 1937. The intervention of Japan would have a crucial impact on the Chinese Civil War (1927–1949). The war between the Japanese and the Chinese nationalist Kuomintang (KMT) severely weakened the latter. This turn of events also enabled the Chinese communist forces to survive at a time when they had been under enormous pressure from the KMT. Indeed, it could be argued that Japan's intervention gave the Chinese communist leader, Mao Tse-tung, the respite he needed to make his theories of rural revolutionary guerrilla warfare work.

For all the communist propaganda surrounding offensives against the Japanese, such as the Campaign of a Hundred Regiments in 1940, the Japanese were little troubled by Maoist insurgency and developed a successful counterinsurgency strategy. The point, however, was that the greater struggle against the KMT meant that the Japanese could not devote sufficient resources to wholly eliminate the communists.

Initially, Japanese commanders treated all irregular opponents as bandits and were left to devise their own methods of restoring order. When it became apparent that large scale sweeping operations were not sufficient to eliminate the bandit threat in Manchuria, the Japanese developed three distinct types of operations, which they characterized as peace preservation, submission, and subjugation. *Peace preservation* involved an element of the hearts-and-minds approach, improving communications and other facilities in an attempt to weaken popular support for the bandits. *Submission* was intended to encourage bandit surrender by means of reward. *Subjugation* involved small, highly mobile units operating against bandits mostly during the winter months.

Faced with rear area security threats after the extension of operations to northern and central China in 1937, the Japanese were content to ignore areas remote from the main towns and communications system and encouraged the puppet China National Government to undertake policing in other areas. Unable to deploy large numbers of troops for internal security per se, Japan's North China Area Army initially concentrated on protecting railways. However, following the communist offensive in 1940, Gen. Yasuji Okamura implemented the so-called three-all campaign: "take all, burn all, kill all." It was brutally effective in military terms, reducing the population of communist-controlled areas by 15 million and the communist forces by 100,000 men, although it served to drive the population toward supporting communists. After 1943 the Japanese were even less able to sustain operations against guerrillas, but still they had succeeded in neutralizing much of the immediate threat.

See also: Chinese Civil War; Kuomintang (KMT); Mao Tse-tung; Okamura, Gen. Yasuji

Further Reading: Beckett, Ian (ed.), *The Roots of Counterinsurgency: Armies and Guerrilla Warfare, 1900–1945* (London, 1988); Lee, C. S., *Counterinsurgency in Manchuria: The Japanese Experience* (Santa Monica, 1967); Li, L., *The Japanese Army in North China, 1937–1941* (Tokyo, 1975).

Kabila, Laurent (1939–)

A guerrilla opponent of Pres. Mobutu Sese Seko of Zaire (former Belgian Congo) for more than 30 years, Kabila finally toppled Mobutu in 1997. Kabila supported Patrice Lumumba, the left-wing prime minister of the newly independent Congo, in 1960. When Mobutu overthrew Lumumba in 1961, Kabila took to the bush and, inspired by the example of Mao Tse-tung, formed the Simba (Lion) movement in 1964. Kabila's forces took Stanleyville (Kisangani) but were ousted by Belgian troops. Che Guevara arrived to help but quickly concluded that Kabila had little potential as a guerrilla leader. Indeed, Kabila's new movement, the People's Revolutionary Party (PRP), had little success until 1996, when the civil war in neighboring Rwanda spilled into Zaire and Kabila became the unexpected beneficiary of the ailing Mobutu's unpopularity. Assisted by Rwanda's new rulers, Kabila entered Kinshasa in May 1997 as Mobutu fled. Zaire was renamed the Democratic Republic of Congo. Kabila's own rule was challenged in August 1998 by his former Rwandan allies, who encouraged a new revolt in eastern Zaire.

See also: Guevara, Ernesto Che; Mao Tse-tung
Further Reading: Young, Crawford, and Thomas Turner, *The Rise and Decline of the Zairean State* (Madison, 1986).

Karen Revolt (1949–1955)

The Karens are a hill tribe mostly inhabiting a plateau east of the Sittang River in Burma (now known as Myanmar). The 1942 Japanese occupation of Burma during World War II exacerbated existing divisions between the majority Burmese population and the minority hill tribes such as the Karens. The British colonial authorities had regarded the 2 million Karens as a "martial race" and recruited them into the police and army. Force 136 of the British Special Operation Executive (SOE) enlisted a large number of Karens for operations against the Japanese and their Burmese allies in the Burma Independence (later National) Army, led by Aung San.

In 1945 Aung San switched sides, and his newly styled Anti-Fascist People's Freedom League (AFPFL) subsequently negotiated a postwar independence from the British in January 1947. Independence came in January 1948. The Karens, however, had no wish to join the federal union that was envisaged and boycotted the elections to the new constituent assembly in April 1947. They established the Karen National Defence Organization (KNDO) to protect their population in a rapidly developing civil war between the AFPFL and its former wartime communist partners.

Following Aung San's assassination in July 1947, his successor, U Nu, offered negotiations on regional autonomy, but Karen militants led by Mahn Ba Zan demanded full independence. Massacres of Karens by Burmese auxiliary police units created further tensions, and amid a series of insurgent challenges to the Burmese government by varying groups, Karen and Kachin army units mutinied in January 1949, seizing Toungoo, Meiktila, Maymyo, and Mandalay. However, the insurgents failed to capture the capital, Rangoon, and became bogged down at Insein.

Lack of coordination between the groups fighting the government and the latter's monopoly of airpower and river transport enabled it to organize successful counterattacks over the next few months. As a result, Meiktila, Maymyo, and Mandalay were recaptured in March and April 1949; Insein was recovered that May. One Karen leader, Naw Seng, fled to China in August 1949 and another, Saw Ba U Gyi, was killed in August 1950, Toungoo having been retaken in March.

The KNDO still controlled much of the Irrawaddy Delta, and the government effort was hindered by incursions of Kuomintang (KMT) troops following their defeat in the Chinese Civil War (1927–1949). Nevertheless, the main threat from the Karens, who had fielded about 10,000 insurgents in 1949, was essentially broken. Large-scale operations between 1953 and 1955 deprived the Karens of their hold on the Mawchi mines and Tenasserim. The Karens had been granted autonomy in 1951, which was finally accepted by most former insurgents in 1964, although Mahn Ba Zan continued the struggle until government amnesty terms were finally accepted in May 1980.

See also: Burma; Chinese Civil War; Kuomintang (KMT); Special Operations Executive (SOE)

Further Reading: Smith, Martin, *Burma: Insurgency and the Politics of Ethnicity* (London, 1991).

Kenyan Emergency (1952–1960)

The Kenyan, or Mau Mau, insurgency enabled the British army to apply the lessons of the Malayan Emergency (1948–1960) in an evolving pattern of post-1945 counterinsurgency. The prime cause of the state of emergency, which was declared on 20 October 1952, was pressure of population. Indeed, Mau Mau frequently called itself the Kenya Land Freedom Army. The greatest pressure was in the so-called White Highlands, where some 3,000 white settlers farmed an average of 3,460 acres each and more than 1.3 million Africans on native land units possessed an average of only 23.6 acres each. As the African population increased, the available land became more and more inadequate to sustain the native people.

The monopoly of political and economic power rested with the settlers, the situation being exacerbated by the arrival of new white immigrants after 1945. African former servicemen took the lead in forging the Mau Mau organization, members being initiated through the administration of secret oaths. Mau Mau was centered in Kenya's largest tribe, the Kikuyu, and two closely related ethnic groups, the Embu and Meru. Other African tribal groups were either indifferent to or opposed Mau Mau. Many Kikuyu also opposed Mau Mau, especially tribal elders and Christian and propertied Kikuyu.

Mau Mau had military and passive wings and was supposedly directed by the "Kenya Parliament" and a central committee based in Nairobi. But the only real organization was in Nairobi. The 12,000 or so Mau Mau in the field—mostly in the Aberdare Forest at the foot of Mount Kenya—had only rudimentary organization. This actually made it difficult for security forces to learn much about the opponent, especially because police had little representation in Kikuyu tribal areas. Less than 12 percent of Mau Mau had firearms, and their methods were characterized by savage attacks on humans and animals with axes and *pangas* (machetes). Most victims of the Mau Mau were fellow Africans. Identifiable leaders were arrested, yet authorities were slow to realize the scale of insurgency.

However, in June 1953 Gen. Sir George Erskine became commander in chief and director of operations. Erskine did not

Thousands of suspected Mau Mau rebels squat on the ground at the Uplands Police Camp in Nairobi, Kenya, after a Mau Mau massacre of other Africans in the Kiambu reserve, April 1953. (UPI/Corbis-Bettmann)

enjoy the extensive political powers given Sir Gerald Templer in Malaya, but he quickly instituted the same coordinated committee structure to ensure that army, police, and civilian agencies worked toward the same objectives. Special emergency regulations were introduced, with the death penalty steadily being extended. More than 78,000 Africans were detained by April 1956; about 1 million Africans were moved to new villages in a resettlement program to further isolate the insurgents from the population.

Erskine was also conscious of the grievances that had led to the insurgency and launched a hearts-and-minds program, including rural public works and agricultural development projects. It was less successful than in Malaya, because neither independence nor significant political concessions were on the table, although the insurgency certainly accelerated progress to independence in 1963. The white settlers also opposed concessions to Africans, and the Kenya Police Reserve (KPR), recruited from settlers, was responsible for a number of atrocities.

Militarily, Erskine first neutralized the Mau Mau organization in Nairobi in "Operation Anvil" (April 1954). A large-scale cordon-and-search operation modeled on those in Palestine between 1944 and 1948, it resulted in the arrest of 16,500 suspects. Erskine also mounted operations in 1955 to force the insurgent groups back into the forests, with troops moving along specially bulldozed tracks and creating cleared fire zones. Bombing of the forests by the Royal Air Force (RAF) did not prove successful, and a lack of firearms encouraged the Mau Mau to avoid firefights. Consequently, small unit operations were instituted. They were spearheaded by tracker teams and pseudo-forces recruited from former Mau Mau and were known as countergangs. Pseudoforces had been an experiment in Malaya but now became far more sophisticated under the direction of Ian Henderson of Special Branch (a plainclothes criminal intelligence unit) and an army field intelligence officer, Frank Kitson.

Kikuyu villages were also increasingly defended by the 25,000-strong Kikuyu Home Guard. The numbers of Mau Mau surrendering increased steadily. For all intents and purposes, Mau Mau was broken by October 1956, when the last leading insurgent, Dedan Kimathi, was captured. However, the state of emergency remained in force until 12 January 1960. During its course, the security forces suffered about 600 dead, of whom 63 were white. Another 32 white civilians were killed and perhaps 2,000 Africans loyal to the authorities. At least 11,500 Mau Mau were killed in action. A total of 1,086 executions had been carried out by April 1956, and 402 Mau Mau prisoners died in captivity, the majority from disease.

See also: British army; Erskine, Gen. Sir George, Hearts and minds; Kitson, Gen. Sir Frank Edward; Malayan Emergency; Mau Mau; Palestine; Police; Pseudoforces; Resettlement; Templer, Field Marshal Sir Gerald
Further Reading: Clayton, Anthony, *Counter-insurgency in Kenya* (Manhattan, 1984).

Khmer Rouge

The Khmer Rouge (Red Khmers) is the Cambodian Communist Party, the Khmer being the people of Cambodia. Under the leadership of Pol Pot, the Khmer Rouge was responsible for the genocide of "Year Zero" when it came to power in 1975. The Khmer Rouge was formed in 1960 and began guerrilla warfare in 1967. It had relatively little success until Gen. Lon Nol seized power in Cambodia in March 1970 and ousted the head of state, Prince Sihanouk. Sihanouk fled to Peking (Beijing) and urged support for the Khmer Rouge. Lon Nol was gravely weakened when the United States withdrew from neighboring South Vietnam in 1973; the Cambodian capital, Phnom Penh, fell to the Khmer Rouge on 8 April 1975. The Khmer Rouge forced the entire population to leave the capital, and in the reign of terror that followed at least 1.4 million people were killed.

Sihanouk returned as head of state of what was now called Democratic Kampuchea but was ousted by the Khmer Rouge in April 1976. Following territorial disputes with Vietnam, the Khmer Rouge was forced back into the jungle by a Vietnamese invasion of Kampuchea in December 1978. The Khmer Rouge joined with noncommunist opponents of the Vietnamese in 1983. Following UN mediation and Vietnamese withdrawal, the Khmer Rouge participated in a coalition government in 1990. However, it boycotted UN-supervised elections in May 1993 and returned to the jungle. The movement fragmented between August 1996 and June 1997, a process that culminated with Pol Pot executing some of his leading followers and his own arrest by the faction wishing to cut a deal with the government. In July 1997 Pol Pot was apparently sentenced to life imprisonment by his erstwhile followers.

In April 1998 it was reported that Pol Pot was being carried with Khmer Rouge forces under Ta Mok, which were fleeing toward the Thai frontier under pressure from a new government offensive. Subsequently, it was reported that Pol Pot had died of a heart attack.

See also: Cambodia; Pol Pot; Vietnam War
Further Reading: Jackson, K. D. (ed.), *Cambodia, 1975–1978: Rendezvous with Death* (Princeton, 1989); Kiernan, Ben, *How Pol Pot Came to Power* (New York, 1985).

Kitchener, Field Marshal Earl (Horatio Herbert) (1850–1916)

Kitchener was one of the leading commanders to emerge from the British army's experience of colonial warfare in the late nineteenth century. He commanded the British and Egyptian forces that reconquered the Sudan in 1898 and was also British commander in chief in the later guerrilla phase of the Second Boer War (1899–1902) in South Africa. While awaiting his commission in the Royal Engineers in 1871, Kitchener attached himself to a French ambulance unit in the latter stages of the Franco-Prussian War (1870–1871). From 1874 to 1881 Kitchener was mostly engaged on archaeological and survey work in Palestine and Cyprus. In 1883 he was selected for service with the Egyptian army, which was reconstituted under British officers following Britain's occupation of Egypt. In 1884–1885 Kitchener served as an intelligence officer during the unsuccessful attempt by Lord Wolseley to relieve Maj. Gen. Charles Gordon, who was besieged by Mahdists at Khartoum in the Sudan.

Following the withdrawal of most British and Egyptian forces from the Sudan, Kitchener was governor of the Red Sea port of Suakin; then in 1892 he became *sirdar* (commander in chief) of the Egyptian army. It fell to Kitchener to avenge Gordon's death by the reconquest of the Sudan between 1896 and 1898, culminating in the defeat of the Mahdists at the Battle of Omdurman on 2 September 1898. Kitchener was made governor-general of the Sudan and was elevated to the peerage as Lord Kitchener of Khartoum.

Following the early British defeats in the Boer War, Kitchener went to South Africa as chief of staff to Lord Roberts and in 1900 succeeded Roberts as commander in chief in South Africa. He therefore presided over the controversial resettlement of Boer civilians in what were called "concentration camps" as a means of isolating Boer commandos from material support. The mobil-ity of commandos led by men such as Christian De Wet and "Koos" De La Rey was further eroded by constructing a network of blockhouses and wired fences. Following the defeat of the Boers, Kitchener effected wide-ranging reforms as commander in chief in India from 1902 to 1909 before returning to Egypt as consul-general. Advanced in the peerage to a viscountcy in 1902, Kitchener received an earldom in 1914. He had been promoted to field marshal in 1909.

Upon the outbreak of World War I in August 1914, Kitchener was appointed Britain's secretary of state for war. Unlike many contemporaries, Kitchener recognized that the war would not be "over by Christmas" and applied himself to a massive expansion of the army. Unfortunately, his austere and autocratic manner, so well suited to colonial rule, was not conducive to smooth civil-military relations in a democratic state at war. Kitchener steadily lost influence with his political colleagues and was eased out of office in December 1915. Sent on a mission to Russia, he was drowned when the ship carrying him hit a mine off the Orkneys in June 1916.

See also: Boer War; British army; Colonial warfare; De La Rey, Gen. Jacobus Hercules; De Wet, Gen. Christiaan Rudolf; Resettlement; Roberts, Field Marshal Earl (Frederick Sleigh); Wolseley, Field Marshal Viscount (Garnet Joseph)
Further Reading: Magnus, Philip, *Kitchener: Portrait of an Imperialist* (London, 1958).

Kitson, Gen. Sir Frank Edward (1926–)

Kitson authored a controversial book called *Low-Intensity Operations* (1971), based on his wide experience in British counterinsurgency campaigns. In it Kitson challenged traditional British approaches to counterinsurgency.

Kitson was commissioned in the Rifle Brigade in 1946. During the Kenyan Emergency (1952–1960), he became one of the leading figures in raising the pseudoforces known as countergangs, which were recruited from former Mau Mau insurgents and would guide security forces in operations against erstwhile colleagues. From Kenya, Kitson moved to Malaya during the latter stages of the Malayan Emergency (1948–1960) and then to Oman, where he participated in the defeat of insurgents on the Jebel Akhdar (Green Mountain) between 1957 and 1959. Kitson then served on Cyprus from 1962 to 1964, experiencing UN peacekeeping operations.

Having already written an account of his service in Kenya, *Gangs and Counter-gangs* (1960), Kitson wrote *Low-Intensity Operations* while a Ministry of Defence–sponsored defence fellow at the University of Oxford from 1969 to 1970. At the time it was published Kitson was commanding 39 Infantry Brigade in Northern Ireland at the very height of the British army's commitment on the streets of Belfast and Londonderry, a factor that added to its controversy. After Northern Ireland, Kitson commanded the School of Infantry from 1972 to 1974. A second volume of memoirs, embodying reflections on the lessons of Kenya, Malaya, Oman, Cyprus, and Northern Ireland, appeared as *Bunch of Five* (1977). As commandant of the Staff College from 1978 to 1980, Kitson was responsible for changes in the syllabus, which for the first time recognized the importance of studying counterinsurgency. Kitson retired in 1985 upon the expiration of his appointment as commander in chief of United Kingdom Land Forces. In retirement Kitson has written on conventional war (*Warfare as a Whole* [1987]) and on military history. He was knighted in 1980.

Kitson starts *Low-Intensity Operations* with the point that the British army, like other major armies, trained mostly for conventional warfare, even though the majority of operations since the end of World War II had been in some form of low-intensity conflict. In recognizing insurgency as the most prevalent form of modern conflict, Kitson therefore believed it was as important to train and educate the army for counterinsurgency as for conventional war.

Kitson's analysis of the nature of insurgency itself differed little from that of other theorists of counterinsurgency, such as Sir Robert Thompson. Indeed, many of Kitson's points about counterinsurgency merely reflected evolving British practice.

However, in one aspect Kitson's response to insurgency differed considerably from the traditional Thompson approach: that is, the question of the relationship between army and police. In traditional British practice the police invariably had primacy over the army, especially in the control of intelligence. Kitson, in contrast, argued that police were usually the first target for insurgent attack and that the army frequently had to rebuild the intelligence organization. It would be better, therefore, to train army officers in advance to take early control of intelligence operations. Coupled with Kitson's call for a radical overhaul of the army's training with regard to counterinsurgency, the issue of military primacy aroused particular controversy primarily because the book's publication coincided with the escalation of the "troubles" in Ulster. Thus, in some quarters, Kitson found himself depicted quite unjustly, almost as a military dictator in the making. Even so, he succeeded in making the British army aware of the need to think more seriously about low-intensity conflict.

See also: British army; Cyprus; Intelligence; Kenyan Emergency; Malayan Emergency; Northern Ireland; Police; Pseudoforces; Thompson, Sir Robert Grainger Ker
Further Reading: Kitson, Frank, *Bunch of Five* (London, 1977).

Komer, Robert William (1922–)

As deputy for pacification to the U.S. military commander in South Vietnam from May 1967 to October 1968, Komer was head of the organization known as Civil Operations and Rural Development Support (CORDS). CORDS brought much-needed coordination to the U.S. pacification effort. Influenced by the British counterinsurgency theorist Sir Robert Thompson, Komer was a deputy special assistant for national security affairs when appointed special assistant for pacification by Pres. Lyndon B. Johnson in February 1966. Komer had served in the United States Army during World War II and with the U.S. Central Intelligence Agency (CIA).

Komer consistently urged that greater priority be given pacification, earning the nickname "Blowtorch" for his abrasive style. His efforts resulted in a decision to reorganize pacification in March 1967, and Komer arrived in Saigon to set up CORDS on 1 May 1967. The greater coordination did bring some improvements in security, but only after the communist Vietcong had suffered heavy losses in the Tet Offensive (1968). Komer left Saigon in October 1968 to become U.S. ambassador in Turkey. He joined the Rand Corporation in 1969 but returned to government as deputy secretary of defense under Pres. Jimmy Carter from 1977 to 1980.

See also: Civil Operations and Rural Development Support (CORDS); Pacification; Tet Offensive; Thompson, Sir Robert Grainger Ker; United States Army; Vietcong; Vietnam War
Further Reading: Komer, Robert, *Bureaucracy at War* (Boulder, 1986); Cable, Larry, *Unholy Grail* (London, 1991).

Korean War (1950–1953)

The Korean War is usually characterized as a classic, limited conventional war, but in fact it did contain guerrilla operations. Indeed, one reason for the initial poor showing of the South Korean army when communist North Korea invaded south in June 1950 was that it had neglected conventional training in order to meet the threat of subversion from the so-called South Korean Labor Party (SKLP). Once the UN had intervened to assist South Korea and driven the communists back across the 38th parallel in autumn 1950, SKLP guerrillas reinforced by stragglers from the North Korean People's Army harassed UN forces. The guerrilla presence was not finally eliminated until March 1952. The Korean War ended in June 1953 based on an armistice

rather than formal peace terms, leaving the relationship between the North and South Korea unresolved.

Between November 1966 and December 1969 there was a second extended guerrilla conflict in South Korea. North Korean guerrillas continually probed the South Korean coast and the formal demilitarized zone (DMZ). However, the communist campaign failed due to its poor coordination and the measured response by UN forces under the operational command of Gen. Charles Bonesteel.
Further Reading: Hastings, Max, *The Korean War* (London, 1987); Bolger, D. P., *Scenes from an Unfinished War* (Leavenworth, 1991).

Kuomintang (KMT)

The KMT or Chinese Nationalist Party was locked in conflict with the Chinese Communist Party (CPC) during the protracted Chinese Civil War (1927–1949). Founded by Dr. Sun Yat-sen, the KMT was a revolutionary socialist party modeled on Russia's Bolsheviks, but Sun Yat-sen never believed that Marxism would work in rural China. After Sun Yat-sen's death in March 1925, leadership of the KMT was assumed by Chiang Kai-shek.

Sun Yat-sen had been prepared to cooperate with the CPC when it was founded in 1921, but Chiang distrusted the communists. Wishing to unite all China under the KMT, Chiang marched against the northern "warlords" in 1926. Discovering that the CPC was establishing a presence in areas cleared of warlord troops, Chiang turned to purge the communists in 1927. In December 1930 Chiang ordered the first of five "encirclement and annihilation" campaigns to eliminate the bases established by communists who had escaped the cities. The first three of these campaigns (in 1930 and 1931) were not conspicuously successful, but the fourth and fifth campaigns (1933 and 1934) overran the CPC's southern base areas. Facing annihilation, the communists began the celebrated "Long

March" to the far northwestern mountains of the Shensi Province in October 1934.

Chiang's subordinates failed to achieve the CPC's final elimination in operations during 1935 and 1936. Consequently, he went north in December 1936 to take personal command, only to be arrested by some of his own officers, who demanded that he form a united front with the communists against the growing Japanese threat. The Japanese army had invaded Manchuria in September 1931, and in July 1937 it launched a full-scale invasion of northern and central China. Chiang reluctantly accepted a united front with the CPC in September 1937, but it ended after a pitched battle in January 1941 between KMT and CPC forces.

Nevertheless, the KMT and the Japanese were too busy fighting each other to worry unduly about the CPC, and that gave the communist leader, Mao Tse-tung, the vital breathing he needed to reorganize. By the time Japan surrendered in August 1945 the KMT had been gravely weakened by the war against the Japanese. Many of its best troops had been killed and its organization greatly reduced. The CPC received captured Japanese arms and equipment from the Soviets and were able to consolidate control of Manchuria, which the Soviets had overrun in August 1945. Chiang tried to wrest back control of Manchuria, but by September 1948 his forces there had been defeated. The communists then went over to the offensive, defeating the KMT in a bitter, two-month battle at Hsuchow (Xuzhou) between December 1948 and January 1949, which cost the KMT an estimated 500,000 men.

Mao entered Peking (Beijing) on 21 January 1949. Chiang had fled to the island of Formosa (Taiwan) in December 1949.

See also: Chinese Civil War; Japanese army; Long March; Mao Tse-tung

Further Reading: Wilson, Dick, *China's Revolutionary War* (New York, 1991); Beckett, Ian (ed.), *The Roots of Counterinsurgency: Armies and Guerrilla Warfare, 1900–1945* (London, 1988).

Kurdistan

The Kurds form a distinct cultural and linguistic group totaling some 20 million people, but their inability to resolve internal rivalries has resulted in their being the largest nation in the world without their own state. They inhabit 250,000 square miles of mountainous Kurdistan, embracing parts of Armenia, Iran, Iraq, Syria, and Turkey. A tribal people, the Kurds came late to nationalism, although the failure of the Western Allies after World War I to honor previous promises of autonomy within the former Ottoman empire led to unrest in the 1920s in the new states of Iran, Iraq, and Turkey.

The Allied occupation of Iran and Iraq during World War II brought new opportunities. A Kurdish rising failed in Iraq in 1945, but the Soviet-sponsored Mahabad Republic was briefly established in Iran in 1946 before Soviet withdrawal led to its collapse in June 1947. With the resulting exile of the veteran Kurdish leader Mustafa Barzani, leadership of the Kurdish Democratic Party (KDP) inside Iraq devolved to the urbanized, left-wing intellectuals Jelal Talabani and Ibrahim Ahmed in the 1950s.

With the establishment of an Iraqi republic by Abd al-Karim Qasim in 1958, the KDP was legitimized and Barzani returned. Increasingly hostile to Kurdish aspirations, Qasim responded to Barzani's demand for autonomy with a full-scale onslaught against the Kurds in September 1961. Autonomy rather than independence remained the Kurdish goal, but that was unacceptable to successive Iraqi governments. Moreover, the Iraqis attempted to exploit internal tribal divisions, recruiting their own Kurdish militia. Moreover, Barzani was not in full control of all those in revolt, Ahmed and Talabani initially establishing the standing military force known as the Peshmarga (Those Who Face Death). Despite eventually mustering 50,000 men, the Kurds were unable to export their campaign from the mountains (although the

Iraqis were equally unable to operate beyond the plains and resorted to indiscriminate aerial bombing).

Negotiations brought temporary cease-fires, and an armistice in March 1970 offered autonomy within four years. Amid mutual recriminations on whether the armistice terms were being fulfilled, fighting erupted again in April 1974. The Iraqis were now better equipped, and the revolt collapsed in April 1975 when the shah of Iran withdrew his previous support for the Kurdish cause. Barzani moved to the United States, and his followers split between a KDP led by his sons and Talabani's Patriotic Union of Kurdistan (PUK). The shah's overthrow in 1979 brought new demands by Iranian Kurds, with which Talabani made common cause. The fighting that broke out inside Iran was then complicated by the onset of the Iran-Iraq War (1980–1988); in that conflict both sides attempted to exploit Kurdish grievances.

Kurdish unrest spread to Turkey in 1984, led by the Kurdistan Workers' Party (PKK), where it continues today. Renewed hostility toward the Kurds in Iraq by Saddam Hussein's government in the aftermath of the Gulf War (1990–1991) caused the UN to establish a protected Kurdish zone around Arbil in northern Iraq in April 1991. American-supervised elections in this protected zone in 1992 were designed to end the rivalry between the KDP and the PUK, but the elections were inconclusive, and fighting broke out in January 1994. In September 1996 Iraqi forces intervened in support of the KDP, enabling it to secure control of the protected zone, although the United States then retaliated against Iraq with missile strikes for its violation of the UN zone. In May 1997 the Turkish army also entered the protected zone, with the cooperation of the KDP, to attack PKK groups.

Further Reading: O'Ballance, Edgar, *The Kurdish Revolt, 1961–1970* (London, 1973).

Lansdale, Maj. Gen. Edward Geary (1908–)

Lansdale became known as a leading counterinsurgency expert in the United States following his service in the Philippines as an adviser to Ramon Magsaysay during the Hukbalahap insurgency (1946–1954) and in South Vietnam as an adviser to Pres. Ngo Dinh Diem. A specialist in intelligence and psychological warfare, Lansdale was depicted as Colonel Hillendale in the novel (later made into a film) *The Ugly American* by William J. Lederer and Eugene L. Burdick and as Alden Pyle in Graham Greene's novel *The Quiet American.*

Prior to World War II, Lansdale worked in advertising. He then became an officer of the United States Army Air Force (USAAF) and served with the guerrilla forces raised by the Office of Strategic Services (OSS) for operations behind Japanese lines in the Philippines. A lieutenant colonel, Lansdale was lecturing on intelligence at the U.S. Air Force's Strategic Intelligence School in 1950 when he met Magsaysay. Upon his appointment as secretary of defense for the Philippines in September 1950, Magsaysay requested that Lansdale be assigned to the Joint U.S. Military Assistance Group (JUSMAG), which was advising the Filipino armed forces fighting the Huk insurgents. Though only a second grade staff officer with JUSMAG, Lansdale became a close and influential adviser to Magsaysay. Lansdale played a special role in the work of the Economic De-velopment Corps (EDCOR), which was responsible for the small but well publicized resettlement scheme introduced by Magsaysay to relocate former Huk insurgents and their families on Mindanao.

Lansdale returned to Washington in 1953 but in June 1954 went to South Vietnam as air force attaché. In reality, Lansdale was head of the clandestine Saigon Military Mission, an organization established by the U.S. Central Intelligence Agency (CIA) to begin to work with Ngo Dinh Diem even before the French had fully withdrawn from French Indochina under the agreement reached at an international conference in Geneva. Under that agreement, Laos and Cambodia became independent and Vietnam was partitioned along the 17th parallel with the understanding that elections would follow to unify the country under a single administration. The United States did not sign the Geneva accords and believed that the communist leader of North Vietnam, Ho Chi Minh, would win any election.

Lansdale was involved in encouraging the movement of refugees south of the 17th parallel and in helping Diem to consolidate his control over the south (intended to be temporary, the arrangement arising from Geneva led to the de facto partition of Vietnam into two separate states). As he had with Magsaysay, Lansdale became a close adviser to Diem and continued to support his cause long after other Americans had concluded the leader was a political liability. As a result, Lansdale's influence over U.S. policy in South Vietnam declined in the early 1960s, Diem being removed by a military coup that the United States tacitly supported in November 1963.

Yet in 1964 the U.S. ambassador in Saigon, Henry Cabot Lodge, asked Lansdale to undertake the coordination of U.S. agencies in South Vietnam involved in civil affairs. Lansdale was rejected as a potential head of the new pacification agency in 1967, that appointment going to Robert Komer.

See also: Ho Chi Minh; Hukbalahap; Komer, Robert William; Magsaysay, Ramon; Office of Strategic Services (OSS); Philippines; Resettlement; Vietnam War
Further Reading: Lansdale, Edward, *In the Midst of Wars* (New York, 1972); Currey, Cecil B., *Lansdale, Edward: The Unquiet American* (Boston, 1988).

Laos

Laos, which gained independence from France in 1954 as a result of the Geneva accords, suffered a prolonged conflict between 1963 and 1975 that resulted in a victory for the communists, who were known as Pathet Lao (Land of the Laos). However, since 1975 the communist government has faced guerrilla resistance from the hill peoples known as the H'mong.

A curious feature of the Laotian conflict during the 1960s and 1970s is that government and communist opposition were initially led by half-brothers: Prince Souvanna Phouma had first accepted autonomy from France in 1949 and then independence; Prince Soupanouvong founded Neo Lao Issara (Lao Freedom Front) in 1950. Renamed Neo Lao Hak Sat (Lao Patriotic Front) in 1956, it was directed by the communist-dominated People's Party of Laos. In 1960 a right-wing military coup forced Soupanouvong to flee to North Vietnam, and both the United States and Soviet Union became increasingly involved in the internal affairs of the country. As a result, another international conference was convened at Geneva. It recognized neutrality for Laos and estab-

lished a coalition government involving the half-brothers. However, the communists, now known as the Pathet Lao (Land of the Laos), withdrew in 1963. Thereafter, annual communist offensives across the Plain of Jars were met by counterattacks from the Royal Laotian Army and its allies among the hill tribes such as the Meo and the H'mong. Indeed, the leader of the 40,000-strong "Secret Army" supported by funding from the U.S. Central Intelligence Agency (CIA) between 1961 and 1967, Vang Pao, was a H'mong officer in the royal army, although Meo and Kha tribesmen also fought with him.

Initially, the North Vietnamese interest was primarily in keeping open the Ho Chi Minh Trail through eastern Laos, which was used to infiltrate war supplies into South Vietnam. The American response was covert use of airpower against the trail between 1965 and 1971. And in February 1971 the South Vietnamese made a limited incursion into Laotian territory designed to cut the trail, but they suffered heavy losses. Increasing North Vietnamese intervention later that year shifted the advantage to the Pathet Lao. Although the half-brothers agreed to a cease-fire in February 1973, a renewed offensive took Vientiane in June 1975, with a communist republic being proclaimed under Soupanouvong in December. Vang Pao and his leading followers then reached an agreement with the Pathet Lao: In return for their departure from Laos, the H'mong would be left alone. However, the Pathet Lao did not keep to the agreement and began to arrest former "Secret Army" members. As a result, the H'mong rose in revolt.

Led by Pa Kao Her, the H'mong guerrillas call themselves Chao Fa (God's Disciples), reflecting a traditional H'mong belief in the periodic appearance of a *chaofa* (messiah). Arms were received from the Chinese in the late 1970s, and although the Thais gave some assistance they have been wary of jeopardizing trading links with Laos. The situation remains a bitter struggle, with communists having used chemical agents against the H'mong.

See also: Ho Chi Minh Trail; Pathet Lao; Vietnam War
Further Reading: Toye, Hugo, *Laos: Buffer State or Battleground* (Oxford, 1968); Brown, M., and J. Zasloff, *Apprentice Revolutionaries* (Stanford, 1986).

Lawrence, Thomas Edward (1888–1935)

The precise role of "Lawrence of Arabia" in the Arab Revolt (1916–1917) against the Ottoman Turkish empire during World War I remains a matter of controversy. However, there is no doubt that Lawrence made a major contribution to the evolution of the theory of guerrilla warfare.

Fascinated by archaeology as a child, Lawrence first visited the Middle East in 1909 as a student at the University of Oxford to write an undergraduate dissertation on the architecture of Crusader castles. After graduating with first-class honors, Lawrence went to Syria in 1911 to work as an archaeologist on an excavation being directed for the British Museum by D. G. Hogarth. In early 1914 he took part in a joint archaeological-topographical expedition in the Sinai Desert. That October Lawrence joined the War Office's geographical section and then transferred to the British military intelligence department in Egypt.

As an archaeologist working in areas under Ottoman control, Lawrence had seen the brutality of Ottoman rule and was sympathetic toward self-determination for the Turks' Arab subjects. And from his work Lawrence was aware of the British negotiations with the Arab *sharif* (governor) of Mecca, Hussein, to induce the Arabs to revolt against the Turks. Yet he was also aware that under the terms of the Sykes-Picot Agreement, Britain and France intended to partition the Ottoman empire after the war. The Arab Revolt began in June 1916. In October 1916 Lawrence joined Hogarth's Arab Bureau in Cairo and became the military adviser to the Arab forces.

An undated photograph of Thomas Lawrence, also known as Lawrence of Arabia, in Arabian dress. (Corbis-Bettmann)

The focus of the Arab campaign led by Hussein's son, Faisal, was to disrupt the Hejaz railway, but following the Arabs' seizure of the port of Akaba in July 1917 Lawrence influenced the shift of the revolt farther north. Ostensibly made to support the British advance into Syria, the Arabs' northern move was actually intended (by Lawrence and by Faisal, to whom Lawrence had revealed the details of the Sykes-Picot Agreement) to give the Arabs greater postwar bargaining power. Lawrence was part of the Arab delegation to the Versailles peace conference, where the Arabs made an unsuccessful attempt to persuade the British and French to reward Arabs with autonomy in Syria and Mesopotamia. In the event, the French received the mandate for Syria, and Britain that for Mesopotamia, although Hussein had been made king of Arabia in December 1916. The British attempt to extend control over Mesopotamia (by now known as Iraq) led to the Iraq Revolt in

1920; Lawrence was appointed as a special adviser to the Colonial Office.

As a result of the revolt, Iraq was given autonomy under Faisal, but Lawrence was thoroughly disillusioned with British policy toward the Arabs and in August 1922 resigned from the Colonial Office. He took the pseudonym Ross and enlisted in the Royal Air Force (RAF) as an ordinary aircraftsman. In 1923 he left the RAF and, this time taking the pseudonym of Shaw, enlisted in the Tank Corps. In 1925 Lawrence reenlisted in the RAF. He retired from the RAF in February 1935, but three months later he died as a result of a motorcycle crash.

Despite seeking the apparent anonymity of service in the ranks of the army and air force, Lawrence had actually maintained his contacts with prominent figures such as Winston Churchill and novelist-poet Robert Graves. He had also sought to cultivate a literary reputation. Lawrence's classic account of the Arab Revolt, *Seven Pillars of Wisdom*, was published by private subscription in 1926 and in a popular abridged edition as *Revolt in the Desert* in 1927. Lawrence also contributed an article on guerrilla warfare to the *Encyclopaedia Britannica* in 1927.

Whatever the truth of Lawrence's claims regarding his role in the Arab Revolt, his writings on guerrilla warfare were an elegant and influential exposition of its potential when waged in a political cause. In Lawrence's case, of course, the cause was Arab nationalism. Stressing the importance of secure base areas and the exploitation of space by small and highly mobile forces, Lawrence recognized the need for good intelligence. However, to him the most important factor in a guerrilla force's survival was popular support, Lawrence claiming that a successful revolt could be accomplished with the active support of only 2 percent of a population provided the remaining 98 percent either sympathized with or acquiesced in the guerrilla cause.

Among Lawrence's three defined functions of command—algebraical, biological, and psychological—the last embraced not only the motivation of guerrillas and populations but also the undermining of an opponent's morale. It is possible that Lawrence's writings had some influence on Mao Tse-tung. Certainly, he influenced the British military theorist Basil Liddell Hart, although Liddell Hart saw Lawrence's military achievements as proof of the value of his own ideas of the "indirect approach" in warfare. Lawrence also influenced the unorthodox British soldier Orde Wingate, who would raise the Special Night Squads against Arab irregulars during the second Arab Revolt (1936–1939) and go on to command the "Chindit" operations behind Japanese lines in Burma during World War II.

See also: Arab Revolt, First (1916–1917); Arab Revolt, Second (1936–1939); British army; Intelligence; Iraq Revolt; Mao Tse-tung; Wingate, Maj. Gen. Orde Charles
Further Reading: Wilson, Jeremy, *Lawrence of Arabia: The Authorised Biography* (London, 1989).

Lenin, Vladimir Ilyich (1870–1924)

Lenin, who masterminded the Bolshevik seizure of power in Russia in October 1917, was a prolific writer on military as well as political theory. Ironically, however, even though Marxist-Leninist ideology has been a potent weapon in insurgency, Lenin himself ascribed no particular importance to guerrilla or partisan warfare in achieving revolution.

Born Vladimir Ilyich Ulyanov, Lenin was introduced to Marxist ideology and revolutionary politics by his older brother, who was executed for plotting the assassination of the Russian tsar. Lenin took a law degree in St. Petersburg in 1891 but was arrested for his political activities and sent to external exile in Siberia in 1895. Leaving Russia in 1900, Lenin based himself mostly in Switzerland, although he frequented London. He was a founder of the Russian Social Democratic Workers' Party in London in 1903 and, when it split, became leader of that faction known as the Bolsheviks. Lenin returned to Russia in disguise during the abortive 1905 revolution, escaping back to Switzerland in 1907. When the pressures of World War I led to the collapse of the tsarist government in February 1917, the German government enabled Lenin to return to Russia across German territory in a sealed train. The Bolsheviks finally seized power in a coup in October 1917 and consolidated control as a result of their victory in the Russian Civil War (1917–1921). Severely wounded in an assassination attempt on his life in August 1918, Lenin died in January 1924.

Lenin's military thought was much influenced by that of the Prussian military theorist of the early nineteenth century, Carl von Clausewitz, whose work Lenin read and annotated in 1915. Like Clausewitz, Lenin was a proponent of mass warfare and saw partisan tactics as merely one of a number of methods that might be utilized by revolutionaries. Certainly, like his first commissar for war, Leon Trotsky, who created the Soviet Red Army during the civil war, Lenin was anxious to draw any partisan groups under the control of the Communist Party machine. This would ensure that they could not encourage the development of independent attitudes dangerous to centralized party authority. Yet Lenin's insistence on a highly centralized and disciplined Communist Party organization was itself to be a significant contribution to the development of guerrilla warfare. This was because insurgent groups inspired by Marxist-Leninist ideology thereby acquired an organizational weapon of enormous potential in the strength of a highly centralized party machine to keep individuals disciplined and focused on the political cause.

See also: Clausewitz, Carl von; Partisans; Russian Civil War
Further Reading: Clark, R. W., *Lenin: A Biography* (New York, 1987); Paret, Peter (ed.), *Makers of Modern Strategy* (Princeton, 1986).

Lettow-Vorbeck, Maj. Gen. Paul Emil von (1870–1964)

Although a regular soldier in the German army, Lettow-Vorbeck was to become one of the most successful guerrilla leaders in history, successfully evading vastly superior numbers of Allied troops deployed against his forces in German East Africa (later Tanzania) during World War I. Born in Saarlouis, Lettow-Vorbeck was commissioned in the Prussian army in 1891 and saw service in China during the Boxer Revolt (1900–1901) and in German South West Africa (later Namibia) during the Herero Revolt (1904–1907), where he served on the staff of Gen. Lothar von Trotha. A lieutenant colonel, Lettow-Vorbeck was posted to command the German forces in German East Africa in January 1914.

Lettow-Vorbeck never had more than 14,000 men under his command, of whom only about 3,000 were Europeans while eventually more than 300,000 British, Imperial, and Allied troops were committed to the conquest of the German colony. Having thrown back the first British attempt to land at Tanga in November 1914, Lettow-Vorbeck took to the interior. Although driven from German East Africa by weight of numbers in November 1917, Lettow-Vorbeck continued his campaign inside the Portuguese colony of Mozambique and then the British colony of Northern Rhodesia. And though Germany itself surrendered to the Allies on 11 November 1918, Lettow-Vorbeck did not do so until hearing the news on 25 November 1918.

The campaign had cost the Allies an estimated £72 million and the British alone more than 63,000 casualties from battle or disease. Lettow-Vorbeck, who had been promoted to major general in the autumn of 1917, returned to a hero's welcome in Germany in January 1919. Subsequently, Lettow-Vorbeck commanded one of the irregular units or *frei corps* against the social revolutionaries known as Spartacists in Hamburg later that year and was then court-martialed for his part in the abortive Kapp military *putsch* (coup) against the government of the Weimar republic in 1920. Taking to politics, Lettow-Vorbeck was a Reichstag deputy from 1929 to 1930; although a right-winger, he was not associated with the Nazis.

See also: German army; Herero Revolt; Trotha, Gen. Lothar von
Further Reading: Gardner, Brian, *German East* (London, 1963); Hoyt, E. P., *Guerrilla* (New York, 1981).

Long March (1934–1935)

The so-called Long March is the most celebrated episode of the Chinese Civil War (1927–1949). Through it, the Chinese Communist Party (CPC) escaped destruction at the hands of the Chinese Nationalist Party or Kuomintang (KMT). Moreover, Mao Tse-tung was able to win sufficient time to revitalize the party and develop the strategy of rural revolutionary warfare that would bring victory in 1949. When Chiang Kai-shek resolved to purge communists from the KMT in 1926, the CPC responded with attempted urban revolts in southeastern Chinese cities such as Nanchang and Canton (Guangzou), but they were easily crushed. Nonetheless, sufficient communists escaped to the southern mountains on the borders between the Hunan and Kiangsi Provinces.

In December 1930 Chiang ordered the first of five "encirclement and annihilation" campaigns to eliminate the communist soviets (base areas). The first three of these campaigns (in 1930 and 1931) were not conspicuously successful but the fourth and fifth campaigns (1933 and 1934) overran the southern base areas. Facing annihilation, the communists began the "long march" from the southern base areas in October 1934. About 120,000 communists began the march and were joined by other surviving communist forces en route to the far northwestern mountains of the Shensi Province. They were under attack from the KMT as well as from local "warlord" and tribal forces. Barely 20,000 reached Shensi in the summer of 1935 after a journey of more than 6,000 miles, but Chiang's subordinates failed to achieve the final elimination of the communists he anticipated in further operations in both 1935 and 1936.

Chiang intended to take personal command but was forced into a uniting with the CPC when the Japanese launched a full-scale invasion of northern and central China in July 1937. The united front ended with a pitched battle in January 1941 between the KMT and the CPC's Fourth Red Army. However, the KMT and Japanese were too busy fighting each other to worry about the CPC; this gave communists the vital breathing room they needed to reorganize after past failures. Thus, it was in the Shensi Province after 1935 that Mao began to emerge gradually as the leading figure in the CPC and to develop his theories of rural guerrilla warfare as a means of achieving ultimate victory.

See also: Chinese Civil War; Japanese army; Kuomintang (KMT); Mao Tse-tung
Further Reading: Wilson, Dick, *China's Revolutionary War* (New York, 1991).

Lyautey, Marshal Louis-Hubert-Gonzalve (1854–1934)

Lyautey was one of the French army's leading exponents of counterinsurgency in the late nineteenth and early twentieth centuries, being especially known for his long tenures as resident-general in Morocco (1912–1916) and (1917–1925).

A royalist in the service of a republic, Lyautey was commissioned in the French cavalry in 1873. He served in Algeria from 1880 to 1882 but then gained notoriety for an 1891 article on the social role of the officer in the journal *Revue des deux mondes* in which he criticized the failure of French officers to take sufficient interest in the welfare of their men. Posted to French Indochina in 1894, Lyautey became associated with the architect of the pacification technique known as *tache d'huile* (oil slick), Joseph-Simon Galliéni. Lyautey followed Galliéni to Madagascar and in 1900 wrote a second article in *Revue des deux mondes*, which became the classic exposition of *tache d'huile*.

Using the analogy of oil spreading slowly over water, *tache d'huile* was a progressive expansion of French administration hand-in-hand with military occupation. In practice *tache d'huile* placed as much emphasis on military measures as on political measures. Implicit in Lyautey's article, too, was the belief that the army itself might be required to move beyond colonial administration to regenerate French society and politics as well. It was a political message that would be echoed in the politicization of the French army in Algeria in the 1950s through the application of the doctrine of *guerre révolutionnaire* (revolutionary war). Lyautey himself had a regimental command from 1902 to 1904 then moved to commands in Algeria from 1904 to 1910. Following command of an army corps in France, he was appointed resident-general in Morocco in 1912, where he applied *tache d'huile* to the consolidation of French control. With one brief interval during World War I, when he served as French minister of war (1916–1917), Lyautey remained in Morocco until August 1925. He was promoted to marshal in 1921.

See also: Algeria; French army; French Indochina; Galliéni, Marshal Joseph-Simon; *Guerre révolutionnaire;* Madagascar; Morocco; Pacification; Politicization of armed forces; *Tache d'huile*

Further Reading: Porch, Douglas, *The Conquest of Morocco* (London, 1982).

Maaten, Maj. Gen. Klaas van der (1861–1944)

Maaten was a captain in the Dutch army in 1896 when he published the three-volume study *De Indische Oorlogen: Een boek ten dienste van den jongen officier en het militair onderwijs* (The Indonesian wars: A book on behalf of the young officer and military education), intended to summarize the lessons of colonial warfare in the Dutch East Indies.

The son of a Dutch impressionist painter, Maaten was educated at the Dutch Royal Military Academy at Breda and commissioned in 1882. He spent most of his career in the East Indies, where the Dutch were involved in the long-running Aceh War (1873–1903). Maaten had considerable understanding of the military characteristics of indigenous cultures the Dutch encountered. He was influenced in this by a celebrated specialist on Islam, Dr. C. Snouck Hurgronje. Indeed, Maaten later wrote a book on Snouck's contribution to the Dutch campaigns, *Snouck Hurgronje en de Atjehoorlog* (Snouck Hurgronje and the Aceh War), which was published posthumously in 1948. In retirement Maaten was a prolific author on military subjects, writing works on colonial policy, colonial defense, and fortification. However, his earliest work, *De Indische Oorlogen,* was his principal contribution to military theory.

A highly perceptive work, it certainly bears comparison with that of his British contemporary, Charles Callwell. However, Maaten's book was largely ignored both in the compilation of the official Dutch manual on colonial tactics issued in 1927 and also in its revised edition of 1947 in the mistaken belief that it was no longer relevant. Maaten himself had been promoted to colonel in 1907 and to major general (general major in the Dutch service) in 1910. He retired in April 1914 and spent his remaining years in Switzerland.

See also: Callwell, Maj. Gen. Sir Charles Edward; Colonial warfare; Dutch army; Dutch East Indies; Manuals
Further Reading: de Moor, J. A., and H. L. Wesseling (eds.), *Imperialism and War: Essays on Colonial War in Asia and Africa* (Leiden, 1989).

MacArthur, Lt. Gen. Arthur (1845–1912)

MacArthur commanded the U.S. forces in the Philippines from May 1900 to July 1901 during the campaign against Filipino insurgents. His son was Douglas MacArthur, who would be commander in chief of Allied forces in the Southwest Pacific during World War II and of UN forces during the Korean War (1950–1953).

Commissioned in a Wisconsin volunteer regiment in 1862, MacArthur saw service in the western theater during the American Civil War (1861–1865). After the war, he became a regular soldier and served in Cuba and the Philippines during the Spanish-American War (1898). MacArthur believed in the need to treat the Filipinos benevolently but also introduced Army Order No. 100 in December 1900 as a means of controlling guerrilla activity. First issued during the Civil War, the Order No. 100 differentiated between the treatment of uniformed partisans and that likely to be meted out to "part-time" guerrillas shielding themselves among a civilian population. MacArthur also began a process of resettlement by moving rural populations into towns so that they could be more easily controlled and protected from guerrilla intimidation. MacArthur thereby offered the population reason to support the U.S. forces and penalties for not doing so.

He quarreled with William Taft, the head of the Philippines Commission, who engineered MacArthur's removal in July 1901. MacArthur was promoted to general in 1906 but the hostility of Taft, by now U.S. president, denied him the post of chief of staff; he retired in 1909.

See also: American Civil War; Cuba; Partisans; Philippines; Resettlement; United States Army
Further Reading: Young, Kenneth Ray, *The General's General* (Boulder, 1996).

Machel, Samora Moïses (1933–1986)

Machel became the leader of the nationalist group Frente de Libertação de Moçambique (FRELIMO) in May 1970 and the first president of Mozambique after its independence from Portugal in June 1975. Machel was born in Xilembene in the Gaza Province and educated by Methodist and Catholic missionaries. Trained as a male nurse, Machel became a committed Marxist and joined FRELIMO in 1962. He was one of the first FRELIMO guerrillas to receive military training in Algeria and led the first group to infiltrate into Mozambique from Tanzania in September 1964. He became FRELIMO's defense secretary in 1966 and its commander in chief in 1968.

After the movement's founder, Eduardo Mondlane, was killed by a parcel bomb in February 1969, Machel emerged from the resulting internal struggle as the dominant figure. FRELIMO did not enjoy whole-

hearted popular support, and after independence Resistançia Naçional Moçambicana (RENAMO) enjoyed considerable success against Machel's government. Rhodesia and then South Africa gave RENAMO covert support, although after Rhodesia's independence Robert Mugabe committed Zimbabwean troops to the defense of the road, rail, and pipeline links to Beira. Nevertheless, Machel was forced to conclude the Nkomati Agreement with South Africa in March 1984, Machel dropping support for the African National Congress (ANC) in return for South Africa repudiating RENAMO. Machel also abandoned some of FRELIMO's Marxist policies, yet RENAMO remained strong. Machel died in an air crash on 19 October 1986 while returning from consultation with other so-called front-line states during a renewed confrontation with South Africa.

See also: African National Congress (ANC); Frente de Libertação de Moçambique (FRELIMO); Mondlane, Dr. Eduardo; Mozambique; Mugabe, Robert Gabriel; Portuguese army; Resistançia Naçional Moçambicana (RENAMO); Rhodesia
Further Reading: Munslow, B. (ed.), *Samora Machel, An African Revolutionary: Selected Speeches and Writings* (London, 1985).

Madagascar

The island of Madagascar occupied an important strategic position off Africa's eastern coast as European powers moved to partition the continent in the late nineteenth century. The French had maintained posts on the island between 1643 and 1674 and temporarily did so during the late eighteenth and early nineteenth centuries. A more permanent presence was established following a punitive expedition in 1827. Yet it was not until the 1880s that the French resolved to take action against the powerful kingdom of Merina, which threatened other tribes under nominal French protection.

The French conquest of the island began in December 1894. The Merina capital of Antananarivo fell in October 1895 but the

French then faced the so-called Menelamba (Red Shawls) Revolt in April 1896; the island was not fully subjugated until 1905. This was accomplished by the application of the *tache d'huile* (oil slick) method of pacification pioneered by Joseph-Simon Galliéni and his assistant, Louis-Hubert-Gonzalve Lyautey. *Tache d'huile* was a progressive extension of French civil administration hand-in-hand with military occupation. Often, as in Madagascar, it implied controlling the local population through its traditional local leaders; the French also made use of the resentment of the Merina by other ethnic groups within the Malagasy population.

During World War II Madagascar, which had remained loyal to the Vichy government after France's defeat by the Germans, was occupied by British forces in May 1942 to forestall possible Japanese invasion. The unsuccessful defense of the island against the British undermined French prestige and stimulated demands for independence. In March 1947 Merina-dominated nationalists rose against the French in the Malagasy Revolt (1947–1949). The revolt was crushed with considerable brutality. Madagascar finally received its independence in June 1960.

See also: French army; Galliéni, Marshal Joseph-Simon; Lyautey, Marshal Louis-Hubert-Gonzalve; Malagasy Revolt; Pacification; *Tache d'huile*
Further Reading: Ellis, Stephen, *The Rising of the Red Shawls* (Cambridge, 1985).

Magsaysay, Ramon (1907–1957)

Magsaysay was the architect of victory over the communist Hukbalahap (Huk) insurgency in the Philippines, serving as secretary of defense from 1950 to 1953 and then as president until his death in an air crash in March 1957. Of mixed blood, Magsaysay was born in Iba, the capital of the Zambales Province of Luzon. Working his way up from mechanic to general manager of a bus company, Magsaysay became an American-trained guerrilla leader against the Japanese during World War II. He was military governor of west-central Luzon in 1945 and entered congress for the same area in 1950. On 1 September 1950 he was appointed secretary of national defense by Pres. Elpidio Quirino.

Magsaysay claimed he had no theories, but he clearly understood the political nature of the Huk insurgency. His ruthless drive against corruption and his determination to win hearts and minds was a convincing sign of progress, and his unannounced visits to army units weeded out the inefficient. Assisted by Americans such as Edward Lansdale, Magsaysay turned the tide against the Huks. However, he met resistance from within the ruling Liberal Party, not least after his troops had prevented electoral fraud in the 1951 elections. When control over the police was taken from him in February 1953, Magsaysay resigned and contested the presidential elections in November 1953 as candidate for the opposition Nacionalistas. Winning the election, Magsaysay presided over the effective end of the Hukbalahap in 1954.

See also: Hukbalahap; Lansdale, Maj. Gen. Edward Geary; Philippines
Further Reading: Greenberg, L. M., *The Hukbalahap Insurrection* (Washington, DC, 1987).

Maji Maji Rising (1905–1907)

The Maji Maji Rising was a major revolt among the Rufifi River tribes in German East Africa. *Maji* is Swahili for "water," the revolt being noted for the tribes' tragic delusion that European bullets would be turned to water and could not harm them. The revolt stemmed from a hut tax, forced labor, and compulsory cultivation of cotton as a cash crop. The German garrison was small when the revolt began in July 1905, but once reinforcements arrived the German response was characterized by brutality. A systematic strategy of scorched earth and famine contributed to starvation and disease among the tribes. Estimates of the native death toll range from 25,000 to 75,000. The last significant leader of the rising, Mpanda, was captured in January 1907.

See also: German army; Herero Revolt
Further Reading: Henderson, W. O., *The German Colonial Empire, 1884–1919* (London, 1993).

Makhno, Nestor (1889–1935)

Makhno was a Ukrainian anarchist who fought a bitter guerrilla campaign against the Bolsheviks during the Russian Civil War (1917–1921). Born in the village of Gulei Polye (Hulyai Pole), Makhno joined the Anarchist Party in 1905 and was imprisoned by imperial authorities for seven years. Returning to the Ukraine in 1917, he organized the Peasant Union and, subsequently, the Insurgent Revolutionary Army.

At the peak of his influence, Makhno had some 25,000 well-armed followers, the majority from Gulei Polye and its immediate vicinity. There were more than 90 competing insurgent groups in Ukraine, and Makhno fought against them as well as the Bolsheviks and the White Russian armies, who remained loyal to the tsar. Faced with the White Russian threat, the Bolsheviks reached a temporary accommodation with Makhno in 1919 and again in 1920 but were able to turn against him in force in November 1920. Known to his followers as "Batko" (Father), Makhno displayed a thoroughly modern understanding of the political and socioeconomic potentials of insurgency. He enjoyed considerable support among the rural population but was as ruthless as the Bolsheviks in eliminating opponents; there were summary executions on both sides. Indeed, at least 200,000 peasants died in the eight months of savagery that ensued before Makhno was forced to take refuge in Romania in August 1921. He died while in exile.

See also: Russian Civil War; Soviet army
Further Reading: Adams, A. E., *Bolsheviks in the Ukraine* (New Haven, 1963); Malet, M., *Nestor Makhno in the Russian Civil War* (London, 1982).

Malagasy Revolt (1947–1949)

The Malagasy Revolt was a large-scale uprising against French rule on the Indian Ocean island of Madagascar off the eastern coast of Africa. It ended in bloody failure. The French had achieved their subjugation of the island between 1895 and 1905, playing off the dominant Merina people against other ethnic groups among the Malagasy population. The Merina remained resistant to the imposition of French culture, and it was among them that nationalism first emerged during and after World War I. There was resentment against French policies, not least compulsory labor conscription, while the island suffered economic privations through its isolation during World War II. French prestige was weakened further by the 1942 British occupation of the island to forestall possible Japanese invasion.

It became apparent, however, that the French would not relinquish their rule after the end of the war, and the Merina-dominated Mouvement Démocratique de la Rénovation Malgache (MDRM), or Democratic Movement for Malagasy Renewal, was founded in February 1946 to work for independence. Other rival nationalist movements appeared, and internal divisions were evident when elements of the MDRM began the revolt on 29 March 1947. It was badly planned, and the rebels were not only poorly armed but oftentimes deluded by drugs or their reliance on religious talismans, believing sheer willpower could overcome French bullets. Although the rebels had some initial success against the small French garrison, the revolt was largely confined to the eastern coast.

Substantial French reinforcements, including elements of the French Foreign Legion, had arrived by July and went to the offensive in early 1948. The last significant rebel leader was taken in February 1949. The French recorded 558,000 rebel surrenders in the course of the revolt; estimates of the dead range from 11,000 to 90,000. There is little doubt that the French reaction was one of considerable brutality, but there were atrocities on both sides, and in some respects the revolt was also a civil war among the Malagasy. The French outlawed the MDRM; in any case, the collapse of the revolt undermined the appeal of militant nationalism. More moderate nationalists emerged in the 1950s, and Madagascar received its independence in June 1960.

See also: French army; French Foreign Legion; Madagascar
Further Reading: Clayton, Anthony, *The Wars of French Decolonisation* (London, 1994).

Malayan Emergency (1948–1960)

The emergency in Malaya between 1948 and 1960 was one of the most significant insurgencies that confronted any Western power immediately after World War II. The lessons learned by the British army in defeating the Malayan Communist Party

(MCP) were crucial in the evolution of modern British counterinsurgency practice as illustrated in the theories of Sir Robert Thompson.

The MCP, founded in 1930, enjoyed its greatest support among the ethnic Chinese minority. Constituting about 38 percent of the population, they had come to Malaya in the nineteenth century as laborers and traders. During the Japanese occupation of Malaya in World War II, the MCP had dominated the Malayan People's Anti-Japanese Army (MPAJA), which received support from the British Special Operations Executive (SOE). MPAJA was supposedly disbanded in December 1945 in return for the legal recognition of the MCP by the restored British colonial authorities. The MCP developed a strong influence

Three British soldiers proudly hold up a banner that had been carried by the communist guerrilla troops, captured during the Malayan Emergency, 4 September 1955. (UPI/Corbis-Bettmann)

among the trade unions, but its appeal remained largely ethnic. Indeed, the Malay majority leaned more toward the emerging United Malayan National Organization, which successfully challenged Britain's postwar plans for a Malay union with some Chinese representation.

With the failure of the union plan, the British proposed a Malay federation with the various states and provinces enjoying some autonomy. This was more acceptable to the Malays, but the Chinese would have fewer rights. The MCP therefore moved to exploit the particular grievances of the half-million-strong Chinese "squatter" population. The squatters had fled the Japanese, then illegally occupied government land in subsistence-oriented communities along the jungle fringes. MPAJA weapons concealed after the war were passed to the new Malayan Races Liberation Army (MRLA), the escalating violence resulting in the declaration of a state of emergency on 17 June 1948.

Initially, the British authorities failed to appreciate the political nature of the threat facing them, the MCP modeling its strategy on that of Mao Tse-tung. The British regarded the insurgency simply as criminal activity, and force was used indiscriminately by army and police. The police commissioner, Nicol Gray, had previously served in Palestine and believed in a paramilitary role. As a result, the scale of the insurgency expanded alarmingly, the MRLA deploying about 7,000 men by 1950. The British were fortunate in that the Malay population remained indifferent to the MCP and that Malaya was geographically isolated from external assistance. Since Malaya was a colony, the British also enjoyed wide powers, and ultimately they were able to give independence to Malaya in 1957 in a way that the MCP could not match.

An economic boom generated by rapidly rising rubber and tin prices, a consequence of Western rearmament during the Korean War (1950–1953), made resources increasingly available to fight the insur-

gency, and the population shared in the prosperity. Another advantage was the inexperience of the MCP's leadership, Chin Peng becoming the party's general secretary on the very eve of the emergency after his predecessor was revealed as a British agent. Indeed, the MCP made the mistake of withdrawing deep into the jungle in 1949 to reorganize for a longer campaign at the very moment when the British most needed a respite. At an equally critical moment in October 1951 the MCP chose to emphasize political mobilization more than military action, a belated recognition that the struggle had been launched prematurely, without the long period of preparatory politicization of the population advocated by Mao.

Whatever their inherent advantages, the British still had to adopt a more appropriate response to Maoist-style insurgency. This began with the appointment of Lt. Gen. Sir Harold Briggs as director of operations in March 1950. The so-called Briggs Plan would, as its first priority, eliminate the MCP's mass political support organization, the Min Yuen, rather than eliminate insurgent groups operating from jungle bases. Another crucial element was to create an elaborate committee structure from a federal war council down through state, district, and even village committees. Representatives from the army, police, civil agencies, and (from January 1955) ethnic communities would sit on the committees. This structure ensured a coordinated response at every stage. The third part of the Briggs Plan was to introduce resettlement in order to separate squatters from insurgents. Eventually, some 500 "new villages" were created to house the squatters, although the application of the same solution to jungle aborigines later in the campaign was abandoned when it became evident that nomadic tribesmen were not socially or economically suited to resettlement.

The inevitable logic of the effort to integrate political and military strategy was to place control of all aspects of the British response in one person. Therefore, following the death of the high commissioner, Sir Henry Gurney, in an ambush and the retirement of Briggs on health grounds, Sir Gerald Templer was made high commissioner and director of operations in February 1952. By force of personality, Templer rejuvenated the campaign. Briggs had already established a special police branch freed of criminal work in May 1950 and had appointed a director to coordinate intelligence at all levels. Templer went farther, establishing a combined intelligence staff. Similarly, as Briggs had created an emergency information service in June 1950, Templer appointed a director-general of information services and established a psychological warfare section.

Templer also gave the squatters in the new villages tangible proof of genuine concern for their welfare by winning hearts and minds. Amenities were increasingly made available, and, to add to the permanent legal title granted the squatters for the land they occupied by December 1951, Templer introduced village councils in May 1952. He also transformed the nature of policing, emphasizing a more traditional British role rather than a paramilitary one. A compulsory home guard was established in new villages in July 1951, and by 1953 Templer felt confident enough to make it solely responsible for village defense. The first "white area"—free of all emergency restrictions—was announced in Malacca in September 1953. Templer also encouraged the growth of the multiracial Alliance Party, led by Tunku Abdul Rahman, which formed the government upon independence in August 1957.

By the time Templer left Malaya in May 1954 the MCP was on the defensive, Britain's successful separation of the insurgents from their core support making it possible to free armed forces for the primary role of striking at insurgent groups in the jungle. Increasingly, it was recognized that the most successful military operations against insurgents were linked to food de-

nial with small units of platoons, sections, and even subsections undertaking deep-penetration patrols into the jungle. The availability of helicopters beginning in 1953 was especially valuable for dropping patrols into the jungle. And with the assistance of aboriginal trackers of the Senoi Pra'aq and others recruited from the Iban tribe in Borneo, the reformed Special Air Service (SAS) pushed surviving insurgents toward the frontier with Thailand. The emergency was declared at an end on 31 July 1960, although insurgent groups continued to exist along the frontier. Chin Peng emerged to surrender to Malaysian authorities in December 1989.

The British had defeated a communist insurgency, but victory was not achieved cheaply or quickly. Insurgent casualties amounted to 13,191, including 2,980 surrenders, and security forces suffered 4,436 casualties; there were 4,668 civilian casualties. The protracted nature of the conflict also cost an estimated $487 million Malay. Nevertheless, a pattern of British postwar counterinsurgency had been established, its lessons enshrined by Thompson in what became known as the five principles.

See also: Briggs, Lt. Gen. Sir Harold Rawdon; British army; Chin Peng; Hearts and minds; Helicopters; Intelligence; Mao Tse-tung; Police; Resettlement; Special Air Service (SAS); Special Operations Executive (SOE); Templer, Field Marshal Sir Gerald; Thompson, Sir Robert Grainger Ker
Further Reading: Short, Anthony, *The Communist Insurrection in Malaya, 1948–1960* (London, 1975); Clutterbuck, Richard, *The Long Long War* (London, 1966); Stubbs, Richard, *Hearts and Minds in Guerrilla Warfare* (Singapore, 1989).

Manuals

Manuals are the principal means by which military doctrine is disseminated through armed forces. Study of successive editions of official manuals, therefore, can show whether lessons have been absorbed from previous campaigns. However, manuals can become outdated, and those based on past experiences might be ignored if new field conditions invalidate previous lessons. Sometimes, manuals are not fully understood in the first place, meaning that local practices continue despite official doctrine.

Manuals on conventional warfare typically outnumber those on counterinsurgency, because regular armies invariably regard their main role as preparing for conventional battles and campaigns—whatever the realities of practical soldiering experience. Often, therefore, preparing manuals on irregular warfare has taken a backseat to writing those on conventional warfare. Despite the British army's constant colonial campaigning throughout the nineteenth century, for example, the War Office waited until 1896 to publish Charles Callwell's celebrated manual *Small Wars: Their Principles and Practice*. It was reissued in 1899 and again in 1906, and it was not effectively superseded until well after World War I.

The next official British manual was *Notes on Imperial Policing*, published in 1934 (ironically the same year Sir Charles Gwynn published *Notes on Imperial Policing* because there had been no satisfactory treatment of colonial warfare since Callwell). Gwynn's series of case studies was probably more widely disseminated than the manual itself. *Imperial Policing* was supplemented by *Duties in Aid of the Civil Power* (1937). Both manuals were combined as *Imperial Policing and Duties in Aid of the Civil Power* (1949).

Useful manuals were produced to disseminate practical local lessons during the Malayan Emergency (1948–1960) and the Kenyan Emergency (1952–1960). In the former case, Sir Gerald Templer oversaw the production of *The Conduct of Anti-Terrorist Operations in Malaya* (1952), a work written by Walter Walker. In the latter campaign, *A Handbook of Anti–Mau Mau Operations* appeared in 1954. Lessons from Malaya were incorporated in a new manual, *Keeping the Peace*, published in 1957 and revised in 1963, and Malaya was also the model for *Land Operations: Counter-Revolutionary Operations* (1969, rev. 1977).

The relevance of the Malay experience so long after the emergency was debatable.

In contrast, due to the lack of any recent American experience, when the United States Marine Corps was required to produce a new study of counterinsurgency in 1960, its author would have certainly benefited from the knowledge enshrined in *Small Wars Manual* of 1935 had he known of its existence. Largely written by Lt. Col. Harold Utley, *Small Wars Manual* drew on the Marines' counterinsurgency experiences in the Caribbean and Central America during the interwar period, including the Nicaragua campaign against Augusto Sandino (1927–1933). Very much a product of its time, the manual addressed the nature of insurgency and the need to win hearts and minds, although there was a certain emphasis on establishing impartial constabularies and on supervising honest elections as a kind of panacea for instability. It was enlarged and revised in 1940, but the Marine Corps was already being drawn toward amphibious warfare, and the practice of small-wars techniques was all but forgotten after World War II.

Other manuals worthy of note include the German army's *Warfare Against Bands*, belatedly published in 1944, and the Dutch army's *Voorschrift voor de uitoefening van de politiek-politionele taak van het leger* (VPTL, or Precepts for the politico-policing tasks of the army), published in 1927 with an additional appendix of case studies known as the *Aanhangsel*. When the Dutch faced a new challenge from Indonesian nationalists in the Dutch East Indies in 1947, Dutch conscripts were issued a digest of the VPTL in comic-book form, *Kennis van het VPTL: een kwestie van leven of dood* (Knowledge of the VPTL: A question of life or death). However, the VPTL was based on the Dutch campaign against Aceh that ended in 1912 and was not very relevant to modern conditions.

See also: British army; Callwell, Maj. Gen. Sir Charles Edward; Dutch army; Dutch East Indies; German army; Gwynn, Maj. Gen. Sir Charles William; Kenyan Emergency; Malayan Emergency; Nicaragua; Sandino, Augusto César; Templer, Field Marshal Sir Gerald; United States Marine Corps (USMC); Utley, Lt. Col. Harold Hickox; Walker, Gen. Sir Walter Colyear

Further Reading: Mockaitis, Thomas, *British Counterinsurgency, 1919–1960* (London, 1990).

Mao Tse-tung (1893–1976)

Mao Tse-tung (Mao Zedong) is arguably the twentieth century's greatest theorist of revolutionary guerrilla warfare. After his victory in the Chinese Civil War (1927–1949), Mao's theories were emulated by revolutionaries in Africa and Southeast Asia, although his theories did not always succeed outside China.

Mao was the son of a prosperous farmer in the Hunan Province and, in fact, always spoke with a pronounced regional dialect. He completed his secondary education and took employment as a library assistant at Peking (Beijing) University in 1917. Mao came into contact with Marxist ideas and was one of the founders of the Chinese Communist Party in 1921. However, he frequently clashed with party leadership and did not establish his own primacy until the 1930s, when the Marxist-Leninist model of urban insurrection favored by the leadership proved inapplicable in an overwhelmingly rural peasant society. Indeed, Mao's ideas gained acceptance only after the communists were driven deep into the interior by Chiang Kai-shek's nationalist Kuomintang (KMT).

Initially, the communists attempted an urban insurrection in 1927 but were driven from the southeastern cities. A series of five campaigns by the KMT between 1930 and 1934 forced the communists to undertake the 6,000-mile so-called Long March to the northwestern Shensi (Shaanxi) Province in order to escape total destruction.

Mao believed the key to short-term survival and long-term success lay in the intimate connection between the concepts of time, space, will, and substitution. Given the weakness of the communists at the conclusion of the Long March in 1935, their only resource was in the geographical remoteness of the mountainous region to which they had retreated. Mao argued such

An official portrait of Mao Tse-tung, 1936. An inscription under the portrait reads, "Great leader chairman Mao will live forever in our hearts." (UPI/Corbis-Bettmann)

"space" could be traded to win "time" necessary for reconstruction, for communists could use the difficult terrain to evade KMT offensives. Time won would be translated into producing "will," by which he meant the forging of a common cause between the party and the population, upon whose support the communists were entirely dependent for ultimate victory. "Substitution," in turn, was connected to the need to survive by using whatever advantages the communists possessed to offset their weaknesses. Thus, skilled use of propaganda might substitute for lack of weapons.

In the short term, guerrilla war offered the best means of survival, but Mao always thought it would be necessary to create a regular army capable of meeting opponents on a conventional battlefield. In isolation, guerrilla warfare could not achieve anything more than tactical gains, and it needed to be incorporated within a wider revolutionary strategy. Mao's emphasis on the political nature of a revolutionary war was influenced partly by the work of the nineteenth-century Prussian theorist Carl von Clausewitz, whose works had long been used at Chinese military academies. It is also conceivable that Mao derived some inspiration from T. E. Lawrence (Lawrence of Arabia).

The whole process would be a protracted struggle spanning three phases of revolution. In practice, however, the phases were likely to merge one into another, and there was no set timetable for the application of each phase. The *prerevolutionary phase* was one of strategic defensive, as communists would be much weaker than their opponents and would have to remain largely on the defensive (though not passive). The aim was to extend the party's organization and to establish an infrastructure before introducing guerrillas into any particular area. Cadres would be infiltrated into key positions through the organization of local groups, such as peasant associations. The peasantry would be convinced that their lives could be improved only by supporting the communists, the cadres identifying the party with popular causes, such as land reform. A limited degree of intimidation might be employed to ensure the acquiescence of the peasantry, as neutrals could not be tolerated, but far more force would be directed at the organization of the opposing authorities. Above all, Mao stressed that the guerrilla "must be in the population as little fishes in the ocean" and must cultivate good relations with the peasantry.

The prerevolutionary phase would lead to the second phase: *strategic stalemate*. Sufficient popular support, sympathy, or acquiescence would allow communists to expand political action into guerrilla warfare in a situation of approximately equal strength between communists and their opponents. Bases would be established and the tempo of recruitment increased, with regular units now being formed and trained for the future. As guerrilla activity increased, the communists would be able to establish a revolutionary administration rivaling that of their opponents. The kind of guerrilla tactics Mao advocated were not innovative and clearly drew on ancient Chinese military classics such as Sun Tzu's *Art of War.*

Finally, the revolution would reach its third and concluding phase: *strategic offensive.* The communists, now stronger than their opponents, would be in a position to launch a mobile conventional war.

It needs to be repeated that Maoist theory evolved relatively gradually and corresponded with the phases of the Chinese Civil War. Thus, Mao's articles published between 1928 and 1936 reflected the early struggle against the KMT, whereas those published between 1936 and 1938 reflected the period of intervention in China by the Japanese army. His most significant articles were "Problems of Strategy in China's Revolutionary War," written in December 1936, and two articles written in May 1938, "Problems of Strategy in the Guerrilla War Against Japan" and "On Protracted War." Elements of the theory also appeared in a 1937 pamphlet, "On Guerrilla War," which was translated into English by Samuel Griffith, an American observer in China. Curiously, no actual copy of the original has ever been located.

Naturally, the communist victory in the Chinese Civil War gave Mao's theories wide currency. However, it is important to stress the significance of Japan's all-out invasion in July 1937. It damaged the KMT to the extent that it could no longer threaten the communists. Thus, the Japanese intervention gave Mao the breathing space he needed to prepare the population politically. The Japanese themselves did not regard the communists as a serious threat, and in any case they could not spare the manpower or resources that would be needed to occupy and control much of the territory the Japanese had overrun. The targeting of railways by the communists in the Campaign of a Hundred Regiments between August and October 1940 did stir Gen. Yasuji Okamura into a more proactive antiguerrilla role in the spring of 1941, but he could not sustain it after Japan entered World War II that December. In fact, Japan's brutality merely strengthened peasant support for the communists, who also benefited by being available to accept Japan's surrender in northern China in 1945. Indeed, the communists were in a far stronger position than the KMT when the civil war resumed. Mao proclaimed the People's Republic of China on 1 October 1949.

Those who emulated Mao tended to overlook the significance of Japan's role in his eventual victory. Instead, they simplistically viewed Maoist theory as a means by which even the weakest revolutionary movement could adopt a form of military and political resistance that could prevail against a vastly superior opponent. Maoist principles were therefore applied in such insurgencies as the Malayan Emergency (1948–1960) and the Hukbalahap (1946–1954). Maoism also influenced African insurgents, such as Amílcar Cabral in Portuguese Guinea between 1961 and 1973 and Robert Mugabe in Rhodesia between 1974 and 1979. The most obvious followers were two Vietnamese theorists of revolutionary war, Truong Chinh and Vo Nguyen Giap. However, both laid greater stress on the mobilization of international opinion in support of the revolution, acknowledging the world had changed from 1930s China. Others, however, did not adjust to changing circumstances. For example, Maoist principles failed in Thailand in the 1980s, and the group known as Sendero Luminoso (Shining Path), founded in Peru in 1980, fragmented after the capture of its leader, Abimael Guzmán, in 1992.

See also: Cabral, Amílcar; Chinese Civil War; Clausewitz, Carl von; Giap, Vo Nguyen; Guinea, Portuguese; Guzmán Reynoso, Prof. Abimael; Hukbalahap; Japanese army; Kuomintang (KMT); Lawrence, Thomas Edward; Long March; Malayan Emergency; Mugabe, Robert Gabriel; Okamura, Gen. Yasuji; Peru; Sendero Luminoso; Sun Tzu; Thailand; Truong Chinh

Further Reading: Mao Tse-tung, *Selected Military Writings* (Peking, 1967); Griffith, Samuel (ed.), *Mao Tse-tung on*

Guerrilla Warfare (New York, 1978); Marks, Tom, *Maoist Insurgency since Vietnam* (London, 1996).

Maori Wars

The Maoris are the indigenous peoples of New Zealand whom the British contacted in the late eighteenth century. In all, the British fought three Maori Wars (1845–1846, 1860–1861, 1863–1870) as settler pressure on Maori lands increased. The Maoris were a warrior society of tribes and clans owing allegiance to individual chiefs. Traditionally, intertribal warfare had been a matter of hand-to-hand fighting with axes and clubs, but the Maoris readily took to firearms introduced by European traders (although they retained their characteristic intimidating practices, including war chants and extensive body tattooing). The Maori *pas* (fortified stockades and earthworks) also proved formidable obstacles to attack, even from artillery. Moreover, since *pa* were regarded as temporary structures, the Maoris would invariably slip away before any assaulting troops breached the defenses.

A British resident had been installed in New Zealand's North Island in 1833 at the request of missionaries. A treaty was then signed with Maori chiefs at Waitangi in February 1840, but the Maoris had little understanding of settlers' desire to acquire legal title to land. The First Maori War, or Flagstaff War, resulted from the rebellion of Hone Heke of the Ngapuhi, whose defiance of British authority was marked by his repeatedly cutting down a flagpole at Kororareka near Auckland. As a result, the British attacked Hone Heke's *pa* at Puketutu in May 1845 but were driven off; sporadic hostilities ended only when the British successfully stormed another *pa* at Ruapekapeka on a Sunday in January 1846 when most defenders were attending divine service.

The Maoris remained peaceful until more settler pressure stimulated a "king" movement in the late 1850s. Thus, when the

British violated the principle of tribal land ownership—purchasing an area along the Waitara River in Taranaki from a minor chief whom the Maoris did not regard as the rightful owner—attempts to survey the land brought renewed conflict. The Second Maori War, or Taranaki War, between March and November 1860, saw an early British reverse at Puketakaurere. There were subsequent British successes in a series of methodical siege operations, but both sides were soon ready to negotiate.

However, conflict resurfaced in April 1863 when Maori opposition to the construction of a military road led to the Third Maori War, or Waikato War. Sir Duncan Cameron chose to launch a costly frontal assault against the Rangiri *pa* in November 1863 but was more successful in reverting to siege tactics against the Gate and Te Ranga *pas* in April and June 1864. Hostilities spread again to Taranaki with the appearance of the messianic Pai Marire, or Hau Hau, and Ringatu sects and became a protracted guerrilla struggle. Te Kooti of the Ringatu and Titokowaru of the Hau Hau were charismatic leaders, and resistance was not finally overcome until 1872.

See also: British army; Colonial warfare

Further Reading: Belich, James, *The New Zealand Wars and the Victorian Interpretation of Racial Conflict* (Auckland, 1986); Ryan, Tim, and Bill Parham, *The Colonial New Zealand Wars* (Wellington, 1986).

Marighela, Carlos (1911–1969)

Marighela was a Brazilian revolutionary who became the principal theorist of urban guerrilla warfare in the 1960s. Marighela was a communist activist for more than 40 years, rising to lead the party's committee in the major city of São Paulo. However, in December 1966 Marighela resigned from the party's executive committee, and in July 1967 he attended a conference of the Cuban-sponsored Organization for Latin American Solidarity (OLAS) in Havana against the wishes of the party leadership. It was now his belief that the kind of armed revolutionary activism being called for by

Fidel Castro and Che Guevara offered better possibilities for overthrowing Brazil's military government than did the party's existing electoral strategy.

Joining with another disaffected communist, Mario Alves, Marighela founded the separate Revolutionary Communist Party of Brazil in early 1968. It was subsequently reorganized as Acçâo Libertadora Nacional (ALN), or Action for National Liberation.

Marighela was well aware of the failures of Guevara's *foco* theory of rural guerrilla warfare. Like Guevara, he rejected Mao Tse-tung's emphasis upon the need for a lengthy period of political preparation of a population for revolution. He also followed Guevara in envisaging his activists as a small, elite group of dedicated and self-sacrificing revolutionaries whose "armed propaganda" would establish a revolutionary situation by undermining the government and security forces and alienating the population from the authorities by forcing government overreaction. However, unlike Guevara, the arena for Marighela's campaign would be the city and not the countryside.

Rural action was not ruled out by Marighela, but the city offered soft targets and safe havens among a teeming population already likely to be politicized by social and economic deprivation. Moreover, action in cities such as Rio de Janeiro, São Paulo, and Belo Horizonte guaranteed a skewed reaction to the actual scale of affairs through media attention. Thus, actions would be designed to be spectacular, targeting Brazilian authorities as well as multinational companies in hopes of weakening the economy by driving out foreign capital. The principal techniques of his urban terror were letter bombings, assassinations, and politically motivated kidnappings. Indeed, in September 1969 ALN kidnapped the U.S. ambassador, Charles Elbrick, demanding the release of 15 captured guerrillas.

Marighela's theories were encapsulated in a handbook of urban guerrilla warfare known as *Minimanual,* published in June 1969. Marighela's expectation was that the authorities would be confronted with choosing either craven capitulation to insurgent demands or overreaction and repression. In the event, authorities opted for the latter and resorted to institutionalized counterterror without restraint. In response, groups like ALN fell back to indiscriminate bombings, which cost them any legitimacy among urban populations.

Few (if any) revolutionaries survived to exploit the situation they engineered. Marighela himself was killed in a São Paulo gun battle on 4 November 1969 amid the intense police activity following Ambassador Elbrick's kidnapping. Alves was arrested in January 1970 and died under torture.

See also: Castro, Fidel; *Foco;* Guevara, Ernesto Che; Mao Tse-tung; Media; Urban guerrilla warfare
Further Reading: Marighela, Carlos, *For the Liberation of Brazil* (Harmondsworth, 1971); Moss, Robert, *Urban Guerrilla Warfare* (London, 1971).

Marion, Brig. Gen. Francis (c. 1732–1795)

Known as the "Swamp Fox," Marion was a highly skilled guerrilla leader who fought the British in the Carolinas during the American War of Independence (1775–1783). Born in Berkeley County, South Carolina, Marion was of Huguenot descent and grew up in the forests and swamps along the Santee River. He served in a Carolinian militia regiment against Cherokees during the Seven Years War (1756–1763), learning many techniques in wilderness warfare.

In the War of Independence he distinguished himself defending Fort Sullivan at Charleston in June 1776 and at Savannah in October 1779 before being directed to wage "forest warfare" against the British following their May 1780 capture of Charleston. The strength of Marion's irregulars varied from as few as 30 to as many as 1,000 as he attempted to win time for the Continental army to reorganize. Skilled in hit-and-run tactics, Marion's refuges were

the swamps of the Santee and Pedee Rivers he knew so well from his youth, hence his nickname. By December 1780, when Marion was promoted to brigadier general, British influence was largely confined to Charleston and its immediate vicinity. The British did launch a determined attack on Marion's base at Snow's Island in March 1781, but he was able to escape. Marion was briefly and unhappily under the command of another noted guerrilla leader, Thomas Sumter, later that year; he and his irregulars were also present at the Battle of Eutaw Springs in September 1781. Marion was elected to South Carolina's senate in 1781 and was appointed to a sinecure post in command at Fort Johnson at the end of the war.

See also: American War of Independence; British army; Sumter, Brig. Gen. Thomas
Further Reading: Bass, Robert, *Swamp Fox* (New York, 1959).

Martí, Farabundo (d. 1932)

Martí was a Salvadoran communist who led an unsuccessful revolt against the military government of Gen. Maximiliano Hernández Martínez in El Salvador in 1932. The insurgent group formed in El Salvador in 1980, Frente Farabundo Martí de Liberación Nacional (FMLN), took its name in commemoration of him. Martí was an adviser to Augusto Sandino in Nicaragua, but Sandino, who was not a communist, broke with him in 1930. The aftermath of Martí's revolt is known as La Matanza (The Massacre) from the severity of the government's repression. Martí himself was captured and executed.

See also: El Salvador; Frente Farabundo Martí de Liberación Nacional (FMLN); Sandino, Augusto César
Further Reading: Dunkerley, J., *The Long War: Dictatorship and Revolution in El Salvador* (London, 1982).

Massu, Gen. Jacques (1908–)

Massu is best known for his command of the French army's Tenth Colonial Parachute Division during the Battle of Algiers in 1957. Educated at the French military academy at Saint Cyr, Massu was serving in North Africa when France fell to the Germans in 1940. He joined Charles de Gaulle's Free French forces and was one of the first French soldiers to return after the Paris liberation in August 1944 and one of the first back into Saigon in French Indochina in October 1945. He was appointed to command the parachute division in 1955 and led it during the Anglo-French operations to seize the Suez Canal in October 1956 before being posted to Algeria.

The tough and stocky Massu had little compunction in destroying the networks of the Front de Libération National (FLN) in the city when the division was ordered into Algiers between February and September 1957. Massu was not much interested in politics, but he was always a convinced Gaullist, and in May 1958 he and the French commander in chief in Algeria, Raoul Salan, demanded de Gaulle's recall to political power. Massu was appointed to command the Algiers division, but his concern with the drift of de Gaulle's Algerian policy led to him criticize his old mentor in a newspaper interview in January 1960; he was recalled to France. After a year of enforced retirement Massu was reinstated as military governor of Metz, having refused to join Salan's attempted coup in Algiers in 1961. He was appointed commander in chief of French forces in Germany in 1966. Massu retired in 1969.

See also: Algeria; Algiers, Battle of; French army; French Indochina; Front de Libération Nationale (FLN); Salan, Gen. Raoul

Further Reading: Massu, Jacques, *La Vraie Bataille d'Alger* (Paris, 1971).

Mau Mau

Mau Mau was the insurgent movement that fought against the British during the Kenyan Emergency (1952–1960) in East Africa. There is still considerable uncertainty as to the origins and the precise meaning of the name Mau Mau. The movement was certainly established within the framework of the legal nationalist party, the Kenya African Union (KAU), by black former servicemen who had served with the British forces in World War II. However, at the time no link was conclusively proven between Mau Mau and the KAU's leading figure, Jomo Kenyatta.

The membership of Mau Mau was characterized by the administration of secret oaths among deeply superstitious tribesmen in Kenya's largest tribe, the Kikuyu, and two closely related ethnic groups, the Embu and the Meru. Mau Mau, however, was not a national uprising, as the other ethnic groups within Kenya were indifferent or firmly opposed to it. Many among the Kikuyu also opposed Mau Mau's methods, even if they sympathized with its political aims. Indeed, the victims of Mau Mau were principally Africans, especially tribal elders and Christian or propertied Kikuyu.

The political aims were best expressed in Mau Mau's alternative title (the Kenya Land Freedom Army), for the insurgency arose largely as a result of pressure on the land. This pressure was greatest in the so-called White Highlands. On average, the 3,000 European settlers in the region owned 3,460 acres each. They lived alongside 1.3 million Africans whose average land holding was but 23 acres. Moreover, most African agriculture was at subsistence level. Africans who worked as resident laborers for the settlers existed on low wages, and their use of the land was subject to many restrictions, such as strict stock control. Further pressure came from the existence of Crown land and forest reserves, thus as the African population increased, the land available to sustain it became more and more inadequate.

Amid increasing violence, a state of emergency was declared on 20 October 1952 following the murder of a Kikuyu chief loyal to the government. Mau Mau had a military wing and a political wing.

Supposedly, it was directed by a shadowy "Kenya Parliament" and a central committee based in Nairobi, but its only real organization was in Nairobi. The military wing was based largely in the Aberdare Forest at the foot of Mount Kenya; although Mau Mau may have numbered 12,000 at its peak in 1953, there was little contact between individual groups or gangs. Thus, when the Mau Mau leader on Mount Kenya, Waruhiu Itote (known as General China), was captured he knew little of the organization in the Aberdare. Indeed, lack of any obvious leadership made it difficult for authorities to dismantle the organization without large-scale detention. Mau Mau was poorly armed and its firearms often homemade. However, *pangas* (machetes) and axes were widely used to mutilate humans and livestock in almost atavistic savagery; activities also included arson and cattle rustling. Most Mau Mau attacks were undertaken under cover of darkness, and in any case the Kenyan police had little representation in the Kikuyu Reserve, and intelligence remained poor.

The British moved to arrest recognized leaders such as Kenyatta but were slow to grasp the scale of the insurgency. It was only in June 1953 that Kenya became an independent military command, with Sir George Erskine being appointed both commander in chief and director of operations. The same kind of coordinated response evident in the British response to the Malayan Emergency (1948–1960) then evolved with the establishment of a committee structure. The Aberdare and Mount Kenya were declared prohibited areas, and a range of emergency measures was introduced. Some 78,000 Africans were detained, and many were put through a program of psychological purification, including the administration of anti–Mau Mau oaths by government-sponsored witch doctors.

Erskine also introduced rural development schemes and resettlement, which affected possibly 1 million Kikuyu. Other reforms included improving native cattle herds and freeing Africans from existing restraints on growing cash crops. However, winning hearts and minds was not as successful as it was in Malaya, because neither independence nor significant political concessions were on offer. Indeed, it would appear that the majority in Mau Mau simply gave up the fight once it became clear that authorities would prevail. They did not change their attitudes toward the British, however, or abandon their sympathy for Mau Mau's aims.

Military pressure on Mau Mau was also steadily increased, with loyal tribesmen being enrolled in a Kikuyu Home Guard and many former Mau Mau recruited into pseudoforces known as countergangs under the direction of Eric Holyoak and Ian Henderson of the Kenyan police's Special Branch and a young seconded army intelligence officer, Frank Kitson.

Mau Mau was effectively defeated by October 1956 with the capture of the last leading insurgent leader, Dedan Kimathi. However, the emergency measures remained in force until 12 January 1960. The security forces had suffered about 600 dead, of whom 63 were white. Another 32 white civilians and possibly 2,000 Africans loyal to the government were killed. At least 11,500 Mau Mau were killed in action and more than 1,000 executed; 402 more died in detention, largely from disease. As a result of the emergency, the White Highlands were opened to African land ownership; more significantly, the British were concerned enough to accelerate progress toward independence. This came on 12 December 1963, Kenyatta being installed as Kenya's first president.

See also: British army; Erskine, Gen. Sir George; Hearts and minds; Intelligence; Kenyan Emergency; Kitson, Gen. Sir Frank Edward; Police; Pseudoforces; Resettlement

Further Reading: Edgerton, Robert, *Mau Mau: An African Crucible* (London, 1990); Furedi, Frank, *The Mau Mau War in Perspective* (London, 1989); Throup, David, *Economic and Social Origins of Mau Mau, 1945–1953* (London, 1987).

McCuen, Col. John Joachim (1926–)

McCuen was the author of *The Art of Counter-revolutionary War* (1966). He was one of a number of theorists attempting to develop a theory of "counterrevolution" capable of meeting the challenge posed by the kind of insurgency associated with Mao Tse-tung.

McCuen was educated at the U.S. Military Academy at West Point and later at Columbia University. He was commissioned in the U.S. army in 1949 and spent much of his military career in West Germany. However, he served as an adviser in Thailand (1957–1958) and was on the staff of the National Defense College in South Vietnam (1968–1969). He then joined the staff of the U.S. Army War College at Carlisle, Pennsylvania, from 1969 to 1972. He served in Indonesia from 1972 to 1974, returning to the Training and Doctrine Command in 1974. McCuen retired from the army in 1976 and entered business. Apart from his principal work, McCuen also wrote articles on French counterinsurgency and on Maoist theory.

In *The Art of Counter-revolutionary War,* McCuen identified four successive phases in the development of Maoist insurgency: subversion, terrorism, guerrilla warfare, and mobile warfare. Accordingly, his own theory precisely mirrored this sequence by suggesting appropriate countermeasures to be taken at each stage. McCuen also believed that there were five strategic principles equally applicable to revolutionary and counterrevolutionary forces: preserving oneself and annihilating the enemy, establishing strategic bases, mobilizing the masses, seeking external support, and unifying the effort.

See also: Mao Tse-tung
Further Reading: McCuen, John, *The Art of Counter-revolutionary War* (London, 1966).

McNamara Line

The McNamara Line was a defensive system established by the United States in 1967 along the demilitarized zone (DMZ) separating North and South Vietnam in an attempt to prevent communist infiltration into the South. The DMZ was a five-mile-wide buffer zone established by the Geneva accords in 1954 on the approximate line of the 17th parallel, although the actual border largely followed the Song Ben Hai River. Some consideration was given in 1965 and 1966 to stationing U.S. forces across the DMZ and in neighboring Laos. However, this was not thought to be politically possible since Laos remained a neutral state and the DMZ was regarded as inviolable under international law. Creating a permanent static defensive line would also have required enormous logistic effort and subjected U.S. forces to constant artillery bombardment from North Vietnam.

The construction of the McNamara Line, between April and September 1967, was a compromise solution in substituting a system of minefields, sensors, and designated "free fire" zones for a permanent garrison. The line was principally conceived by Robert Fisher of the so-called Jasons, a group of systems analysts who advised U.S. Secretary of Defense Robert McNamara on technical issues relating to the war in Vietnam. In the event, it was not possible to prevent continued infiltration through Laos, and the concept of the McNamara Line was discredited by the ability of North Vietnamese communists to concentrate large forces around Khe Sanh prior to launching the Tet Offensive in January 1968.

See also: Cordon sanitaire; Laos; Tet Offensive; Vietnam War
Further Reading: Krepinevich, Andrew, *The Army and Vietnam* (Baltimore, 1986).

Media

The media has had an increasing impact on the conduct of insurgency and counterinsurgency since 1945. Take, for example, the case of the United States in Vietnam between 1965 and 1973. It is widely assumed that hostile coverage in the American media played a significant part in turning domestic public opinion against the war. Yet the American media, if anything, tended to follow rather than direct public mood back home and thus merely reinforced views that were already held. Combat per se was not usually shown in close-up on American TV, although the overall coverage did reflect how the war lacked any coherent pattern. What affected public opinion more was the casualty rate—the "body count." Support for the Vietnam War in the United States fell approximately 15 percent each time U.S. casualties increased by a factor of ten (for example, from 1,000 to 10,000). Yet one might argue that the impact of the body count was magnified by media coverage.

Similarly, the British army suffered only 57 dead during its campaign in Aden between 1964 and 1967. Yet the effect was almost certainly accentuated by greater media attention, that is, when compared to the higher losses suffered in earlier campaigns such as the Malayan Emergency (1948–1960) and the Kenyan Emergency (1952–1960). This was especially so when 23 deaths occurred on a single day as a result of a police mutiny in June 1967.

A number of issues are raised by media involvement in insurgencies. In democratic societies, of course, media invariably assert the public's right to know the truth in pursuing freedom of the press. However, in any conflict short of a major war, there is not the same likelihood that the media will see its duty as supporting what might be termed national interests. Indeed, the media might be more interested in pursuing a good story or getting good images than in preserving objectivity.

Occasionally the media will trivialize events and may not understand military affairs. Yet security forces also have their agenda in wishing to win a campaign with minimum casualties and, as a result, will wish to preserve operational security. But in doing so the security forces will invariably separate the public's desire to know from the public's right to know. The security forces will also wish to discredit the insurgents and will wish to use the media for its own propaganda purposes. Insurgents, of course, thrive upon publicity in the course of waging what the Brazilian theorist of urban guerrilla warfare, Carlos Marighela, described as "armed propaganda." Insurgents will wish to demonstrate their own capabilities and to derive maximum political benefit from media exposure in terms of recruiting support, suggesting weakness in government, and bringing a sense of vulnerability to the public. Indeed, the insurgent needs the media as much as the media needs the insurgent.

Faced with insurgency, therefore, democratic societies face particular difficulty in balancing censorship against wider freedoms. In the case of Britain, for example, a total of 45 different TV programs relating to Northern Ireland were subject to censorship of some kind between 1968 and 1983. There was also consistent media opposition to the government's prohibition of broadcasting interviews with terrorists or anyone thought to support terrorism. As a result, terrorist spokesmen appeared on the screen, but their words were spoken by actors in voiceovers. By contrast, in the Irish Republic (Eire), the state broadcasting company, RTE, was prohibited from interviewing or even reporting on interviews with people belonging to certain organizations. The Irish press was also prohibited from publishing or printing documents that could be regarded as incriminating, treasonable, or seditious. However, the danger of imposing such excessive controls—especially in terms of withholding information—may merely encourage the media to seek more from insurgents.

See also: Aden; Marighela, Carlos; Northern Ireland; Propaganda; Terrorism; Vietnam War
Further Reading: Young, Peter (ed.), *Defence and the Media in Time of Limited War* (London, 1991).

Mexico

Mexico has frequently witnessed guerrilla warfare, the result of foreign intervention and internal conflict. During the Mexican War (1846–1848), the United States Army encountered guerrillas inside Mexico; its units also crossed into Mexican territory on occasion in pursuit of Apaches during the American Indian Wars. French Emperor Napoleon III took advantage of internal disorder within Mexico and the American Civil War (1861–1865) to attempt the conquest of Mexico between 1861 and 1867. The French were harassed by the guerrillas of Benito Juárez, one of the more celebrated episodes being the destruction of a force from the French Foreign Legion at Camerone (El Camarón) in April 1863.

Mexico enjoyed stability, albeit under the dictatorial rule of Gen. Porfirio Díaz, from the 1870s onward. However, in November 1910, Díaz was overthrown by a revolution led by Francisco Madero. Chaos ensued, the United States occupying the port of Vera Cruz between April and November 1914 after American seamen were arrested by forces under Victoriano Huerta, who had murdered Madero in 1913. U.S. intervention weakened Huerta's regime, but U.S. recognition of a former Madero supporter, Venustiano Carranza, disgusted another former supporter of Madero, Pancho Villa. Villa launched a raid on Columbus, New Mexico, in March 1916. Some 12,000 U.S. troops under the command of Brig. Gen. John Pershing were committed in a vain pursuit of Villa until February 1917.

Another figure to emerge from the chaos was Emiliano Zapata, who fought with Villa against both Huerta and Carranza. He was assassinated by Carranza's agents in 1917. Villa was assassinated in 1923. Order was effectively restored with the emergence of the Institutional Revolutionary Party in 1929. Indeed, no other party won even a state gubernatorial election in Mexico for another 60 years. The long rule of a single party bred its own frus-

trations, and in January 1994 the so-called Zapatista Army for National Liberation (EZLN), taking its name from Zapata, began a revolt in the southern state of Chiapas. Led by "Marcos," the movement claimed to represent the rights of indigenous Mayan natives. There has been a tenuous cease-fire since negotiations began with the government in October 1995. A Marxist group known as the Popular Revolutionary Army (EPR) also emerged in the central states of Oaxaca and Guerrero in June 1996.

See also: American Civil War; American Indian Wars; French Foreign Legion; Pershing, Gen. John Joseph; United States Army

Further Reading: Meyer, M. C., and W. L. Sherman, *The Course of Mexican History* (Oxford, 1987).

Mina, Francisco Espoz y (1781–1836)

Mina was a Spanish guerrilla leader opposing French occupation during the Peninsular War (1808–1814). A farmer's son from Navarre, he joined a guerrilla band led by his nephew in 1809 and became its leader when the latter was captured by the French in March 1810. Under Mina's command, the group expanded from 400 men to more than 7,000 by 1813. Mina, who became commander-general of Navarre, claimed in his memoirs to have inflicted 40,000 casualties on the French. During the Carlist War (1833–1840), Mina fought for Queen Isabella against those supporting her uncle, Don Carlos, the rival claimant to the Spanish throne. Subsequently, Mina moved abroad, ironically ending his days in France.

See also: French army; Peninsular War; Suchet, Marshal Louis-Gabriel, Duc d'Albufera

Further Reading: Tone, John L., *The Fatal Knot: The Guerrilla War in Navarre and the Defeat of Napoleon* (Chapel Hill, 1994).

Mitchell, Lt. Col. Colin (1925–1996)

Known to journalists as "Mad Mitch," Mitchell commanded the First Battalion, Argyll and Sutherland Highlanders, during the latter stages of the British campaign in Aden (1964–1967). Enlisting in the Home Guard at the age of only 14, Mitchell joined the Argylls in 1943 and saw service in Italy in the closing months of World War II. Service followed in Palestine, the Korean War (1950–1953), the Kenyan Emergency (1952–1960), Cyprus, and Borneo during the Malaysian/Indonesian Confrontation (1962–1966).

The aggressive Mitchell had a flair for publicity and, to the irritation of other units, ensured that his beloved battalion received maximum coverage during its tour in Aden. He also quarreled with the army commander in Aden, Maj. Gen. Philip Tower. Following police mutinies on 20 June 1967 whereby 23 British servicemen were killed, the nationalist insurgents gained control of Aden's Crater District. Mitchell became a national hero when he reoccupied Crater in a model operation in the early hours of 4 July without the loss of a single man. The Argylls did not leave Crater until four days before final British withdrawal in November 1967.

The subsequent selection of the Argylls for reduction as part of defense cuts in 1968 was widely seen as pique on the part of the Labour government, which had abandoned Aden. In reality, the Argylls were the junior Scottish battalion. Such was the public outcry that the battalion was retained at company strength and fully restored by Conservatives in 1972. Mitchell himself was denied the Distinguished Service Order (DSO) for his services in Aden as a result of Tower's antipathy and retired from the army. He was Conservative MP for West Aberdeenshire from 1970 to 1974 but decided not to seek reelection.

See also: Aden; British army; Confrontation, Indonesian/Malaysian; Cyprus; Kenyan Emergency; Palestine; Police
Further Reading: Mitchell, Colin, *Having Been a Soldier* (London, 1969).

Mondlane, Dr. Eduardo (1920–1969)

Mondlane founded the nationalist group Frente de Libertação de Moçambique (FRELIMO), which fought Portuguese control of Mozambique in 1962. The son of a minor chief of the Thonga tribe, Mondlane was educated by Methodist missionaries before winning a scholarship at the University of Witwatersrand in South Africa. In 1948 he left for the United States, gaining a degree from Oberlin College in 1953, followed by a doctorate from Northwestern University. After a year's research at Harvard, Mondlane worked for the United Nations. He became assistant professor of anthropology at Syracuse University in New York in September 1961 but left in June 1962 to establish FRELIMO's headquarters in Tanzania.

FRELIMO was formally founded in September 1962. It was always subject to internal conflict, and Mondlane was assassinated by a parcel bomb in February 1969. After Mondlane's death, FRELIMO grew steadily more oriented toward the Soviet Union, notably after the emergence of Samora Machel as leader in 1970.

See also: Frente de Libertação de Moçambique (FRELIMO); Machel, Samora Moïses; Mozambique; Portuguese army
Further Reading: Mondlane, Eduardo, *The Struggle for Mozambique* (Harmondsworth, 1969).

Montoneros

Montoneros was one of several groups waging urban guerrilla warfare in Argentina during the 1970s. Whereas Ejército Revolucionario del Pueblo (ERP) was Trotskyist, Montoneros owed nominal allegiance to the former president, Juan Perón Sosa, who had been exiled in 1955. Perón returned to power in September 1973 but died in July 1974; government was then assumed by his widow, "Isabelita." However, the Peróns proved less radical than the guerrilla groups had anticipated, and in turn the government repudiated the Montoneros. As a result, violence increased once more, and in March 1976 the army took control. The subsequent institutionalized counterterror of the dirty war (1976–1977) destroyed the Montoneros.

See also: Argentina; Dirty war; Ejército Revolucionario del Pueblo (ERP); Urban guerrilla warfare
Further Reading: Kohl, J., and J. Litt, *Urban Guerrilla Warfare in Latin America* (Cambridge, MA, 1974); Gillespie, R., *Soldiers of Peron* (Oxford, 1982).

Moplah Rebellion (1921–1922)

The Moplah Rebellion was an Islamic revolt in the Malabar coastal region of southwestern India. The Islamic Mappilla people had frequently proved troublesome to the British authorities, with frequent agrarian disturbances occurring between 1858 and 1919. A Muslim group calling itself the Khilafat Volunteers emerged in 1921 initially to oppose Hindu landlords. When the police tried to arrest its leaders in August 1921, widespread rioting broke out. An area of more than 2,000 square miles was affected. Martial law was declared, but in retaining the right to try suspected rebels the civilian authorities actually undermined any advantage gained from immediate punishments inflicted by military courts.

The British retained control of the key centers of Malappuram and Calicut and dispersed the main Mappilla concentration. However, the rebels' recourse to guerrilla tactics in the jungle forced the British to deploy nine British and Indian battalions and to undertake extensive small-unit patrolling. The rebellion was declared at an end in February 1922. The official figures for rebel losses were put at 2,339 killed and 1,652 wounded, with 5,955 being captured.

See also: British army; India
Further Reading: Townshend, Charles, *Britain's Civil Wars* (London, 1986).

Morice Line

The Morice Line was the physical barrier erected by the French in 1957 to prevent infiltration by the Front de Libération Nationale (FLN) into Algeria from neighboring Tunisia. Named after the French defense minister, André Morice, the line stretched 200 miles, from the Mediterranean Coast into the Sahara. Completed in September 1957, the line consisted of an eight-foot-high electric fence charged with 5,000 volts. The fence was bolstered by a 50-yard "killing zone" sown with antipersonnel mines. Electronic sensors detected any attempt to cut through.

At night the line was floodlit, and there was a cleared track behind the killing zone for routine patrols and mobile reaction forces in the event of an infiltration attempt. The line was also covered by automatically ranged 105mm howitzers. A very large number of French troops was required to police the line, but by January 1958 the French reckoned to have prevented 35 percent of the infiltration attempts, 80 percent by April. As a result, FLN forces inside Algeria were steadily isolated from external assistance. The similar but less extensive Pedron Line was constructed along the frontier between Algeria and Morocco.

See also: Algeria; French army; Front de Libération Nationale (FLN)
Further Reading: Horne, Alistair, *A Savage War of Peace* (London, 1977).

Morocco

Morocco came under French control between 1912 and 1934. The French established a protectorate in March 1912 partly in response to the use of Moroccan territory by Arab and Berber groups raiding into neighboring French Algeria. The first French resident-general was Louis-Hubert-Gonzalve Lyautey, who had made his reputation in Madagascar. Lyautey remained in Morocco, with the exception of a brief period during World War I, until 1925. He introduced the *tache d'huile* (oil slick) method of pacification, whereby military action joined a hearts-and-minds campaign offering protection, free medical assistance, and subsidized markets. Lyautey also ruled through traditional Islamic leaders whenever possible.

However, there were frequent challenges to French rule, one of the most serious being the extension to French territory in 1924 of the Rif Revolt of Abd el-Krim from neighboring Spanish Morocco. The French cooperated with the Spanish (Abd el-Krim actually surrendered to the French in May 1926). Final pacification of the Atlas Mountains in southern Morocco was not completed until March 1934. After World War II, nationalist agitation by the Istiqlal Party led to riots in 1947 and 1952. As violence increased, the French forced the Sultan, Mohammed V, to abdicate in August 1953 due to his links with the nationalists. However, he was restored in March 1955, and negotiations led to Morocco becoming independent in March 1956 (although some French troops remained until 1960). The attempt by Mohammed's son, King Hassan II, who ascended to the throne in 1961, to occupy the former Spanish territory of Western Sahara in 1975–1976 led to the continuing conflict with the Popular Front for the Liberation of Saguiet el Hamra and Rio de Oro (POLISARIO).

See also: Abd el-Krim, Mohammed ben; Algeria; French army; Hearts and minds; Lyautey, Marshal Louis-Hubert-Gonzalve; Pacification; Popular Front for the Liberation of Saguiet el Hamra and Rio de Oro (POLISARIO); *Tache d'huile;* Western Sahara
Further Reading: Porch, Douglas, *The Conquest of Morocco* (London, 1982).

Moros

The Moros are an Islamic people occupying the islands of Jolo and Mindanao in the Philippines. They constantly resisted Spanish rule from 1578 until 1898 and then equally resisted the United States Army and the Philippine Constabulary after 1898 and until the 1930s. They again took up arms against Pres. Ferdinand Marcos in the 1970s.

John Pershing made strenuous efforts to understand Moro culture both as a U.S. army captain on Jolo between 1901 and 1903 and then as governor of the Moro Province from 1909 to 1913. However, he miscalculated, pressing for Moro disarmament in 1911, and he was compelled to storm the Moro strongholds of Bud Dajo and Bud Bagsak. He also countered the fanatical *juramentados,* who took oaths to kill Christians, by having them buried with pig carcasses.

Yet the Moros remained suspicious of Christian domination of the autonomous administration established by the United States in 1935 and of the independent Filipino government after 1946. Similarly, the influx of a non-Muslim population into Mindanao played a significant part in stimulating the unrest that led the Marcos government to impose martial law in September 1972. Martial law merely led to the reemergence of Moro nationalism in the form of the Moro National Liberation Front (MNLF), led by Nur Misuari, and its military wing, the Bangsa Moro. The Moros occupied Jolo City at one point in January 1974, and following a cease-fire in December 1975 Marcos promised a degree of autonomy. However, Marcos conditioned the agreement on a referendum of all the southern population agreeing to autonomy for the Moros. This threatened to give the larger Christian population an effective veto over the deal, and fighting broke out again in October 1977. However, the Moro movement fragmented as different factions looked for assistance from Libya, Egypt, and Saudi Arabia. Some Moros even approached the resurgent communist insurgents of the indigenous New People's Army (NPA).

As a result of the split among the Moros, the communists became a greater threat to Marcos in the 1980s. When Marcos was toppled by a remarkable display of "people's power" in February 1986, the new government of Corazon Aquino offered a cease-fire to the Moros. It was not accepted.

See also: Pershing, Gen. John Joseph; Philippines; United States Army
Further Reading: George, T. J. S., *Revolt in Mindanao: The Rise of Islam in Philippines Politics* (Singapore, 1980).

Movimento Popular de Libertação de Angola (MPLA)

The Popular Movement for the Liberation of Angola (MPLA) was founded in the capital of the Portuguese colony of Angola, Luanda, in December 1956 by Dr. Agostinho Neto. Its leadership was dominated by *mesticos* (those of mixed race) like Viriato da Cruz and *assimilados* (assimilated Africans) like Neto. Most had been educated by either Methodist or Catholic missionaries. It drew its rank-and-file support, however, from the Mbundu tribe, whose traditional territory surrounded Luanda. As in other nationalist movements in the Portuguese colonies, however, there were splits in MPLA. Neto emerged as undisputed leader only in 1963, and there were internal conflicts in 1972 and 1974.

MPLA's ideology was strongly Marxist-Leninist. Its first 350 guerrillas were trained in Algeria; thereafter recruits were also trained in Bulgaria, Czechoslovakia, and the Soviet Union. MPLA rose in revolt in early 1961, but its early efforts were unsuccessful. A more sustained military campaign was begun by infiltrating into the Cabinda enclave from the neighboring Congo Republic in 1963. However, MPLA was soon forced to move its bases to Zambia through its failure to raise local support in Cabinda. MPLA opened an "eastern front" in the Moxico and Bié regions during 1966–1967, but its efforts there were badly damaged by the Portuguese army, and by 1974 it had retired once more to the Congo Republic and was reduced to long-range bombardment of Portuguese targets with mortars and rockets.

MPLA's claim that it controlled 50 percent of Angola at the campaign's peak in the east was false, and it is doubtful if more than a small proportion of its estimated 3,000–5,000 guerrillas ever operated permanently in Portuguese territory. Civil war broke out between MPLA and its nationalist rivals, Frente Nacional de Libertação de Angola (FNLA) and União Nacional para a Independência Total de Angola (UNITA), even before the Portuguese withdrew in November 1975. South Africa and the United States did provide some limited assistance to FNLA and UNITA, but the course of the civil war was determined by a massive Soviet airlift of Cuban troops to Angola between October 1975 and January 1976. FNLA disappeared but UNITA, led by Jonas Savimbi, continued to fight the MPLA government. The Cubans finally withdrew in 1991; MPLA won new elections in September 1992. This led to a renewal of guerrilla war by UNITA. Eventually, UNITA joined with MPLA, forming the Government of National Unity and Reconciliation in April 1997.

See also: Angola; Frente Nacional de Libertação de Angola (FNLA); Neto, Dr. Agostinho Antonio; Portuguese army; Roberto, Holden; Savimbi, Jonas; Uniao Nacional para a Independência Total de Angola (UNITA)

Further Reading: Bender, G. J., *Angola under the Portuguese* (London, 1978); Marcum, John A., *The Angolan Revolution* (Cambridge, MA, 1969 and 1978), 2 vols.

Mozambique

Mozambique was the last of the Portuguese colonies in Africa to experience insurgency, the nationalist group Frente de Libertação de Moçambique (FRELIMO) mounting its first attack on 25 September 1964. FRELIMO formed the government of Mozambique upon Portuguese withdrawal in June 1975 but has faced continuing opposition from the guerrilla movement Resistançia Naçional Moçambicana (RENAMO). The Portuguese had anticipated the likely start of operations by FRELIMO, which had been founded by Dr. Eduardo Mondlane in 1962. Consequently, the Portuguese army had reinforced the colony. The Portuguese also derived advantages from the natural barrier of the Rovuma River between Mozambique and FRELIMO's bases in Tanzania. In addition, FRELIMO was heavily dependent upon the support of the minority Makonde tribe of the Mueda Plateau and had to cross hostile Macua territory to reach it.

Friction was apparent within FRE-LIMO, with Comite Révolucionário de Moçambique (COREMO), or the Mozambican Revolutionary Committee, being an early breakaway movement. Mondlane was killed by a parcel bomb in February 1969, and there were further divisions before Samora Machel emerged as Mondlane's successor in May 1970. FRELIMO, therefore, had little success even when extending its operations to the Niassa region, where the Nyanja tribe proved more cooperative, in 1967. The Portuguese response was vigorous, not least under the direction of Gen. Kaulza de Arriaga between 1969 and 1973. Among other measures, Arriaga pressed ahead with resettlement and "social promotion" programs designed to win hearts and minds by providing farms, medical centers, schools, and cattle dips. FRELIMO did score a major success, however, in switching the focus of operations to the Tete Province in 1968.

Tete was vital as the site of the major Cabora Bassa Dam project. When completed in 1975, the dam would be the largest source of hydroelectric power in Africa. The Portuguese were taken by surprise, and although they prevented disruption of construction, their largely defensive role enabled Tete to become a base for Zimbabwe African National Union (ZANU) guerrillas operating against Rhodesia in 1972. FRELIMO began to infiltrate south and east from Tete that same year, reaching the Zambezia region for the first time in 1974. Despite these setbacks, the Portuguese had not lost the struggle when revolution back in Portugal in April 1974 signaled the end of colonial involvement.

Agreement was reached with FRE-LIMO in September 1974, and Mozambique became independent in June 1975. However, RENAMO emerged in 1976, first with Rhodesian and then South African support, although after Rhodesia's independence in 1980 Robert Mugabe committed Zimbabwean troops to the defense of the

road, rail, and pipeline links to Beira. Nevertheless, Machel was forced to conclude the Nkomati Agreement with South Africa in March 1984, Machel dropping support for the African National Congress (ANC) in return for South Africa repudiating RENAMO. Machel also abandoned some of FRELIMO's Marxist policies before his death in an air crash in October 1986, but RENAMO had already seized control of an estimated 85 percent of the country. RENAMO remains a formidable opponent of the FRELIMO government.

See also: African National Congress (ANC); Arriaga, Gen. Kaulza Oliveira de; Frente de Libertação de Moçambique (FRELIMO); Machel, Samora Moïses; Mondlane, Dr. Eduardo; Mugabe, Robert Gabriel; Portuguese army; Resistançia Naçional Moçambicana (RENAMO); Rhodesia; Zimbabwe African National Union (ZANU)
Further Reading: Newitt, Marlyn, *A History of Mozambique* (London, 1995); Rich, Paul, and Richard Stubbs (eds.), *The Counter-insurgent State* (London, 1997).

Mugabe, Robert Gabriel (1924–)

Mugabe emerged as the dominant figure of the Zimbabwe African National Union (ZANU), fighting against the white government of Rhodesia in 1974. He became prime minister of an independent Zimbabwe in April 1980 and executive president in December 1987.

A laborer's son who became a teacher, Mugabe joined Joshua Nkomo's National Democratic Party in 1960. Two years later, the party was renamed the Zimbabwe African People's Union (ZAPU). Mugabe was detained by the Rhodesian authorities in 1964, by which time ZANU had been founded by the Rev. Ndabaningi Sithole as a breakaway movement from ZAPU. However, Sithole was increasingly outmaneuvered by more radical elements, and Mugabe effectively became leader of ZANU after his release from detention in 1974. Mugabe and Nkomo forged the Patriotic Front in 1976, although the unity was largely fictional. Indeed, whereas ZAPU appealed primarily to the minority Ndebele population and Nkomo was an orthodox

Marxist, ZANU appealed to the majority Shona. Moreover, Mugabe followed the military theories of Mao Tse-tung. In the February 1980 elections that followed the settlement reached at the Lancaster House conference in London, ZANU triumphed.

See also: Mao Tse-tung; Nkomo, Joshua; Rhodesia; Zimbabwe African National Union (ZANU); Zimbabwe African People's Union (ZAPU)
Further Reading: Mugabe, Robert, *Our War of Liberation* (Gweru, 1983).

Mujahideen

The mujahideen (warriors of God) are Islamic fundamentalist guerrillas who first emerged in opposition to the Soviet-backed Marxist government of Afghanistan in the 1980s. A Marxist government came to power in Afghanistan in 1978 but split between two factions, Khalq (People's Party) and Parcham (Flag Party). In December 1979 the Soviets intervened in support of the latter. Soviet forces remained in Afghanistan until February 1989, by which time the conflict with the guerrillas had cost at least 13,000 lives. The Soviet army encountered opposition from the beginning, but the mujahideen constituted an alliance of at least seven different Sunni Muslim resistance groups that came together more formally in 1985. Largely based in Pakistan, the mujahideen became increasingly effective, not least after their receipt of Stinger antiaircraft missiles from the United States.

Once the Soviets withdrew, the mujahideen closed on the Afghan capital of Kabul. Kabul duly fell in April 1992, but the mujahideen fragmented, and civil war continues. Currently, Kabul is controlled by Taleban (Religious Students Movement), which seized the capital in September 1996.

See also: Afghanistan; Soviet army
Further Reading: Roy, O., *Islam and Resistance in Afghanistan* (Cambridge, 1986).

Namibia

Namibia has been a frequently contested territory. Known as German South West Africa from 1884 until 1920, it was the scene of the bloody Herero Revolt (1904–1907) against German rule. It was occupied by the South African army during World War I, and South Africa continued to administer what was called South West Africa against rising nationalist opposition. Indeed, the struggle between South Africa and the South West Africa People's Organization (SWAPO) lasted from 1966 until the independence of Namibia in 1990. South African forces also used the territory as a base form striking against other nationalists in neighboring Angola in the 1980s.

The German army's suppression of the Herero and Nama peoples involved systematic employment of scorched-earth tactics, described by Gen. Lothar von Trotha as a policy of *schrecklichkeit* (dreadfulness). In 1915, however, the German garrison was overrun by South African forces, and South Africa was then granted the League of Nations mandate to administer the territory in 1920 as an integral part of South Africa itself. In 1946 South Africa requested that the United Nations, the successor to the League, allow permanent incorporation. However, the UN refused and directed instead that the territory be placed under international trusteeship pending full independence. South Africa refused to do so and, indeed, introduced some of its apartheid policies (racial segregation) into South West Africa.

In October 1966 the UN General Assembly formally revoked the mandate; in June 1968 it renamed the territory Namibia and then demanded its independence. South Africa responded by formally incorporating the territory in 1969, but in July 1971 the International Court of Justice ruled that South Africa's occupation was illegal. A Herero organization known as the South West African National Union (SWANU) emerged in 1959 but was soon eclipsed by the appearance of SWAPO in April 1960, which appealed to the far more numerous Ovambo people. Led by Sam Nujoma, SWAPO opened a guerrilla campaign in August 1966, infiltrating into Namibia from Zambia by way of the 250-mile-long Caprivi Strip. The South African Police (SAP) and South African army had some success in combating SWAPO, but the situation deteriorated when the Portuguese left Angola in November 1975.

A civil war had broken out between the three nationalist factions that had fought the Portuguese even before they left. Indeed, South African forces were committed to Angola to assist União Nacional para a Independência Total de Angola (UNITA) in August 1975. However, the Soviet airlift of Cuban troops to Angola tilted the balance toward hard-line Marxists in the Movimento Popular de Libertação de Angola (MPLA). The South Africans withdrew from Angola in March 1976, and

SWAPO established bases there. Subsequently, there were a number of major South African raids from Namibia into Angola, as in May 1978, August 1981, and December 1983. Assistance was also given to UNITA. As a result, Angola was compelled to negotiate the Lusaka Accords in February 1984, dropping support for SWAPO in return for a cessation of South African raids. In turn, this facilitated negotiations between South Africa and SWAPO, and agreement on independence was reached in November 1988. It was also linked to the disengagement of Cuban troops from Angola. The UN supervised a cease-fire in Namibia in April 1989 and the subsequent elections of November 1989. SWAPO won the elections, and Namibia received its independence on 21 March 1990; Nujoma became president.

See also: Angola; German army; Herero Revolt; Movimento Popular de Libertação de Angola (MPLA); South African army; South West African People's Organization (SWAPO); Trotha, Gen. Lothar von; União Nacional para a Independência Total de Angola (UNITA)
Further Reading: Beckett, Ian, and John Pimlott (eds.), *Armed Forces and Modern Counter-insurgency* (London, 1985).

Nasution, Gen. Abdul Haris (1918–)

Nasution was an Indonesian nationalist and theorist of guerrilla warfare who fought against the Dutch in the Dutch East Indies between 1947 and 1949. Born in Kotanopan on Sumatra, Nasution was educated at the Dutch military academy in Bandung and joined the Royal Dutch Indies Army or Koninklijk Nederlandsch-Indisch Leger (KNIL) in 1941. Following the Japanese occupation of the Dutch East Indies during World War II, the Dutch attempted to reestablish control, launching a "police action" against the nationalists in June 1947. Nasution led the nationalist forces on Java until Indonesian independence in December 1949. He became chief of staff of the new Indonesian army in 1950 and minister of defense in 1959.

There had long been tension between the Indonesian armed forces and the Indonesian Communist Party. After Pres. Kusno Sosro Sukarno became seriously ill, the communists attempted a coup in September 1965. They aimed to eliminate the military leadership, and although six generals were murdered, Nasution escaped. Together with Gen. T. N. J. Suharto, Nasution led the army in suppression of the revolt. Estimates vary, but as many as 500,000 communists or suspected communists perished as the army seized effective control. The army also took the opportunity to end the Indonesian/Malaysian Confrontation (1962–1966).

Sukarno remained president but was eased from office in 1967; Suharto became acting president and then both president and supreme commander in 1968. Nasution was chairman of the People's Consultative Congress from 1966 until 1972. Nasution's book on guerrilla warfare, *Fundamentals of Guerrilla Warfare,* was originally published in 1953. Nasution worked independently of the theories of Mao Tse-tung. However, it bears a striking similarity to Maoist thought in its exposition of people's war and in Nasution's belief that the ultimate aim of the guerrilla should be the creation of a conventional army.

See also: Confrontation, Indonesian/Malaysian; Dutch army; Dutch East Indies; Mao Tse-tung
Further Reading: Nasution, Abdul Haris, *Fundamentals of Guerrilla Warfare* (London, 1956).

National Liberation Front (NLF)

The NLF was the hard-line Marxist nationalist group that fought against the British in Aden between 1964 and 1967. NLF emerged in June 1963, whereas the rival Front for the Liberation of Occupied South Yemen (FLOSY) did not appear until May 1965. Backed by the republican government that had come to power in neighboring Yemen in 1962, NLF began its campaign with a grenade attack that injured the

British high commissioner on 10 December 1963. NLF had a cell-like structure that made it difficult to obtain intelligence on its organization. Its first attacks were frequently amateurish but became steadily more effective. The favored methods were grenades and sniping. Often, carefully staged riots were designed to lure troops into the range of snipers.

The number of terrorist incidents rose from 286 in 1965 to 2,900 in 1967. The British response was not as assured as in some other postwar campaigns, the Labour government being uncomfortable with the perceived colonial role. As it became clear that the NLF was also winning the internal struggle with FLOSY, Arab officials of the British-sponsored Federation of South Arabia as well as some of the rulers of the outlying emirates, sultanates, and sheikhdoms threw in their lot with the NLF. NLF won the short civil war following the British withdrawal from Aden in November 1967. Subsequently, the NLF government of what was now known as the People's Democratic Republic of Yemen (PDRY) provided bases for the Popular Front for the Liberation of the Occupied Arabian Gulf (PFLOAG) operating in the Dhofar Province of Oman.

See also: Aden; British army; Dhofar; Popular Front for the Liberation of the Occupied Arabian Gulg (PFLOAG)
Further Reading: Harper, Stephen, *Last Sunset* (London, 1978).

Navarre, Gen. Henri-Eugène (1898–1983)

Navarre was the last French commander in chief in French Indochina from 1953 to 1954 and the architect of the disastrous decision to occupy and hold Dien Bien Phu. The son of a leading academic at Toulouse University, Navarre served in World War I and World War II. After World War II, Navarre served in Algeria and Germany before being appointed to succeed Raoul Salan in Indochina in May 1953.

Described as "air-conditioned" by one of his leading subordinates, Maj. Gen.

René Cogny, Navarre wanted to bring the communist Vietminh to battle. He intended to accomplish this by dropping parachute troops into Dien Bien Phu, which lay on the frontier between Laos and northern Vietnam, about 170 miles west of Hanoi. This would interdict the Vietminh supply lines into northern Laos and demonstrate French commitment to the Laotian government. At the same time, a garrison at Dien Bien Phu would assist the Meo peoples in resisting the communists and help reestablish French control over the region's opium crop, which provided the Vietminh considerable financial benefit. Establishing a "mooring-point" in communist-controlled territory would also force the Vietminh commander, Vo Nguyen Giap, to commit his forces to attacking the French fortified positions. The first French unit led by Col. Marcel Bigeard dropped on Dien Bien Phu on 20 November 1953.

The difficulty was that Dien Bien Phu was dominated by surrounding hills and so isolated that it could only be supplied by air. It was assumed that the Vietminh would not be able to bring artillery and antiaircraft batteries into the area. In the event, this proved tragically wrong, for Giap concentrated more than 37,000 men and more than 300 heavy guns against the French. As the Vietminh buildup became apparent, Navarre chose to reinforce the garrison rather than withdraw it in order to take on Giap. The French eventually committed about 10,800 men to Dien Bien Phu. After 55 days, the surviving French surrendered on 7 May 1954. The French had lost almost 2,000 dead, the Vietminh an estimated 8,000 dead and 15,000 wounded. The Geneva conference that led to French withdrawal from Indochina began on the day after Dien Bien Phu's surrender. Navarre retired from the army and entered the construction industry.

See also: Algeria; Bigeard, Gen. Marcel; Dien Bien Phu, Battle of; French army; French Indochina; Laos; Salan, Gen. Raoul
Further Reading: Fall, Bernard, *Hell in a Very Small Place* (London, 1966).

Neto, Dr. Agostinho Antonio (1922–1979)

Neto was the leader of Movimento Popular de Libertação de Angola (MPLA), which fought against the Portuguese army for the independence of Angola between 1961 and 1974. Born in Bengo, Neto was the son of a Methodist minister. He went to Portugal to study medicine but was imprisoned there between 1955 and 1957 for his political activities. Returning to Angola in 1959 to work as a doctor, Neto was again detained by the Portuguese. He escaped to Morocco in 1962.

The hard-line Marxist MPLA was founded in Luanda in December 1956, the leadership being dominated by *mesticos* (those of mixed race) such as Viriato da Cruz and *assimilados* (assimilated Africans) like Neto himself. When the Portuguese withdrew from Angola in November 1975, civil war broke out between MPLA and its nationalist rivals, Frente Nacional de Libertação de Angola (FNLA) and União Nacional para a Independência Total de Angola (UNITA). MPLA emerged as the victor thanks to the intervention and support of Cuban troops airlifted to Luanda by Soviet aircraft. Neto became president of Angola until his death, when he was succeeded by José Eduardo dos Santos. Neto also had a reputation as a poet.

See also: Angola; Frente Nacional de Libertação de Angola (FNLA); Movimento Popular de Libertação de Angola (MPLA); Portuguese army; União Nacional para a Independência Total de Angola (UNITA)
Further Reading: Marcum, John A., *The Angolan Revolution* (Cambridge, MA, 1969 and 1978), 2 vols.

Nicaragua

The Central American state of Nicaragua was the scene of one of the most significant guerrilla conflicts in the first half of the twentieth century. This guerrilla campaign, waged by Augusto Sandino against the Nicaraguan Guardia Naçional (National Guard) and its United States Marine Corps allies between 1927 and 1933, later inspired

the Sandinistas to bring down the government of Anastasio Somoza Debyle between 1974 and 1979. In turn, the victory of the Sandinistas led the United States to support the guerrilla campaign fought against the new government by former Somoza supporters, known as the Contras, between 1981 and 1989.

Nicaragua became independent from Spain in 1821 but did not become a separate republic until 1838, having been linked with both Mexico and a short-lived Central American state. It suffered frequent periods of instability and was often viewed by Americans as a target for annexation. Indeed, the American adventurer William Walker installed himself as president of Nicaragua in July 1856 but was defeated and forced to flee to the United States in May 1857. Walker was executed on another filibustering expedition in Honduras in 1860. There were nine subsequent U.S. interventions in Nicaragua between 1867 and 1912. Moreover, after the United States intervened to supervise new elections in August 1912, an American legation guard remained as guarantor of stability until August 1925.

Traditional rivalries between conservative and liberal factions resumed almost immediately thereafter, and U.S. Marines relanded in May 1926. The United States brokered a deal allowing for the disarming of rival factions and new elections. However, in July 1927 Sandino, at the time a relatively minor liberal leader in the province of Nueva Segovia, attacked the Marine garrison at Ocotal. Sandino's motivation was to rid Nicaragua of the American presence, his movement being announced in September 1927 as the Ejercito Defensor de la Soberania Nacional (EDSN), or Defending Army of the National Sovereignty of Nicaragua.

Sandino's ideology was vague, and he was more religious mystic than revolutionary, even though his initial advisers included communists like the Salvadoran Farabundo Martí and the Venezuelan Gus-

Victorious Sandinista rebels ride through downtown Managua, singing and celebrating their victory over Somoza, 19 July 1979. (UPI/Corbis-Bettmann)

tavo Machado. Nonetheless, if not a precursor of modern revolutionaries in ideological terms, Sandino's tactics were forward-looking. There was considerable sophistication in the targeting of American-owned companies, and Sandino enjoyed considerable international publicity. Although running an effective administration in Nueva Segovia, Sandino was unable to disrupt the presidential elections in 1928 and 1932. At one point, the United States had almost 4,000 men in Nicaragua and experimented with using airpower against Sandino's columns. The U.S. intervention proved increasingly unpopular at home, however, and the Americans withdrew in January 1933, having arranged new negotiations between Sandino and the liberal government of Juan Sacasa. In return for amnesty, Sandino laid down his arms and

retired to an agricultural collective. A year later, he was arrested and executed on the orders of the director of the National Guard, Anastasio Somoza García, the nephew of Sacasa.

Two years after Sandino's death, Somoza ousted Sacasa and seized power in Nicaragua. Somoza was assassinated in 1956 but control passed to his son, Luis Somoza Debyle. When Luis died in 1967, the presidency was assumed by his younger brother, Anastasio Somoza Debyle. The tight hold on power maintained by the Somoza dynasty alienated even the more privileged members of Nicaraguan society, and conservative and liberal factions mounted periodic challenges to the family. The Frente Sandinista de Liberación (FSLN), or Sandinista National Liberation Front, was formed in July 1961, but the Sandinistas (as they became known) enjoyed little initial success. But in the early 1970s a deteriorating economic situation stimulated support for the Sandinistas. This was coupled with widespread disillusionment with the government following its failure to cope with the aftermath of a major earthquake in Managua in 1972 and rumors that Somoza had pocketed international aid funds. The Sandinistas opened a more sustained guerrilla campaign in the Matagalpa Mountains in December 1974.

Somoza's response was to impose martial law. Recognizing the potential for exploiting general disaffection with the government, the Sandinistas modified their Marxist ideology in 1978 to extend their popular appeal. Riots and strikes became commonplace as more of the population vented displeasure with Somoza and his National Guard throughout the year. The Sandinistas began a new offensive in May 1979 and closed on Managua. On 17 July 1979 Somoza fled to the United States. He was assassinated in Paraguay in 1980.

The United States was alarmed at the prospect of Marxist control of Nicaragua and especially feared that the Sandinistas would now supply arms to the Frente Farabundo Martí de Liberación Nacional (FMLN) in El Salvador. An economic embargo was imposed on Nicaragua, and military assistance was channeled to opponents of the Sandinistas, many of whom were former national guardsmen. Several different groups, collectively known as the Contras and numbering about 15,000, began a guerrilla campaign against the Sandinistas from bases in both Honduras and Costa Rica in 1981. The U.S. Senate voted to suspend U.S. military assistance to the Contras in 1984; nonmilitary aid was resumed in June 1985. However, the deputy director for political and military affairs on Pres. Ronald Reagan's National Security Council, Lt. Col. Oliver North, sought to continue supporting the Contras by diverting funds received from illegal arms sales to Iran; the affair,

known as Iran-Contra, became public knowledge in November 1986.

Meanwhile, the Contadora Group of Central and South American countries had been seeking ways to achieve peace in Nicaragua since 1983. Agreement was finally reached in 1989, and new elections were held in February 1990. These resulted in a sweeping electoral defeat for the Sandinistas at the hands of a 14-party coalition known as the Union Nacional de la Oposición (UNO), or the National Opposition Union.

See also: Contras; Frente Farabundo Martí de Liberación Nacional (FMLN); Martí, Farabundo; Sandinistas; Sandino, Augusto César; United States Marine Corps (USMC)
Further Reading: Selser, G., *Sandino* (New York, 1981); Robinson, William, and Kent Norsworthy, *David and Goliath: Washington's War Against Nicaragua* (London, 1987).

Nkomo, Joshua (1917–)

Nkomo was the leader of the Zimbabwe African People's Union (ZAPU) fighting for the independence of Rhodesia between 1972 and 1979. The son of a teacher, Nkomo originally intended to become a social worker. Drawn into nationalist politics, he founded a group known as the African National Congress (not to be confused with that in South Africa) in 1957. Banned on a number of occasions, Nkomo's movement became the National Democratic Party in 1960 and ZAPU in 1962.

Nkomo was imprisoned from 1964 to 1974. After his release he joined the short-lived Zimbabwe Liberation Council in 1975 with other nationalists, including the Rev. Ndabaningi Sithole. Sithole had previously split from ZAPU, founding the Zimbabwe African National Union (ZANU) in 1963, but had been outmaneuvered by more radical elements within ZANU led by Robert Mugabe. In 1976 Nkomo forged the so-called Patriotic Front with Mugabe. ZAPU appealed primarily to the minority Ndebele people. Accordingly, following the negotiated end of white rule, ZAPU lost the subsequent British-supervised elections to ZANU in February 1980. Nkomo served in Mugabe's cabinet after independence in April 1980 but was dismissed two years later. However, in 1988 ZAPU was merged into ZANU and Nkomo became Zimbabwe's co–vice president two years later.

See also: Mugabe, Robert Gabriel; Rhodesia; Zimbabwe African National Union (ZANU); Zimbabwe African People's Union (ZAPU)

Further Reading: Moorcraft, Paul, and Peter McLaughlin, *Chimurenga* (Marshalltown, 1982).

Northern Ireland

"The Troubles" in Northern Ireland (Ulster) since 1969 represent one of the longest conflicts since the end of World War II. They are the result of intransigence of two communities in Northern Ireland, the Protestant majority (wishing to remain part of the United Kingdom) and nationalists among the Catholic minority (wishing to be part of a united Ireland).

Northern Ireland was created by the Anglo-Irish Treaty of 1921, whereby the six counties of Antrim, Armagh, Down, Fermanagh, Londonderry, and Tyrone were separated from the Irish Free State. Northern Ireland remained a part of the United Kingdom but with its own parliament at Stormont. Its boundaries were drawn in such a way as to guarantee Protestant primacy. Effectively, too, the Royal Ulster Constabulary (RUC) and its reserve, the Ulster Special Constabulary (or B Specials), was largely Protestant. By the mid-1960s Northern Ireland enjoyed a generally relaxed security situation. The Irish Republican Army (IRA) had begun a campaign of subversion in 1956, but it petered out by 1962. Living standards had improved with an extension of welfare and education. This stimulated the growth of a Catholic middle class, and Capt. Terence O'Neill of the ruling Unionist Party, who became prime minister of Northern Ireland in 1963, believed that he could draw these Catholics into Ulster's public life. However, O'Neill merely created rising expectations among the Catholics—about 38 percent of the popula-

tion—over the continuing discrimination in employment and housing. This expectation found expression in the Northern Ireland Civil Rights Association (NICRA), formed in February 1967.

NICRA, which demanded reform of the local government franchise and legislation against discrimination, organized its first civil rights march in August 1968. It claimed to be nonsectarian but embraced nationalist groups such as the Derry Citizens Action Committee and People's Democracy. Opposed by hard-line Protestants such as the founder of the Free Presbyterian Church, the Rev. Ian Paisley, NICRA's marches became increasingly violent. O'Neill introduced a reform package in November 1968, but it was rejected by People's Democracy. The latter organized a march from Belfast to Londonderry on 4 January 1969, which was met by a violent Protestant counterprotest at Burntollet Bridge.

Despite further reforms introduced by O'Neill, the violence escalated, and in May 1969 he resigned. O'Neill's successor, Maj. James Chichester-Clark, announced an amnesty for anyone arrested on public order offenses. However, the concessions to the Catholics convinced Protestants that they needed to reassert their own rights. The Protestant "Apprentice Boys" march in Londonderry on 12 August 1969 resulted in more confrontation. Catholics erected barriers around "Free Derry," and the RUC became exhausted and demoralized by its failure to restore order. On 14 August the British government of Harold Wilson deployed troops to contain communal violence in Londonderry. On 19 August 1969 tactical control passed from the police to the British army.

Initially, the army was welcomed by many within the Catholic population, and the barricades were removed. Wilson sought to reassure the Protestants that Ulster would remain part of the United Kingdom unless the majority willed otherwise but also emphasized the need for more reforms. In October the Hunt Committee recommended disbanding the B Specials. This sparked riots in Protestant areas; the first RUC man to be killed in "the Troubles" on 11 October 1969 was a victim of this Protestant backlash. However, the Catholic community was increasingly resentful of the slow pace of reform, of the relationships developing between British soldiers and some Catholic girls, and of the arms searches being conducted in Catholic areas.

The first street clash between the army and Catholic youths occurred in Belfast on 1 April 1970. Initially, the IRA had been surprised by the developments. Indeed, in September 1969 the so-called Belfast Brigade of the IRA broke away from the old-style, southern-based leadership of the "Officials" to form the Provisional IRA (PIRA). PIRA killed its first British soldier on 6 February 1971. Later, the Irish Republican Socialist Party was also to break with the Officials in December 1974, its military wing being the Irish National Liberation Army (INLA). The Officials declared a cease-fire in February 1972.

Wilson's Conservative successor, Edward Heath, refused to send additional troops. As a result, Chichester-Clark resigned in March 1971 and was replaced by Brian Faulkner. Faulkner was a pragmatist and favored offering the Catholics a limited share in government. However, renewed violence caused Faulkner to seek something else to satisfy his more militant supporters. As a result, he urged the introduction of internment. The army did not favor this solution, yet Heath, seeing little alternative other than the imposition of direct rule from London, agreed. Introduced on 9 August 1971, internment proved a failure due to defective intelligence on PIRA. It provoked considerable resentment among the Catholic community, culminating in the deaths of 13 civilians in the "Bloody Sunday" incident in Londonderry on 30 January 1972. Direct rule followed on 24 March 1972. Stormont was prorogued, and Faulkner resigned in protest. Internment

was scaled down, and Heath briefly opened negotiations with PIRA, although the cease-fire endured only from 26 June to 9 July 1972. At the same time, however, the British were determined to do something about the "No-go" areas that had been set up in Catholic areas. Consequently, on 31 July 1972 "Operation Motorman" removed the barricades.

With direct rule, the security situation improved. In 1973 the government brought forward a plan for a Northern Ireland Assembly, to be elected by proportional representation, and a 12-strong power-sharing executive. An all-Ireland dimension was added with a proposed Council of Ireland. The Executive itself took office on 1 January 1974, but Faulkner's decision to participate split the Unionist Party, Paisley forming the new Democratic Unionist Party (DUP). The Executive was brought down in May 1974 by a general strike led by the Ulster Workers Council. That event was backed by Protestant paramilitary groups such as the Ulster Freedom Fighters (UFF) and Ulster Defence Association (UDA), which had recently emerged. PIRA again declared a cease-fire between 22 December 1974 and 22 November 1975; Wilson, by now back in office, responded by releasing remaining internees.

An additional political initiative was a constitutional convention, but the May 1975 elections were won by hard-line Protestants, and the convention's recommendation to restore Stormont led to its dissolution in March 1976. A policy of "Ulsterization" was announced in January 1977 by which the RUC and the Ulster Defence Regiment (UDR), created in 1970, would take over more of the policing responsibility from the army. A short-lived "Peace People" movement also emerged, but the attempt to organize all-party talks failed. A new phase began in 1978 with the so-called dirty protest by republican prisoners against the withdrawal of special category status. Successive British governments were not prepared to decriminalize paramilitaries in this way. PIRA then orchestrated hunger strikes, which were called off after ten prisoners died. One, Bobby Sands, had been elected to the House of Commons before his death, marking a move by PIRA toward a dual political and military strategy. This was articulated as one of "a ballot paper in one hand and an Armalite in the other." Thus, the nationalist political party closely associated with PIRA, Sinn Féin (Ourselves Alone), challenged the constitutional nationalist party, the Social Democratic and Labour Party (SDLP), for the Catholic vote.

Prime Minister Margaret Thatcher, whose Conservative government was elected in 1979, continued to seek a new political initiative. A Northern Ireland Assembly was elected in October 1982, but it was boycotted by all parties except the DUP and the small, nonsectarian Alliance Party. As a result, Thatcher sought an accord with the Irish Republic, concluding the Hillsborough or Anglo-Irish Agreement on 15 November 1985. This allowed for a joint governmental consultative office in Ulster and an intergovernmental conference in which the republic could represent Ulster Catholics. Protestants reacted strongly against Hillsborough. The DUP now left the assembly, and it was dissolved in June 1986.

The political impasse was breached thanks only to January 1990 talks about devolution for Ulster. However, the talks ended in deadlock in November 1992. The British and Irish governments signed the Downing Street Declaration in December 1993, both committing to a settlement based on nonviolence and consent. In February 1993 the British had also begun talks with PIRA. On 1 September 1994 a new PIRA cease-fire came into effect, only to end in February 1996. The end of the cease-fire followed the British decision to hold elections for a consultative body to proceed to all-party talks on the basis of conditions laid down by the U.S.-sponsored Mitchell Commission of December 1995. A peace forum was elected in May

1996 and negotiations began the following month; they included representatives of the Protestant paramilitaries that had declared a cease-fire in October 1994. PIRA declared another cease-fire in July 1997, and as a result Sinn Féin was permitted to join the talks in September 1997. The DUP left the talks, but the Official Unionists' United Unionists Party (UUP) remained. A deadline for agreement was set by the British and Irish governments for April 1998. An agreement was signed on 10 April 1998 allowing for the recognition of the principle of consent, an assembly, and power-sharing executive, a North-South ministerial council, a council of the Isles, and a commitment to disarmament of paramilitaries. It was submitted to a referendum on 22 May 1998 and approved by a large majority. However, splits within the republican movement led to a new atrocity at Omagh in August 1998 in which a bomb killed 28 people. The new executive was due to begin work in September 1998. As of February 1997 "the Troubles" had resulted in 3,211 deaths in Northern Ireland.

See also: British army; Intelligence; Ireland; Irish Republican Army (IRA); Police
Further Reading: Arthur, P., and Jeffery Keith, *Northern Ireland since 1969* (Oxford, 1988).

North-West Frontier

Service along the North-West Frontier on the India-Afghanistan border provided practical instruction in colonial warfare to generations of British army soldiers. The mountains of the Hindu Kush, some 200 miles northwest of the Indus River, separate Central Asia from southern Asia. Almost 600 miles in length, the mountain chain frequently reaches 20,000 feet in height. The means of crossing the Hindu Kush and the lesser Sulaiman Range to its immediate south were a series of high mountain passes such as the Khyber, Bolan, and Kurram through the Sulaiman. Between the Indus River and the Hindu

Kush was what the British referred to as tribal territory. This was principally inhabited by the martial Pathan peoples, who took little notice of the formal frontier between India and Afghanistan and owed allegiance to separate tribes and clans such as the Afridi, Wazir, Mahsud, and Mohmand. However, there were also other peoples, such as the Ghilzai, with similar subgroups in what has been described as "an ethnological jigsaw of frightening complexity."

The British, who had established themselves in Bengal, Madras, and Bombay during the eighteenth century, did not show particular interest in events beyond the Indus until the 1830s. British mediation was being sought by the emir (ruler) of Afghanistan, Dost Mohammed, who had recently defeated the Sikh army. The Sikhs supported the previous Afghan ruler, Shah Shuja, whom Dost Mohammed had deposed in 1810. However, the British were well disposed toward the Sikhs and concluded that Dost Mohammed was too friendly toward the Russians. As a result, they resolved to depose Dost Mohammed and replace him with Shah Shuja. What became known as the First Afghan War (1838–1842) saw the British army invade Afghanistan in December 1838 by way of the Bolan. It occupied Kabul in August 1839. However, the Afghans rose against the British in December 1841, and the British army was cut to pieces as it retreated from Kabul. The British left Afghanistan alone for another 30 years.

However, by the 1870s the Russians were rapidly advancing in Central Asia. The British became determined to maintain Afghanistan as a buffer against Russian expansion and in 1876 sought to persuade Amir Sher Ali, one of Dost Mohammed's sons, to exclude Russian envoys from Kabul. When Sher Ali declined to do so, the British launched the Second Afghan War (1878–1881), sending three columns into Afghanistan by way of the Bolan, Khyber, and Kurram Passes in November 1878. Kabul was again occupied, in

May 1879, and the Afghans accepted a British envoy in the capital. British troops were withdrawn, but in September 1879 the British envoy was murdered. Lt. Gen. Sir Frederick Roberts reoccupied Kabul in October 1879 and a nephew of Sher Ali, Abdur Rahman, was installed as amir in July 1880. The British again withdrew from Afghanistan in March 1881 but retained a degree of influence over Afghan affairs. Abdur Rahman retained the throne until his death in 1907, and the British did not reenter Afghanistan again until the Third Afghan War (1919), when the Afghans sought greater freedom of action.

During the Second Afghan War, the British had pushed the frontier of India forward to Quetta in Baluchistan; they also occupied the Kurram and secured permanent access to the Khyber. In 1893 Abdur Rahman accepted a new boundary along the so-called Durand Line, which gave the British control of still more tribal territory. Coupled with the British annexation of Burma in 1886, India's frontiers now stretched for more than 4,700 miles. The North-West Frontier Province in particular gave soldiers constant problems but also an unrivaled practical military training ground. When political initiatives failed to exact satisfaction for a kidnapping, murder, or border raid, a punitive expedition was mounted. In 1888, 1890, and 1891, for example, expeditions were mounted against the Black Mountain tribes; in 1895 the British garrison in Chitral was besieged and had to be relieved. In 1897 the "Mad Mullah of Swat" raised virtually all the frontier against the British. The Malakand garrison held off a determined attack in July 1897, but the garrison in the Khyber was overwhelmed. Expeditions had to be mounted against the Mohmand, Orakzai, and Afridi in order to suppress the rising.

There were other serious tribal uprisings on the frontier in the 1930s, to which the British responded with the use of airpower. One occurred in Waziristan in 1936 after the emergence of the religious fanatic known as the Fakir of Ipi. In July 1947 the North-West Frontier Province voted overwhelmingly to join the new state of Pakistan.

See also: Afghanistan; Airpower; British army; Colonial warfare; India; Roberts, Field Marshal Earl (Frederick Sleigh)

Further Reading: Swinson, Arthur, *North-West Frontier* (London, 1967); Elliott, J. G., *The Frontier, 1839–1947* (London, 1968).

Office of Strategic Services (OSS)

The OSS was formed during World War II (June 1942) to coordinate U.S. efforts supporting resistance movements in German-occupied Europe and Japanese-occupied Southeast Asia. It succeeded the Office of Coordination of Information established by Col. William "Wild Bill" Donovan in July 1941. In practice, OSS was bedeviled by rivalries and intrigues that tend to proliferate in the world of secrets. Thus, it clashed with the Federal Bureau of Investigation (FBI), which jealously guarded its own role in security affairs, and with the U.S. commander in the Southwest Pacific, Douglas MacArthur, who wanted to run his own organization independent of OSS. On occasions, relations were also strained between OSS and the British Special Operations Executive (SOE), notably in Greece and Southeast Asia. In the case of French Indochina, for example, SOE supported the French authorities even as OSS assisted Ho Chi Minh's Vietminh. Partisan units were also raised by OSS agents in Europe, as was "Detachment 101" (from Karen tribesmen) in Burma. These units, rather than the United States Army's long-range penetration units, such as the Rangers and Special Service Force, were the real forerunners of the postwar U.S. Special Forces (Green Berets), which were revived in 1952. OSS, which had at least 13,000 operatives during World War II, was replaced after the war by the U.S. Central Intelligence Agency (CIA).

See also: Burma; French Indochina; Green Berets; Ho Chi Minh; Partisans; Special Operations Executive (SOE); United States Army; Vietminh
Further Reading: Harris-Smith, R., *OSS* (Los Angeles, 1972); Smith, B. F., *The Shadow Warriors* (New York, 1983).

Okamura, Gen. Yasuji (1884–1966)

Okamura was commander of the Japanese North China Area Army, which fought Chinese communist guerrillas under Mao Tse-tung during World War II. The communists had launched the so-called Campaign of a Hundred Regiments against the Japanese army in August 1940. This convinced the Japanese of the need to suppress what they had previously regarded as mere banditry. Okamura, who had helped plan the Japanese invasion of Manchuria in 1931, took over the North China Area Army in July 1941 and ordered a "security strengthening campaign" and what he also referred to as "pacification by prolonged occupation."

Japanese methods during the next 18 months were brutally efficient, based on the three principles of "take all, burn all, kill all." However, the momentum of the Japanese campaign could not be sustained when resources were increasingly diverted to the main conflict with the nationalist Kuomintang (KMT) and to the war in the Pacific. In November 1944 Okamura was promoted to command all Japanese forces in China. He surrendered to the KMT at Nanking in September 1945. He acted as military adviser to the KMT when the Chinese Civil War (1927–1949) resumed between the nationalists and communists; that enabled him to avoid trial as a war criminal.

See also: Chinese Civil War; Japanese army; Kuomintang (KMT); Mao Tse-tung
Further Reading: Lee, C. S., *Counterinsurgency in Manchuria: The Japanese Experience* (Santa Monica, 1967).

Organisation d'Armée Secrète (OAS)

OAS, or the Secret Army Organization, was the terrorist group created by dissident French army officers to oppose Charles de Gaulle's policy of giving Algeria its independence. De Gaulle announced his intention of allowing Algerian self-determination in September 1959, creating immediate unease among French soldiers as well as *colons* (European settlers) in Algeria. The existence of OAS surfaced in January 1961 when a *colon* lawyer who had expressed support for de Gaulle was murdered.

Following a failed coup led by Gen. Raoul Salan against de Gaulle in Algeria in April 1961, those who escaped arrest took over the direction of OAS. Salan, for example, became the overall commander. Col. Yves Godard, one of the architects of the army's victory over the nationalist Front de Libération Nationale (FLN) in the battle of Algiers in 1957, became chief of the OAS "general staff." Intending to create general instability in Algeria, OAS used *plastique* (plastic explosive), often to devastating effect. Hit squads known as Delta Commandos led by a former lieutenant in the French Foreign Legion, Roger Degueldre, assassinated opponents of the organization.

Salan was content to restrict operations to Algeria, but others (including two former colonels, Antoine Argoud and Charles Lacheroy, who helped develop the French theory of counterinsurgency known as *guerre révolutionnaire*), advocated extending the campaign to France itself. Thus, Salan was unhappy with an assassination attempt on de Gaulle in Paris in September 1961, which came close to succeeding. The OAS aroused public anger when one of its bombs killed a four-year-old in February 1962. The French police were steadily closing in, and Salan was arrested in April 1962. Some continued the struggle for a few months more, but Algeria duly became independent in July 1962.

See also: Algeria; Algiers, Battle of; French army; French Foreign Legion; Front de Libération Nationale (FLN); Godard, Col. Yves; *Guerre révolutionnaire*
Further Reading: Henissart, Paul, *Wolves in the City* (London, 1970).

Pacification

In the context of guerrilla warfare, *pacification* means far more than simply suppressing guerrillas by military means. It has long been recognized that guerrillas can be undermined by offering populations security against guerrilla intimidation and positive reasons to support government. Thus, *pacification* implies combining military and political or socioeconomic measures in order to redress popular grievances.

The French army doctrine of *tache d'huile* (oil slick), developed by Joseph-Simon Galliéni in French Indochina and Madagascar at the end of the nineteenth century, combined military and political action. Similarly, the United States Marine Corps promoted "civic action" during its campaigns in the Caribbean and Central America before and after World War I. As a result, the Marines coupled antiguerrilla military action with the construction of schools, roads, and harbors. Agricultural and industrial development projects were started, and there was even enforcement of sanitation regulations.

With American advice, the government of South Vietnam attempted civic action projects such as the Hop Tac (Cooperation) program in 1964 and the Revolutionary Development, or Rural Construction, program in 1965. However, these efforts were halfhearted and badly coordinated until the United States created the organization known as Civil Operations and Revolutionary Development Support (CORDS)

in 1967; it was renamed Civil Operations and Rural Development Support in 1970. The U.S. Marines also launched a pacification program in South Vietnam, the so-called county fair operations, offering medical and other assistance to villagers in a relaxed, "county fair" atmosphere. However, in South Vietnam pacification could not make up for the government's illegitimacy in the eyes of much of the population.

In many cases *pacification* can mean a greater emphasis on military rather than political action. It is significant that the British army has always used the phrase "winning hearts and minds" rather than "pacification" to describe its approach to civic action, implying a greater willingness than some other armies to subordinate the military response to the political response.

See also: British army; Civil Operations and Rural Development Support (CORDS); French army; French Indochina; Galliéni, Marshal Joseph-Simon; Hearts and minds; *Tache d'huile;* United States Marine Corps (USMC); Vietnam War
Further Reading: Hunt, R. A., *Pacification* (Boulder, 1995).

Palestine

Palestine has been contested by Arabs and Jews for much of the twentieth century. There have been four conventional wars (1948–1949, 1956, 1967, and 1973) between the Arab states and the Jewish state of Israel established in 1948. The Israeli army has intervened in Lebanon on two occasions (1978 and 1982) and still maintains a "security zone" in southern Lebanon. There was also the sporadic War of Attrition between Egypt and Israel along the Suez Canal from 1969 to 1970. In addition, the state of Israel has faced a continuing challenge from Arab guerrilla and terrorist groups such as the Palestine Liberation Organization (PLO). A serious uprising known as the Intifada (literally, "Shuddering") occurred within Israeli-occupied territory between 1987 and 1993. Jewish terrorist groups fought the British between 1944 and 1948 prior to the establishment of Israel; British control of Palestine was also challenged before World War II during the Arab Revolt (1936–1939).

The roots of the modern conflict in Palestine lie in the events of World War I, when Britain and France gave contradictory promises to Arabs and Jews in order to enlist their support in the war against the Ottoman empire of Turkey. Whereas the British encouraged the first Arab Revolt (1916–1917) against the Turks by promising a degree of postwar autonomy, they and the French promised Zionists a national home in Palestine. In the event, the British and French divided Turkey's Middle East territories, with League of Nations mandates for Palestine, Iraq, and Transjordan (later Jordan) passing to Britain and Syria and that for Lebanon to France. Jewish immigration into Palestine increased after World War I, confronting the British with the problem of reconciling differing Jewish and Arab demands. Arab opposition to immigration led to the Second Arab Revolt in July 1936. Partition of Palestine was recommended by the Peel Commission in July 1937, but in February 1939 the British resolved on independence within ten years. However, this resolution did not include partition, and the British announced new restrictions on Jewish immigration.

British intentions were undermined in the immediate aftermath of World War II by U.S. support for lifting all restrictions on immigration and a separate Jewish state. British police had already been attacked by Irgun Zvai Leumi and the Stern Gang dur-ing the war; the Jewish groups wanted to pressure Britain into withdrawal. The official representative of the Jewish community, the Jewish Agency, also lost patience with the British. It therefore committed its own military forces, Hagana (Defense) and Palmach (Shock Companies), to a joint military campaign with Irgun and the Stern Gang in October 1945. The bombing of the King David Hotel in Jerusalem by Irgun in July 1946 broke the Jewish Agency's resolve, however, and it withdrew from the campaign. Irgun and the Stern Gang continued, and their highly efficient terrorist campaign confronted the British, as Menachem Begin of Irgun always intended, with a direct choice between total repression and withdrawal. The British turned over the problem to the United Nations in February 1947, and in September Britain announced it would withdraw from Palestine by 15 May 1948.

The UN revived the concept of partition, but in May 1948 the new state of Israel was attacked by the forces of the Arab League (Egypt, Syria, Lebanon, Iraq, Transjordan, and Saudi Arabia). Astonishingly, the Israelis won the so-called War of Independence, consolidating control over all of Palestine with the exception of the West Bank of the Jordan River and the Gaza Strip. The Israelis faced crossborder raids from Arab guerrillas known as fedayeen (commandos) based in Gaza during the early 1950s. Consequently, when the British and French resolved to oppose the nationalization of the Suez Canal by Egypt's Pres. Gamal Abdel Nasser in 1956, the Israelis cooperated, launching an attack into Gaza and the Sinai Desert. British and French withdrawal in turn compelled the Israelis to do the same in the Sinai.

PLO attacks against Israel began in the early 1960s. However, in June 1967 the Israelis responded to Nasser's closure of the Strait of Tiran, which led to the main Israeli port of Elat, with a preemptive strike against Egypt, Syria, and Jordan. Israel's stunning victory in the Six Day War resulted in the occupation of the Sinai, Gaza, the West Bank, and the Golan Heights on the Syrian border. Apart from artillery bombardments across the Suez Canal that characterized the aforementioned War of Attrition, Arab responses more often than not came in the form of terrorism. Egypt and Syria attacked Israel yet again in October 1973 in the October, or Yom Kippur, War, but the Israelis survived early reverses to drive back their assailants. Defeat led Egypt's Pres. Anwar Sadat to negotiate a peace deal with Israel in March 1979, by which the Israelis evacuated Sinai by April 1982. The PLO had been expelled from Jordan in 1970 and moved its bases to Lebanon.

Continuing PLO terrorist attacks from Lebanon brought Israeli interventions in 1978 and 1982. In turn, Israel's continued occupation of the West Bank and Gaza caused increased frustration among Palestinians under Israeli control; the Intifada began in December 1987. It focused new attention on the problem; ultimately, Israeli negotiations with the PLO resulted in the establishment of a Palestinian administration for parts of Gaza and the West Bank in September 1993. It is clear, however, that tensions remain high.

See also: Arab Revolt, First (1916–1917); Arab Revolt, Second (1936–1939); Begin, Menachem; British army; Irgun Zvai Leumi; Israeli army; Palestine Liberation Organisation (PLO); Palmach; Stern Gang; Terrorism
Further Reading: Pimlott, John (ed.), *The Middle East Conflicts* (London, 1983).

Palestine Liberation Organization (PLO)

The PLO is an umbrella organization comprising a number of different Palestinian groups. It is regarded by the Arab League as the sole representative of Palestinian Arabs and their aspirations for the liberation of Palestine from Israeli control.

The PLO was founded in June 1964 at a meeting in Cairo of the Palestinian National Council, itself a government-in-exile. Among the groups that joined the PLO

was al-Fatah (Conquest), whose leader, Yasser Arafat, was to become chairman of the PLO as a whole in 1969. Other groups associated with PLO have included the Popular Front for the Liberation of Palestine (PFLP), the Arab Liberation Front (ALF), and Black September, which carried out the 1972 terrorist attack against Israeli athletes during the Summer Olympics in Munich.

After Israel defeated the Arab states in the Six Day War in June 1967, PLO terrorism and guerrilla action became the principal means by which Arabs struck back at Israel. However, the PLO's destabilizing presence led to its expulsion from Jordan in September 1970. It shifted its bases to Lebanon, prompting major interventions by the Israeli army in 1978 and 1982. The PLO was forced to move its headquarters to Tunisia. However, in July 1988, King Hussein of Jordan ceded to the PLO his claims to the West Bank, which had been occupied by Israel since 1967. In November 1988 the PLO declared the independence of a Palestinian state based on the occupied West Bank, yet at the same time it recognized Israel's right to exist in the expectation that that gesture would facilitate negotiations.

The PLO has frequently suffered internal splits. In recent years its leadership of the Palestinian cause has been challenged by hard-line Islamic groups such as Hamas (Zeal), which came to particular prominence during the Palestinian uprising, or Intifada (literally, "Shuddering"), in Israeli-occupied Gaza and the West Bank in 1987. The PLO also lost its remaining bases in southern Lebanon in July 1991 when it was expelled by the Lebanese army. Nonetheless, as part of the wider Middle East peace process sponsored by the United States, the PLO was able to take over administration of some parts of Gaza and the West Bank in September 1993. The PLO has not found this an easy task, however, and the peace process remains tenuous.

See also: Israeli army; Palestine; Terrorism
Further Reading: Cobban, H., *The PLO* (Cambridge, 1984).

Palmach

The name Palmach is derived from Plu-goth Mahatz (Shock Companies). Palmach was the Jewish Agency's strike force in Palestine during World War II; thus it was the forerunner of the Israeli army's special forces after the state of Israel was created in 1948. Palmach developed from the Special Night Squads that were raised by British officer Orde Wingate to protect the oil pipeline from Haifa into Iraq against Arab sabotage during the Arab Revolt (1936–1939). It was loosely associated with Hagana (Defense), the principal military arm of the Jewish Agency.

During World War II, Palmach helped British army operations against the Vichy French authorities in Syria in 1941. Between November 1944 and June 1945 Hagana and Palmach were directed by the Jewish Agency to neutralize the extremists in Irgun Zvai Leumi and the Stern Gang, whose terrorism was jeopardizing the agency's political campaign to persuade British authorities to augment Jewish immigration into Palestine. When the Jewish Agency lost patience with British policy, Hagana and Palmach were committed in October 1945 to a joint terrorist campaign against the British known as Tenuat Hameri (United Resistance Movement). The alliance was dissolved in August 1946 following Irgun's bombing of the King David Hotel in Jerusalem.

As the British began their withdrawal from Palestine in autumn 1947, Hagana and Palmach began preparing for the coming struggle against the Arabs. Palmach had about 3,000 men in 1947, expanding to ten battalions by early 1948. It fought gallantly in trying, unsuccessfully, to hold the Old City of Jerusalem against the Arab Legion in May 1948.

See also: Arab Revolt, Second (1936–1939); British army; Irgun Zvai Leumi; Israeli army; Palestine; Stern Gang; Wingate, Maj. Gen. Orde Charles
Further Reading: Katz, S. M., *Israeli Special Forces* (Osceola, 1993).

Partido Africano da Independência de Guiné e Cabo Verde (PAIGC)

PAIGC, or the African Party for the Independence of Guinea and Cape Verde, was the nationalist movement that fought for the independence of Portuguese Guinea and the Cape Verde Islands between 1963 and 1974. PAIGC was founded in 1956 by a Cape Verdean *mestico* (mixed race), Amílcar Cabral. The Cape Verde Islands off the coast of West Africa were administratively linked to Portuguese Guinea.

Initially, PAIGC recruited urban *assimilados* (assimilated Africans), Bissau waterfront workers, and rootless youths drifting into the city from the countryside. Many of the latter were from the Balante tribe, who made up about one-third of the population of Portuguese Guinea. However, there was always an uneasy relationship between the Balante rank-and-file and the Cape Verdean leadership. This was especially so because PAIGC's revolutionary egalitarianism fit uneasily with the traditional animist beliefs of the Balante. Indeed, a short-lived rival to PAIGC known as Frente para a Libertação e Independência de Guine (FLING), or the Front for the Liberation and Independence of Guinea, was particularly marked by its animosity to Cape Verdeans. In 1973, internal rivalries within PAIGC were marked by Cabral's assassination.

PAIGC's ideology was certainly resisted by Islamic peoples such as the Fula, and at least half of the Portuguese troops in Guinea were locally recruited Africans. PAIGC established its headquarters in Conakry in the neighboring Republic of Guinea and began guerrilla operations into Portuguese territory in January 1963. PAIGC had some success and in 1971 claimed that it had established "liberated zones" covering 50 percent of the colony. In fact, under the energetic leadership of Gen. Antonio de Spinola from 1968 onward, the Portuguese reduced the war to a low-level stalemate. With the military coup in Portugal in April 1974, the fighting rapidly ceased, and Portuguese Guinea became independent as Guinea-Bissau in September 1974. The Cape Verde Islands chose to become a separate independent state in July 1975.

See also: Cabral, Amílcar; de Spinola, Marshal Antonio Sebastião Ribeiro; Guinea, Portuguese; Portuguese army

Further Reading: Newitt, Marlyn, *Portugal in Africa* (London, 1981).

Partisans

A partisan is not the same as a guerrilla, although they use similar tactics. The partisan is most often defined as a regular soldier who is undertaking irregular, guerrillalike operations on the flanks or rear of an opposing regular army. However, a partisan can also be any member of a large, organized, and disciplined force that has the characteristics of a regular army yet wages guerrillalike warfare.

This August 1944 photograph shows President Josip Broz Tito of Yugoslavia directing actions of the partisans from his cave home-headquarters during World War II. (UPI/Corbis-Bettmann)

Russian partisans who harassed the French in 1812 during Napoleon's epic retreat from Moscow are examples of the first definition. They were regular Russian troops detached from the main Russian army specifically for the purpose. Similarly, Russian partisans in World War II were regular troops who were trapped behind German lines by the speed of the German advance into Russia in 1941. Accordingly, they resorted to irregular warfare against German lines of communication.

In contrast, the partisans led by Josip Broz Tito, who fought the Germans in Yugoslavia during World War II, are an example of the second definition. They were not regular troops, although they did include former Yugoslav soldiers; still, they became large, organized, and disciplined military forces.

In many respects, partisan warfare emerged from the development of light infantry tactics in the eighteenth century. The word *partisan* derives from the French *partis* (foraging parties); at the time, it conveyed a type of skirmishing likely to be undertaken by light infantry or light cavalry. Increasingly, armies recruited special irregular units to operate in support of conventional operations. The Habsburg empire in Austria, for example, raised units among the Croat and Magyar peoples of the frontier regions who were thought to have a special flair for irregular warfare. Similarly, the British army employed colonists and Indians against the French in North America during the French and Indian War; it also hired Hessian mercenaries, who were accustomed to light infantry tactics, during the American War for Independence.

In the case of the French retreat from Moscow, the Russian partisans were often Cossacks, the descendants of the warrior horsemen of the Don and Volga Valleys. The best known Russian partisan, Denis Davydov, commanded the First Regiment of Cossack Partisans. Based on the experience of the French Revolutionary and Napoleonic Wars (1792–1815), most of

the military theorists of the nineteenth century, such as the Prussian Carl von Clausewitz, believed that guerrillas could not succeed in defeating a conventional opponent. Accordingly, partisan warfare as advocated by theorists such as Davydov and another Prussian, Carl von Decker, was thought to be the most appropriate use of irregular tactics: Partisans were regulars who happened to be detached from the main army and remained under proper military discipline.

V. I. Lenin ascribed no particular importance to partisans or guerrillas in achieving revolution in Russian. And even though the tradition of partisan warfare was revived during the Russian Civil War (1917–1921), the Bolsheviks were suspicious of what they termed *partizanshchina* (partisan spirit). For example, Leon Trotsky, who took the title People's Commissar for War and Chairman of the Supreme Military Soviet in March 1918, believed that partisans were no substitute for the regular Red Army and that their existence encouraged attitudes dangerous to centralized authority. Joseph Stalin was equally suspicious of the possible political independence of partisans. It is not surprising, therefore, that Soviet partisans were kept firmly under army and especially Communist Party control when partisan warfare was resurrected as a result of Stalin's public broadcast on 3 July 1941.

A central staff for the partisan movement was established under Lieutenant Gen. P. U. Ponomarenko, and partisan operations were carefully coordinated with those of the Soviet army. However, the Germans enjoyed such success against the partisans that by 1943 perhaps 400,000 of the 500,000 Russian partisans used may well have been lost. The Germans did not garrison large parts of the Russian interior, and most German commanders were unconcerned by partisan operations behind them. Antipartisan missions were left to second-rate Italian, Rumanian, and Hungarian units or those that were locally raised. Russian partisans did come into play after Hitler ordered last-ditch resistance and prohibited retreat after the German offensive stalled, but by that time partisans increasingly were being reabsorbed into the Soviet army.

The Germans regarded Yugoslavia, which they invaded in April 1941, as strategically and economically important, and they directed seven major offensives against Tito's partisans between November 1941 and August 1944. However, many German troops were elderly, since the best units were deployed on the Eastern Front. Moreover, the Germans could not entirely rely on the Italian army, deployed in Dalmatia and Montenegro, or on the forces raised by the puppet Ustashi regime in Croatia. For all that, it was still a brutal struggle. Tito had formed the First Proletarian Brigade as the basis for a partisan army in December 1941. By 1943 the communists had 200,000–300,000 men. In the autumn of 1944 Soviet and Bulgarian forces entered Yugoslavia in a coordinated drive with Tito's forces. Tito entered Belgrade in October 1944, and another offensive cleared the Adriatic Coast by April 1945. Tito's partisans succeeded largely without external assistance, but it is doubtful they would have if Germany had not been waging war on other fronts.

See also: Clausewitz, Carl von; Davydov, Denis Vasilevich; Decker, Gen. Carl von; French army; German army; Italian army; Russian army; Russian Civil War; Soviet army; Tito, Marshal Josip Broz; Yugoslavia
Further Reading: Heilbron, Otto, *Partisan Warfare* (London, 1962).

Pathet Lao

The Pathet Lao was the communist nationalist movement formed in Laos in 1950. The protracted Laotian conflict (1963–1975) saw both government and communist opposition led by royal half-brothers. Prince Souvanna Phouma accepted a French offer of autonomy for Laos within the French Union in 1949. However, Prince Soupanouvong founded Neo Lao Issara (Lao Freedom Front) in 1950. Renamed Neo Lao

Hak Sat (Lao Patriotic Front) in 1956, the front was really directed by the communist-dominated People's Party of Laos. Soupanouvong subsequently agreed to Laos becoming neutral, and he participated in coalition governments with his half-brother. His communist partners, now known as the Pathet Lao (Land of the Laos), withdrew from the coalition in 1963.

Thereafter, annual communist offensives across the Plain of Jars were met by counterattacks from the Royal Laotian Army and its Meo allies. The United States provided covert support to the Laotian government and also undertook bombing missions over Laos. However, North Vietnamese support shifted the advantage to the Pathet Lao in 1971. Although a cease-fire was agreed to in 1973, a renewed Pathet Lao offensive took the Laotian capital, Vientiane, in June 1975. A communist republic was proclaimed under Soupanouvong that December.

See also: Laos
Further Reading: Brown, M., and J. Zasloff, *Apprentice Revolutionaries* (Stanford, 1986).

Peninsular War (1808–1814)

The Peninsular War was waged in Spain and Portugal following the French invasion of the Spanish Peninsula in February 1808. The Spanish and Portuguese armies were assisted by the British army, and after May 1808 the French were also opposed by Spanish guerrillas. Indeed, the word *guerrilla* (literally, "little war") derived from the Peninsular War.

The popular rising against the French was provoked by the forced abdication of the Spanish king in May 1808 and his replacement by French Emperor Napoleon's own brother, Joseph Bonaparte. At the same time, however, the precise motivation for opposing the French could vary from region to region. The first groups emerged in Galicia and Aragon. In Navarre there was a highly complex mix of political, social, and religious factors behind the emergence of guerrilla groups, whose development in

Navarre had more to do with the local perception that the French threatened traditional autonomy than with any conscious demonstration of Spanish nationalism.

Prominent guerrilla leaders included Juan Diaz Porlier (El Marquesito), Jean de Mendietta (El Capuchino), Juan Palarea (El Medico), Juan Martin Diaz (El Empechinado), and Francisco Espoz y Mina. The size of the guerrilla bands grew considerably, with Mina, for example, commanding more than 7,000 men in Navarre by 1811. In all, there may have been as many as 30,000 guerrillas operating against the French. As a result, the French were forced to disperse large numbers of men through the countryside as the guerrillas improved their organization and effectiveness. The French were also compelled to introduce more extreme measures in order to try to pacify the countryside. The guerrillas certainly helped to weaken French morale and provided the British, commanded by the Duke of Wellington, with invaluable intelligence. They also disrupted the French command and logistic systems. However, the guerrillas would have been defeated if not for British logistic support. The French also had to concentrate their main forces against Wellington, and it was Wellington's army—not the guerrillas—who ejected the French from Spain in February 1814. Nonetheless, the existence of the guerrillas gave the Spanish people the important psychological satisfaction of being able to claim a part in their own liberation.

See also: French army; Mina, Francisco Espoz y; Suchet, Marshal Louis-Gabriel, Duc d'Albufera
Further Reading: Gates, David, *The Spanish Ulcer* (London, 1986); Tone, John L., *The Fatal Knot: The Guerrilla War in Navarre and the Defeat of Napoleon* (Chapel Hill, 1994); Alexander, Don, *Rod of Iron: French Counterinsurgency Policy in Aragon During the Peninsular War* (Wilmington, 1985).

Pershing, Gen. John Joseph (1860–1948)

Pershing is best known as the commander in chief of the United States Expeditionary Force in France during World War I. However, he saw earlier service against the Moros in the Philippines and led the American pursuit of Pancho Villa into Mexico in 1916 following Villa's raid on Columbus, New Mexico. A graduate of West Point, Pershing was nicknamed "Black Jack" after serving with a Negro cavalry company.

As a captain, Pershing was posted to Jolo in the Philippines between November 1901 and July 1903. He made every effort to cultivate links with the Moros and received the unique distinction of being made a Moro *datu* (chief). Coming to the notice of U.S. Pres. Theodore Roosevelt, Pershing was promoted to brigadier general in 1906 over 862 more senior officers. He was governor of the Moro Province, embracing Jolo and Mindanao, from November 1909 to December 1913, instituting a number of civic action projects. However, even Pershing assumed that the Moros would be willing to assimilate American cultural values, and he miscalculated in trying to disarm the Moros in September 1911. As a result, he was forced to storm the two major Moro strongholds of Bud Dajo and Bud Bagsak. He also countered the fanatical Islamic *juramentados*, who took oaths to kill Christians, by having them buried with pig carcasses.

Pershing led a punitive expedition into Mexico between March 1916 and February 1917 but failed to trap Villa. When he took the expeditionary force to France later in 1917, Pershing was successful in maintaining its independence from the other Allied armies. After the war, Pershing was United States Army chief of staff from 1921 to 1924. His war memoirs, published in 1931, won the Pulitzer Prize.

See also: Mexico; Moros; Philippines; United States Army
Further Reading: Smythe, D., *Guerrilla Warrior* (New York, 1973); Vandiver, Frank, *Black Jack* (College Station, 1973), 2 vols.

Peru

Peru, like other states in Latin America, has experienced periods of military government since 1945. However, it was relatively untouched by insurgency until the 1980s. Indeed, a *foco*-style insurgency in 1965 collapsed almost immediately. A new and serious challenge then emerged in 1980 in the form of Sendero Luminoso (Shining Path).

Unusually, Peru was subject to a radical rather than a conservative military coup in 1968, led by Gen. Juan Velasco Alvarado. Velasco began a program of land reform and nationalization intended to benefit disadvantaged groups such as Andean Indians. The cause of the Indians had previously been championed by the Alianza Popular Revolucionaria Americana (APRA), or American Popular Revolutionary Alliance. APRA briefly formed a government in 1962 before being overthrown by the military.

The centrist Acción Popular (Popular Action Party) led by Fernando Belaúnde Terry came to power in 1963, only to be overthrown in turn by Velasco. However, Velasco was overthrown by more conservative officers in 1975, and the reform process was halted. APRA remained the largest opposition party yet became more moderate. Therefore, as the Peruvian economy deteriorated, new revolutionary movements appeared, even though the military surrendered power in 1980 to a civilian government led once more by Belaúnde.

The most prominent of the new revolutionary movements was Sendero Luminoso, which emerged in the mountainous Ayacucho Province under the leadership of Abimael Guzmán. Another group that emerged in the 1980s was Movimiento Revolucionario Tupac Amarú (MRTA), or Tupac Amarú Revolutionary Movement, which took its name from an Indian leader executed by the Spanish in 1780. (The Tupamaros—an urban guerrilla group in Uruguay during the 1970s—were named for the same hero.) Whereas Sendero Luminoso, whose military campaign began in 1982, largely followed the rural revolutionary guerrilla warfare principles of Mao Tsetung (albeit in the context of a regional

urban insurrection), MRTA operated primarily as an urban guerrilla group in the capital, Lima, from 1984 onward.

Belaúnde's government failed to bring inflation under control, and the scale of insurgency escalated steadily with yet another group, Commandos Revolucionarios del Pueblo (Popular Revolutionary Commandos), announcing their arrival in 1985. National elections went ahead in 1985, and APRA returned to power for the first time since 1962. Its leader, Alan García, promised new reforms and secured a ceasefire with MRTA, but Sendero Luminoso continued its campaign; MRTA also resumed attacks after a year. While grappling with Peru's economic problems, not least the crippling levels of foreign debt, García attempted to eradicate excesses by soldiers and police. However, inflation continued to rise, and as criticism of his policies rose within APRA, García actually resigned as party leader in December 1988 while remaining president.

The 1990 elections were unexpectedly won by Alberto Fujimori, a Peruvian of Japanese extraction, and his Cambio 90 (Change 90) movement. Fujimori's response to continued violence was a "self-coup" in April 1992 whereby he dismissed Congress and took dictatorial powers. Fujimori's hard-line stance was rewarded when Guzmán was captured in September 1992. In January 1994 Sendero Luminoso fragmented when Guzmán offered peace terms from his prison cell. Fujimori was returned to power in the 1995 elections with 64 percent of the vote. However, his government suffered a setback in December 1996 when MRTA, which for all intents and purposes appeared to be extinct, seized the Japanese ambassador's residence in Lima. The incident occurred during a reception for 500 guests from the diplomatic community, most of whom were taken hostage. After a prolonged standoff during which MRTA demanded the release of imprisoned guerrillas in return for releasing the hostages, the Peruvian armed forces stormed the residence. The end of the siege of the residence and the elimination of the MRTA guerrillas involved was a vindication for Fujimori's refusal to surrender to their terms. Peru thus remains on course to defeat insurgency, but the internal conflict has cost an estimated 27,000 lives and $23 billion since 1982.

See also: Foco; Guzmán Reynoso, Prof. Abimael; Mao Tse-tung; Sendero Luminoso; Tupamaros; Urban guerrilla warfare

Further Reading: Palmer, David Scott (ed.), *The Shining Path of Peru* (London, 1992); Marks, Tom, *Maoist Insurgency since Vietnam* (London, 1996).

Philippines

The 7,000 islands of the Philippine archipelago have witnessed three significant periods of insurgency during the twentieth century. The first was between the United States Army and Filipino guerrillas between 1899 and 1902 and followed the U.S. decision to annex the Philippines. The second was the communist Hukbalahap insurgency against the newly independent government of the Philippines between 1946 and 1954. The third is the ongoing struggle of the communist New People's Army (NPA) since 1969 and that of the Moro National Liberation Front (MNLF) since 1972. The United States also faced periodic insurgencies in the Philippines between 1902 into the 1930s, and the United States Armed Forces in the Far East (USAFFE) sponsored guerrilla opposition to Japanese occupation during World War II.

Ruled by Spain from the sixteenth century, Filipinos rose against Spanish control in August 1896. It was an insurrection encouraged by the United States, which arranged for the exiled nationalist leader, Emilio Aguinaldo, to return to the Philippines in May 1898 just after the beginning of the Spanish-American War (1898). The U.S. Fleet destroyed the Spanish naval presence on 1 May 1898, and with assistance from insurgents the American forces took Manila in August 1898. Ostensibly, the war was fought for Cuban independence from Spain, but in December 1898 the peace treaty provided for U.S. annexation of Philippines, Puerto Rico, and Guam. Perhaps not surprisingly, the continued American presence conflicted with Aguinaldo's aspirations, and fighting broke out with U.S. forces in February 1899.

News reached the United States the day before the U.S. Senate narrowly voted to ratify the peace terms. In all, 70,000 U.S. troops were needed to suppress Aguinaldo's uprising, and the conflict cost 4,300 American lives and almost $170 million. Worse yet, the American press played up alleged atrocities by U.S. troops, notably the campaigns of Brig. Gen. J. Franklin Bell on Batangas and Brig. Gen. Jacob Smith on Samar between September 1901 and May 1902. Indeed, Aguinaldo, who was captured in March 1901, had set out consciously to influence the 1900 U.S. presidential election, in which the Republican incumbent, William McKinley, was opposed by an anti-imperialist Democrat, William Jennings Bryan.

The commander of the U.S. forces from May 1900 to July 1901, Maj. Gen. Arthur MacArthur, believed in the need for benevolence yet introduced Army Order No. 100 in December 1900. Dating from the American Civil War (1861–1865) Order No. 100 differentiated, for purposes of punishment, between uniformed partisans and "part-time" guerrillas hiding among civilian populations. MacArthur also introduced resettlement of populations as a means of separating them from insurgents. Civic action programs complemented resettlement, offering the general population positive reasons to support U.S. administration. An example was the work of Brig. Gen. John Pershing among the Moros on Jolo and Mindanao between 1909 and 1913 in starting a general store, industrial training stations, and a homestead for squatters. However, American cultural values would still be resisted, as when the Moros revolted against the abolition of slavery in 1903 and against Pershing's attempt to disarm them in 1911. Although the main insurgency was contained by May 1902, periodic outbreaks had to be addressed by the American-led Philippine Constabulary. A major uprising among Sakdal peasants occurred as late as 1935.

The Hukbalahap also drew on traditional peasant grievances in the central Luzon Plain. Indeed, even as the communist leadership espoused land redistribution, peasant supporters appeared content with the limited aim of achieving larger shares in crops, as landlords traditionally took up to 50 percent. Moreover, population growth and progressive subdivision of land had put even greater pressure on tenants. The communists had the advantage of being able to exploit such grievances through their wartime role, the Hukbalahap having originated in March 1942 as the Hukbo ng Bayan lagan sa Hapon (People's Anti-Japanese Army).

The Democratic Alliance (DA) formed by the National Peasants' Union (PKM) and the Huks won all the central Luzon seats in the April 1946 elections, but Pres. Manual Roxas debarred the elections on the grounds of fraud. Negotiations broke down, and the renamed Hukbong Mapagpalaya ng Batan (HMB), or People's Liberation Army, took to the hills. Faced with an insurgency inspired by the principles of Mao Tse-tung, Roxas resorted to a strategy of military coercion. His successor, Pres. Elpido Quirino, attempted negotiations, but they also broke down, and Huk successes continued. However, in September 1950 Quirino appointed a former USAFFE guerrilla leader, Ramon Magsaysay, secretary for national defense. Magsaysay launched a hearts-and-minds program to win over the population. The despised police force was integrated into the army (but with better pay to discourage looting), and it was barred from using excessive force.

Civic action programs were begun, including a well-publicized resettlement project for former Huks and their families on Mindanao. With the assistance of American advisers like Edward Lansdale, Magsaysay reorganized the army into self-sufficient battalion combat teams for undertaking sustained, small-unit actions. The Huks were forced to take the defensive, and by 1954 9,695 had been killed, 1,635 wounded, and 4,269 captured. In addition, 15,866 Huks had surrendered, including the Huk leader, Luis Taruc. Magsaysay went on to become president of the Philippines in November 1953, and by the time he died in a March 1957 air crash the Huk uprising had been broken.

There was a brief Huk revival between 1965 and 1970, but it had little impact. Yet growing opposition to the rule of Pres. Ferdinand Marcos, who took office in 1965, prompted Marcos to declare martial law in September 1972. His principal opponents were the MNLF and the NPA. Moro opposition to Marcos stemmed from continuing resentment at the Catholic domination of government in Manila and the influx of non-Muslims into Mindanao. The Moros occupied Jolo City at one point in January 1974, and following a December 1975 cease-fire Marcos promised a degree of autonomy. However, Marcos conditioned the agreement on a referendum of all the southern population agreeing to autonomy for the Moros. This in effect gave the larger Christian population a veto to kill the deal, and fighting broke out again in October 1977. However, the Moro movement fragmented, with different factions looking for assistance from Libya, Egypt, and Saudi Arabia.

With the split among the Moros, the communists became a greater threat to Marcos in the 1980s. The NPA emerged in 1969 as the military wing of the Communist Party of the Philippines (CPP). In classic Maoist style, the NPA gradually built a sophisticated web of political support that enabled it to fill the vacuum left by the split in the Moros. By 1980 the NPA had an estimated 24,000 activists and had spread from Luzon to other islands affected by poverty and deprivation, such as Samar, Panay, Negros, and Mindanao. However, NPA intimidation brought about a popular backlash, which led to the growth of a government-sponsored militia.

Yet the NPA suffered even as Marcos was toppled through a remarkable display of "people's power" in February 1986, for the new government adopted a more considered political response to communist insurgency. This was largely masterminded by a former army officer, Victor Corpus, who had defected to the NPA in 1970 but returned to the government side in 1976 and was released from detention after the fall of Marcos. Codenamed "Lambat Bitag" (Net Trap) and introduced in 1989, the new strategy was one of "gradual constriction" of communist areas by a combination of military pressure and social reform. Neutralization of the NPA infrastructure was accorded first priority. The scale of insurgency has decreased significantly despite the failure of post-Marcos governments to introduce genuine land reform.

See also: Bell, Gen. J. Franklin; Hearts and minds; Hukbalahap; Lansdale, Maj. Gen. Edward Geary; MacArthur, Lt. Gen. Arthur; Magsaysay, Ramon; Mao Tse-tung; Moros; Partisans; Pershing, Gen. John Joseph; Resettlement; Smith, Brig. Gen. Jacob Hurd; Taruc, Luis; United States Army
Further Reading: Gates, J. M., *Schoolbooks and Krags* (Westport, 1973); Greenberg, L. M., *The Hukbalahap Insurrection* (Washington, DC, 1987); Corpus, Victor, *Silent War* (Manila, 1989); Marks, Tom, *Maoist Insurgency since Vietnam* (London, 1996).

Phoenix program

The Phuong Hoang (Phoenix) program was a controversial attempt to eliminate the infrastructure of the communist Vietcong in South Vietnam between 1967 and 1973. It was promoted by Robert Komer's Civil Operations and Rural Development Support (CORDS) organization. Evolving from the existing Special Platoons established in Quang Ngai Province in 1965, the Intelligence Coordination and Exploitation Program (ICEX) was launched in June 1967, utilizing South Vietnamese as well as U.S. Central Intelligence (CIA) resources.

On 20 December 1967 ICEX was renamed Phoenix.

The intent was to coordinate all intelligence activities in the South Vietnamese countryside to enable provincial security committees to identify and arrest Vietcong agents. It was estimated that the Vietcong might have as many as 70,000 such agents. Little progress was made, however, since the South Vietnamese disliked sharing intelligence with Americans. The South Vietnamese government also did not wish to involve its National Police, whose task was seen more as preventing coups. The shock resulting from the communist Tet Offensive in early 1968 revived Phoenix. As a result, as part of the so-called Accelerated Pacification Campaign, the South Vietnamese did commit police, regional and popular forces, provincial reconnaissance units, and the people's self-defense force to the program.

Americans attached to the program were to be phased out by January 1969, yet in practice about 650 Americans remained closely involved. A monthly quota of Vietcong agents to be eliminated, established in August 1969, unfortunately gave Phoenix a reputation as an assassination program. And though Komer's successor as director of CORDS, William Colby, ordered American advisers to report any indiscriminate killing, clearly some abuses occurred. Intelligence was also often unreliable, and too many of those who were eliminated turned out to be lower-level agents and not the higher Vietcong leaders that were targeted. Phoenix purportedly neutralized 81,740 Vietcong agents by August 1972, of whom 26,369 were killed. In fact, Phoenix did cause the communists heavy grassroots losses, but they came far too late in the war to make any real difference. The program ended in March 1973.

See also: Civil Operations and Rural Development Support (CORDS); Intelligence; Komer, Robert William; Police; Tet Offensive; Vietcong; Vietnam War
Further Reading: Moyar, Mark, *Phoenix and the Birds of Prey* (Annapolis, 1997); Valentine, D., *The Phoenix Program* (New York, 1990).

Pol Pot (1928–1998)

Pol Pot was the leader of the communist Khmer Rouge in Cambodia from 1962 until 1979 and remained the most important figure within the movement until 1997. Born Saloth Sar in the Kompong Thom Province, Pol Pot has also been known as Pol Porth and Tol Saut. A shadowy figure, he was briefly a novice in a monastery and studied technical education in France from 1949 to 1953. Returning to Cambodia, Pol Pot had become general secretary of the Khmer Rouge by 1962.

Following the fall of the Cambodian capital, Phnom Penh, to the communists in April 1975, Pol Pot became the prime minister of what was now called Democratic Kampuchea. The despotic rule of the Khmer Rouge, which may have resulted in at least 1.4 million deaths by 1977, was ended by the Vietnamese invasion of Kampuchea. Pol Pot and his colleagues slipped into the jungle after the Vietnamese took Phnom Penh in January 1979 and waged a guerrilla war against the government the Vietnamese had installed. Supposedly, Pol Pot was displaced as leader of the Khmer Rouge in 1979, retired in 1985, and resigned entirely from any party posts in 1989. However, he is believed to have continued to wield the major influence over the movement.

The Khmer Rouge joined a fragile coalition with other, noncommunist groups opposed to the Vietnamese in June 1983. Under a plan put forward by the United Nations, the Vietnamese withdrew from Cambodia in 1989 and a peace agreement was reached, paving the way for a coalition government and new elections in 1993. However, the Khmer Rouge boycotted the elections and resumed its guerrilla campaign, only to become increasingly fragmented.

Pol Pot executed his own defense minister in June 1997 but was arrested by other elements within the Khmer Rouge and, apparently, sentenced to life imprisonment. In April 1998 it was reported that Pol Pot was being carried with Khmer Rouge forces under Ta Mok fleeing toward the Thai frontier under the pressure of a renewed government offensive. Subsequently, it was reported that he had died of a heart attack.

See also: Cambodia; Khmer Rouge
Further Reading: Chandler, David, *Brother Number One* (Boulder, 1992); Kiernan, Ben, *The Pol Pot Regime* (New Haven, 1996).

Police

Insurgency inevitably begins with political subversion as opposed to an outright military assault against authorities. Thus, police rather than armed forces typically encounter insurgent groups first. Indeed, it might be argued that effective policing should impede the escalation of subversion into full-scale insurgency. Police forces have a great advantage over other security services in possessing detailed knowledge of localities. Nonetheless, although police have tended to be paramilitary gendarmerie, this has not always been the case, and colonial police forces often appeared primarily concerned with protecting the government and administration rather than ordinary citizens.

The Palestine police, for example, primarily recruited from the Arab population and was commanded by British personnel. Less than 4 percent of the officers spoke Hebrew. Accordingly, the force was unable to respond adequately to terrorist action by Irgun Zvai Leumi and the Stern Gang in Palestine between 1944 and 1947 because it could not gain the confidence of the Jewish community. Indeed, a report by Sir Charles Wickham in December 1946 recommended abandoning the police force's paramilitary mobile role and reverting to British-style foot patrols.

The Palestinian police had been modeled on the paramilitary Royal Irish Constabulary (RIC), whose successor in Northern Ireland in 1921 was the Royal Ulster Constabulary (RUC). When violence escalated in Northern Ireland in 1969, the RUC was unwelcome in many Roman Catholic areas because it was a predominantly Protestant force. Similarly, the Kenya Police was ill-equipped to deal with the emergence of the Mau Mau among the Kikuyu tribal areas during the Kenyan Emergency (1952–1960) because it normally left policing there to a tribal force.

The paramilitary role sometimes performed by police can also result in the failure to carry out what might be termed "normal" policing, a vital aspect of police work because it conveys to the population that there is a semblance of normalcy as well as central control of events. In the Malayan Emergency (1948–1960), for example, initial deployment of paramilitary police jungle squads left too few police for normal police activities. Thus, when assuming command of the Malayan police in December 1951, Sir Arthur Young insisted on a more traditional British approach. Accordingly, he introduced the so-called Operation Service to win the cooperation of the population. It was symbolized by a new badge displaying clasped hands. However, Young was less successful when sent to Kenya in 1954, because the white-settler Kenya Police Reserve (KPR), in particular, proved reluctant to relinquish its paramilitary role, so much so that it formed its own, unofficial units.

Police difficulties in countering subversion may be increased if insurgency begins with a deliberate assault on the police and its intelligence agencies. On Cyprus between 1955 and 1959, for example, the Greek-Cypriot nationalist group Ethniki Organosis Kyprion Agoniston (EOKA), led by George Grivas, deliberately targeted Greeks in the police force. In particular, EOKA eliminated Greeks serving in Special Branch, which was the traditional intelligence section established within British-style police forces. It thus became difficult to recruit Greek-Cypriots, and the police had to rely more heavily on Turkish-Cypriots. They, of course, did not offer the same depth of knowledge regarding the Greek community.

In much the same way, carefully targeted terrorism by the Vietcong deterred many candidates from joining the South Vietnamese police. In any case, the police had alienated itself from many South Vietnamese because it was popularly identified with tax and rent collection and gross corruption. And in Aden, the Aden State Police was entirely unreliable during the British campaign against the National Liberation Front (NLF) between 1963 and 1967. In fact, elements of both the South Arabia Police and Federal Armed Police mutinied in June 1967.

Failure to contain subversion usually results in the expansion of police forces, and hasty expansion can result in poorly trained police officers. The classic example is the RIC's recruitment of former servicemen between 1919 and 1921 for the "Black and Tans" and the Auxiliary Division, both notorious for excesses against the population. Former servicemen were also recruited by the Palestinian police, and some police veterans in turn went on to serve in other British colonial emergencies. In Cyprus, for example, additional police were seconded from Britain itself.

In addition to expanding police forces once emergencies develop, administrations introduce armed forces to support the police. This can bring possible friction in command-and-control arrangements. In the typical British practice, it is understood that the army only supports the police, yet tensions are inevitable. There was friction, for example, between the commissioner of police, Nicol Gray, and the director of operations, Lt. Gen. Sir Harold Briggs, in the early stages of the Malayan Emergency. Most often these tensions arise over the control of intelligence, the bailiwick of Special Branch in British colonies. However, in 1971 Gen. Sir Frank Kitson challenged this tradition in his book *Low-intensity Conflict*. Based on his experiences in Malaya, Cyprus, and Kenya, he argued that policemen were incapable of providing the operational intelligence soldiers needed to make actual contact with insurgents in the field.

The British army has often had to rebuild intelligence networks in the wake of insurgent attacks on police. The best solution has been to ensure close coordination of intelligence agencies. And even though the British army typically mounted the responding campaign, as in Kenya and Northern Ireland, it wanted to hand operations back to local police as soon as possible. Yet disagreement between police and army has by no means been confined to British campaigns. For example, there were frequent clashes between the Portuguese army and the security police (DGS) in Mozambique between 1964 and 1974 and between the Rhodesian army and the British South Africa Police (BSAP) in Rhodesia between 1972 and 1979.

See also: Aden; Briggs, Lt. Gen. Sir Harold Rawdon; British army; Cyprus; Ethniki Organosis Kyprion Agoniston (EOKA); Grivas, Gen. George Theodorou; Intelligence; Irgun Zvai Leumi; Kenyan Emergency; Kitson, Gen. Sir Frank Edward; Mau Mau; National Liberation Front (NLF); Northern Ireland; Palestine; Portuguese army; Rhodesia; Stern Gang; Vietcong

Further Reading: Holland, Robert (ed.), *Emergencies and Disorder in the European Empires after 1945* (London, 1994); Killingray, David, and David Anderson (eds.), *Policing and Decolonisation: Nationalism, Politics, and the Police, 1917–1965* (Manchester, 1992).

Politicization of armed forces

Counterinsurgency campaigns impact the security forces involved. A particular danger is politicization of armed forces, which can then turn on their own government. In the case of the French army, for example, regular soldiers came to believe that French politicians failed them in not assuming full responsibility for the military outcome of political decisions. Thus, the army blamed the politicians of the Fourth Republic for the defeat in French Indochina between 1946 and 1954. The advocates of the new French doctrine of counterinsurgency known as *guerre révolutionnaire,* which evolved in the mid-1950s, believed that the challenge of communist-inspired insurgency could only be met by an equally strong ideological commitment on the part of its opponents.

Thus, when the French faced the Front de Libération Nationale (FLN) insurgency in Algeria between 1956 and 1962, the army insisted that French politicians not betray the continuation of French Algeria. When the army deemed that politicians were not committed to the concept, they effectively engineered the fall of the Fourth Republic in May 1958 and the return to power of Charles de Gaulle. However, when de Gaulle in turn contemplated Algerian independence, elements within the army, led by Raoul Salan, attempted a military coup in Algiers in April 1961. In the event, regulars were not followed by conscripts, and the coup collapsed. Those, like Salan, who escaped arrest formed the Organisation d'Armée Secrète (OAS) to assassinate de Gaulle.

Another example of politicization occurred within the Portuguese army during its campaigns in Angola, Portuguese Guinea, and Mozambique between 1961 and 1974. It also involved an element of bifurcation in that a split developed between regular soldiers and conscripts. Elite units such as paratroops and commandos undertook much of the fighting, whereas conscripts were mostly used in civic action programs. The greatest bifurcation obtained in the officer corps, which had greatly expanded to meet the demands of the conflict. A particular problem was the need to conscript large numbers of university graduates or *milicianos,* who tended to fill static garrison posts while career officers led the fighting units. When *milicianos* were given accelerated promotion in July 1973 as a means to persuade them to prolong military careers, younger career officers formed the Armed Forces Movement (MFA) in September 1973 to publicize their grievances. There was a general feeling in the army that Portugal suffered from social, economic, and political stagnation. Thus, when the former commander in chief in Portuguese Guinea, Antonio de Spinola, was dismissed as the army's deputy chief of staff in March 1974 for criticizing government policy, MFA responded with a military coup on 25 April 1974. The new military government became increasingly radical, and Portugal rapidly divested itself of its African colonies.

See also: Algeria; Bifurcation; de Spinola, Marshal Antonio Sebastião Ribeiro; French army; French Indochina; Guerre révolutionnaire; Organisation d'Armée Secrète (OAS); Portuguese army; Salan, Gen. Raoul
Further Reading: Porch, Douglas, *The Portuguese Armed Forces and the Revolution* (London, 1977); Martin, M. L., *Warriors and Managers* (Durham, 1981).

Popular Front for the Liberation of Saguiet el Hamra and Rio de Oro (POLISARIO)

Properly known as Frente Popular para la Liberación de Saguira el Hamra y Rio de Oro, POLISARIO is the insurgent group that has been fighting against Morocco in the former Spanish territory of Western Sahara since 1976. Western Sahara was claimed by Morocco and Mauritania, but they agreed to partition the territory once the Spanish withdrew. Meanwhile, POLISARIO's demands for an independent Western Sahara, which emerged in 1973, were supported by Algeria and then Libya. In December 1974 the United Nations referred the matter to the International Court of Justice, which in October 1975 ruled that the Western Saharan population should be given the right of self-determination.

The Moroccan response to the court decision was the so-called Green March of unarmed civilians to occupy Western Sahara. In November the Spanish agreed to withdraw, and Morocco and Mauritania duly partitioned the territory in December 1975. POLISARIO formally declared the existence of the Sahrawi Arab Democratic Republic on 27 February 1976 under the presidency of Mohammed Abd al-Aziz. An economic crisis led to a military coup in Mauritania in July 1978, and it renounced all claim to Western Sahara in July 1979. However, Morocco occupied the vacated

Mauritanian portion of the territory and has continued to fight POLISARIO, whose government-in-exile was recognized by the Organization of African Unity (OAU) in February 1982.

At the height of the fighting, between 1979 and 1981, POLISARIO fielded heavy weapons and an estimated 10,000 men. A UN-sponsored cease-fire in 1989 broke down after ten months over the interpretation of who would be entitled to vote in any referendum on self-determination. However, the cease-fire was revived in September 1991 pending a referendum on self-determination. It has yet to be held.

See also: Morocco; Western Sahara
Further Reading: Hodges, Tony, *Western Sahara: The Roots of a Desert War* (Westport, 1983).

Popular Front for the Liberation of the Occupied Arabian Gulf (PFLOAG)

PFLOAG was the Marxist group that waged the insurgency in the Dhofar Province of Oman between 1968 and 1975. The original opposition to the near-feudal rule of Sultan Said bin Taimur came from a group known as the Dhofar Liberation Front (DLF), led by Mussalim bin Nufl. DLF was a small group backed by the exiled imam (religious leader) of Oman and by Saudi Arabia, which had territorial claims on part of Oman. DLF aimed to overthrow the sultan and began a sabotage campaign in Dhofar in 1962.

Technically, the insurrection dated from 9 June 1965, following DLF's first "congress." In November 1967 the British withdrawal from Aden brought a Marxist government to power in what was now called the People's Republic of South Yemen (PDRY). PDRY was quick to offer support to the DLF, and at a second congress in August 1968 the nationalist followers of Mussalim were ousted by hard-line Marxists. DLF became PFLOAG, its title subsequently amended in 1971 to denote the Popular Front for the Liberation of Oman and the Arabian Gulf. The movement received Soviet and Chinese weapons, and some of its guerrillas were trained in China and North Korea. PFLOAG enjoyed some initial successes until Said was overthrown in July 1970 by his son, Qaboos bin Said.

Qaboos turned to the British for support, and in a model counterinsurgency campaign PFLOAG was subjected to a combined military and political strategy that deprived it of support among the Dhofari population. Indeed, PFLOAG's Marxist ideology undermined two fundamental principles of Dhofari life: Islam and the tribal system. Significantly, the first large insurgent group to surrender to the government in September 1970 was led by the most experienced of the former DLF guerrillas, Salim Mubarak. They became the nucleus of the first *firqat* unit, a pseudoforce enlisted to fight erstwhile colleagues.

PFLOAG was also hampered by its weak and rudimentary command structure, which made its decisionmaking slow and ineffective. Its increasing failure was characterized by its adoption of yet another title, the Popular Front for the Liberation of Oman (PFLO), in August 1974. This implied that the former aim (sparking insurrection throughout the Arabian Gulf) had been forced into the background by the sheer need to survive in Dhofar. From an estimated peak strength of 2,000 active fighters in its People's Liberation Army and 3,000 part-time militia in 1968, PFLOAG had declined to about 800 activists and 1,000 militia by 1974. By December 1975 PFLOAG was broken, although clearing operations continued until mid-1976; the last contact with armed guerrillas occurred in 1979.

See also: British army; Dhofar; *Firqat;* Pseudoforces
Further Reading: Beckett, Ian, and John Pimlott (eds.), *Armed Forces and Modern Counter-insurgency* (London, 1985).

Portuguese army

The Portuguese were the first European colonial power to arrive in Africa, but their penetration of the interior was limited until the late nineteenth century. Pacification of the colonies of Portuguese Guinea, Angola, and Mozambique by the Portuguese army continued until the 1930s. In the case of Portuguese Guinea, frontiers were not established until 1886, and sporadic resistance continued until 1936. In Angola there was constant warfare, especially in the Dembos region, the target of 15 major Portuguese military expeditions between 1631 and 1919. In Mozambique, there were no less than 27 separate revolts between 1878 and 1904 alone.

Revolts were usually put down by African levies in the *guerra preta* (black war). In emergencies, however, the colonies could be reinforced from Portugal, as happened during World War I when German forces, operating from German South-West Africa (later Namibia) and German East Africa (later Tanzania), mounted incursions into Angola and Mozambique respectively. On most occasions, however, the Por-

Portuguese troops on patrol in Estima, Mozambique, uncover a land mine laid by guerrilla forces from the Mozambique Liberation Front, 16 September 1973. (UPI/Corbis-Bettmann)

tuguese enjoyed superiority of firepower over African opponents. The campaigns of the nineteenth century also saw some talented soldiers emerge, such as Artur de Paiva, Pereira d'Eça, António Enes, Mouzinho de Albuquerque, and Henrique de Paiva Couceiro.

When revolt resurfaced in Angola in March 1961, the army had not seen a major action since World War I, and within a few months it suffered a humiliating defeat when the Indian army overran the small Portuguese garrison in Goa, India. Even though caught by surprise, the Portuguese had little difficulty suppressing the initial outbreak, as the rebels were poorly armed. The Portuguese also had the advantage of drawing on the experiences of other European armies since 1945. However, pending buildup of their troop levels, the Portuguese withdrew into defended outposts and relied largely on airpower to contain the revolt as it spread through Angola. As a result, the initiative was largely surrendered to the insurgents (as was the case in Portuguese Guinea, where fighting began in January 1963). Portuguese troop strength reached 30,000 in Guinea by 1967 and 60,000 in both Angola and Mozambique by 1971 and 1974 respectively. Eventually, 50 percent of Portuguese forces were African.

The increase in Portuguese strength permitted a more active role after 1968. Central to the new strategy was the resettlement of populations to separate them from insurgents. The new defended villages were known as *senzalas do paz* or *dendandas* (in Angola) and *aldeamentos* (in Mozambique). Resettlement had actually begun first in Guinea in 1964 and was extended to Angola in 1967. When Antonio de Spinola arrived in Guinea as commander in chief in 1968 he initiated a new, coordinated hearts-and-minds strategy based on villages. His counterpart in Mozambique, Kaulza de Arriaga, also instituted an energetic program of civic action. In Angola, some 70 percent of the Portuguese forces were devoted to such programs. There were extensive propaganda campaigns, and pseudoforces were raised from insurgents who had been captured or deserted. The pseudoforces were known as Grupos Especiais de Paraquedistas (GEP) in Mozambique and as *flechas* (arrows) in Angola. The overall problem, however, was that the Portuguese lacked sufficient resources for a comprehensive program of hearts and minds, and as independence was not an offer on the table they could not satisfy wider African aspirations.

Another feature of the post-1968 enhanced approach was more effective deployment of forces available. Airpower was now used to seal off infiltration and supply routes across frontiers and as a quick-response force. Even more important, helicopters were used to land elite units behind identified insurgent concentrations and supply routes. Although helicopters were not always available in sufficient numbers, at its best the combination of light bombers, helicopters, and reinforced ground patrols achieved many successes during dry-season operations. Yet modern technology was not always the remedy, and so cavalry was used extensively in Angola, where the terrain was too difficult for vehicles. And empty beer bottles slung on wires were a successful substitute for sophisticated sensors as early-warning devices around Portuguese outposts. Small-unit operations with 30-man patrols also increasingly substituted for less-effective, large-scale sweeps. The Portuguese occasionally threatened hot pursuit into neighboring countries, but they were generally reluctant to incur the international criticism that would surely follow. (However, they did attempt an abortive landing of armed exiles in the Republic of Guinea in November 1972.)

The Portuguese methods were sufficient to produce stalemate in Guinea and low-intensity stalemate in Angola, yet the Portuguese were coming under increasing pressure in Mozambique. However, the price of success was not only international criticism, which damaged Portugal's prestige, but also increasing expenditure, which damaged the domestic economy, as well as politicization of the army. Defense expenditures as a proportion of national budget rose from 25 percent in 1960 to 42 percent by 1968. The Portuguese also suffered 11,000 dead by 1974. At home, opposition to the colonial campaigns led to an estimated 110,000 conscripts failing to report for service by 1974.

Compounding the situation, the Portuguese government gave *milicianos* (university graduates) accelerated promotion in July 1973, hoping to encourage conscripts to prolong military careers. Disillusioned career officers formed the Armed Force Movement (MFA) shortly afterward to articulate grievances. When the popular de Spinola was dismissed as deputy chief of staff for criticizing colonial policy in March 1974, MFA overthrew the government on 25 April 1974. Independence followed swiftly for Portugal's African colonies.

See also: Airpower; Angola; Arriaga, Gen. Kaulza Oliveira de; de Paiva Counceiro, Henrique Mitchell; de Spinola, Marshal Antonio Sebastião Ribeiro; Guinea, Portuguese; Hearts and minds; Helicopters; Mozambique; Politicization of armed forces; Pseudoforces; Resettlement
Further Reading: Beckett, Ian, and John Pimlott (eds.), *Armed Forces and Modern Counter-insurgency* (London, 1985); Cann, John, *Counterinsurgency in Africa: The Portuguese Way of War, 1961–1974* (Westport, 1997).

Propaganda

Propaganda can be defined as any of the methods used by governments or organized groups to exert psychological influence over populations and their actions. In insurgencies, propaganda is vital to both sides—government and insurgents—because the protracted nature of modern insurgency makes it important to maintain the determination and will to prevail. For insurgents, there is a need to reinforce their ideological appeal to their own members as well as the general population. Thus, insurgent groups will use propaganda to not only undermine the authorities but also indoctrinate followers to enforce cohesion and solidarity. The government will use propaganda in communicating its message

to not only undermine the insurgents but also project a certain image to the population and the international community.

In the case of insurgent groups, internal cohesion and solidarity might be achieved via rituals or oaths, as the Mau Mau did during the Kenyan Emergency (1952–1960). External influence might come via leaflets, radio and television broadcasts, and (as with the Tupamaros in Uruguay in the early 1970s), kidnappings of foreign business people (who are ransomed for food to be distributed to the poor). Indeed, the principal theorist of urban guerrilla warfare, Carlos Marighela, characterized his methods as "armed propaganda." But terror and intimidation for propaganda purposes might also be employed to demonstrate the power of an insurgent group and to undermine the authorities, for example, via selective targeting of government officials and police.

Authorities possess a similar range in options; for example, air-dropped propaganda leaflets have been a feature of many rural campaigns. And the British army, in most campaigns since 1945, eventually incorporated propaganda specialists in a coordinated response. Thus, in the Malayan Emergency (1948–1960), the Emergency Information Service was established in June 1950 with a director-general of information services being appointed in October 1952. By 1954 more than 100 million leaflets were being distributed annually in Malaya.

As a general rule that applies to authorities and insurgents alike, propaganda must be credible in order to be effective.

See also: Kenyan Emergency; Malayan Emergency; Marighela, Carlos; Media; Tupamaros; Urban guerrilla warfare
Further Reading: Carruthers, Susan, *Winning Hearts and Minds* (London, 1995); Dine, Philip, *Images of the Algerian War* (Oxford, 1994).

Pseudoforces

Pseudoforces are units of former insurgents that take up arms against erstwhile colleagues. They have been a common feature of insurgencies since 1945, because rank-and-file members of many insurgent groups do not have the same degree of ideological commitment as the leaders; indeed, they may have been intimidated into joining insurgents in the first place. The British made some use of surrendered enemy personnel (SEPs) in the Malayan Emergency (1948–1960), but it was really the young Frank Kitson, together with Ian Henderson and Eric Holyoak, who demonstrated the potential of pseudoforces by raising "countergangs" from former Mau Mau during the Kenyan Emergency (1952–1960). The British similarly raised the *firqat* in the Dhofar campaign in Oman (1970–1975), eventually employing more than 1,600 men in 21 different units based on tribal affiliations.

The Portuguese army also raised pseudoforces during its campaigns in Africa between 1961 and 1974, such as the *flechas* (arrows) in Angola. The concept was also used in Rhodesia, a pilot scheme being begun in the Zambezi Valley in October 1966. However, since the insurgents had little support there and were easily contained, there was little scope for developing the idea further. When insurgent activity escalated in Rhodesia 1972, pseudoforces were revived, with the first being deployed in January 1973. From this, Ron Reid-Daly developed the Selous Scouts as a combat-tracker unit.

Pseudo-operations were always dangerous and required a constant source of new defectors in order to enable the pseudoforce to keep up to date on insurgents' internal security measures. In Rhodesia, the Selous Scouts appear sometimes to have attacked protected villages in order to prove their bona fides in the course of seeking to sow distrust within the insurgent groups.

See also: British army; Dhofar; *Firqat;* Kenyan Emergency; Kitson, Gen. Sir Frank Edward; Malayan Emergency; Portuguese army; Reid-Daly, Lt. Col. Ron; Rhodesia; Selous Scouts; Special Air Service (SAS)

Further Reading: Kitson, Frank, *Gangs and Countergangs* (London, 1960); Jeapes, Tony, *SAS Secret War* (London, 1996).

Puller, Lt. Gen. Lewis Burwell (1898–1971)

Known as "Chesty" for his barrel chest, Puller came to notice while serving with the United States Marines in Haiti and Nicaragua between the world wars. Indeed, Puller won two of his five Navy Crosses for his service in these counterinsurgency campaigns. Born in Virginia and educated at Virginia Military Institute, Puller left in 1917 to enlist in the Marines during World War I. He did not see wartime action and received a reserve commission in 1919. However, he reenlisted as an ordinary marine and served during the Cacos Revolt on Haiti (1919–1924), working with the American-raised gendarmerie. Puller was commissioned again in 1924 and was posted to Nicaragua in 1928.

Attached to the Nicaraguan National Guard, Captain Puller led the celebrated "M" Company in the campaign against Augusto Sandino. Sandino even placed a price on his head. "M" Company operated from Jinotega as a 30- to 40-man patrol with light equipment carried on a few pack mules. For speed, Puller dispensed with flank guards, and in the event of ambush he relied on firepower provided by a light machine gun, six automatic weapons, and four rifles fitted with grenade launchers. In September 1932 Puller covered 150 miles in only ten days, killing 30 guerrillas in four engagements.

During the World War II campaign against the Japanese in the Pacific, Puller commanded the First Battalion of the Seventh Marine Regiment on Guadalcanal (1942) and the First Marine Regiment on Peleliu (1944). Puller again commanded the First Marine Regiment during the Korean War (1950–1953). He was promoted to brigadier general in 1951 and to major general in 1953; he retired as a lieutenant general in 1955.

See also: Nicaragua; Sandino, Augusto César; United States Marine Corps (USMC)

Further Reading: Davis, Burke, *Marine!* (Boston, 1966).

R

Reid-Daly, Lt. Col. Ron (1933–)

Reid-Daly commanded the pseudoforce known as the Selous Scouts in Rhodesia from 1973 to 1979. The intention of the pseudoforce, developed from an earlier combat-tracker unit, was to recruit former guerrillas who surrendered or were captured by security forces to take up arms against erstwhile colleagues. Reid-Daly had served as a noncommissioned officer with a Rhodesian squadron attached to the British army's Special Air Service (SAS) during the Malayan Emergency (1948–1960), and the Scouts were based on British experience as well as the Portuguese Army's *flechas* (arrows) as observed by Daly. Raised between November 1973 and January 1974, the unit was named Selous Scouts in March 1974. The name derived from the celebrated big-game hunter Frederick Selous, who had guided the original white pioneer column into what became Southern Rhodesia in 1890. Reid-Daly's unit operated both as intelligence-gatherers and hunter-killers. However, there was some friction between the Selous Scouts and the army as well as between the Scouts and the police.

In Malaya, Reid-Daly had been under the command of Peter Walls, and he remained close to Walls. However, when Walls became commander of the Combined Operations Headquarters in March 1977, Reid-Daly did not enjoy the same easy relationship with the new army commander, Lt. Gen. John Hickman. Indeed, it became evident to Reid-Daly in January 1979 that his telephone was being bugged by the army's intelligence department. Hickman had authorized this in August 1978 following allegations that the Scouts were involved in ivory poaching. Reid-Daly confronted Hickman, and as a result Reid-Daly was court-martialed for insubordination, reprimanded, and retired. Hickman, however, was himself sacked in March 1979. Reid-Daly moved to South Africa and became commander of the army in the "independent homeland" of Transkei.

See also: Intelligence; Malayan Emergency; Police; Pseudoforces; Rhodesia; Selous Scouts; Special Air Service (SAS); Walls, Lt. Gen. Peter
Further Reading: Reid-Daly, Ron, and Peter Stiff, *Selous Scouts: Top Secret War* (Cape Town, 1982).

Resettlement

Resettlement of civilian populations is a principal means employed by armies since 1945 for separating populations from guerrillas and their influence. Indeed, such separation is usually considered an absolute prerequisite to any campaign to win the hearts and minds of a population. Separation can be achieved by erecting a physical barrier against guerrilla infiltration, such as the French army's Morice Line in Algeria in 1957, the McNamara Line in South Vietnam in 1967, or the so-called *cordon sanitaire* of border minefields in Rhodesia between 1974 and 1979. However, a frequent alternative has been the resettlement of populations to defended locations.

Resettlement was widely practiced by European armies in colonial warfare during the nineteenth century. Known then as reconcentration, the technique was being used simultaneously, for example, by the British army in the Boer War (1899–1902) and by the United States Army in the Philippines. In the case of the Boer War, the mobility of Boer commandos was restricted by the lavish use of lines of blockhouses linked by wire entanglements; Boer women and children were incarcerated in "concentration camps." Farms, crops, and livestock were destroyed systematically to deny commandos supplies. The Spanish also used similar methods when faced with an insurrection on Cuba between 1896 and 1898.

Reconcentration was largely intended to impose physical control over a population likely to support guerrillas. Resettlement also had this function, but when the British revived the concept during the Malayan Emergency (1948–1960) they recognized that the implicit guarantee of security from guerrilla intimidation could provide the basis for winning popular support for the government. In Malaya, the key to success for the authorities was winning their contest with the Malayan Communist Party (MCP) for the allegiance of the so-called squatter community. (The squatters, some 500,000 ethnic Chinese, occupied illegal settlements on government-owned land at the fringes of the jungle.)

As part of the strategic plan developed by Lt. Gen. Sir Harold Briggs after his appointment as director of operations in 1950, the squatters were moved into 509 "new villages." Strict food controls were introduced to ensure that communist sympathizers could not continue to support guerrillas in the field; other restrictions further isolated the guerrillas. However, the villages were also provided with medical and other facilities, and in December 1951 the squatters received legal title to land they occupied. Village councils were established in May 1952, and responsibility for village defense eventually passed to a home guard drawn from villager-recruits. Thus, resettlement proved a major factor in the defeat of insurgency.

At the same time, the British realized that the squatters happened to be socially and economically susceptible to resettlement. But the same did not apply to the nomadic aboriginal population of the deeper jungle (and thus the attempt to resettle them was quickly abandoned). The same flexibility was shown by the British during the Dhofar campaign in Oman between 1970 and 1975, when the target population was again nomadic. In this case, wells were sunk in an arid country and became a natural focus for the population. Other facilities were then introduced around the wells to demonstrate to the Dhofari tribes the potential benefits of supporting the authorities.

The danger with resettlement is that authorities can be accused of oppression unless the policy is carried out humanely. Unfortunately, many armies have regarded it simply as a means of physical control and not as an opportunity for winning hearts and minds. Thus, in the case of South Vietnam, the South Vietnamese government ignored the advice of the British Advisory Mission headed by one of the architects of the Briggs Plan, Robert Thompson. As a result, the so-called strategic hamlets program, which began in January 1962, created 7,200 strategic hamlets with a population of 8.7 million by July 1963. By the time the computerized Hamlet Evaluation System was established in 1967, there were 12,750 strategic hamlets spread across 244 districts and 44 provinces of South Vietnam. Much of the resettlement had been undertaken without adequate preparation and without adequate protection for the resettled population. Moreover, the South Vietnamese peasantry was being moved from ancestral lands to which it had great attachment. As a result, resettlement in South Vietnam was a failure. (The French were not much more successful in Algeria.)

Failure was also the rule in Portugal's African colonies between 1961 and 1974. The new villages were variously known as *senzalas do paz* or *dendandas* in Angola and as *aldeamentos* in Mozambique and Portuguese Guinea. About 1 million people were resettled in both Angola and Mozambique, some 120,000 in Guinea. And though African tribal leaders who had reason to fear guerrilla intimidation welcomed resettlement on occasion, more often it was resented as a disruption of traditional tribal society. The villages were often badly sited and lacked the advertised facilities. The new lands were not only agriculturally less productive but also subject to depredations by wildlife. As a result, rural agriculture suffered; there is also evidence in Mozambique that there was inadequate sifting of the population, which meant that insurgents could infiltrate the villages with the help of supporters. This led to continued penetration of the settlements by the guerrillas.

Similarly, the protected villages increasingly introduced in Rhodesia after 1974 (eventually accommodating at least 350,000 and conceivably as many as 750,000 Africans) often lacked proper facilities, even basic sanitation. The villages were inadequately defended by poor-quality Guard Force units or district security assistants who may have ignored the fact that food was being smuggled to guerrillas by a population that was, in any case, insufficiently screened for possible insurgent reporters. Again, resettlement struck at tribal values, and crops cultivated some distance from villages were left unprotected at night and were subject to animal depredations. In effect, resettlement in Rhodesia was too punitive in intent.

Such a record, compared to the success of the British in Malaya, suggests that resettlement failed not in concept but in execution. Thus, the policy of resettlement is not doomed if it is carried out by authorities with sufficient care and preparation.

See also: Algeria; Angola; Boer War; Briggs, Lt. Gen. Sir Harold Rawdon; British army; Colonial warfare; Cordon sanitaire; Cuba; French army; Guinea, Portuguese; Hamlet Evaluation System (HES); Hearts and minds; Malayan Emergency; McNamara Line; Morice Line; Mozambique; Philippines; Rhodesia; Strategic hamlets; Thompson, Sir Robert Grainger Ker; United States Army; Vietnam War
Further Reading: Beckett, Ian, and John Pimlott (eds.), *Armed Forces and Modern Counter-insurgency* (London, 1985).

Resistance

Resistance is a term usually used to characterize various activities intended to undermine German occupations in Europe and Japanese occupations in Southeast Asia during World War II. It did not always occur immediately after occupation, for populations sometimes needed time to overcome the shock of defeat and adjust to new circumstances. In the case of occupied Europe, resistance could be an extension of violent prewar rivalries between certain political groups. Certainly, all kinds of individuals joined the resistance, whether they be active partisans or merely collaborators; everyone had to make a choice. As a result, the politics of resistance varied widely. In Europe nationalists might resist German occupation yet regard communism as a greater threat than Nazism and thus collaborate.

Japanese occupation of Southeast Asia also stimulated indigenous nationalism but in two entirely different ways. Some joined anti-Japanese movements such as the Malayan People's Anti-Japanese Army (MPAJA), the Hukbalahap in the Philippines, and the Vietminh in French Indochina. Others joined Japanese-sponsored movements such as the Indian National Army and Burma Independence Army or served in supposedly autonomous administrations established by the Japanese in states like Burma, the Dutch East Indies, and the Philippines because they seemed to offer the independence previously denied them by European colonial powers. Communists often played a particularly equivocal role in resistance until the invasion of the Soviet Union by the Germans in June

1941 transformed their war overnight from an "imperialist" conflict to a vital struggle against fascism.

The nature of resistance itself varied according to the terrain of the occupied country. Thus, whereas large scale guerrilla warfare was possible in the wastes of Russia or in the mountains of Yugoslavia or Greece, it would have been suicidal in a small, low-lying country such as Denmark. However, resistance could equally mean publishing clandestine newspapers or even listening to radio broadcasts of the British Broadcasting Company (BBC). In Norway, school teachers went on strike in protest against the attempt to impose a new school syllabus.

German and Japanese occupation policies varied in intensity. In Europe, for example, Austria was effectively treated as part of Germany itself, whereas the Netherlands was treated to a limited extent as a possible ally. By contrast, Poland and occupied parts of Russia were subject to the most ruthless exploitation. As a result, the extent of direct German control varied, and in many cases the Germans worked through the local police or units raised from the occupied territories. However, sooner or later it often became apparent that German or Japanese occupation was far from benign. Thus, in German-occupied Russia, despite the recruitment of anti-Soviet units from among non-Russian groups in areas like Ukraine, Byelorussia (Belarus), and the Baltic states, German brutality succeeded in legitimizing the appeal even of Stalin's totalitarian regime.

One of the most useful activities undertaken by resistance groups was gathering intelligence on German and Japanese forces, as was assisting escapes of Allied personnel (such as downed airmen) from occupied territory. In Western Europe resistance groups helped some 33,000 Allied servicemen escape German capture, including 10,000 airmen as well as 10,000 prisoners of war who walked out of Italian prison camps when the Italians suddenly capitulated in September 1943. Sabotage, of course, could be effective, such as the attack on the heavy water plant at Vemork, Norway, in February 1943 and the sinking of the remaining stocks of heavy water aboard the Tinnso ferry in February 1944; both imposed crucial delays on the German attempt to produce an atomic bomb. The most successful sabotage was that carried out by the French resistance on the German communications system in preparation for the Allied invasion of Normandy in June 1944. Larger scale military action by resistance groups was often less successful, as in the case of the insurrection by the Polish Home Army in Warsaw in August 1944 or the Slovak rising in Prague in May 1945. Similarly, attempts by the French *maquis* to establish a "liberated zone" in the Savoy and Vercours areas failed in the summer of 1944, and Italian partisans likewise failed making a similar attempt in autumn 1944.

The German and Japanese armies developed effective methods to counter partisan warfare. The Germans, for example, did not attach great importance to the operations of Soviet partisans in rear areas, and the success of the Yugoslav partisans led by Josip Broz Tito owed much to Germany's involvement in a much wider war, Yugoslavia being a secondary theater of operations. Rather similarly, the communist forces of Mao Tse-tung survived in China primarily because the Japanese could not devote the time and resources required to eliminate them while engaging a wider struggle against the nationalist Kuomintang (KMT) in China proper and against Britain and the United States in the wider war.

However, in any respects, the success of resistance should not be measured in conventional terms of military gains or successful sabotage. First, it was important in political terms, for it often determined the character of postwar political development of states in Europe and Southeast Asia. Second, it was significant in psychological terms because it helped sustain the morale of people under occupation by giving them hope of eventual liberation and by enabling them to claim a share in that liberation.

See also: Burma; Dutch East Indies; French Indochina; German army; Hukbalahap; Japanese army; Kuomintang (KMT); Mao Tse-tung; Office of Strategic Services (OSS); Partisans; Philippines; Special Operations Executive (SOE); Vietminh; Yugoslavia
Further Reading: Foot, M. R. D., *Resistance* (London, 1976); Beckett, Ian (ed.), *The Roots of Counter-insurgency: Armies and Guerrilla Warfare, 1900–1945* (London, 1988).

Resistançia Naçional Moçambicana (RENAMO)

RENAMO, or Mozambique National Resistance, emerged in Mozambique in 1976 in opposition to the Frente de Libertação de Moçambique (FRELIMO) government of Samora Machel. Originally, RENAMO was established by Rhodesia's central intelligence organization, which aimed to undermine Machel's support for the guerrillas of Robert Mugabe's Zimbabwe African National Union (ZANU). Following Rhodesia's independence as Zimbabwe, Mugabe committed forces to Mozambique in support of Machel. However, South Africa then extended support to RENAMO, forcing Machel to conclude the Nkomati Agreement in March 1984, by which South Africa withdrew support for RENAMO in return for Machel dropping his support for the African National Congress (ANC, not to be confused with the South African group of the same name).

However, by the time of Machel's death in an air crash in October 1986 RENAMO controlled an estimated 85 percent of Mozambique. RENAMO has benefited from FRELIMO's relatively narrow base of support among the Makonde tribe and from the resistance of other tribal leaders to FRELIMO's Marxist ideology and its attempted suppression of traditional cultural and religious practices. Indeed, RENAMO has generally cooperated with traditional tribal leaders and is especially strong in the Zambezia Province. Despite some modification by Machel of FRELIMO's policies before his death, RENAMO remains a powerful opponent of FRELIMO. RENAMO has been led since 1983 by Afonso Dhlakama as both president and supreme commander.

See also: African National Congress (ANC); Frente de Libertação de Moçambique (FRELIMO); Machel, Samora Moïses; Mozambique; Mugabe, Robert Gabriel; Rhodesia; Zimbabwe African National Union (ZANU)
Further Reading: Rich, Paul, and Richard Stubbs (eds.), *The Counter-insurgent State* (London, 1997).

Rheault affair

The Rheault affair, which occurred in South Vietnam in 1969, was one of several incidents whereby Americans began to suspect the true nature of the war was being concealed from them. In particular, the incident suggested that U.S. Special Forces (Green Berets) were implicated in war crimes. Col. Robert Rheault and seven colleagues from the Fifth Special Forces Group (SFG) were accused in July 1969 of the premeditated murder of a suspected communist double agent. The Vietnamese person in question worked for one of the so-called B-Teams of the Green Berets and was thought to be compromising the Gamma project, a hazardous intelligence-gathering operation along communist infiltration routes into South Vietnam. Rheault and his men were arrested and detained at Long Binh. However, members of the U.S. Central Intelligence Agency (CIA), who were involved in wider special forces operations, would be compromised if compelled to testify against Rheault. This led the White House to insist that it would not be in the public interest to prosecute the case. As a result, the charges were dismissed; Rheault retired from the army in September 1969.

See also: Green Berets; Special Forces; United States Army; Vietnam War
Further Reading: Westmoreland, William, *A Soldier Reports* (New York, 1976).

Rhodesia

The guerrilla war in Rhodesia between 1972 and 1979 is a good illustration of how

A four-man paramilitary Rhodesian security patrol keeps watch inside the gates of Protected Village No. 10 in October 1979. The patrol sought guerrillas that may have tried to take refuge in the village as well as protecting the village from guerrilla attacks. (UPI/Corbis-Bettmann)

external political considerations can determine outcomes irrespective of security forces' military successes. The war as a whole was fought against the background of complicated political events, which often had a direct impact on operations. For example, guerrillas in Robert Mugabe's Zimbabwe African National Union (ZANU) and Joshua Nkomo's Zimbabwe African People's Union (ZAPU) operated from sanctuaries in Mozambique and Zambia respectively, and thus Rhodesians mounted operations across frontiers at times to put pressure on the guerrillas' hosts. In turn, the survival of Rhodesia was jeopardized by the withdrawal of the Portuguese from Mozambique in 1974, and many feared that if South Africa overtly supported Rhodesia it would lead to a dangerous escalation of conflict in southern Africa. The situation was complicated by the Soviet Union and the Chinese People's Republic, who gave

support to the guerrillas, and by the splits in the nationalist movement itself. (Indeed, Rhodesia's white prime minister, Ian Smith, would reach an internal settlement with three different nationalist leaders in March 1978; see below.)

In defiance of the British Labour government, which was dedicated to African majority rule, Rhodesia's whites (led by Smith) issued a unilateral declaration of independence from Britain on 11 November 1965. The British rejected the use of force and resorted largely to ineffectual economic sanctions. Negotiations between Smith and the British failed in 1966 and 1968. The initial efforts of ZANU and ZAPU to infiltrate from Zambia were easily contained by Rhodesia's British South Africa Police (BSAP). However, this early success led the police to resist the increasing dominance of the Rhodesian army after the scale of the war increased as a result of

ZANU's infiltration through Mozambique in December 1972. Eventually, a combined operations headquarters (Comops) was established under the command of Lt. Gen. Peter Walls in March 1977, but rivalry between police and army persisted.

This led to a lack of coordination of intelligence, a major drawback as manpower was limited. White conscription was steadily increased, but in fact the majority of the security forces were African, especially from the Kalanga tribal group. Following the internal settlement, black conscription was introduced in January 1979. Usually, however, only about 25,000 men could be put in the field at any one time, and many were needed for static guard duties on important installations, such as railways. To compensate for the manpower shortage, the Rhodesians adopted a strategy of mobile counteroffensive characterized by the fire force concept. It utilized a combination of light aircraft, heliborne infantry, and paratroopers as a means of concentrating firepower and mobility. Other specialized units were developed (such as Ron Reid-Daly's Selous Scouts) as pseudoforces. The kill ratio was always favorable to the Rhodesians, yet they did not have the resources to prevent infiltration. Indeed, according to Rhodesian estimates the number of guerrillas able to operate inside the country rose from a mere 350 in 1974 to 12,500 by 1979.

The Rhodesians attempted to prevent infiltration with a cordon sanitaire of border minefields and to separate the guerrillas from the African population via resettlement. Neither was entirely successful, and in general the Rhodesian approach to winning hearts and minds left much to be desired. The emphasis was on broadening African representation in government (as in the case of the internal settlement) rather than on improving the lot of rural Africans; the preference was for control rather than concession. By the end of the war, rural administration had broken down in many tribal areas, and although the guerrillas had not succeeded in establishing any liberated areas, they had been effective at political subversion.

Whether the security forces could have continued to contain the insurgency is therefore arguable, as Rhodesia's resources were stretched dangerously thin, especially after the Portuguese withdrew from Mozambique. The South Africans pressed Smith into negotiations with Nkomo in 1975, but they (as well as a separate South African and U.S. initiative) failed to produce a settlement acceptable to all parties in 1977. Smith thus reached an internal settlement in March 1978 with three nationalist leaders, including Bishop Abel Muzorewa and the Rev. Ndabaningi Sithole. Sithole had broken away from Nkomo to form ZANU in 1963 but was outmaneuvered by Mugabe.

Following elections, Muzorewa became the first black prime minister of what was now called Zimbabwe-Rhodesia, but the result was denounced by Nkomo and Mugabe, who had created the fragile Patriotic Front in 1976. British Prime Minister Margaret Thatcher's new Conservative government had agreed at the 1979 Commonwealth conference to promote new negotiations, and Muzorewa concluded he would not get better terms. Nkomo and Mugabe were also willing to negotiate, given their escalating casualties and growing internal tensions, and the economies of their host states were being severely damaged by Rhodesian raids. The Lancaster House conference (London, September–December 1979) resulted in a British-supervised cease-fire on 28 December 1979. New elections were held in February 1980, which were won by Mugabe, and Zimbabwe received full legal independence on 18 April 1980.

Officially, the war had cost the lives of 410 white civilians, 691 black civilians, 954 members of the security forces, and 8,250 guerrillas. The actual death toll, however, may have exceeded 30,000.

See also: Cordon sanitaire; Fire force; Hearts and minds; Intelligence; Mugabe, Robert Gabriel; Nkomo, Joshua;

Police; Pseudoforces; Reid-Daly, Lt. Col. Ron; Resettlement; Selous Scouts; Special Forces; Walls, Lt. Gen. Peter; Zimbabwe African National Union (ZANU); Zimbabwe African People's Union (ZAPU)

Further Reading: Moorcraft, Paul, and Peter McLaughlin, *Chimurenga* (Marshalltown, 1982); Cilliers, J. K., *Counterinsurgency in Rhodesia* (London, 1985); Godwin, Peter, and Ian Hancock, *Rhodesians Never Die* (Oxford, 1993).

Roberto, Holden (1925–)

Roberto was the leader of Frente Nacional de Libertação de Angola (FNLA), the nationalist group that fought the Portuguese army in Angola between 1961 and 1974. It then lost the subsequent civil war in 1975 to the rival Movimento Popular de Libertação de Angola (MPLA). FNLA's main support was among the Bakongo tribe; Roberto was the nephew of one of the tribe's traditional kingmakers. Educated by Baptist missionaries in the Belgian Congo (Zaire), Roberto worked for the Belgian administration before founding FNLA's precursor, União das Populaçôes de Angola (UPA) in 1954. FNLA was created by a union of UPA and another group in March 1962.

UPA's attacks into Portuguese territory began in March 1961, and Roberto formed a government-in-exile in 1963. He claimed to have 10,000 men by 1971, although it is unlikely he had more than 6,000. Moreover, FNLA was only sporadically active from its bases in Zaire, although it did maintain groups within the heavily forested Dembos region of northern Angola. Roberto's "foreign minister," Jonas Savimbi, broke from FNLA in 1964 to found the separate União Nacional para a Independência Total de Angola (UNITA) in 1964. FNLA also lost the support of the Organization of African Unity (OAU), which dropped its recognition of the government-in-exile in 1968. As a result, Roberto was forced to rely mostly on the support of his brother-in-law, President Mobutu of Zaire, and some limited support from the United States. As the Portuguese prepared to withdraw in 1974, FNLA and UNITA forged an alliance, but MPLA won the civil war through the inter-

vention of Cuban troops airlifted into Angola by the Soviet Union. Although UNITA continued to fight the MPLA government, FNLA disappeared.

See also: Angola; Frente Nacional de Libertação de Angola (FNLA); Movimento Popular de Libertação de Angola (MPLA); Neto, Dr. Agostinho Antonio; Portuguese army; Savimbi, Jonas; União Nacional para a Independência Total de Angola (UNITA)

Further Reading: Marcum, John A., *The Angolan Revolution* (Cambridge, MA, 1969 and 1978), 2 vols.

Roberts, Field Marshal Earl (Frederick Sleigh) (1832–1914)

Nicknamed "Bobs," Roberts was one of the most prominent soldiers to emerge from the British army's colonial campaign in the late nineteenth century. A general's son, Roberts was born at Cawnpore, India, and educated at Eton College, the Royal Military College at Sandhurst, and the East India Company (EIC) College at Addiscombe. Roberts was commissioned in the Bengal Artillery in December 1851. He served on the North-West Frontier and won the Victoria Cross during the Indian Mutiny (1857).

In 1875 Roberts became quartermaster-general in India and then led the Kurram Field Force into Afghanistan in October 1878 during the first phase of the Second Afghan War (1878–1881). When a British mission was massacred at Kabul in September 1879, Roberts led the Afghan Field Force to reoccupy Kabul. Then, when a British force was defeated at Maiwand in July 1880 and the British garrison in Kandahar besieged, Roberts secured his reputation by leading a celebrated relief expedition from Kabul to Kandahar. Roberts was commander in chief in India from 1885 to 1893 and was promoted to Field Marshal in 1895. He then took over command of the British forces in South Africa in December 1899 after early British defeats in the Second Boer War (1899–1902).

Succeeded in South Africa by Lord Kitchener, Roberts returned home to become commander in chief of the British army in January 1901, succeeding his great rival, Lord Wolseley. Roberts was retired when the post was abolished in February 1904. Subsequently, he campaigned unsuccessfully for the introduction of conscription in Britain. Roberts died visiting Indian troops serving in France during World War I.

See also: Afghanistan; Boer War; British army; Colonial warfare; India; Kitchener, Field Marshal Earl (Horatio Herbert); North-West Frontier; Wolseley, Lord
Further Reading: James, David, *The Life of Lord Roberts* (London, 1954).

Rogers, Maj. Robert (1732–1795)

Rogers led Rogers's Rangers, the celebrated irregular unit raised in 1756 during the earliest colonial phase of the American Indian Wars. Born in Methuen, Massachusetts, Rogers was brought up in Concord, New Hampshire. He served with the colonial militia during King George's War (known in Europe as the War of Austrian Succession) from 1744 to 1748. War with the French and their Indian allies resumed in 1755. Hostilities in what was called the French and Indian War in North America preceded the outbreak of the Seven Years War in Europe (1756–1763). Rogers again entered the militia as a means of avoiding a counterfeiting charge. Rogers's frontier skills resulted in his being given command of an independent company of rangers by the British in March 1756. Two years later, his command was raised to nine companies.

One of Rogers's best-known exploits was the raid on the Abenaki village of St. Francis in October 1759. Rogers received the surrender of Detroit in 1760. He also took part in the relief of Detroit during the native rebellion known as Pontiac's War in 1763. Rogers was never a capable administrator, and he went to England in 1765 not only to seek a new appointment but also to avoid his many creditors. He received the command of Fort Michilimackinac on the shores of Lake Michigan, but in December 1767 he was arrested and charged with embezzlement and treasonable contact with the French. He was acquitted in October 1768; Rogers returned to England, only to be imprisoned for debt. He returned to North America at the beginning of the American War of Independence (1775–1783) and was detained by the Americans as a suspected loyalist. He escaped and raised the Queen's American Rangers to fight for the British. However, he was removed from command in 1777, ending his days living in poverty in London.

See also: American Indian Wars; American War of Independence; British army
Further Reading: Cuneo, John, *Robert Rogers of the Rangers* (2d ed., Ticonderoga, 1988).

Roguet, Gen. C. M. (1800–1877)

The son of a French general, Roguet was a page to Emperor Napoleon in 1815 and aide-de-camp to Emperor Napoleon III in 1851. Commissioned in the French engineers, he transferred to the infantry and was promoted to general in 1845. He is best known for his studies on street fighting and on the suppression of the Vendéan Revolt by the French republic between 1793 and 1796. Three studies, *L'emploi de la force armée dans les émeutes* (The employment of force in riots, 1832), *Guerres d' Insurrection* (Insurrectionary wars, 1839), and *Répression des émeutes* (Suppression of riots, 1848), were published for internal circulation in the army. However, a book on urban insurgency, *Avenir des Armée Européenes ou le Soldat Citoyen* (The future of European armies or the citizen soldier), was published in Paris in 1850. Roguet's study of the French campaign against the Vendée, *De la Vendée Militaire* (On military Vendée), had also been published in Paris in 1833.

Roguet's ideas on street fighting were embodied in the army's standing orders, although it would appear that his approach to street fighting and counterinsurgency was regarded as overintellectual. Yet his analysis of the brutal French republican response to the rising in the Vendée has been described as remarkably modern in its emphasis on making military action subordinate to political action as well as the necessity for winning hearts and minds. In part, Roguet also drew on the experiences of Louis-Gabriel Suchet in Spain during the Peninsular War (1808–1814) in suggesting how lessons of the past might be translated into current French practice in Algeria.

See also: Algeria; French army; Hearts and minds; Peninsular War; Suchet, Marshal Louis-Gabriel, Duc d'Albufera; Vendéan Revolt

Further Reading: Griffith, Paddy, *Military Thought in the French Army, 1815–1851* (Manchester, 1989); Holmes, Richard, *The Road to Sedan* (London, 1984).

Russian army

The Imperial Russian Army bequeathed a series of lessons to the Soviet army, which was created by the Russian Revolution in 1917 in both the promotion and the suppression of guerrilla war. The tradition of partisan warfare inherited by the Soviets, of course, could be traced to the French Revolutionary and Napoleonic Wars (1792–1815), when the French retreat from Moscow in 1812 had been harassed by Russian partisans led by men such as Denis Davydov. However, the Russian army had also fought a series of campaigns during the expansion of Russia into the Caucasus and Central Asia during the nineteenth century. Such campaigns were fought against guerrillas such as Shamil in the Caucasus (1834–1859) and against relatively organized native armies such as those of the khanates of Kokand and Bukhara (1870s and 1880s).

As was the case in nineteenth-century colonial warfare generally, the greatest problem was more often climate and terrain rather than opponents. Indeed, it has been calculated that the Russians suffered only 2,000 battle casualties during Central Asian campaigns between 1847 and 1873. The city of Tashkent, for example, was taken by only 2,000 Russians in June 1865 when defended by 30,000 men, and 40,000 Bukharans were defeated by only 3,000 Russians in 1866.

But the fanatical Islamic monastic military order known as the Murids and led by Shamil proved a more difficult adversary. Count Vorontsov instigated "slow strangulation" in the 1840s, cutting off the guerrillas from the population with a combination of military and political action to restore the proprietary and social rights of tribal leaders that had been usurped by the Murids. The process was completed by Prince Baryatinsky in the 1850s through a systematic penetration of Shamil's mountain bases. The Russian governor-general of Turkestan, K. P. Kaufman, extended control over the Central Asian khanates in much the same way between 1867 and 1882. However, the Russians were prepared to be ruthless, as when M. D. Skobelev massacred the defenders of Gok Tekke in January 1881.

There were subsequent uprisings against Russian control, such as the Andijan Revolt in Turkestan in the 1890s, and large-scale unrest resurfaced in Turkestan and on the Turkmen Steppes during World War I. Indeed, in many respects, the Soviets repeated the mistakes of tsarist predecessors in ignoring demands from non-Russian minorities for autonomy.

See also: Davydov, Denis Vasilevich; Partisans; Shamil; Soviet army

Further Reading: Beckett, Ian (ed.), *The Roots of Counterinsurgency: Armies and Guerrilla Warfare, 1900–1945* (London, 1988); Allen, W. E., and P. Muratoff, *Caucasian Battlefields* (Cambridge, 1953).

Russian Civil War (1917–1921)

The Russian Civil War resulted from the Bolsheviks' coup d'état against the Russian provisional government in Petrograd (St. Petersburg) in November 1917. The provisional government had replaced that of Tsar Nicholas II in March 1917, but it erred in attempting to continue Russia's participation in World War I against Germany and Austria-Hungary. Protsarist "White" forces emerged in December 1917 to attempt to wrest back power from the Bolshevik "Red Army," but the situation was greatly complicated by the appearance of other groups opposed equally to Whites and Bolsheviks. In Ukraine, for example, there were more than 90 groups fighting the Bolsheviks in 1919, including forces loyal to Simon Petliura's All Ukrainian Military Committee of the Central Rada (Council), those loyal to the German-backed government of Paul Skoropadsky, and those of the anarchist Nestor Makhno. White forces under Gen. Anton Denikin were also active in Ukraine from August to December 1919; Polish forces also entered the region during the separate Russo-Polish War (1920), which resulted in Poland securing its independence.

In the Caucasus, the Bolsheviks overran the three short-lived republics of Azerbaijan, Armenia, and Georgia between 1920 and 1921; this in turn enabled them to suppress a rising by the mountain tribes of Daghestan. The White forces in the Caucasus had originally been led by the provisional government's former commander in chief, Gen. Lavr Kornilov. However, Kornilov was killed in May 1918 and was succeeded by Denikin. His forces were eventually pushed out of the Caucasus and Ukraine although Gen. Peter Wrangel continued to hold the Crimea against the Bolsheviks until November 1920.

In northern Russia, the Bolsheviks were compelled to recognize Finnish independence and fought unsuccessfully to hold the Baltic states of Latvia, Lithuania, and Estonia, all of which slipped from their grasp by August 1920. British and French forces landed at Murmansk, and Japanese and U.S. forces landed at Vladivostock, in interventions against the Bolsheviks, the Japanese and the Czech Legion assisting Adm. Alexander Kolchak in establishing a White government in Siberia. This endured until Kolchak's capture and execution in February 1920. There were also peasant, or Green, uprisings against the Bolsheviks, such as the Antonov Revolt in the Tambov region in 1921.

The Bolsheviks ultimately prevailed against the myriad threats due to a lack of coordination among opponents.

See also: Antonov Revolt; Lenin, Vladimir Ilyich; Makhno, Nestor; Soviet army

Further Reading: Adams, A. E., *Bolsheviks in the Ukraine* (New Haven, 1963); Kenez, P., *Civil War in South Russia* (Berkeley, 1971 and 1977), 2 vols.; Radkey, O. H., *The Unknown Civil War in Soviet Russia* (Stanford, 1976); Lincoln, W. Bruce, *Red Victory* (New York, 1989).

Salan, Gen. Raoul (1889–1984)

Salan was one of the French army's most decorated soldiers and was commander in chief in French Indochina from 1951 and 1953 and in Algeria from 1956 to 1958. Ultimately, however, he led the attempted military coup against Charles de Gaulle in Algiers in April 1961, then led the terrorist group Organisation d'Armée Secrète (OAS), which tried to assassinate de Gaulle.

Salan fought as an officer-cadet at the very end of World War I before being commissioned in 1919. He served with the army's intelligence section in Indochina; he was on an intelligence mission in Ethiopia at the outbreak of World War II. The ambitious Salan's mysterious and inscrutable manner gained him two nicknames "Le Mandarin" (The Mandarin) and "Le Chinois" (The Chinese); he never was entirely trusted. Having initially served for the Vichy French administration in West Africa, Salan switched to the Free French in 1942. He became deputy to Jean de Lattre de Tassigny in Indochina, succeeding him as commander in chief in December 1951. However, Salan could not prevent the continuing decline in French fortunes and was replaced by Henri Navarre in May 1953. He was appointed to Algeria in December 1956 but was recalled by de Gaulle in December 1958 for attempting to influence the Algerian elections.

As military governor of Paris, Salan increasingly voiced his disagreement with de Gaulle's intention to quit Algeria, and he was retired in 1960. Salan first went to Algiers but then moved to Spain, returning to Algiers in April 1961 to lead the abortive coup against de Gaulle. Salan escaped when the coup collapsed and remained at large until April 1962. Salan had been sentenced to death in absentia in May 1961 for his OAS activities, but the sentence was now commuted to life imprisonment. He was from prison released in an amnesty in 1968.

See also: Algeria; de Lattre de Tassigny, Jean-Marie-Gabriel; French army; French Indochina; Navarre, Gen. Henri-Eugène; Organisation d'Armée Secrète (OAS)
Further Reading: Horne, Alistair, *A Savage War of Peace* (London, 1977).

Sandinistas

Popularly known as the Sandinistas, the Frente Sandinista de Liberación Nacional (FSLN), or Sandinista National Liberation Front, was the revolutionary guerrilla group that came to power in Nicaragua in 1979, only to lose power in a 1990 election. Founded in 1961, the movement took its name from Augusto Sandino, who had been executed by the Nicaraguan National Guard on the instructions of Anastasio Somoza García in 1934. Somoza then seized power in 1936, only to be assassinated in 1956. He was succeeded by his son, Luis Somoza Debyle, who in turn was succeeded by his brother, Anastasio Somoza Debyle, in 1967.

As the Somoza dynasty enriched itself, so it increasingly alienated large sections of

Nicaraguan society. The formation of FSLN in July 1961 by Carlos Fonseca and Silvio Mayorga was inspired by Fidel Castro's success in toppling the regime of Fulgencio Batista on Cuba two years earlier. However, FSLN had little initial success. A premature attempt to capitalize on the unrest following the National Guard's massacre of demonstrators in the Nicaraguan capital, Managua, in January 1967 led to a major military setback seven months later and the death of Mayorga. Indeed, it took Somoza's rumored pocketing of international aid following the Managua earthquake in 1972 to stimulate further popular unrest; FSLN then began to gain wider popular support.

A new phase of FSLN's campaign opened when it took the U.S. ambassador hostage in December 1974. The ambassador and others were released in return for the release of a number of prisoners (including FSLN's leader, Daniel Ortega), a $2 million ransom, and increased wages for industrial and agricultural workers. Somoza's subsequent declaration of a state of siege escalated the fighting in the Matagalpa Mountains, where FSLN was based. Fonseca was killed in 1976. Somoza's murder of a popular newspaper editor in January 1978 led to widespread rioting, which developed into virtual insurrection in Nicaragua's main urban centers through that summer. FSLN began a new offensive in February 1979, and with the guerrillas nearing Managua, Somoza fled to the United States on 17 July. He was assassinated in Paraguay in September 1980.

The Sandinista government then faced insurgency in turn from the U.S.-backed contras operating from Honduras and Costa Rica. FSLN did not modify its Marxist policies enough to widen its base of support; it also came into conflict with Miskito natives on the Atlantic Coast. Ultimately, Ortega accepted the peace proposals put forward by the so-called Contadora Group of Latin American states, which had been seeking ways to achieve peace in Nicaragua since 1983. Agreement was finally reached in 1989, and new elections were held in February 1990. However, they resulted in a sweeping electoral defeat for the Sandinistas at the hands of a 14-party coalition known as the Union Nacional de la Oposición (UNO), or the National Opposition Union.

See also: Castro, Fidel; Contras; Cuba; Nicaragua; Sandino, Augusto César

Further Reading: Weber, H., *Nicaragua: The Sandinista Revolution* (London, 1981); Christian, Shirley, *Nicaragua: Revolution in the Family* (New York, 1985); Robinson, William, and Kent Norsworthy, *David and Goliath: Washington's War Against Nicaragua* (London, 1987).

Sandino, Augusto César (1893–1934)

Sandino was a Nicaraguan radical whose campaign against the United States Marine Corps and the Nicaraguan National Guard between 1927 and 1933 demonstrated a remarkable understanding of the political and socioeconomic potential of guerrilla warfare. The illegitimate son of a moderately wealthy liberal landowner, Sandino left Nicaragua in 1920 to work abroad. He became politicized by labor disputes while employed as a mechanic by an American-owned oil company at Tampico, Mexico, and returned to Nicaragua in June 1926. Working for another American company at a gold mine in Nueva Segovia, Sandino organized his first group of followers in October 1926 to support the liberal vice-president of Nicaragua, Juan Sacasa.

Traditional enmities between liberal and conservative political factions had resumed with the 1925 departure of the U.S. Marine legation guard that had been stationed in Nicaragua as guarantor of stability since 1912. Sacasa and the moderate conservative president, Carlos Solórzano, had been ousted in October 1925 by the ultraconservative Emiliano Chamorro. Fighting broke out, and U.S. Marines relanded in May 1926. Chamorro was persuaded to resign, but the Americans were suspicious of Sacasa's links with Mexico and installed a former conservative president, Adolfo Diaz. Sacasa then

A photograph of General Augusto César Sandino taken in Nicaragua, ca. 1920. (UPI/Corbis-Bettmann)

ica's domination of its internal affairs, his movement being pointedly called Ejército Defensor de la Soberania Nacional (EDSN), or Defending Army of the National Sovereignty of Nicaragua.

The Americans initially referred to him as a "mule thief" and later cast him in the role of Marxist revolutionary. Sandino did enjoy the support of communist advisers, such as the Venezuelan Gustavo Machado and the Salvadoran Farabundo Martí, but his ideology was more religious mysticism than revolutionary. Thus, he rejected the idea of land redistribution, judging there was already enough unused land in public ownership; he broke from Machado and Martí in 1930. Yet if Sandino was not a precursor of revolutionary guerrillas in ideological terms, his military methods did look to the future.

Forced by American airpower to quit his original base on El Chipote Mountain, Sandino was constantly on the move and kept his bands as dispersed as possible. EDSN enjoyed popular support and established at least a rudimentary administration to collect food and funds in "assessments." Sandino also showed a high degree of political sophistication in targeting American-owned companies, such as the banana plantations of the Standard Fruit Company, during a time of labor unrest and also attempted to disrupt the 1928 and 1932 elections. Ironically, the first was won by one of Sacasa's former commanders, José María Moncada, the second by Sacasa himself. Sandino's cause received some good international publicity, yet he failed to enlist actual support when he slipped out of Nicaragua to visit Mexico in July 1929.

The commitment of almost 4,000 U.S. Marines to the campaign against Sandino did not prove popular among Americans. Following the deaths of eight Marines repairing telephone lines in December 1930, it was announced that the majority would be withdrawn by June 1931, the remainder after the 1932 election. The conduct of the war thus increasingly devolved to the

proclaimed himself the legitimate president and continued the struggle. More U.S. forces were landed in December 1926, and a peace agreement was concluded whereby Diaz would remain president but would be judged ineligible to stand at the next election in 1928. It was also agreed that liberal and conservative factions would disarm.

Initially, the disarmament went well, but on 16 July 1927 Sandino responded to calls to lay down his weapons by attacking the U.S. Marine garrison at Ocotal with between 500 and 600 guerrillas. He was eventually put to flight after a 16-hour firefight, which included a Marine air attack that is sometimes claimed to be the first organized dive-bombing attack in history. Sandino's motivation was to rid Nicaragua of Amer-

American-trained Nicaraguan National Guard. By January 1933 the U.S. Marines had sustained 47 killed in more than 150 separate engagements, with another 89 deaths coming from other causes (such as disease). The National Guard, which was 2,650-strong by 1933, suffered 75 dead in more than 500 engagements and claimed to have killed 1,115 of Sandino's guerrillas.

Negotiations between Sandino and Sacasa commenced shortly after the last Marines withdrew on 2 January 1933. An agreement was reached on 2 February 1933, whereby Sandino laid down arms in return for complete amnesty; he retired to run an agricultural cooperative in the Coco River valley. A year later, on the night of 21–22 February 1934, he was arrested and executed while visiting Managua by National Guardsmen acting under the instructions of their director, Anastasio Somoza García. Somoza, who was Sacasa's nephew, ousted his uncle and seized power for himself in 1936. The Somoza dynasty was eventually overthrown in 1979 by the Sandinistas, who derived their name from Sandino.

See also: Airpower; Martí, Farabundo; Nicaragua; Puller, Lt. Gen. Lewis Burwell; Sandinistas; United States Marine Corps (USMC)
Further Reading: Selser, G., *Sandino* (New York, 1981); Macaulay, N., *The Sandino Affair* (Durham, 1985).

Santa Cruz y Marcenado, Don Alvaro Navia Osoric, Marqués de (1684–1732)

Santa Cruz was a leading Spanish soldier during the early eighteenth century who gained considerable experience fighting irregulars in Spain during the War of Spanish Succession (1702–1714). He also fought Austrian irregulars in Sicily in 1718 and the Moors in North Africa. His 12-volume work of military theory, *Réflections militaires et politiques* (Military and political reflections), published at the Hague between 1724 and 1730, included sections on what later generations would refer to as counterinsurgency. Indeed, Santa Cruz advo-

cated the kind of hearts-and-minds approach familiar in the works of twentieth-century practitioners. He cautioned, for example, against trying to alter the traditions and customs of a people under occupation and also recommended that amnesty be extended to a population as soon as military resistance had ceased.

See also: Spanish army
Further Reading: Duffy, Christopher, *The Military Experience in the Age of Reason* (London, 1987).

Savimbi, Jonas (1934–)

Savimbi is the leader of União Nacional para a Independência Total de Angola (UNITA). He fought the Portuguese army in Angola between 1966 and 1974 and then, after losing the subsequent civil war, continued his struggle against the Marxist government of the Movimento Popular de Libertação de Angola (MPLA). The son of a railway worker, Savimbi received a medical degree in Portugal before returning to Angola. He joined Holden Roberto's Frente Nacional de Libertação de Angola (FNLA) and became the foreign minister in Roberto's provisional government. However, he broke from Roberto in 1964 and founded UNITA two years later.

Whereas FNLA's traditional support was among the Bakongo people, UNITA's appeal was to the Ovimbundu and Chokwe peoples of southern Angola. UNITA was originally based in Zambia but was expelled after its attacks on the Benguela rail line threatened the Zambian economy. Thereafter, UNITA was the only nationalist movement operating entirely in Portuguese territory. Savimbi allied with Roberto once more when the Portuguese withdrew, but MPLA won the civil war in 1975–1976 through the intervention of Cuban troops airlifted to Angola in Soviet aircraft. FNLA dissolved, but Savimbi continued to fight MPLA. Indeed, he cooperated with the South African army in its operations against South West African People's Organization (SWAPO) bases in Angola.

In December 1988 the international agreement for Namibia's independence provided for the removal of the Cubans from Angola. Negotiations between MPLA and UNITA resulted in a cease-fire and new elections in September 1992. They were won by MPLA, and Savimbi resumed his guerrilla campaign; pressure from the United Nations brought new negotiations in October 1993. UNITA then joined the Government of National Unity and Reconciliation in April 1997. Savimbi continues to distance himself from this process.

See also: Angola; Frente Nacional de Libertação de Angola (FNLA); Movimento Popular de Libertação de Angola (MPLA); Namibia; Roberto, Holden; South African army; South West African People's Organization (SWAPO); União Nacional para a Independência Total de Angola (UNITA)
Further Reading: Windrich, Elaine, *The Cold War Guerrilla* (Westport, 1992).

Selous Scouts

The Selous Scouts were a pseudoforce raised from former guerrillas by Ron Reid-Daly, a former soldier with Britain's Special Air Service (SAS), in Rhodesia between November 1973 and January 1974. The unit was named Selous Scouts in March 1974 after the white big-game hunter Frederick Selous, who guided the original pioneer column into what became Southern Rhodesia in 1890. Following the beginning of insurgency in 1966 in Rhodesia, the Rhodesian army made an initial evaluation of the possibility of organizing a pseudoforce, but it was not felt that the security situation was sufficiently serious to warrant it. When the scale of insurgency escalated in 1972, however, the concept was revived. Reid-Daly modeled the Scouts on the British army's experience of pseudo-operations in the Malayan and Kenyan Emergencies, and the *flechas* (arrows) of the Portuguese army.

The Scouts were initially under the control of the British South Africa Police (BSAP) Special Branch, with the intention of gathering intelligence on guerrillas. They passed under the control of the army-dominated combined operations headquarters (Comops) in 1977. But friction developed between the Scouts and the army and between the Scouts and the BSAP. Tensions were so high that Reid-Daly's telephone was tapped by the army's intelligence department after some army officers alleged that the Scouts were involved in ivory poaching. This led to a confrontation between Reid-Daly and the army commander, Lt. Gen. John Hickman, in January 1979 and to Reid-Daly's retirement.

Many military and police officers doubted the merit of releasing captured guerrillas who would otherwise face the full force of the law, and there was disquiet when the Scouts attacked protected villages to preserve their bona fides in the course of seeking to sow distrust among the guerrillas. The generally unkempt appearance of the Scouts also led to them being nicknamed "armpits with eyeballs." Nevertheless, the Scouts claimed credit for 68 percent of all guerrilla kills as their original combat-tracker role was supplanted by a more active hunter-killer role. They also figured in some of the raids made by the Rhodesians against guerrilla concentrations in Zambia and Mozambique, as in the successful three-day battle waged by only 100 Scouts to overrun a guerrilla camp at New Chimoio in Mozambique in September 1979. The camp was defended by 6,000 guerrillas and their East German advisers, but they were put to flight with an estimated 3,000 dead.

See also: British army; Hot pursuit; Intelligence; Portuguese army; Pseudoforces; Reid-Daly, Lt. Col. Ron; Rhodesia; Special Forces
Further Reading: Reid-Daly, Ron, and Peter Stiff, *Selous Scouts: Top Secret War* (Cape Town, 1982).

Seminole Wars (1816–1858)

The Seminoles of Florida proved skillful guerrilla opponents of the United States Army during the American Indian Wars. Technically, Seminoles were not a separate tribe, mostly being Lower Creek refugees from U.S. territory who moved into Spanish Florida. Indeed, in Spanish, *seminole* meant "runaway" or "separatist." In turn, the Seminoles had given refuge to runaway slaves. They fought with the British during the Anglo-American War of 1812–1814.

The First Seminole War (1816–1818) was essentially an American retaliatory action against Seminole raids. The future president, Andrew Jackson, ended the raids by unilaterally invading Spanish Florida in 1818 and seizing Pensacola. In 1819 Florida was ceded to the United States by Spain. As U.S. president between 1829 and 1837, Jackson initiated a policy of native removal whereby the five Civilized Tribes (Cherokee, Creek, Choctaw, Chickasaw, and Seminole) were removed westward to Indian Territory (modern Oklahoma).

Led by Osceola, many Seminoles resisted removal. The Second Seminole War (1835–1842) thus began with the destruction of Maj. Francis Dade's column in the Wahoo Swamp of the Withlacoochie River in December 1835. Seven different U.S. commanders failed to conclude the war, including future U.S. presidential candidate Maj. Gen. Winfield Scott. Another future U.S. president, Brig. Gen. Zachary Taylor, was more successful in penetrating the swamps and Everglades in 1836 and 1837. Taylor's storming of the Seminole stronghold at Lake Okeechobee in December 1837, and the seizure of Osceola while under a flag of truce by Maj. Gen. Thomas Jesup, broke organized Seminole resistance. Osceola died in detention at Fort Moultrie, South Carolina. However, the Seminoles resorted to guerrilla warfare, and the frustrated Taylor, who had succeeded Jesup in overall command, asked to be relieved from the task in April 1840. Thus the Second Seminole War, which was declared at an end in August 1842, cost the United States an estimated $14 million and resulted in the removal of some 3,800 Indians.

About 500 Seminoles evaded removal and were allowed to remain on unsettled land. However, the ambush of an American surveying party in December 1855 resulted in the Third Seminole War (1855–1858). This ended in May 1858 with the removal of another 125 Seminoles to the west; the 100 or so who remained withdrew even deeper into the swamps.

See also: American Indian Wars; United States Army
Further Reading: Prucha, Francis, *The Sword of the Republic* (Toronto, 1969); Walton, George, *Fearless and Free* (Indianapolis, 1977); Mahon, John K., *The History of the Second Seminole War, 1835–1842* (Gainesville, 1967).

Sendero Luminoso

Sendero Luminoso (Shining Path) is a guerrilla group founded in Peru in 1980, which enjoyed considerable success until the capture of its leader, Abimael Guzmán, in 1992. Guzmán was professor of philosophy at the National University of San Cristóbal de Huamanga at Ayacucho, in mountainous southeastern Peru, when he founded Sendero Luminoso. Guzmán rejected what had become the usual pattern of urban guerrilla warfare in Latin America since the 1960s, drawing instead upon Mao Tse-tung's theories of rural revolutionary warfare. Indeed, Sendero Luminoso drew support from the Quechua natives of the Ayacucho region when it began its campaign in 1982. However, most of the victims of Sendero Luminoso, whose campaigns cost an estimated 23,000 lives by 1992, were natives. That in itself was a violation of Mao's belief in the necessity for winning over the people so that in effect guerrillas were fish swimming in the sea of people.

Moreover, in practice Sendero Luminoso was more a provincial urban insurgency than it was a rural insurgency. Sendero Luminoso's influence spread beyond Ayacucho; indeed, targets in the Peruvian capital, Lima, were increasingly attacked from 1983 onward. In 1985 Sendero Luminoso succeeded in blacking out Lima's power supplies during a visit by Pope John Paul II. The escalating violence and the emergence of other guerrilla groups caused Pres. Alberto Keinya Fujimori to take virtual dictatorial powers in April 1992. An enhanced security effort brought Guzmán's arrest in September 1992. Sentenced to life in prison, Guzmán offered permanent peace terms from his cell in January 1994. This had the effect of fragmenting Sendero Luminoso, although it still poses a threat to Peru.

See also: Guzmán Reynoso, Prof. Abimael; Mao Tse-tung; Peru; Urban guerrilla warfare

Further Reading: Palmer, David Scott (ed.), *The Shining Path of Peru* (London, 1992); Marks, Tom, *Maoist Insurgency since Vietnam* (London, 1996).

Senussi

The Senussi were a nomadic tribal confederation inhabiting parts of Tunisia and Libya in North Africa; it had originated as an Islamic religious sect founded by Ben Ali Senussi in the 1850s. They occasionally clashed with the French army during the late nineteenth century and fought the Italian army when the Italians ousted Ottoman Turkey from Libya in 1911–1912. In fact, Senussi opposition forced the Italians to abandon much of Libya by June 1915.

Meanwhile, Turkey had entered World War I against Britain and France in October 1914, and the sultan at Constantinople declared a jihad (holy war). In addition to the success against the Italians, this had the effect of encouraging the Grand Senussi, Sayed Ahmed, to begin operations against the French in Tunisia and the British in Egypt. Khalifa ben Asker was thrown back by the French in October 1915 and again in June 1916, and the French won a decisive engagement at Agadès in March 1917. In the east the attempted Senussi invasion of Egypt, led by the Turkish officer Nuri Bey and the German-trained Ja'far Pasha, was repulsed in December 1915. The British army's Western Frontier Force then pushed the Senussi back into Libya, capturing Ja'far Pasha and severely wounding Nur Bey at Agagiya in February 1916.

The Italians did not begin their reconquest of the interior of Libya until 1921. It was a bitterly fought campaign; the Italians relied on armored cars, motorized infantry, and airpower to counter the Senussi irregulars, now led by Omar Mukhtar. Tribal rivalries within the Senussi were exploited by the Italians, who also slaughtered the herds of sheep on which the tribes depended. Eventually, 12,000 Senussi were brought into concentration camps; there were deportations and executions. Wells were poisoned, mustard gas was dropped from the air, and a 200-mile-long fence was erected to seal off the Senussi from refuge in Egyptian territory. The capture and execution of Omar Mukhtar in September 1931 finally broke the Senussi resistance.

See also: British army; French army; Italian army

Further Reading: Whittam, John, *The Politics of the Italian Army* (Hamden, 1977).

Shamil (c. 1797–1871)

Shamil (or Shamyl) was the spiritual and military leader of the Murids, a fanatical Islamic monastic military order in the Caucasus that fought the Russian army from 1834 to 1859. Arising from a movement within Islam known as Sufi'ism, the Murids had an estimated 20,000 men in the mid-1840s. Early Russian attempts to crush Shamil's revolt via large scale military operations failed. Count Vorontsov then instigated "slow strangulation" in the 1840s to separate the guerrillas from the population via a series of military outposts. The Russians also launched a political offensive to restore the proprietary and social rights of traditional tribal leaders usurped by the Murids. Prince Baryatinsky completed the gradual penetration of Shamil's stronghold in the Daghestan Mountains in the 1850s. Shamil, who had allied with the Ottoman Turks during the Crimean War (1854–1856) against Russia, surrendered in August 1859. He was exiled to Kaluga, St. Petersburg, and then Kiev. Shamil died while on a pilgrimage to Mecca.

See also: Chechens; Russian army

Further Reading: Allen, W. E., and P. Muratoff, *Caucasian Battlefields* (Cambridge, 1953); Geyer, Dietrich, *Russian Imperialism* (New Haven, 1987).

Simson, Col. Hugh James (1886–1941)

Simson authored one of the classic British texts on counterinsurgency during the interwar period: *British Rule and Rebellion* (1937). Commissioned in the Royal Scots in 1906, Simson served in World War I as an interpreter with the Japanese forces at Tsingtau, China, in 1914; after serving in France he was briefly an instructor to the American Expeditionary Force. Simson also accompanied Allied forces intervening in the Russian Civil War. Simson obtained regimental and staff appointments after the war, including a spell as brigade major at Aldershot (1924–1927) and one with the independent brigade in China (1927). Promoted lieutenant colonel in 1927, Simson was British military attaché in Tokyo from 1930 to 1932 before returning to the War Office. In September 1936 he was appointed brigadier general on the general staff in Palestine, although with the rank of colonel. Simson retired in March 1937.

He based his analysis primarily on the earliest phase of the Arab Revolt (1936–1939) in Palestine, which he had witnessed, although he made some limited reference to the British army's experience in Ireland between 1919 and 1921. Simson identified the growing politicization of what he referred to as "subwar," which was characterized by guerrilla use of terror tactics and propaganda to undermine the police and wage a political-psychological campaign against the government. Simson suggested governments needed to respond to subwar with equal political sophistication, and he urged the coordination of all aspects of the response on the part of civil, police, and military agencies. In particular, Simson saw the need for coordination of intelligence.

Yet Simson favored prompt action by authorities to prevent the spread of insurgency, and so he regarded martial law as a viable option. The emphasis on martial law was likely to attract military readers to Simson's book, but in fact Sir Charles Gwynn's *Imperial Policing* (1934) found greater favor with the British army during the interwar period.

See also: Arab Revolt, Second (1936–1939); British army; Gwynn, Maj. Gen. Sir Charles William; Intelligence; Ireland; Manuals; Police
Further Reading: Simson, H. J., *British Rule and Rebellion* (London, 1937); Charters, David, *The British Army and Jewish Insurgency in Palestine, 1945–1947* (London, 1989).

Smith, Brig. Gen. Jacob Hurd (1840–1918)

Known to his troops as "Hell Roaring Jake," Smith was a controversial U.S. army commander on the island of Samar, the Philippines, between September 1901 and May 1902. Smith was born in Jackson, Ohio, and educated at a commercial institute in New Haven, Connecticut. At the outbreak of the American Civil War (1861–1865) Smith enlisted in a Kentucky regiment in the Union Army. Reaching the rank of captain, Smith was invalided out after being seriously wounded at Shiloh. However, he was commissioned as a captain in the U.S. Thirteenth Infantry in 1867 in recognition of his wartime services. Supposedly he was at the last engagement of the American Indian Wars, at Wounded Knee in December 1890, although he was assigned to the U.S. Nineteenth Infantry at the time. Promoted lieutenant colonel in 1898, Smith was again seriously wounded at San Juan on Cuba during the Spanish-American War (1898).

Promoted brigadier general of volunteers in 1900 and of the army in 1901, Smith took a notably hard line toward the Filipino insurgents who had begun to fight the American presence in February 1899. Smith served briefly as chief of staff to J. Franklin Bell on Batangas before being posted to Samar. Following the massacre of Company "C" of the U.S. Ninth Infantry at Balangiga in September 1901, Smith ordered that no prisoners be taken and that all males over the age of ten be executed. Bell's equally hard methods on Batangas were the subject of a U.S. Senate hearing; Smith was court-martialed and admonished in May 1902. In

July he was retired by direction of the president. Smith returned to a hero's reception in San Francisco in August 1902.

See also: American Indian Wars; Bell, Gen. J. Franklin; Philippines; United States Army
Further Reading: Gates, J. M., *Schoolbooks and Krags* (Westport, 1973); Miller, S. C., *Benevolent Assimilation* (New Haven, 1982).

Somaliland

Somaliland (now Somalia) on the Horn of Africa's eastern coast saw a prolonged guerrilla war waged against the British army by Mohammed-bin-Abdullah Hassan, whom the British dubbed the "Mad Mullah," between 1899 and 1920. Ultimately, the mullah's power was broken by the use of airpower.

Somaliland was established as a British protectorate in 1885 when troops from Aden occupied Berbera. The Italians also had interests in the area, and the boundaries between British and Italian Somaliland were set in 1894. The territory was largely waterless desert and thorn scrub and had little importance in itself. However, the Horn had strategic importance for the British sea route to India. Somaliland was also a necessary ancillary to the garrison at Aden, which depended on meat supplies caravanned to Berbera. The British position was threatened by the emergence of the mullah at the head of a fanatical, quasireligious movement in the Ogaden Desert in the 1890s. Indeed, in October 1902 the mullah put to flight a force of locally raised native levies sent against him by the British. Reinforcements were rushed to Somaliland; more yet were sent when a force of the King's African Rifles was overrun at Gumburu in April 1903. But the mullah was badly mauled after choosing to fight in the open at Jidbali in April 1904 and was pushed back out of British territory.

He accepted limited autonomy within Italian territory but continued to make periodic raids on tribes friendly to the British. The cost of defending Somaliland became increasingly prohibitive; the British thus withdrew to the coast in March 1910, only to reoccupy the interior two years later. The mullah proved troublesome once more in 1918, and to save costs the British decided to bomb the ring of stone forts the mullah had constructed around Taleh. The operation, undertaken with Royal Air Force (RAF) light bombers, finally began in January 1920. The forts proved more resilient than anticipated, yet the mullah was forced to disperse his armed bands and withdraw toward Italian territory. The Somaliland Camel Corps was committed in pursuit, and the mullah's forces disintegrated. This cheap and rapid success in "aerial policing" led the British to use it elsewhere.

See also: Aden; Airpower; British army
Further Reading: Beckett, Ian, *Johnnie Gough, VC* (London, 1989); Beckett, Ian (ed.), *The Roots of Counterinsurgency: Armies and Guerrilla Warfare, 1900–1945* (London, 1988).

South African army

The South African army enjoyed considerable success in its counterinsurgency operations from 1966 to 1984. The initial internal nationalist challenge to white rule from the African National Congress (ANC) and the more militant Pan-Africanist Congress (PAC) between 1961 and 1964 was easily contained by the South African Police (SAP). The nationalists were forced to regroup outside South Africa and infiltrate back through neighboring Rhodesia and the Portuguese colonies of Angola and Mozambique. In 1967 SAP units were therefore deployed in Rhodesia, and an average of about 2,000 South Africans remained there until August 1975.

South African army personnel were also seconded to Rhodesia from the 1970s until 1980. The principal army effort, however, was in South West Africa (Namibia) against the guerrillas of the South West African People's Organisation (SWAPO). The first SWAPO group infiltrated Namibia from Zambia through the Caprivi Strip in late 1965, and the first clash between them and South African forces came in August 1966.

Technically, the army was initially acting only in support of SAP, and it was not until 1974 that it assumed responsibility for operations. The new factor was the Portuguese withdrawal from Angola, which gave SWAPO direct access to Namibia.

SWAPO claimed that the South Africans had 100,000 men in Namibia by 1980, but the number never exceeded 40,000. Increasingly, they included African units raised from the San, Ovambo, Okavango, and East Caprivi peoples in what was eventually called the South West Africa Territory Force. South African forces were also committed to the Angolan Civil War in support of Jonas Savimbi's União para a Independência Total de Angola (UNITA) between August 1975 and March 1976. The border with Angola was then sealed with a cordon sanitaire of fences, minefields, and free-fire zones, and there was an attempt to introduce a hearts-and-minds program in Namibia proper to undermine the appeal of SWAPO. Resettlement was introduced in the Caprivi and Okavango areas.

The South Africans also mounted hot-pursuit and preemptive-strike operations against guerrilla concentrations in Zambia, Botswana, and Angola. "Operation Protea," for example, was a successful, 13-day strike 100 miles into Angola in August 1981; it may have killed around 1,000 Cuban, SWAPO, and Angolan troops. A pseudoforce known as the Buffalo Battalion also operated inside Angola, and the South Africans continued to assist UNITA.

The Marxist government in Mozambique was undermined by South African support for Resistançia Naçional Moçambicana (RENAMO). South African military success was rewarded in 1984 by the Lusaka and Nkomati Accords. In February 1984 under the Lusaka Agreement the Angolans dropped support for SWAPO in return for the cessation of South African raids, and in March 1984 the Nkomati Agreement saw Mozambique drop its support of the ANC in return for South Africa ending support for RENAMO.

It was international pressure, therefore, and not military action by the guerrillas that led to wider agreements on independence for Namibia in 1990 and the emergence of a new South Africa in 1994.

See also: African National Congress (ANC); Angola; Cordon sanitaire; Hearts and minds; Mozambique; Namibia; Pseudoforces; Resistançia Naçional Moçambicana (RENAMO); Rhodesia; Savimbi, Jonas; South West African People's Organization (SWAPO); União Nacional para a Independência Total de Angola (UNITA)

Further Reading: Beckett, Ian, and John Pimlott (eds.), *Armed Forces and Modern Counter-insurgency* (London, 1985).

South West African People's Organization (SWAPO)

SWAPO was the Marxist guerrilla group that fought the South African forces in Namibia between 1966 and 1990, forming the government of Namibia upon independence. SWAPO was originally formed in 1957 as the Ovamboland People's Congress (renamed SWAPO in April 1960). Its support was among the Ovambo tribe, which represented about 46 percent of the African population of the territory. SWAPO, which was led by Sam Nujoma, set up headquarters in Tanzania and bases in Zambia so that it could infiltrate Namibia through the Caprivi Strip, a 250-mile-long corridor linking Zambia to Namibia but bordered by both Angola and Botswana.

The first SWAPO guerrillas infiltrated Namibia at the end of 1965, with the first clash between them and the South African Police (SAP) coming in August 1966. The South Africans were able to close off the Caprivi Strip, but Ovamboland remained strongly pro-SWAPO; martial law was introduced there in February 1972. However, the Portuguese withdrawal from Angola in 1974–1975 provided SWAPO with new bases along the 1,000-mile frontier between Angola and Namibia. By 1978 SWAPO had increased its strength to about 10,000 men trained and equipped by the Soviet, Cuban, and other Eastern bloc personnel in

Angola. SWAPO also received the backing of the UN General Assembly in December 1976, the UN deeming South Africa's occupation of Namibia to be illegal.

But the South African army was now introduced to support SAP, and anti-SWAPO forces were raised from other tribes. South African raids into Angola ultimately forced the Angolans to drop their support for SWAPO in the Lusaka Accords in February 1984 in return for a cessation of the raids. This facilitated negotiations between South Africa and SWAPO, and agreement was reached on independence in November 1988—linked in turn to the withdrawal of Cuban troops from Angola. The UN supervised a cease-fire in April 1989 and also elections, which SWAPO won, in November 1989. Namibia became independent on 21 March 1990, with Nujoma as its first president.

See also: Angola; Namibia; South African army
Further Reading: Soggot, D., *Namibia: The Violent Heritage* (New York, 1986).

Soviet army

The popular association of the Soviet army (formally Red Army) with guerrilla warfare stems from the partisan warfare waged against the invading Germans on the Eastern Front during World War II. Less apparent is the Red Army's waging of counterguerrilla campaigns to establish and maintain communist rule after 1917. Yet in recent years the Soviet war against the mujahideen in Afghanistan (1979–1989) caused the old notions to resurface.

There was a tradition of partisan warfare in the old Imperial Russian Army prior to 1917, but the Bolshevik leader V. I. Lenin ascribed no particular prominence to partisans or guerrilla warfare in achieving revolution. Moreover, the first people's commissar for war after the Bolshevik seizure of power in 1917, Leon Trotsky, believed partisan warfare to be a weapon of the weak rather than the strong; he thought it encouraged attitudes that were dangerous to centralized authority. As a result, *partizanshchina* (partisan spirit) was discouraged, and even though there was some Bolshevik partisan activity during the Russian Civil War (1917–1921), the establishment of a conventional regular Red Army took precedence.

Stalin, who came to power after Lenin's death in 1924, was as suspicious as Trotsky, his rival, regarding the potential independence of partisans. Thus, a Soviet guide to insurrection published in 1928 devoted only one chapter to guerrilla warfare, and even then it was the work of a young Vietnamese revolutionary named Ho Chi Minh. Little appeared thereafter, and when partisan warfare was resurrected in July 1941 in response to the German invasion its value was seen in the political presence of partisans in German rear areas. In any case, Soviet partisans were kept firmly under party control and were entirely subordinated to the requirements of conventional military operations by the Red Army.

The Red Army was far more innovative in terms of counterguerrilla warfare. Indeed, a Soviet marshal executed by Stalin in 1937, M. N. Tukhachevsky, is sometimes held up as one of the founders of modern counterinsurgency. His work, which appeared in a series of articles in 1926, was based largely on his suppression of the Antonov Revolt (1921) in Tambov Province in the Volga region. The revolt was but one of a series of Green, or peasant, uprisings at the same time. In Ukraine, more than 90 separate anti-Bolshevik guerrilla groups had emerged by 1919, the most significant being that led by the anarchist Nestor Makhno. Makhno was not overcome until 1921.

Bolsheviks also faced a challenge from Islamic guerrillas in the Caucasus and Central Asia. In the Caucasus, for example, Chechens rose against the Bolsheviks in 1920, 1928, 1936, and 1942. Even more serious was the Basmachi Revolt (1918–1933), which particularly affected Turkestan. The Basmachi provided Red Army commanders such as M. V. Frunze with considerable experience in counterinsurgency. The lessons were applied against the Ukrainian People's Army and the Lithuania Freedom Army between 1945 and 1952 and ultimately provided some guidance for the Red Army in Afghanistan after 1979.

The Soviet response to insurgency was marked by ruthlessness and cynicism. Marxist-Leninist ideology was often the stimulus to popular revolt. This was the case with the Basmachi, who resented the suppression of Islamic culture (whereas collectivization of agriculture was a factor in the Antonov Revolt). The Soviets generally failed to appreciate the economic, social, and traditional factors underlying such movements, and their initial response was often purely military. The arrival of the Red Army and of the secret police invariably resulted in excesses. The failure of such methods to curb insurgency therefore resulted in temporary political concessions to undermine popular support for guerrillas. Thus, food requisitioning was suspended in the Tambov region in 1921, and Islamic courts and schools were reopened in Central Asia in 1921 and 1922.

Bolsheviks also sought to cultivate elements with whom they could work, Frunze in particular skillfully exploiting tribal rivalries when confronting the Basmachi between 1919 and 1920. However, political concessions did not imply any slackening in the ruthlessness applied to the guerrillas themselves. The Soviet version of resettlement, for example, was deportation, as in the case of 350,000 Lithuanians deported between 1945 and 1952. As guerrillas became isolated from their support, they could be broken into smaller concentrations by the use of artillery, armored cars, and airpower. Tukhachevsky's articles reflected this pattern of military repression tempered by political concession.

The swift military suppressions of East Berlin in 1953, Hungary in 1956, and Czechoslovakia in 1968 did not require the Soviets to display the full range of tech-

niques learned during the 1920s. However, in Afghanistan after 1979 the army devoted itself to reexamining the techniques of Frunze in Turkestan. Airpower certainly remained an integral component in the Soviet response in Afghanistan; helicopters especially were used as gunships and as a means to deploy troops to high ground or to cut off guerrilla groups. The Soviets also encouraged infantry to take the fight to the guerrillas rather than remaining inside armored personnel carriers when under attack. However, the Soviets did not have a monopoly in firepower, for the mujahideen were far better armed than earlier guerrilla opponents, eventually receiving American-supplied Stinger antiaircraft missiles.

The Red Army, which had about 116,000 men in Afghanistan by 1986, did not lose control of the major urban centers or strategic routes, but it increasingly suffered morale problems. Ultimately, of course, the Soviets withdrew from Afghanistan (February 1989) after suffering an estimated 13,000 dead. The collapse of the communist system of the former Soviet Union has exposed additional internal weaknesses in the Red Army (or Russian army as it became known in 1991). Thus, its handling of renewed Chechen unrest between 1994 and 1996 was largely ineffective.

See also: Afghanistan; Airpower; Antonov Revolt; Basmachi Revolt; Chechens; Frunze, Mikhail Vasilyevich; German army; Helicopters; Ho Chi Minh; Lenin, Vladimir Ilyich; Makhno, Nestor; Mujahideen; Partisans; Russian army; Russian Civil War; Tukhachevsky, Marshal Mikhail Nikolaievich
Further Reading: Beckett, Ian (ed.), *The Roots of Counterinsurgency: Armies and Guerrilla Warfare, 1900–1945* (London, 1988); Isby, David, *War in a Distant Country, Afghanistan: Invasion and Resistance* (London, 1989).

Spanish army

The Spanish army had a mixed record in countering guerrilla opponents in Spanish colonies during the nineteenth and early twentieth centuries. It did not succeed in holding Spanish possessions in Latin America between 1808 and 1826, partly because it needed to concentrate on the Peninsular

War (1808–1814) against the French back in Spain. It did succeed in suppressing insurrection on Cuba between 1868 and 1878, but its attempted suppression of a renewed Cuban revolt between 1896 and 1898 and a revolt in the Philippines between 1895 and 1898 helped bring on the Spanish-American War (1898). As a result of U.S. intervention, Spain lost Cuba and the Philippines, confining its empire to North Africa. Spanish rule was challenged there in the 1920s, and the Spanish army suffered a major defeat at the hands of the Rif leader, Abd el-Krim at Anual, in Spanish Morocco in July 1921. Only the intervention of French forces in 1925 enabled the Spanish to overcome the Rifs. Thereafter, the most pressing military conflict was the Spanish Civil War (1936–1939).

Cuban insurgents were poorly armed, and in the so-called Long War between 1868 and 1878 most Spanish casualties came from disease. Indeed, yellow fever alone killed an estimated 30,000 Spanish troops. There were an estimated 44,000 Spanish deaths, again mostly from disease, between 1895 and 1898 on Cuba. The most controversial aspect of the later Cuban campaign was the appointment of Valeriano "Butcher" Weyler as captain-general in February 1896 in succession to Martinez Campos. Weyler revived a system used in the earlier campaign, constructing successive *trochas* (fortified lines) from west to east. He then used small, mobile columns to comb and penetrate the forests and jungles from specially cleared roads. However, Weyler also exerted control over the population through a range of emergency laws (including the death penalty) and resettlement of the population. American condemnation of resettlement led to Weyler's removal in October 1897.

As for North Africa, the Spanish Foreign Legion was created in September 1920 to assist in the pacification of Spanish Morocco. Commanded after June 1923 by Francisco Franco, the Legion suffered more than 8,000 casualties in 845 separate actions

against the Rifs between 1920 and 1926. At Anual, Gen. Fernandes Silvestre and more than 12,000 others lost their lives when Abd el-Krim caught the Spanish army dispersed and forced it to retreat in panic. The Spanish then suffered another defeat at Sidi Massaoud in April 1924, but Abd el-Krim's incursions into French territory resulted in joint Franco-Spanish military action. This led to el-Krim's surrender in May 1926.

When civil war broke out in Spain in July 1936, Franco, who now commanded the Spanish "Army of Africa," transferred his troops to the mainland to aid the nationalist cause against the republican government. However, the civil war was largely a conventional conflict.

See also: Abd el-Krim, Mohammed ben; Anual, Battle of; Cuba; Peninsular War; Resettlement; Santa Cruz y Marcenado, Don Alvaro Navia Osoric, Marquès de; Spanish Civil War; Weyler, Gen. Valeriano, Marqués de Tenerife

Further Reading: Costeloe, M. P., *Response to Revolution: Imperial Spain and the Spanish American Revolutions, 1810–1840* (Cambridge, 1986); Payne, Stanley, *Politics and the Military in Modern Spain* (London, 1967); Preston, Paul, *Franco: A Biography* (London, 1994).

Spanish Civil War (1936–1939)

The Spanish Civil War began with a revolt by the Spanish army against the republican government under the Popular Front in July 1936. The struggle, which cost an estimated 750,000 lives, was largely a conventionally fought war. However, it did provide some theorists such as Tom Wintringham with an understanding of guerrilla tactics. Gen. Francisco Franco, who brought his troops to the mainland from Spanish Morocco in support of the revolt, initially employed mobile columns like those used in North Africa against the Rifs of Abd el-Krim. However, the nationalist army soon developed along conventional lines. The republicans, who were supported by more than 32,000 foreign volunteers serving in the so-called International Brigades, equally failed to develop guerrilla units, for the conservative military leadership doubted the military value of guerrilla tactics and the political leadership distrusted the potential political independence of guerrilla groups. The republican Fourth Guerrilla Corps, for example, was trained by Soviet advisers for sabotage missions rather than guerrilla operations.

All the decisive actions in the war were conventional battles. Franco, who was proclaimed head of state by the nationalists in October 1936, consolidated control first in western and southern Spain. In 1937 Franco gained control of Bilbao in the north, though he failed to cut off the republican government in Madrid. With Italian and German assistance, Franco renewed his offensive in 1938 and effectively cut republican territory in half. Soviet assistance for the republicans was withdrawn, and Franco took Barcelona in January 1939 and Madrid in March 1939 to complete control.

See also: Spanish army; Wintringham, Thomas Henry
Further Reading: Preston, Paul (ed.), *Revolution and War in Spain, 1931–1939* (London, 1984); Carr, Raymond, *The Spanish Tragedy* (London, 1993).

Special Air Service (SAS)

The SAS was formed by David Stirling in 1941 as a unit for raiding airfields behind German lines in North Africa during World War II. It cooperated closely with another specialized British army unit, the Long Range Desert Group (LRDG), and was originally known as "L" Detachment, Special Air Service Brigade. The First and Second Special Air Service Regiments were formed in January and April 1943 respectively and served in Sicily, Italy, and northwest Europe. After the war, the title was revived as 21st SAS, part of the reserve Territorial Army. In 1950, however, a new unit called the Malayan Scouts (SAS) was formed to hunt down guerrillas in the deep jungle during the Malayan Emergency (1948–1960). In 1952 it was renamed 22nd SAS. The regiment served in Borneo during the Indonesian/Malaysian Confrontation (1962–1966) and in Oman during the Dhofar campaign between 1970 and 1975.

It was officially deployed to Northern Ireland in 1976.

The SAS also has an antiterrorist role, as demonstrated by its spectacular assault on the Iranian embassy in London during a hostage crisis in May 1980. It also supports conventional operations, as in the Falklands War (1982) and the Gulf War (1991). As to counterinsurgency, the SAS played a vital role in Borneo, winning the confidence of the aboriginal tribes of the area and identifying targets for the clandestine Claret operations inside Indonesian territory. In the Dhofar campaign, SAS personnel were at the heart of the British Army Training Team (BATT), which raised the pseudoforce known as the *firqat* from insurgents who surrendered, deserted, or were captured and then persuaded to take up arms against erstwhile colleagues.

See also: British army; Confrontation, Indonesian/Malaysian; Dhofar; *Firqat;* Malayan Emergency; Northern Ireland; Pseudoforces; Special Forces
Further Reading: Geraghty, Tony, *Who Dares Wins: The Story of the Special Air Service* (London, 1980); Jeapes, Tony, *SAS Secret War* (London, 1996).

Special Forces

Due to the unconventional nature of guerrilla warfare and insurgency, regular armies have increasingly formed specialized units to meet guerrillas on level terms. Often, special forces mirror guerrilla organization and tactics, although most have origins in the raiding and commando units formed to operate behind enemy lines during World War II. Special forces need specialized skills in handling weapons, explosives, and communications equipment as well as language and survival skills. Thus, special forces must be able to adapt quickly to different environments, since guerrillas may have better knowledge of the terrain. (In Rhodesia between 1974 and 1979, for example, the Selous Scouts became adept at locating water-bearing roots in arid country.)

Special forces can be engaged in five principle roles. First, they gather intelligence through surveillance, deep patrolling, or even penetration of enemy territory. The British army's Special Air Service (SAS), for example, spent long periods on patrol in the jungle during the Malayan Emergency (1948–1960) in order to locate guerrilla groups. Second, special forces are frequently involved in the organization of pseudoforces recruited from guerrillas who have deserted, surrendered, or been captured and then persuaded to fight erstwhile colleagues. This was one role taken by the SAS in forming the *firqat* during the Dhofar campaign in Oman between 1970 and 1975. The third and closely related role is to organize local defense forces and to direct civic action projects. For example, in South Vietnam between 1961 and 1971 the Green Berets organized the Montagnard tribesmen of the Central Highlands into the Civilian Irregular Defense Group (CIDG) or "cidgees."

Fourth, special forces operate clandestinely when governments do not wish security-force operations to be politically attributable. The SAS was involved in the secret Claret operations inside Indonesian territory during the Indonesian/Malaysian Confrontation (1962–1966). Similarly, their involvement in the Dhofar campaign enabled that conflict to be largely hidden. It is possible, however, for special forces operations to attract undue political attention if conducted out of uniform (unless confined strictly to surveillance). This is because operating out of uniform may raise the suspicion that the teams are exceeding the law, as in the case of the alleged "shoot to kill" policy deployed in Northern Ireland during the 1970s and 1980s. There is also the danger that special forces develop such self-belief in their skills and elite status that tensions surface with the police and army. This was certainly the case with the Selous Scouts.

Finally, special forces can be deployed purely in a hunter-killer role, as was increasingly the case with the Green Berets in Vietnam after 1965, especially once con-

trol over CIDG passed to the South Vietnamese army (ARVN) in 1971.

See also: British army; Civilian Irregular Defense Group (CIDG); Confrontation, Indonesian/Malaysian; Dhofar; *Firqat;* Green Berets; Malayan Emergency; Northern Ireland; Pseudoforces; Rhodesia; Selous Scouts; Special Air Service (SAS); United States Army; Vietnam War
Further Reading: Mockaitis, Thomas, *British Counter-insurgency in the Post-imperial Era* (Manchester, 1995); Geraghty, Tony, *Who Dares Wins: The Story of the Special Air Service* (London, 1980); Jeapes, Tony, *SAS Secret War* (London, 1996); Paddock, A. H., *U.S. Army Special Warfare: Its Origins* (Washington, DC, 1982).

Special Operations Executive (SOE)

SOE was created in July 1940 to coordinate British attempts to organize subversion and resistance in German-occupied Europe during World War II. Its founders, L. D. Grand and J. C. F. Holland, consciously modeled SOE on the original Irish Republican Army (IRA) as encountered by the British army between 1919 and 1921. Colin Gubbins, the initial head of SOE's operations division and later the organization's director, had also served in Ireland with Holland. SOE's remit was extended to Japanese-occupied Southeast Asia after December 1941. SOE, which came under the authority of the Ministry of Economic Warfare, had about 13,000 men and women attached to it by 1944.

As with similar organizations such as the U.S. Office of Strategic Services (OSS), SOE did not always enjoy good relations with other government agencies, especially as it frequently operated beyond real executive control. The relationship between SOE and OSS was not even harmonious. In Greece, for example, SOE wished to promote a restoration of monarchy after the war, whereas OSS was influenced to some degree by the anti-imperialist sentiments of the Greek communists. In the Far East, SOE ran Force 136, which assisted the Karens and the Malayan Anti-Japanese People's Army (MPAJA) to fight the occupying Japanese forces. Ironically, MPAJA later transformed into the Malayan Anti-

Races Liberation Army (MRLA), the military wing of the Malayan Communist Party (MCP), which fought the British during the Malayan Emergency (1948–1960).

See also: British army; Ireland; Irish Republican Army (IRA); Karen Revolt; Malayan Emergency; Office of Strategic Services (OSS); Resistance
Further Reading: Foot, M. R. D., *SOE in France* (London, 1966); Foot, M. R. D. (ed.), *War and Society* (London, 1973); Foot, M. R. D., *Resistance* (London, 1978);.

Stern Gang

Lehame Herut Israel (LEHI), or Fighters for the Freedom of Israel, was founded in 1940 by Avraham Stern to fight British authorities in Palestine. It became popularly known as the Stern Gang; Stern was killed in a police raid in February 1942. A true revolutionary, Stern was ready to enlist the support of both Arabs and Germans in an anti-imperialist front against the British. Originally, he was a member of Irgun Zvai Leumi but broke away to form LEHI. After his death, leadership devolved to Yitzhak Shamir, who in 1983 succeeded the former leader of Irgun, Menachem Begin, as Israeli prime minister.

Both Irgun and LEHI were opposed by the Jewish Agency, which was recognized as the official representative of the Jewish population in Palestine. As a result, the Jewish Agency's own forces, Hagana (Defense) and Palmach (Shock Companies), were used against LEHI and Irgun in 1944. However, when the Jewish Agency lost patience with British restrictions on Jewish immigration, it patched up differences with LEHI and Irgun and launched a joint military campaign against the British in October 1945. The Jewish Agency withdrew following Irgun's bomb attack on the King David Hotel in Jerusalem in July 1946; Irgun and the Stern Gang continued alone.

Compared with Irgun's 1,500 activists, LEHI had only about 150. Its favored methods were taxi or truck bombs. Like Irgun, LEHI had an effective propaganda arm. It had its own radio station in Palestine; one of its fronts in the United States was the Political Action Committee for Palestine. With the announcement of British withdrawal in September 1947, LEHI increasingly turned its attention to the forthcoming struggle with the Arabs for Israel's survival.

See also: Begin, Menachem; British army; Irgun Zvai Leumi; Palestine; Palmach
Further Reading: Zadka, Saul, *Blood in Zion* (London, 1995); Charters, David, *The British Army and Jewish Insurgency in Palestine, 1945–1947* (London, 1989).

Strategic hamlets

Strategic hamlets were the protected villages introduced in South Vietnam in 1962 as the basis of a resettlement program to separate the rural population from the communist guerrillas of the Vietcong.

An old concept, resettlement had been revived during the Malayan Emergency (1948–1960) with considerable success. A total of 509 "new villages" had been constructed by the British to house the 500,000-strong ethnic Chinese "squatter" community most susceptible to communist influence. One of the architects of resettlement in Malaya was Robert Thompson. Thompson was invited to make a report on the situation in South Vietnam by Pres. Ngo dinh Diem in 1960 and then became head of the British Advisory Mission to South Vietnam (BRIAM) in 1961. Diem had already begun an "agroville" program of rural community development in 1959 but was now intent on a wider resettlement program modeled partly on Thompson's ideas and partly on Israeli kibbutzim. At Diem's request, Thompson provided an outline plan for the pacification of the Mekong Delta region in November 1961. However, this was at odds with the recommendations of the U.S. Military Assistance Advisory Group (MAAG), which favored a resettlement campaign centered initially on the so-called War Zone D northeast of the capital, Saigon.

As a result, the choice for the first strategic hamlets experiment—"Operation Sunrise"—fell on Binh Duong Province north of Saigon in March 1962, but Diem also decided to adopt the Delta pacification plan as well; he established the Interministerial Committee on Strategic Hamlets in February 1962. However, it soon became clear that Diem and his brother, Ngo dinh Nhu (who chaired the committee), regarded resettlement as a means of extending physical control over the countryside and not as an opportunity to win the hearts and minds of the population. Thus, no less than 3,225 strategic hamlets with a population of 4.3 million people were supposedly completed by September 1962, out of the 11,316 planned. By July 1963 there were 7,200 with a population of 8.7 million; ultimately, the computerized Hamlet Evaluation System (HES) in 1967 included 12,750 hamlets spread across the whole of South Vietnam.

The entire program had been undertaken too hastily and without adequate protection for the resettled population. In any case, unlike the ethnic Chinese in Malaya, the South Vietnamese had a great attachment to ancestral lands and greatly resented being moved. After the overthrow and murder of Diem and Nhu in November 1963, the new South Vietnamese government modified the program to some extent, but strategic hamlets remained a perversion of the original concept of resettlement. They were thus a failure and did not result in any fundamental change in the political attitude of the rural population toward the government in Saigon.

See also: Hamlet Evaluation System (HES); Hearts and minds; Malayan Emergency; Resettlement; Thompson, Sir Robert Grainger Ker; Vietnam War
Further Reading: Thompson, Robert, *Defeating Communist Insurgency* (London, 1966); Gravel, Senator, *The Pentagon Papers* (Boston, 1971).

Suchet, Marshal Louis-Gabriel, Duc d'Albufera (1770–1826)

One of the 26 marshals of France created by Emperor Napoleon I, Suchet was one of the few successful French commanders during the Peninsular War (1808–1814) in Spain, evolving effective counterinsurgency strategies against Spanish guerrillas.

The son of a silk manufacturer, Suchet was born in Lyons. He joined the local National Guard at the start of the French Revolutionary and Napoleonic Wars (1792–1815) in 1792. Soon transferring to a volunteer regiment as an ordinary private, he was elected lieutenant colonel just 16 months later. He came to the notice of Napoleon during the siege of Toulon and served under him in Italy, although he was never a close confidante of the future emperor. Suchet received a divisional command in 1805, fighting at Austerlitz and Jena. He was given command of the Third Corps in Spain in April 1809 (which was later designated the Army of Aragon). As governor of Aragon, Suchet was careful to work through a locally raised gendarmerie and the local administration.

Suchet sought what he referred to as "peaceful coexistence" with the Spanish population and was reasonably successful in keeping Aragon relatively passive. However, he did not have sufficient troops to keep the whole of Aragon under complete control, especially when he was directed in 1810 to extend his jurisdiction to Navarre, Catalonia, and Valencia. Suchet successfully occupied Catalonia in 1811 and took Valencia in January 1812. Created marshal in July 1811, Suchet became Duke of Albufera in January 1812 and was named commander in chief of the Army of Catalonia and Aragon in April 1813. However, Suchet's troops were progressively diverted from him as crises surfaced elsewhere. He concluded an armistice with the British commander in chief in Spain, the Duke of Wellington, in April 1814 and pledged loyalty to the restored Bourbon monarchy. Suchet was appointed to command at Strasbourg but declared his support for Napoleon when the emperor escaped from Elba in March 1815. As a result, he was struck from the list of French peers after Napoleon's defeat and retired. In 1819 he was readmitted to the peerage but took no further part in public life.

See also: French army; Peninsular War; Roguet, Gen. C. M.
Further Reading: Alexander, Don, *Rod of Iron: French Counterinsurgency Policy in Aragon During the Peninsular War* (Wilmington, 1985).

Sumter, Brig. Gen. Thomas (1734–1832)

Known as the "Carolina Gamecock," Sumter was one of the most prominent guerrilla opponents of the British army during the American War of Independence (1775–1783). Of Welsh extraction, Sumter was born in Virginia and served with the Virginian militia against Cherokee natives in 1762. Moving to South Carolina in 1765, Sumter opened a store and became a magistrate. He served against the British and their Cherokee allies as a captain with a volunteer unit between 1776 and 1778 before resigning his commission. However, the destruction of his property by an American loyalist unit commanded by a British officer, Banastre Tarleton, brought Sumter back into the war. Forming a guerrilla unit, Sumter began operations in July 1780. Sumter, who was promoted brigadier general in the South Carolina militia in October 1780, was by no means uniformly successful and was badly wounded in November 1780.

Sumter was not popular with some American leaders such as Francis Marion, and he disliked having to cooperate with other American forces. He also drew criticism for paying his men in plunder under an arrangement he called "Sumter's law." Indeed, the prohibition placed on plundering by the restored South Carolinian administration in August 1781 persuaded Sumter to retire from command. He re-

signed his commission in February 1782, serving several terms in the South Carolina House of Representatives and also in the U.S. Congress. Frequently in debt, he was granted a lifetime moratorium from state debts by the South Carolina legislature in 1827.

See also: American War of Independence; British army; Marion, Brig. Gen. Francis; Tarleton, Gen. Sir Banastre
Further Reading: Hoffman, R., Thad Tate, and Peter Albert, *An Uncivil War* (Charlottesville, 1985).

Sun Tzu (fl. c. 350 B.C.)

Sun Tzu of Ch'i was conceivably the author of the Chinese military classic *The Art of War,* which influenced the tactical methods of Mao Tse-tung in the twentieth century. It is not entirely clear whether Sun Tzu actually existed, although he may have been one of the itinerant military advisers at a time of warring independent kingdoms prior to the unification of China by the Qin dynasty in 221 B.C. It was once thought that *The Art of War* dated from about 500 B.C., but it is now believed to date from between 400 and 320 B.C. Various commentaries added to the text date from the second to the eleventh centuries A.D.

The text first became known in the West through a translation by a French Jesuit missionary in 1772. The emphasis in *The Art of War* is on the economic use of force and the way in which deception and surprise could achieve success without the necessity of fighting at all. In many respects, Mao's tactical thought merely paraphrases Sun Tzu's dictums.

See also: Mao Tse-tung
Further Reading: Sun Tzu, *The Art of War* (Oxford, 1963); Handel, Michael, *Masters of War* (London, 1992).

Taber, Robert

The American Robert Taber authored *The War of the Flea,* an account of rural revolutionary guerrilla warfare. The entire first edition, published in 1964, was supposedly bought out by the U.S. armed forces so they might appreciate the nature of the insurgency being encountered in South Vietnam. Indeed, Taber provided a guide to Mao Tse-tung's principles of guerrilla warfare and other rural variants, including Fidel Castro's campaign on Cuba between 1956 and 1959. Taber had particular experience in the latter.

Born in Illinois, Taber held a variety of manual jobs; he was a merchant seaman during World War II before becoming a journalist. He was the first reporter to conduct a television interview with Castro in the Sierra Maestra Mountains in 1957, and after Castro's victory he worked for the Cuban newspaper *El Mundo.* He was wounded during the abortive invasion by American-backed Cuban exiles at the Bay of Pigs in Cuba in April 1961. In the second edition of *The War of the Flea* (1968), Taber acknowledged that in light of the failure of Che Guevara's *foco* theories, he had underestimated the difficulties facing rural guerrillas in a world being transformed by urbanization. However, he still believed that the United States would face significant guerrilla challenges in Central and Latin America.

See also: Castro, Fidel; Cuba; Vietnam War
Further Reading: Taber, Robert, *The War of the Flea* (London, 1970).

Tache d'huile

Tache d'huile (oil slick) was a pacification technique developed by the French army in the late nineteenth century. It was principally associated with Joseph-Simon Galliéni and his leading protégé, Louis-Hubert-Gonzalve Lyautey. Galliéni perfected the technique in French Indochina between 1892 and 1896 and then as governor-general of Madagascar from 1896 to 1905. Lyautey then introduced Galliéni's methods to Morocco between 1912 and 1925.

Galliéni was partly inspired by the earlier methods of Thomas-Robert Bugeaud in Algeria during the 1840s. The analogy used was that of oil spreading slowly over water, the classic exposition of the technique being an article by Lyautey in the *Revue des deux mondes* in 1900. *Tache d'huile* therefore implied the gradual extension of French administration hand-in-hand with military occupation. Firm military action would be followed by economic and administrative reconstruction of the state by French military administrators. Hearts and minds would be won over by providing the population with protection and such facilities as free medical assistance and subsidized markets. At the same time, the French would work through traditional rulers whenever possible.

In practice, however, there was as much emphasis on military as on political measures, and the French application of force could be utterly ruthless. Moreover, French culture was always intended to predominate over indigenous culture. Also implicit in the theory was a belief that the army itself might be required to move beyond colonial administration and regenerate French society and politics. Thus, *tache d'huile* was something of a precursor of a later theory, *guerre révolutionnaire,* which applied to Algeria in the 1950s and led to the politicization of the French army. Thus, recognizing the need for a greater political response to insurgency in *guerre révolutionnaire* in itself acknowledged the failure of *tache d'huile* when confronted by revolutionary nationalism in French Indochina between 1946 and 1954.

See also: Algeria; Bugeaud, Marshal Thomas-Robert; French army; Galliéni, Marshal Joseph-Simon; *Guerre révolutionnaire;* Hearts and minds; Lyautey, Marshal Louis-Hubert-Gonzalve; Madagascar; Morocco; Pacification; Politicization of armed forces

Further Reading: Paret, Peter (ed.), *Makers of Modern Strategy* (Princeton, 1986); Beckett, Ian (ed.), *The Roots of Counter-insurgency: Armies and Guerrilla Warfare, 1900–1945* (London, 1988).

Tamils

The Tamils are a Dravidian people inhabiting southern India and northern and eastern Sri Lanka (known as Ceylon prior to 1972). In the case of Sri Lanka, the Hindu Tamils form about 18 percent of the population, whereas the Buddhist Sinhalese represent about 74 percent. Tamils migrated to Sri Lanka in antiquity but were also introduced as plantation labor after the British established control of the island in the Kandyan Wars (1803–1818). The Tamils enjoyed a degree of advantage under British rule, which ceased with Ceylon's independence in 1948. Indeed, Tamils of Indian origin were technically rendered stateless by being denied citizenship by both Ceylon and India.

Sinhalese governments progressively sought to raise the status of the Sinhalese majority, for example, by replacing English with Sinhalese as the official language in 1956. As a result, ethnic violence steadily increased, and Tamil demands for autonomy grew. These demands were manifested during the 1970s when several groups called for the establishment of the separate state of "Eelam." The most militant was the Liberation Tigers of Tamil Eelam (LTTE), popularly known as the Tamil Tigers. LTTE was founded by a radical student, Vellupillai Prabakharan, in 1972 in response to the adoption of a republican constitution for the new Sri Lanka, which institutionalized Sinhalese domination. The Indian government and that of the Indian state government of Tamil Nadu encouraged the separatists despite the Marxist orientation of most Tamil separatist groups in Sri Lanka and the potential dangers of encouraging similar Tamil separatism in India itself.

There was an abortive cease-fire between June 1985 and January 1986; with violence escalating rapidly thereafter, India intervened in August 1987, dispatching the Indian Peacekeeping Force (IPKF) to northern Sri Lanka. However, LTTE refused to disarm, and the Indians were forced to undertake large scale military operations against them. LTTE was confined to the Jaffna Peninsula but not destroyed, and IPKF was withdrawn in March 1990. Subsequently, the Tigers assassinated the former Indian prime minister, Rajiv Gandhi, in May 1991, as well as the Sri Lankan president, Ranasinghe Premadasa. IPKF's withdrawal led to a deterioration in the security situation; the conflict, which has cost at least 18,000 lives since 1983, continues.

See also: India
Further Reading: Mohan, Ram, *Sri Lanka: The Fractured Island* (Harmondsworth, 1989).

Tarleton, Gen. Sir Banastre (1754–1833)

The red-haired Tarleton earned a bloodthirsty reputation as the leader of a loyalist cavalry unit during the American War of Independence (1775–1783). The son of a wealthy Liverpool merchant, Tarleton attended Oxford University before being commissioned in the British army in April

1775. He volunteered for North America and served with a number of British cavalry regiments before being given command of the loyalist British Legion with the rank of lieutenant colonel and commandant in 1778.

Sent to South Carolina in 1780, Tarleton came into his own and enjoyed a number of successes against American guerrilla leaders such as Thomas Sumter and Francis Marion. He was known to the Americans as "Bloody" Tarleton, especially after giving no quarter—"Tarleton's quarter"—to those American rebels captured at Waxhaws in May 1780. However, he was defeated, despite commanding the larger force, by Daniel Morgan at Cowpens in January 1781; he offered his resignation. It was not accepted, and Tarleton performed well at Guilford Court House in March 1781, losing two fingers of his right hand in the engagement. Tarleton was interned with the rest of the Earl of Cornwallis's army after its surrender at Yorktown in October 1781 but was paroled to England in 1782. Tarleton was MP for Liverpool on several occasions, returning to active service in 1790. He commanded the military district of Cork from 1803 to 1808. Promoted a full general in January 1812, Tarleton received a baronetcy in November 1815.

See also: American War of Independence; British army; Marion, Brig. Gen. Francis; Sumter, Brig. Gen. Thomas
Further Reading: Bass, Robert, *The Green Dragoon* (London, 1957).

Taruc, Luis (1913–)
Taruc was the leader of the Hukbalahap insurgency in the Philippines from 1946 to 1954. The son of a peasant farmer, Taruc was born at San Luis in Pampanga. Unable to support his university studies, Taruc joined his brother's tailor shop in 1934. In 1935 he became a full-time organizer for the Socialist Party, rising to become secretary-general three years later. Taruc became head of the Hukbalahap military

committee in 1942 and was instrumental in forming the National Peasants' Union (PKM) in 1945, contesting the 1946 elections for the Democratic Alliance (DA).

His subsequent career reflected the deep divisions among the Huks, for he was always closer to the rank-and-file peasant membership than to the communist intellectuals in Manila. The latter aspired to control the Huks but were resisted by field commanders like Taruc. Indeed, when he resigned as Huk commander in chief in March 1951, Taruc discovered he had already been dismissed by the politburo the previous August. Becoming head of the organization department, Taruc was ordered to the distant Cagayan Valley in October 1951. Disillusioned with the campaign, he called for negotiations in September 1952 and was dismissed from the politburo in August 1953. Taruc entered negotiations with the government and surrendered in May 1954. Initially sentenced to twelve years in prison in August 1954, Taruc was then tried for the murder of a wartime governor who collaborated with the Japanese and was sentenced to life in June 1958. He was released in 1968 but was rearrested when Pres. Ferdinand Marcos imposed martial law in 1972.

See also: Hukbalahap; Magsaysay, Ramon; Philippines
Further Reading: Taruc, Luis, *He Who Rides the Tiger* (New York, 1967).

Taylor, Col. John Rodgers Meigs (1865–1949)
As head of the U.S. army's military information department in the Philippines, the then Captain Taylor authored a full-length, five-volume study of the guerrilla campaign fought on the islands between 1898 and 1902. He also prepared a pamphlet on the campaign of Brig. Gen. J. Franklin Bell on Batangas between September 1901 and May 1902. Taylor had been awarded a Silver Star for gallantry in the Philippines in March 1899; he received two more for services during a relief expedition to China in

1900 (launched to rescue the European legations besieged in Peking [Beijing] by the Boxer rebels). Taylor retired due to ill health in 1914 as a major but then served as librarian at the U.S. Army War College until 1919. He received promotion to colonel (retired) in 1918.

Unfortunately, the controversies surrounding Bell and the conduct of the American campaign generally led to the suppression of Taylor's work by William H. Taft, who headed the Philippines Commission and resented Taylor's criticism of the American civil administration. In any case, it has been argued that Taylor was more interested in collecting documents than in analyzing them; thus the work has the appearance of a somewhat fragmented compendium. As a result, the army's 1905 field service regulations gave scant attention to the problems of guerrilla warfare beyond a recapitulation of legal constraints. Similarly, the 1911 infantry drill regulations devoted only two pages out of 528 to the subject. Thus, guerrilla warfare was dismissed as a minor battlefield irritant—arguably to the lasting detriment of its comprehension within the U.S. army.

See also: Bell, Gen. J. Franklin; MacArthur, Lt. Gen. Arthur; Philippines; Smith, Brig. Gen. Jacob Hurd; United States Army
Further Reading: Linn, B. M., *Guardians of Empire: The U.S. Army and the Pacific, 1902–1940* (Chapel Hill, 1997); Gates, J. M., *Schoolbooks and Krags* (Westport, 1973).

Templer, Field Marshal Sir Gerald (1898–1979)

Templer was high commissioner and director of operations in Malaya from February 1952 to May 1954, a crucial period during the Malayan Emergency (1948–1960). Templer was born at Colchester and educated at the Royal Military College in Sandhurst. Commissioned in the Royal Irish Fusiliers, Templer served on the Western Front and in the Caucasus during World War I. He also saw service in Palestine during the Arab Revolt (1936–1939). He rose rapidly in rank during World War II, becoming the youngest lieutenant general in the British

army; but he then chose to step down in rank in order to command the Fifty Sixth and Sixth Armoured Divisions in combat. He was seriously injured in an accident but recovered to become director of military government in the British-occupied zone of West Germany in 1945. Templer was director of military intelligence and then vice chief of the general staff before being appointed to Malaya.

Surprised by the outbreak of the Malayan communist insurgency, the British had begun to develop an effective response after Lt. Gen. Sir Harold Briggs was appointed director of operations in March 1950. Briggs's first priority was to eliminate the political infrastructure of the Malayan Communist Party (MCP). He also established a committee structure to ensure coordination of civil and military responses and introduced resettlement for the ethnic Chinese "squatter" community most sus-

Sir Gerald Templer displays a pamphlet containing facts about his new appointment as British high commissioner in Malaya during a press conference in January 1952. (UPI/Corbis-Bettmann)

ceptible to communist influence. However, the implementation of the so-called Briggs Plan merely escalated the guerrillas' efforts, and morale in the security forces was damaged by Briggs's retirement due to ill health and the death of the high commissioner, Sir Henry Gurney, in an ambush in October 1951. The logic of the attempt to integrate political and military strategies was that a single individual should control all aspects of the government response—thus Templer in the dual role.

By force of his formidable personality, Templer rejuvenated the campaign. Briggs had already appointed a director to coordinate intelligence, and Templer went further in establishing a combined intelligence staff. Briggs had also created an emergency information service, and so Templer appointed a director-general of information services and created a new psychological warfare section. Templer also gave the squatter population positive reasons to support the government, coining the phrase "winning hearts and minds" to signify his intentions. Amenities were increasingly made available, squatters received legal title to lands they occupied in December 1951, and village councils were established in May 1952.

Templer also insisted on transforming the Malayan police from a paramilitary role to one reflecting the more traditional image of British police. A compulsory home guard was established in the new villages, and in September 1953 Templer was confident enough to declare Malacca the first "white area" free of all emergency restrictions. Another important Templer contribution was his encouraging the development of the multiracial Alliance Party that led Malaya to independence in August 1957. Templer went on to become chief of the imperial general staff from 1955 to 1958. Knighted in 1949, he was promoted field marshal in 1956. Templer also founded Britain's National Army Museum.

See also: Briggs, Lt. Gen. Sir Harold Rawdon; British army; Hearts and minds; Intelligence; Malayan Emergency; Police; Resettlement

Further Reading: Cloake, John, *Templer: Tiger of Malaya* (London, 1985).

Terrorism

Terrorism should not be confused with revolutionary guerrilla warfare or insurgency. The confusion arises from the fact that terror is a tactical method that can be used by revolutionary guerrillas and insurgents. Moreover, groups possessing similar ideologies and methods have been labeled urban guerrillas and international terrorists. Even the United Nations has failed to arrive at an agreed definition of terrorism. However, terrorism generally differs from guerrilla warfare (even urban guerrilla warfare) in the motivations behind it.

Guerrilla warfare since 1945 has increasingly been characterized as a combination of military and political methods intended to overthrow the government of a state. By contrast, terrorism is more often a premeditated use or threat of indiscriminate violence exercised without humanitarian constraint. Terrorism is intended to influence a subnational, national, or international audience but often may simply perpetuate violence for its own sake without an obvious political aim.

The origins of modern terrorism lie arguably in the activities of German and Russian revolutionaries during the mid- and late nineteenth century. A systematic terror campaign waged by Russian anarchists culminated in the assassination of Tsar Alexander II in 1881. Then in the late 1960s terrorism made its presence felt as terrorists realized that technological advances, especially in communications and transportation, made the international community vulnerable to extreme violence for political ends.

There were more than 900 terrorist incidents between 1968 and 1975 alone, causing more than 800 deaths. The terrorism rate has continued to grow since at an average of 12–15 percent per year, with the United States becoming an increasing target. In

1990, for example, attacks on Americans or American interests represented 42 percent of 456 total incidents; that rose to 55 percent of 557 total incidents in 1991. Thus, groups with little or no political legitimacy or military power have become significant players on the international stage through the use of terror. The hijacking of three aircraft to Dawson's Field in Egypt and their subsequent destruction in September 1970 was a significant factor in bringing the Palestine Liberation Organization (PLO) the recognition it craved for the Palestinian cause after Israeli military victories over the Arab states had extinguished expectations for Palestinian success.

Terrorist groups have been many and varied. Some have been motivated by nationalism or separatism such as the Sikh Dal Khalsa in India or the Basque Euskadi Ta Askatasun (ETA) in Spain. Others have been clearly revolutionary, such the Brigate Rosse (Red Brigade) in Italy and Action Directe (Direct Action) in France. While paying lip service to nationalist or revolutionary causes, others have actually been sponsored, as instruments of foreign policy, by states such as Cuba, Libya, Iraq, Syria, Iran, and North Korea. The Palestinian Abu Nidal Organization, for example, has received backing from Libya, Iraq, and Syria. Still more curious have been ideological mercenaries such as the Sekigun Wa (Japanese Red Army), which carried out a massacre at Lod Airport, Israel, in May 1972.

Yet terrorism is not confined to the political left, and the philosophy of terrorism has been remarkably uniform across the political spectrum. Whether the identified enemy is vaguely defined as imperialism or capitalism or something else, there is a common belief that violence is a cleansing force for the soul. It might be described as a kind of liberation theology for violence. It is perhaps not entirely coincidental that so many Western terrorist groups originated in the late 1960s amid the radicalism and pseudointellectualism associated with the New Left, the drug culture, Black Power, and the antiwar movement during Vietnam. The small and short-lived Symbionese Liberation Army (SLA) in the United States originated at the University of California–Berkeley, the Red Brigades in the sociology department at the University of Trento, and West Germany's Rote Armee Fraktion (Red Army Faction, popularly known as the Baarder-Meinhof Gang), in the psychology department at the University of Heidelberg. Yet the profile of middle-class dropout as terrorist changed in the 1980s, with terrorists becoming less well educated, less politically aware, and more obviously rooted in street gangs and other criminal elements.

In many ways, terrorists' methods are strikingly similar to those of urban guerrillas. Certainly, the emphasis on "armed propaganda"—brought to light by the Brazilian theorist of urban guerrilla warfare Carlos Marighela—accords with the intent of most terrorist acts. Thus, Marighela believed that the creation of an atmosphere of terror would compel authorities to introduce a range of repressive measures that would provoke a spontaneous reaction on the part of the population against government. For the terrorist, the familiar currency of assassination, bombing, kidnapping, hostage-taking, and hijacking is intended to not only undermine the fabric of society but also ensure full media attention. In this regard, the worse the carnage, the greater the publicity, although paradoxically only 15–20 percent of terrorist incidents involve fatalities, and less than 1 percent involve more than ten fatalities, for terrorists primarily want people to watch rather than perish.

Terrorism poses particular difficulty for liberal democracies, which must balance the need to impose adequate security measures against the democratic rights of citizens. Some states have even chosen to appease terrorism. Other states recognize so-called political crimes, making it difficult to extradite terrorists for trial elsewhere.

And though there are a number of international conventions on terrorism, few are binding. Better exchange of intelligence has assisted the fight against terrorism, as has new technology such as electronic detection and tagging of explosives. Most Western states have also developed appropriate crisis management organizations and specialized antiterrorist squads to deal with terrorist incidents.

In theory, terrorism should not prove a mortal danger to a healthy society. Even in societies with manifest social, economic, and political grievances, terrorism has not been sustainable due to the remoteness of terrorists from the exploited. Indiscriminate violence also tends to drive ordinary citizens toward supporting authorities, and most citizens of liberal democracies want terrorism defeated. In any event, governments must find levels of responses that are effective in stopping terrorism yet acceptable to general populations.

See also: Marighela, Carlos; Media; Palestine Liberation Organisation (PLO); Urban guerrilla warfare
Further Reading: Laqueur, Walter, *The Age of Terrorism* (London, 1987); Wilkinson, Paul, *Terrorism and the Liberal State* (London, 1986); Long, David, *The Anatomy of Terrorism* (New York, 1990).

Tet Offensive

The Tet Offensive was a major surprise attack launched by the communist Vietcong (VC) and the North Vietnamese army (NVA) against South Vietnam in January 1968, coinciding with the celebration of Tet (the lunar new year).

In military terms, Tet was a huge defeat for the communists, yet it proved to be a major political success in that it undermined U.S. resolve in Southeast Asia. The communist leadership in Hanoi agreed to Tet after much internal disagreement. Indeed, the North Vietnamese commander in chief, Vo Nguyen Giap, clearly miscalculated in prematurely launching an all-out offensive, as it allowed the Americans to bring to bear the full weight of superior firepower for the first time since U.S.

ground forces landed in 1965. Giap made the same mistake against the French in Indochina in 1951.

The apparent intention of the offensive was to encourage a popular uprising to bring about the collapse of the South Vietnamese government (GVN) and the South Vietnamese army (ARVN). Following a diversionary attack against the U.S. base at Khe Sanh on 21 January 1968, assaults were mounted on 30–31 January on 36 provincial capitals, 64 district capitals, and five cities by more than 84,000 men, the VC using the holiday to infiltrate the centers undetected. However, communist resistance was wiped out swiftly everywhere except in Saigon and Hue. The communists were finally driven from Hue on 25 February, and the siege of Khe Sanh was lifted on 14 April 1968. Tet failed to result in a general uprising, and

An American military police officer bends over the outstretched body of a Vietcong guerrilla on the grounds of the U.S. embassy in Saigon, 31 January 1968. (UPI/Corbis-Bettmann)

communist actions in towns they controlled temporarily were characterized by atrocities against civilian populations. In all, the communists may have suffered 45,000 casualties; the offensive all but destroyed the VC as an effective combat force (although that very fact removed a potential rival to leadership in Hanoi).

Yet TV images of a VC squad breaking into the U.S. embassy compound in Saigon had a profound effect on American audiences, who till then had believed the war was being won. Then came the request from the American commander in South Vietnam, William Westmoreland, for an additional 200,000 troops as a result of Tet; an administration task force concluded on 4 March that there was no certainty such reinforcement would improve the military situation. Faced with mounting domestic opposition to the war, Pres. Lyndon B. Johnson announced on 31 March 1968 that he would not seek reelection. Johnson also offered to halt bombing of North Vietnam in order to encourage negotiations; a cessation was announced on 31 October 1968, with peace talks due to begin in Paris after the presidential election in November.

See also: French Indochina; Giap, Vo Nguyen; Vietcong; Vietnam War; Westmoreland, Gen. William Childs
Further Reading: Wirtz, J. T., *The Tet Offensive* (New York, 1991); Ford, R. E., *Tet 1968: Understanding the Surprise* (London, 1995); Braestrup, Peter, *Big Story* (New Haven, 1983).

Thailand

Thailand was subjected to a running communist insurgency between 1965 and 1983 that ultimately resulted in victory for the government and its security forces. The Thai Communist Party (CPT) was originally a creation of ethnic Chinese and Vietnamese prior to World War II and was heavily influenced by the example of Mao Tse-tung's success in China in 1949. Increasingly dominated by Maoists, the CPT at its 1961 congress resolved to launch a "people's war"; it opened the campaign in August 1965.

Limited support came from the communist Pathet Lao in neighboring Laos, and support for insurgency would prove strongest in northeast Thailand, where there was a strong sense of regional identity and tension between Thais and the H'mong hill tribes. Facing insurgency, the Thai government contributed troops to the war against communism in South Vietnam and covert assistance to the government of Laos. It also established a Communist Suppression Operations Command (CSOC) under the direction of Saiyud Kerdphol. Unfortunately, Saiyud's attempts to coordinate the government response encountered considerable opposition within the Royal Thai Army, which remained addicted to counterproductive, large-scale search-and-destroy operations. U.S. economic assistance, directed through an Accelerated Rural Development (ARD) scheme, also failed to reduce the level of insurgency because it did not address the need for simultaneous political development in the northeast.

The general political instability in Thailand, which resulted in coups in 1973 and 1976, also hampered progress in combating insurgency. However, the CPT's Maoist methods were equally inappropriate for a society largely concentrated in regional urban centers. An internal debate within CPT as to whether to change strategy caused divisions, which were exacerbated by disagreements regarding the Sino-Vietnamese War in 1979. Meanwhile, a new response to insurgency was developed after 1973 by the deputy commander of the Thai Second Army, Prem Tinsulanonda, building on Saiyud. In 1976 Prem assumed command of the Thai Second Army; he became army commander in chief in September 1978 and prime minister in February 1980. Prem made CSOC, now called Internal Security Operations Command (ISOC), an integral part of the chain of command rather than merely an advisory body. Emphasis was also placed on political as well as military measures. CPT's error in condemning the monarchy, which remained immensely popular, assisted in establishing a 13,000-strong militia known as "Rangers." CPT headquarters were captured in early 1982, and by mid-1983 CPT ceased to be a significant threat.

See also: Laos; Mao Tse-tung; Pathet Lao; Vietnam War
Further Reading: Marks, Tom, *Maoist Insurgency since Vietnam* (London, 1996).

Thompson, Sir Robert Grainger Ker (1916–1992)

Thompson was the leading British theorist on counterinsurgency after World War II, his "five principles" becoming immensely influential within the British army. Thompson developed his ideas from his experiences in the Malayan Emergency (1948–1960). From 1961 to 1965 he was head of the British Advisory Mission to South Vietnam (BRIAM) and was identified with the initiation of the strategic hamlets program. Thompson was also an unofficial adviser to U.S. Pres. Richard Nixon on Vietnam between 1969 and 1973.

The son of a clergyman, Thompson was educated at Marlborough and Sidney Sussex, University of Cambridge. Thompson joined the Malayan Civil Service (MCS) in 1938; during World War II he served in the Royal Air Force. He was attached as air liaison officer to Orde Wingate's Chindits for their long-range penetration raids behind Japanese lines in occupied Burma. He was awarded the Distinguished Service Order (DSO) and, unusually for an airman, the Military Cross (MC). Thompson returned to Malaya and was assistant commissioner for labour and Chinese affairs in Perak when the state of emergency was declared in June 1948. Thompson therefore had intimate knowledge of the ethnic Chinese "squatter" community most susceptible to the influence of the Malayan Communist Party (MCP).

He helped establish the improvised jungle patrol units known as Ferret Force and in 1950 became staff officer (civil) to the newly appointed director of operations, Lt. Gen. Sir Harold Briggs. Thompson contributed to what became known as the Briggs Plan, which recognized the political as opposed to the military challenge posed by the MCP and the communists' exploitation of the squatters' socioeconomic grievances. The first priority was to eliminate the communist political infrastructure and effectively separate squatters from communist influence through a revival of the old concept of resettlement, with the squatters being moved into 509 "new villages." Physical control was a precursor to winning hearts and minds with modern amenities, representative local government, and, above all, legal entitlement to lands that squatters occupied.

Equally essential to British success was the establishment of complete civil-military coordination, especially in the key areas of intelligence and psychological warfare. With responsibility for local security increasingly devolved to the people, army units were freed to strike guerrilla groups who were isolated from their supporters among the squatters. During the course of the emergency, Thompson became coordinating officer (security) in 1955, deputy secretary of defence in 1957, and, in 1959, permanent secretary for defence in the Malayan administration.

The hard-won lessons of Malaya were well encapsulated in what became known as Thompson's five principles of counterinsurgency. They became very influential within the British army well into the 1980s, although they were not formally published until the appearance of Thompson's book *Defeating Communist Insurgency* (1966), which specifically compared Malaya to Vietnam. The five principles are the need for government to have a clear political aim; to function within the law; to establish an overall plan whereby all political, socioeconomic, and military responses are coordinated; to give priority to the elimination of political subversion; and to secure one's base areas before conducting a military campaign. Implicit within Thompson's theories was the British tradition of police primacy over the military; in the context of military operations, Thompson also stressed the need for small-unit operations to meet and defeat guerrillas in their own element.

Thompson was invited to visit Saigon by South Vietnam's President, Ngo dinh Diem, in April 1960 and was appointed to head BRIAM in September 1961. BRIAM eventually consisted of Thompson and four others drawn from either the MCS or the Malayan police. U.S. Pres. John F. Kennedy thought highly of Thompson, and they would meet in April 1963. Thompson's views were also welcomed by civilian counterinsurgency experts around Kennedy such as Roger Hilsman. However, American officials in South Vietnam and the U.S. military establishment did not believe that lessons from Malaya could apply to Vietnam and resented Thompson's access to Diem. At Diem's request, Thompson produced an outline plan for pacification in November 1961; it targeted the Mekong Delta region as the first priority for a resettlement program, as the communist Vietcong (VC) were weakest there. A February 1962 paper by Hilsman embodied many of Thompson's ideas. However, Thompson's proposals conflicted with those of the U.S. Military Assistance Advisory Group (MAAG), which wanted to give priority to so-called War Zone D northeast of Saigon, where VC infrastructure was strongest. The compromise was "Operation Sunrise" in March 1962, which began resettlement in Binh Duong Province north of Saigon, coupled with Diem's adoption of the Delta pacification plan.

However, it became clear that Diem and his brother, Ngo dinh Nhu, had their own interpretation of resettlement; they saw it merely as a means of extending physical control over the rural population. As a result, 3,225 strategic hamlets with a population of 4.3 million had been established by September 1962 alone—without adequate preparation or protection. And though

Thompson had some impact on the *chieu hoi* (open arms) amnesty program to encourage defections from the VC, his influence with the South Vietnamese all but disappeared with the overthrow and murder of Diem and Nhu in November 1963. Thompson was able to persuade U.S. Pres. Lyndon B. Johnson's defense secretary, Robert McNamara, of the benefits of appointing a single individual to coordinate American efforts in Vietnam, much as Gen. (later Field Marshal) Sir Gerald Templer had played a proconsular role in Malaya. Yet when Gen. Maxwell Taylor was given such an appointment in 1964, he did not have the same powers enjoyed by Templer and chose not to exercise those he did have. With its usefulness clearly expended, BRIAM was wound down in March 1965.

Thompson's frustration over lost opportunities in Vietnam was apparent in *Defeating Communist Insurgency*. However, Pres. Richard Nixon read Thompson's *No Exit from Vietnam* (1969) and invited him to meet in October 1969. Thompson counseled against any further escalation of the war, thereby reinforcing Nixon's decision to begin a policy of "Vietnamization." Thompson visited Vietnam on Nixon's behalf in December 1969 and undertook further missions for Nixon in July 1972 and August 1973. Thompson continued to write, including *Revolutionary War in World Strategy, 1945–1969* (1970), and the memoirs *Make for the Hills* (1989). Thompson was knighted in 1965.

See also: Briggs, Lt. Gen. Sir Harold Rawdon; British army; Burma; Hearts and minds; Hilsman, Roger; Intelligence; Kitson, Gen. Sir Frank Edward; Malayan Emergency; Resettlement; Strategic hamlets; Templer, Field Marshal Sir Gerald; Vietnam War; Wingate, Maj. Gen. Orde Charles
Further Reading: Thompson, Robert, *Make for the Hills: Memories of Far Eastern Wars* (London, 1989); Thompson, Robert, *Defeating Communist Insurgency* (London, 1966).

Tito, Marshal Josip Broz (1892–1980)

"Tito" (Hammer) was the cover name adopted by the general secretary of the Yugoslavian Communist Party (CPY), Josip Broz, who led the Yugoslav partisans against the German army in World War II and then ruled Yugoslavia until his death.

The son of a Croat father and a Slovene mother, Tito was trained as a metal worker. He served with the Austro-Hungarian army during World War I and was a Russian prisoner of war when the Russian Revolution broke out in 1917. Converted to communism, he worked as an agent for the Soviet Comintern during the interwar period. When Germany invaded Yugoslavia in April 1941, resistance was mounted by the Cetnik movement of Serbian nationalist-monarchist Draza Mihailovic as well as Tito's communists. Tito and Mihailovic met in September and October 1941 but failed to agree on a joint strategy; in November 1941 Mihailovic concluded that communism was a greater threat to the future of Serbia than was German occupation. As a result, he began to cooperate with the Germans, although he continued to receive Allied supplies until mid-1943.

Tito's forces therefore became the Germans' principal target. Seven major offensives were launched against the partisans between November 1941 and summer 1944. Tito, who formed the First Proletarian Brigade as the nucleus of his partisan army in December 1941, had recruited perhaps 150,000 men by November 1942 and 200,000–300,000 by 1943. He also built a network of People's Liberation Committees as a means of mobilizing the population, but the process of spreading communist political influence was also assisted by the frequent need to shift the partisans' bases to avoid German offensives. In June 1942, for example, the third German offensive forced Tito to retreat some 200 miles, from southeastern Bosnia to Bihac, Croatia. Similarly, the fourth German offensive (January–April 1943) pinned Tito on the Narenta River, forcing him to break out into the Durmitor Mountains. The seventh and last German offensive (May 1944) came close to capturing Tito's headquarters at Drvar, Bosnia, and forced him to relocate to the island of Vis in the Adriatic.

Although Tito's partisans succeeded in liberating Yugoslavia largely on their own without much external assistance, the German troops they faced were mostly elderly and second-rate, and German efforts were bedeviled by rivalries with the Italians, although that made the struggle no less brutal. Soviet forces crossed into Yugoslavia in autumn 1944 for a coordinated drive with Tito on Belgrade. Tito entered the city on 27 October 1944 and mounted an offensive that cleared Yugoslavia by April 1945. Tito, who had been proclaimed marshal by the Yugoslav National Antifascist Liberation Council in November 1943, became president of communist Yugoslavia. He proved too independent-minded for the Soviet leadership, and Yugoslavia was expelled from the Soviet bloc in 1948. While he lived, Tito's status was sufficient to hold the rival nationalities within Yugoslavia together, but the federal structure came under increasing pressure after his death in 1980; it finally disintegrated in 1991.

See also: German army; Partisans; Yugoslavia
Further Reading: Auty, Phyllis, *Tito* (London, 1970); Maclean, Fitzroy, *Tito* (London, 1980).

Toussaint L'Ouverture, Pierre François Dominique (c. 1743–1803)

Toussaint was president of the short-lived Haitian republic, which resisted French rule on the Caribbean island during the French Revolutionary and Napoleonic Wars (1792–1815). "L' Ouverture" (The Opening) was a nickname acquired as a result of his military talents.

Born to a slave family on the French island of Saint Domingue or San Domingo (Haiti), Toussaint was a coachman who learned to read and write with the help of a missionary. He served with the slave army that rose against French republican rule in 1791 and then entered the Spanish service on the eastern part of the island known as

Hispaniola in 1793. However, after the French abolished slavery, Toussaint helped to defend the island against British attack in 1794. He became a French general in 1797 and then life president of the new Haitian republic in 1801. But Napoleon resolved to reoccupy Haiti and dispatched an army there in 1802. Toussaint was seized during negotiations and sent to France, where he died in prison near Besançon in April 1803. Much of the French expeditionary force on Haiti succumbed to yellow fever.

See also: French army
Further Reading: Korngold, Ralph, *Citizen Toussaint* (2d ed., Westport, 1979).

Trinquier, Col. Roger (1908–)

During the mid-1950s Trinquier became one of the architects of *guerre révolutionnaire,* the French army's new counterinsurgency doctrine. Trinquier had served as a French liaison officer in China between 1938 and 1945 and helped form the army's first colonial parachute battalion in French Indochina in 1947. He spent much of the French war in Indochina (1946–1954) behind the lines of the communist Vietminh; his knowledge of communist insurgency techniques was thus invaluable. In Algeria, Trinquier headed the Dispositif de Protection Urbane (DPU), a covert intelligence-gathering unit tasked with dividing up the city of Algiers into controlled sectors under the surveillance of trusted householders, who were usually former Muslim soldiers in the French forces. It played an integral part in the French victory over the Front de Libération Nationale (FLN) in the so-called Battle of Algiers (January–September 1957). Trinquier then succeeded Marcel Bigeard in command of the elite Third Colonial Parachute Regiment.

Trinquier's involvement in the *colon* (European settler) agitation that helped topple the French Fourth Republic in May 1958 led to his recall from Algeria. Trin-

quier retired and became a mercenary leader in the attempt by the Katanga (Shaba) Province to break from the former Belgian Congo in 1960. As a result, he was not available to lend his support to the attempted army coup in Algiers in April 1961 against Charles de Gaulle's policy of self-determination for Algeria. After his Congo days, Trinquier became a viticulturist; he encapsulated his thoughts on the principles of *guerre révolutionnaire* in his 1963 book *Modern Warfare.*

See also: Algeria; Algiers, Battle of; Bigeard, Gen. Marcel; French army; French Indochina; Front de Libération Nationale (FLN); *Guerre révolutionnaire;* Vietminh
Further Reading: Trinquier, Roger, *Modern Warfare: A French View of Counterinsurgency* (New York, 1963).

Trotha, Gen. Lothar von

Von Trotha directed the suppression of the Herero Revolt (1904–1906) in German South West Africa (Namibia). Von Trotha assumed command in June 1904 after the failure of his predecessor, Maj. Theodor Leutwin, to contain the revolt. This failure was due partly to the lack of German troops in the colony, and so von Trotha brought an additional 2,000 men with him. A vigorous strategy of encircling the main Herero force and the obliging compliance of the Hereros in trying to hold a defensive position at Watersberg allowed von Trotha to bring superior firepower to bear. Thus, he was able to rout the Hereros on 11 August 1904. Von Trotha had left one sector deliberately weak and the bulk of the Hereros broke out as he intended into the Omaheke Desert.

In October 1904 von Trotha announced a policy of *schrecklichkeit* (dreadfulness), a systematic strategy of shooting Herero males and forcing the aged, women, and children back into the desert and starvation. However, von Trotha's brutality and failure to contain the subsequent Hottentot Revolt in Namaland resulted in his recall in June 1906. Von Trotha reportedly died of a heart attack while dancing in a ballet tutu at an Imperial Guards ball.

See also: German army; Herero Revolt; Namibia
Further Reading: Bridgeman, J. M., *The Revolt of the Hereros* (Los Angeles, 1981).

Truong Chinh (1909–1989)

Truong Chinh was a leading Vietnamese theorist of revolutionary guerrilla warfare, largely influenced by the principles of Mao Tse-tung. Truong's first work, *Primer for Revolt: The August Revolution* (1945), was an analysis of the Vietminh's seizure of Hanoi following the Japanese surrender in August 1945 before the French could re-assert control over French Indochina. Truong recognized the value of initial cooperation with noncommunist nationalists, who could be subsequently swept aside; he also thought that an avowedly patriotic program could help build popular support for communists.

Truong's second work, *Resistance Will Win* (1947), was intended to prepare the Vietminh for a longer struggle against the French. It drew largely on Maoist concepts and only marginally restyled Mao's three phases of revolution. Thus, whereas Mao spoke of strategic defensive, equilibrium, and strategic offensive, Truong spoke of contention, equilibrium, and general counteroffensive. There was also the same emphasis upon the total mobilization of the masses at all levels, and Mao's concept of substitution was also evident, wherein Truong envisaged the struggle as one of opposing "strengths": thus Vietnamese *political* strength might prevail over French *military* strength. Truong departed from Mao in a much greater emphasis on mobilizing international opinion in support of the revolution, reflecting the greater opportunities already available for the projection of the revolutionary cause in the global arena. The better-known Vo Nguyen Giap largely reiterated Truong's ideas.

See also: French Indochina; Giap, Vo Nguyen; Mao Tse-tung; Vietminh
Further Reading: Chinh, Truong, *Primer for Revolt* (New York, 1963).

Tukhachevsky, Marshal Mikhail Nikolaievich (1893–1937)

Tukhachevsky was a leading modernizer in the Soviet army, responsible for developing a theory of mechanized warfare as well as one of counterinsurgency. Indeed, some claim he is the father of modern counterinsurgency, although it is not clear that his theories became known outside the Soviet Union. Tukhachevsky's ideas on counterinsurgency derived from his experiences in suppressing the Antonov Revolt (1921) in the Tambov Province of the Volga region and the Basmachi Revolt (1918–1933) in Turkestan.

A lieutenant in the Imperial Russian Army during World War I, Tukhachevsky was captured by Germans in 1915 but escaped in 1917, throwing in his lot with the Bolsheviks during the Russian Civil War (1917–1921). He rose rapidly to command Soviet forces during the Russo-Polish War (1920). Tukhachevsky moved to the Tambov in May 1921, deploying a 3,000-strong strike force of cavalry, armored cars, and motorized infantry to match the mobility

An undated photograph of Marshal Mikhail Nikolaievich Tukhachevsky, who was executed for treason in 1937. (Popperfoto/Archive Photos)

of Antonov's insurgents. By June Tuk-hachevsky had destroyed Antonov's forces, leaving the secret police to hunt down the remnants. Tukhachevsky also briefly commanded the Soviet First Army in Turkestan. His thoughts on counterin-surgency appeared in an article, "Borba s Kontrrevoliutsionnim Vosstaniam" (Strug-gle with counterrevolutionary uprisings), in *Voina i Revoliustsiia* (War and revolu-tion) in 1926.

Within the limits of an ideology that compelled him to attribute "banditry" to the inspiration of *kulaks* (wealthier peasants), Tukhachevsky displayed an understanding of the political requirements of counterin-surgency. Thus, he stressed the need to ac-count for local culture and religion and the value of appointing a single individual with full authority over all aspects of the authori-ties' response to insurgency. He suggested raising local forces and, if possible, employ-ing those who surrendered or were cap-tured in pseudoforces against erstwhile col-leagues. The object of military action was to break guerrilla concentrations into smaller groups that could be defeated in detail. Tukhachevsky also suggested measures to win the hearts and minds of the population, but in typical Bolshevik fashion he regarded political concessions as temporary measures that could be rescinded once the insurgency was broken. Thus, he also advocated the eviction of "bandit" families, the confisca-tion and redistribution of their property, the general application of a doctrine of collec-tive guilt, and the widespread use of deten-tion and deportation. Tukhachevsky thus re-flected the Bolshevik pattern of military repression tempered by temporary political concession.

Tukhachevsky became the Red Army's chief of staff in 1925 and deputy commissar for defense in 1931. He oversaw the mecha-nization of the Red Army and the introduc-tion of paratroopers, stressing the need for offensive operations and deep penetration of enemy lines in mechanized warfare. He was created a marshal in September 1935

but then fell victim to Stalin's purge of the army. Accused of treasonable contact with the German army, Tukhachevsky was ar-rested in May 1937. He was executed on 12 June 1937.

See also: Antonov Revolt; Basmachi Revolt; Hearts and minds; Russian army; Russian Civil War; Soviet army
Further Reading: Butson, T. G., *The Tsar's Lieutenant, the Soviet Marshal* (New York, 1984); Paret, Peter (ed.), *Makers of Modern Strategy* (Princeton, 1986); Beckett, Ian (ed.), *The Roots of Counter-insurgency: Armies and Guerrilla Warfare, 1900–1945* (London, 1988).

Tupamaros

Popularly known as the Tupamaros, the Movimiento de Liberación Nacional (MLN), or National Liberation Movement, was an urban guerrilla group operating in Uruguay between 1963 and 1973. The name Tupamaros derived from Tupac Amarú, an Indian leader executed by the Spanish in 1780, and has since been adopted by an-other urban guerrilla group in Peru known as the Movimiento Revolucionario Tupac Amarú (MRTA), or Tupac Amarú Revolu-tionary Movement. Uruguay was unusual in Latin America in the mid-1960s in that it remained a democracy. However, the pros-perity that had underpinned democracy came to an end when world demand for the country's main product—wool—declined during the late 1950s. Prices fell, and Uruguay began to suffer unemployment and inflation. Labor unrest increased in the country's capital and single large center, Montevideo, as living standards declined and bureaucratic corruption increased.

MLN was founded by young, middle-class radicals led by Raul Sendic in 1963. Initially, MLN cultivated a Robin Hood image, conducting a series of bank raids and seizing food, which it distributed to the poor living in shanties surrounding Montevideo. The first armed clashes with the police did not occur until December 1966, but violence escalated steadily there-after. A state of emergency was declared in June 1968, with MLN adding kidnap-pings and seizure of radio stations to its repertoire. Often the victims were businessmen employed by U.S.-owned companies, but MLN also kidnapped and murdered Dan Mitrione, a U.S. Agency for International Development (AID) expert attached to the Uruguayan police, in August 1970. The British ambassador, Geoffrey Jackson, was taken then released in September 1971 after being held for nine months.

Influenced by the theories of Abraham Guillén, MLN intended to provoke an extreme reaction from the armed forces, which might result in some kind of spontaneous popular insurrection. Pres. Juan Maria Bordaberry declared a state of internal war in April 1972; that allowed him to bring the armed forces fully into the conflict. Within six months a ruthless campaign of counterterror had broken MLN, albeit at the price of jettisoning democracy, for the army overthrew the government in February 1973. However, MLN did not survive to exploit the situation it had engineered, and military control was such that insurrection was impossible even if MLN had enjoyed wide support.

See also: Guillén, Abraham; Media; Peru; Urban guerrilla warfare
Further Reading: Porzecanski, A. C., *Uruguay's Tupamaros: The Urban Guerrilla* (New York, 1973); Beckett, Ian, and John Pimlott (eds.), *Armed Forces and Modern Counterinsurgency* (London, 1985).

Tyrolean Revolt (1809)

The revolt against French occupation of the Austrian Tyrol in 1809 was one of a series of popular insurrections that the French faced during the French Revolutionary and Napoleonic Wars (1792–1815). The Tyrol had a certain tradition of popular revolt and had resisted the attempted reforms of Joseph II of Austria in the 1780s, including the imposition of more taxes and conscription as well as the suppression of lay monasteries. Indeed, Joseph's apparent concessions to Jewish and Protestant groups were particularly disliked in the staunchly Catholic Tyrol.

After Austria's defeat by the French at Austerlitz in 1805, control of the Tyrol was handed over to a French ally, Bavaria. The Bavarians attempted to debase the Austrian currency and to impose new taxes and conscription. The revolt was begun with Austrian encouragement in April 1809 by Andreas Hofer and Josef Speckbacher, drawing on the *schützbünde* (local militia). Hofer succeeded in defeating the Bavarians at Berg in August 1809, but the French then resumed control of the Tyrol and drove the rebels into the mountains. Hofer was betrayed to the French and executed in 1810. The Tyrol was restored to Austria in 1814.

See also: French army; Hofer, Andreas
Further Reading: Eyck, F. G., *Loyal Rebels: Andreas Hofer and the Tyrolean Uprising of 1809* (New York, 1986).

União Nacional para a Independência Total de Angola (UNITA)

UNITA, or the National Union for the Total Independence of Angola, one of several nationalist groups fighting the Portuguese in Angola, was founded by Jonas Savimbi in 1966. Initially, Savimbi had been the "foreign minister" of the provisional government established by Holden Roberto of the Frente Nacional de Libertação de Angola (FNLA), but he broke away in 1964. Whereas FNLA appealed primarily to the Bakongo peoples of northern Angola, Savimbi established his support among the Ovimbundu and Chokwe peoples of southern Angola.

UNITA was originally based in Zambia, but its attacks on the Benguela railway threatened the Zambian economy, and the movement was expelled. Thereafter, it became the only one of the nationalist groups fighting the Portuguese to operate entirely inside Angola. UNITA had only about 300 guerrillas as late as 1970 and was concerned more with political than military action. Savimbi was advised by the Chinese, and UNITA was sometimes known as the "Black Chinese." To some extent, too, UNITA enjoyed a tacit agreement with the Portuguese, as it became increasingly hostile to the Marxist Movimento Popular de Libertação de Angola (MPLA). With the withdrawal of Portuguese forces in 1975, a civil war broke out, with Savimbi allying once more with Roberto against MPLA.

(Though UNITA received some limited assistance from the South African army, the war was won by the massive intervention of Cuban forces airlifted to Angola in Soviet aircraft.)

FNLA dissolved, and Savimbi continued to fight MPLA and Cuban forces. He even cooperated with South African operations aimed at the South West Africa People's Organization (SWAPO), which had made its base in Angola. In December 1988 an international agreement on independence for South West Africa (Namibia) provided for the removal of Cuban troops from Angola. Negotiations between UNITA and MPLA resulted in a cease-fire and new elections in September 1992. These were won by MPLA, and UNITA resumed its guerrilla campaign. However, pressure from the United Nations brought new negotiations in October 1993, and UNITA joined the Government of National Unity and Reconciliation in April 1997, although Savimbi has distanced himself from the process.

See also: Angola; Frente Nacional de Libertação de Angola (FNLA); Movimento Popular de Libertação de Angola (MPLA); Portuguese army; Roberto, Holden; Savimbi, Jonas; South African army; South West African People's Organization (SWAPO)
Further Reading: Windrich, Elaine, *The Cold War Guerrilla* (Westport, 1992).

United States Army

Although the United States did not expand overseas much before the Spanish-American

War (1898), Americans were not strangers to projecting military and naval power overseas. Indeed, the United States Army did have a quasicolonial role prior to 1898, as the American Indian Wars had provided American soldiers with enormous experience of irregular tactics. The war between the United States and Mexico (1846–1848) and the American Civil War (1861–1865) also had many instances of guerrilla warfare. And during the American War of Independence (1775–1783), Americans such as Francis Marion and Thomas Sumter proved themselves skilled guerrillas.

Yet the U.S. army showed little interest in the techniques of guerrilla and counterguerrilla war, as its professional focus was firmly fixed on the theories of conventional war as experienced in Europe. In consequence, little was learned, and the U.S. army remained wedded to the concept of what might be termed "real war" to the detriment of its ability to meet the challenge of modern insurgency as experienced in Vietnam between 1965 and 1973.

Apart from coastal defense, the army's only fixed mission after 1783 was to police a moving frontier as the United States expanded westward across the North American continent. Between 1866 and 1890 alone, for example, the U.S. army fought more than 1,000 separate engagements with "hostile" natives. However, the tendency was to regard those engagements as a rather tiresome distraction from the study of conventional war. Of course, there were often setbacks, not least the defeat of George Custer's Seventh Cavalry at the Little Big Horn in June 1876 and, in earlier times, the even worse defeat of Arthur St. Clair on the Wabash in November 1791. However, the tribes had little long-term prospect of sustaining opposition to the inexorable movement of population and the advance of technology such as the railroads. Mexican guerrillas had not proved troublesome, and the experience of irregular war in the Mexican theater was disparate, making lessons difficult to evaluate.

Mostly, natives were fought as if they were conventional opponents, although George Crook made considerable efforts to understand the Apaches when campaigning in Arizona in the 1870s and 1880s. Thus, the only real attention to irregular warfare was in the context of discussing legal niceties to be extended to captured irregulars during the American Civil War. The Union army's Order No. 100 (April 1863) differentiated between treatment accorded uniformed partisans versus irregulars shielding themselves among the population, the latter being regarded as forfeiting any protection if captured.

American cultural attitudes often made it difficult to comprehend the nature of irregular opponents. The fact that Americans had themselves fought for independence meant some opponents were cast in an almost heroic image. Thus, in 1870 one American radical referred to Custer, Philip Sheridan, and Eugene Baker as the only true "savages" on the Great Plains. Even so, Americans often displayed a contempt for indigenous cultures, as manifested in the instructions issued by George Washington for the 1791 campaign for the extermination of hostile natives or the sentiments occasionally expressed by successive commanders in chief, William Tecumseh Sherman and Sheridan, regarding the extermination of Indians on the Great Plains.

The irony was that the army's frontier experiences rendered it largely unfit for conventional war, requiring urgent modernization when the Spanish-American War broke out in 1898. Victory there led to the annexation of the Philippines, yet the U.S. army was then confronted with Filipinos waging the same kind of guerrilla warfare that had been used against the Spanish. The commander in the Philippines from May 1900 to July 1901, Maj. Gen. Arthur MacArthur, favored a policy of benevolence toward the Filipinos yet reintroduced Order No. 100 in December 1900. The army was also compelled to introduce the kind of resettlement that inflamed

American public opinion against Spanish rule when used on Cuba between 1896 and 1898. The pacification campaigns of Brig. Gen. J. Franklin Bell on Batangas and Brig. Gen. Jacob Smith on Samar between September 1901 and May 1902 proved especially controversial. Still, there were American officers like John Pershing, who was interested in comprehending indigenous society, but even Pershing assumed the Moros would be willing to assimilate American cultural values at the expense of their own. Thus, Moros were offended by the understandable American efforts to suppress slavery, much as Cubans resented the equally understandable harsh sanitation regime imposed by Maj. Gen. Leonard Wood between 1899 and 1902 since they had little understanding of the requirements necessary to avoid disease.

A theoretical basis for what might be termed "benevolent pacification" had been provided in the 1890s by Capt. John Bigelow in winning hearts and minds through civic action programs. And in attempting to pursue the Mexican revolutionary Pancho Villa, Pershing demonstrated the lessons of the past by emulating Crook's mounted mobile columns that pursued Apaches. Bell, who had become army chief of staff on the basis of his Philippines experience, was also able to advise Pres. Theodore Roosevelt on the practical problems of any new pacification on Cuba in 1906. However, there was no real attempt to disseminate lessons more widely. Captain J. R. M. Taylor's study of the Philippines campaign between 1898 and 1902 was suppressed due to the political controversies surrounding it. Thus, the 1905 field service regulations and the 1911 infantry drill regulations gave little attention to guerrilla warfare.

It could be argued that the army was aware of the basis requirements of counterguerrilla warfare through its experiences to an extent that did not require qualification. The reality was that officers remained seduced by the prospect of major conventional conflict and had tired of pacification. The defense of the Philippines against Japan became a more significant preoccupation after World War I. A more professionally rewarding study to career soldiers was also provided by participation in World War I. Indeed, the army did not return to the serious study of irregular warfare; less than 1 percent of successive editions of field service regulations in the 1940s were devoted to counterguerrilla warfare.

A study was undertaken during the Korean War (1950–1953), but there was to be no extended statement of counterguerrilla doctrine until 1961. Thus, while successive manuals often appeared to address guerrilla warfare in their titles, guerrillas were regarded as something that could be addressed through conventional operations or as partisans acting in support of conventional operations. Of course, there were unconventional operations during World War II, with American officers leading guerrillas in Japanese-occupied Southeast Asia, and the units raised by the Office of Strategic Services (OSS) represented the forerunners of the army's special forces, the Green Berets, which were revived in 1952. However, the Green Berets had a long struggle for recognition within the military establishment.

Indeed, the thrust behind the new counterinsurgency doctrine of the 1960s was from civilian advisers in the Kennedy administration such as Roger Hilsman. The army's own doctrine remained that of conventional operations in World War II. Indeed, even after the Vietnam War, some American soldiers were arguing that there had been too much rather than too little emphasis on counterinsurgency. In practice, however, the army in Vietnam, as manifested by the head of Military Assistance Command–Vietnam (MAC–V), William Westmoreland, believed that its mission was to fight the "main force" war against the North Vietnamese army (NVA) and not the "other war" against the guerrillas of the Vietcong. It is a debate not yet concluded.

See also: American Civil War; American Indian Wars; American War of Independence; Baker, Maj. Eugene M.; Bell, Gen. J. Franklin; Crook, Maj. Gen. George; Cuba; Custer, Lt. Col. George Armstrong; Green Berets; Hilsman, Roger; Korean War; MacArthur, Lt. Gen. Arthur; Mexico; Office of Strategic Services (OSS); Pershing, Gen. John Joseph; Philippines; Smith, Brig. Gen. Jacob Hurd; Taylor, Col. John Rodgers Meigs; Vietnam War; Westmoreland, Gen. William Childs

Further Reading: Dupuy, R. E., and W. H. Baumer, *The Little Wars of the United States* (New York, 1968); Gates, J. M., *Schoolbooks and Krags* (Westport, 1973); Paddock, A. H., *U.S. Army Special Warfare: Its Origins* (Washington, DC, 1982); Sarkesian, S. C., *America's Forgotten Wars* (Westport, 1984); Utley, Robert, *Frontier Regulars* (2d ed., Bloomington, 1977); Cable, Larry, *Conflict of Myths* (New York, 1986); Krepinevich, Andrew, *The Army and Vietnam* (Baltimore, 1986).

United States Marine Corps (USMC)

It can be argued that the USMC always took counterguerrilla warfare more seriously than the U.S. army, because the Marines rather than the army were primarily responsible for policing American interests overseas after World War I if not before. Marines had landed in Japan, China, Formosa, and the Korean Peninsula on many occasions in the latter half of the nineteenth century. U.S. intervention in Central and Latin America was frequent. Between 1867 and 1900, for example, Marines went ashore on Haiti no less than eight times, and by 1912 there had been nine interventions in Nicaragua. Even though the army was primarily responsible for the policing of the Philippines and Cuba after 1898, Marines policed Haiti from 1915 to 1934 and the Dominican Republic from 1916 to 1924. A USMC legation guard remained in Nicaragua from 1913 to 1925; the Marines returned to Nicaragua from 1926 to 1933 for the campaign against Augusto Sandino.

The lessons were encapsulated in the USMC *Small Wars Manual* (1935, reissued in 1938 and 1940). However, the USMC had other professional interests with amphibious warfare after the creation of the Fleet Marine Force in 1933, and the beaches of the Pacific proved more seductive as a subject for study after World War II. As a result, no time was allocated to small wars at the USMC training establishment in Quantico, Virginia, again until 1960. Nonetheless, based on its traditions, USMC understanding of counterinsurgency would prove far superior to that of the army in Vietnam between 1965 and 1973.

As was the case with the U.S. army, there were difficulties for the USMC given the predominant American cultural attitudes toward irregular opponents. The "Tiger of Seibo," Capt. Charles Merkle, for example, committed suicide in October 1918 while awaiting trial for excesses in the Dominican Republic. Controversy also surrounded the 3,250 deaths resulting from the suppression of the *cacos,* who revolted in Haiti in 1919; the Marines suffered but 13 combat deaths during the entire occupation. This revolt surfaced when Maj. Smedley Butler enforced a little-used law, compelling Haitians to undertake regular road maintenance. This attitude toward indigenous cultures tended to complicate the second characteristic of the USMC and the overall American style of counterinsurgency, which emphasized civic action and constructing impressive public works. Unfortunately, however, insistence on fiscal and political integrity often proved too great a cultural shock to many communities in the Caribbean. In turn, this undermined a third strand of the USMC approach, which was a desire to effect long-term stability through the panacea of holding free and fair elections in circumstances where democratic ideals were little understood. The establishment of efficient gendarmerie went hand-in-hand with this process, as it was intended that they should ultimately take over the principal policing role. Thus, gendarmerie were established on Cuba and Haiti and in the Dominican Republic and Nicaragua. After U.S. withdrawal, however, dictators invariably emerged from the gendarmerie (for example, Rafael Trujillo in the Dominican Republic in 1930 or the Somoza dynasty in Nicaragua in 1936).

U.S. marines during the 1913–1925 Nicaraguan campaign. (Corbis-Bettmann)

Americans did recognize that separating insurgents from the population was an essential prerequisite of success, yet whereas resettlement was a feature of U.S. Army policy in the Philippines, the *Small Wars Manual* rejected that approach. So-called zones of refuge became absolutely necessary. In pure military terms, then, the Marines sought to ensure their mobility but without losing any reliance upon firepower and technology. Intensive patrols from fixed garrisons were a feature of the USMC presence in the Caribbean during the 1920s and 1930s, such as those in Nicaragua by Lewis Puller and his National Guard "M" Company or Capt. Merritt Edson's patrol some 400 miles up the Coco River in 1928. Airpower was also utilized in Haiti and the

Dominican Republic and became even more significant against Sandino in Nicaragua. The USMC even experimented with a fixed-wing rotary aircraft to lift heavy equipment in Nicaragua in June 1932.

An early study of the lessons of small wars written by Maj. Samuel Harrington appeared in *Marine Corps Gazette* as early as 1921–1922. By 1924–1925 seven hours of formal instruction in small wars techniques was being imparted at Quantico by a veteran of the Dominican Republic, Lt. Col. W. P. Upshur. A study of tactics in Nicaragua in 1931 by Maj. Roger Peard also indicated an early preference for what might be termed reconnaissance by fire. Another contributor to the *Marine Corps*

Gazette in 1931 and 1933, Lt. Col. Harold Utley, also pointed to the value of good intelligence and of maintaining good relations with local populations. By this time, Utley was teaching a 19-hour course at Quantico; small-wars instruction eventually reached 45 hours by 1938. Utley and others compiled the *Small Wars Manual,* which reflected the emerging characteristics of USMC practice.

If the author of the 1960 USMC study *Anti-guerrilla Warfare* was initially unfamiliar with the *Small Wars Manual,* there was still at least a body of experience upon which he could draw. Thus, in their area of responsibility in South Vietnam (Corps Tactical Zone I), Marines began experimental county-fair operations in late 1965, screening local populations in cordon-and-search operations while providing entertainment and medical treatment. More than 46,000 people were screened during 1966, and more than 20,000 of them received some form of medical treatment. "Golden fleece" operations were also conducted to safeguard the annual harvest, and the marines established Combined Action Platoons (CAPs) in 1965. CAPs, teaming 15 marines and 34 members of the South Vietnamese Popular Forces (PF), were tasked with attacking the political infrastructure of the communist Vietcong, protecting the government's own infrastructure, collecting intelligence, and training more militia. CAPs were a tactical success (though not as successful as sometimes suggested), and they could survive only in the presence of conventionally deployed marine forces.

In any case, Military Assistance Command–Vietnam (MAC-V) was largely unimpressed with USMC "oil spot" techniques, and the Marines had wider commitments to the defense of the demilitarized zone (DMZ). Unfortunately, therefore, pacification, one of the most important elements of any counterinsurgency campaign, for the most part remained in the hands of the South Vietnamese Army (ARVN).

See also: Airpower; Cuba; Manuals; Nicaragua; Pacification; Puller, Lt. Gen. Lewis Burwell; Sandino, Augusto César; United States Army; Utley, Lt. Col. Harold Hickox; Vietnam War

Further Reading: Fuller, S. M., and W. H. Cosmas, *Marines in the Dominican Republic, 1916–1924* (Washington, DC, 1974); Heinl, R. D., *Soldiers of the Sea* (Baltimore, 1991); Langley, L. D., *The Banana Wars* (Lexington, 1985); Schmidt, H. R., *The U.S. Occupation of Haiti, 1915–1934* (Rutgers, 1971); Nalty, B. C., *The U.S. Marines in Nicaragua* (Washington, DC, 1961); Cable, Larry, *Unholy Grail* (London, 1991); Schaffer, Ronald (ed.), *The Small Wars Manual* (reprint of 1940 ed., Mahattan, 1989).

Urban guerrilla warfare

Urban guerrilla warfare emerged in the late 1960s, initially in Latin America. Prior to that time most revolutionary guerrilla warfare had traditionally been conducted in rural environments—mountains, jungles, and forests, places where guerrillas used difficult terrain to offset the greater strengths of their opponents. The shift to urban environments was a recognition that the world had changed. Increasing industrialization and urbanization meant that even in Third World countries populations were more likely to be concentrated in urban centers.

The discrediting of Che Guevara's *foco* theory of rural revolutionary guerrilla warfare was one of the major factors in the emergence of urban guerrilla warfare in Latin America. Although Fidel Castro referred to cities as the "graveyard" of revolutionaries, the Venezuelan guerrilla leader Moses Moleiro remarked that a peasant revolt was no longer possible when society was no longer peasant-based. By 1967 at least 50 percent of the population in every state in Latin America, with the exception of Peru, was urban. In some states, like Argentina and Uruguay, more than 70 percent of the population lived in urban areas, with 40 percent and 46 percent respectively in their capital cities of Buenos Aires and Montevideo alone. With high unemployment, high inflation, and younger populations concentrated in urban slums and shanties, the widespread sense of deprivation appeared ripe for revolutionary exploitation. In addition, the city provided a wealth of "soft" targets, and revolutionary action in densely populated areas would draw maximum publicity from the media. Moreover, revolutionaries could exist anonymously within the teeming urban populations.

Of course, Marxists had long regarded the urban proletariat as the basis for insurrection, yet the success of Mao Tse-tung's principles of rural revolutionary war in China proved immensely seductive. There had been some recourse to urban terror in campaigns since 1945, such as that by Irgun Zvai Leumi and the Stern Gang against the British in Palestine between 1945 and 1947; by Ethniki Organosis Kyprion Agoniston (EOKA) against the British on Cyprus between 1955 and 1959; by the Front de Libération Nationale (FLN) against the French in Algiers between 1954 and 1962; and even in Latin America, by Fuerzas Armadas de Liberación Nacional (FALN) in Venezuela between 1963 and 1965. Indeed, the leader of EOKA, George Grivas, had written an account of his campaign that offered significant pointers to future urban guerrillas, although he intended it as a kind of primer for Western governments facing communist insurgency.

Even though the disastrous outcomes of urban actions by the FLN in Algiers in 1957 and FALN in Venezuela later should have served as warnings of the inherent dangers, urban guerrilla warfare was increasingly attractive. Youth populations were becoming politicized and radicalized in the Western world through disillusionment with the U.S. role in Vietnam, the rise of the New Left, the drug culture, and, in the United States, Black Power. And other alternatives to violence appeared unlikely to succeed in view of U.S. intervention in the Dominican Republic in 1965. Thus, a theory of urban guerrilla warfare began to emerge, as did international terrorism. However, whereas urban guerrillas and international terrorists used the same methods and often shared ideologies, urban guerrillas can generally be differentiated from terrorists in their motivations: Whereas the urban guerrilla still intended to overthrow government and achieve political change, the terrorist not only rejected the political process as a whole but frequently perpetuated violence for its own sake.

The kind of idealized, ennobling, and morally cleansing form of revolutionary violence preached by popular radical philosophers like the Frenchman Herbert Marcuse and the Martinique-born Algerian Franz Fanon greatly contributed to the blinkered psyche of many emerging urban guerrillas and terrorists. Urban guerrilla warfare itself found expression in the works of the Spaniard Abraham Guillén and the Brazilian Carlos Marighela. Like Guevara, Marighela rejected Mao's emphasis on the need for lengthy political preparation of populations for revolution. He also followed Guevara in envisaging the guerrillas as a small, elite group of dedicated and self-serving revolutionaries. Yet neither Marighela nor Guillén satisfactorily explained how such a small group could build mass popular support. Indeed, Marighela assumed it would follow the "armed propaganda" of guerrillas, who would alienate authorities from populations by forcing authorities to overreact, thereby affecting all involved. The key, therefore, would be maximum media attention through the use of urban terror techniques such as bombs, assassinations, and politically motivated kidnappings. American diplomats and businessmen were the favored kidnap targets, as their capture would focus attention on guerrilla claims of undue political, financial, and military influence being exercised by the United States and would help drive out foreign capital. Confronted with a choice between capitulation and repression, authorities would thus resort to repression. Confronted with the government's repressive policies, the people would in turn spontaneously rise against their oppressors.

Numerous urban guerrilla groups thus emerged, including Marighela's Acção Libertadora Nacional (ALN), or Action for National Liberation in Brazil; the Montoneros and Ejército Revolucionario del Pueblo (ERP) in Argentina; and the Tupamaros in Uruguay. However, Marighela and other urban guerrillas miscalculated, for in every case urban guerrilla warfare provoked such violent reactions from authorities that the guerrillas did not survive to exploit the political situations they created. In the face of institutionalized counterterror, the urban guerrillas were forced into indiscriminate bombing, regardless of their chances for winning popular support. The result was that populations to some degree welcomed at least the initial stages of counterterrorist policies introduced by governments. Democracy was generally sacrificed in the event, but the guerrillas did not benefit from its disappearance. By the mid-1970s, then, all urban guerrilla groups had been destroyed. More recent revolutionary groups have since learned these lessons and endeavor to find the balance between rural and urban actions.

See also: Algiers, Battle of; Argentina; Castro, Fidel; Ejército Revolucionario del Pueblo (ERP); Ethniki Organosis Kyprion Agoniston (EOKA); *Foco;* Front de Libération Nationale (FLN); Fuerzas Armadas de Liberación Nacional (FALN); Grivas, Gen. George Theodorou; Guevara, Ernesto Che; Guillén, Abraham; Irgun Zvai Leumi; Mao Tse-tung; Media; Montoneros; Stern Gang; Terrorism; Tupamaros; Venezuela

Further Reading: Hughes, D. C. (ed.), *The Philosophy of the Urban Guerrilla: The Revolutionary Writings of Abraham Guillén* (New York, 1973); Marighela, Carlos, *For the Liberation of Brazil* (Harmondsworth, 1971); Moss, Robert, *Urban Guerrillas* (London, 1972); Kohl, J., and J. Litt, *Urban Guerrilla Warfare in Latin America* (Cambridge, MA, 1974).

Utley, Lt. Col. Harold Hickox (1885–1951)

Utley was one of the principal authors of the United States Marine Corps (USMC) instructional *Small Wars Manual* (1935). Born in Springfield, Illinois, Utley was commissioned in the USMC in 1907. He served at Cuba in 1908 and served several tours

aboard U.S. naval vessels. In August 1915 Utley was posted to Haiti and remained there until 1917, when he briefly joined the USMC brigade in the Dominican Republic. Promoted to temporary major in 1917, Utley served in Washington before being attached to the gendarmerie on Haiti from 1919–1921. Having commanded Marine forces in eastern Nicaragua against the guerrillas of Augusto Sandino, Utley then moved to the USMC training center in Quantico, Virginia.

In 1932 the course on small-wars techniques taught by Utley increased to 19 hours. Utley was responsible for much of the early draft of the *Small Wars Manual,* which was called "The Tactics and Technique of Small Wars." It drew on the work of British colonial-warfare theorist Charles Callwell and that of Samuel Harrington and E. H. Ellis, who had contributed articles to the *Marine Corps Gazette* in 1921–1922. Utley had written three articles for the *Marine Corps Gazette* under the same title, "The Tactics and Technique of Small Wars," in 1931 and 1933, addressing general issues, intelligence, and staff functions. However, the historical examples Utley utilized in the 1935 and 1938 editions of *Small Wars Manual* were deleted from the final revision in 1940.

The manual outlined five phases of small-war operations: the initial landing; reinforcement and initial military operations; assumption of administration; policing leading to the supervision of "free and fair" elections; and withdrawal, by which time the locally raised gendarmerie would assume the policing function. It has been argued that there were inherent contradictions and inconsistencies in *Small Wars Manual* arising from the attempt to blend benevolence with military realities. Nonetheless, it was a remarkable document for its time.

See also: Callwell, Maj. Gen. Sir Charles Edward; Manuals; Nicaragua; Sandino, Augusto César; United States Marine Corps (USMC)

Further Reading: Schaffer, Ronald (ed.), *The Small Wars Manual* (reprint of 1940 ed., Manhattan, 1989).

Valentini, Lt. Gen. Georg Wilhelm Freiherr von (1775–1834)

Valentini was the author of *Abhandlung über den Kleinen Krieg und über den Gebrauch der Leichten Truppen* (Treatise on small wars and the use of light troops), published in Berlin in 1799. It addressed small wars within the context of the French Revolutionary Wars (1792–1799). However, Valentini did not consider the Vendéan Revolt (1793–1796) to be a small war, and his work was in the tradition of light infantry tactics treated by earlier authors such as Johann von Ewald. A regular soldier in the Prussian army, Valentini became chief of staff to a number of leading generals; he ended his career as chief of the army's educational service in 1828.

See also: Ewald, Lt. Gen. Johann von; Vendéan Revolt
Further Reading: Laqueur, Walter, *Guerrilla* (London, 1977).

Vendéan Revolt (1793–1796)

The French republican armies' brutal suppression of the popular revolt in the Vendée region between 1793 and 1796 resulted in an estimated 400,000 deaths. Vendée was a remote agricultural region south of the Loire River with a conservative and staunchly Catholic population resistant to the republic's anticlerical ideology. But the imposition of conscription quotas in February and March 1793 provided the actual stimulus for a largely spontaneous popular revolt.

Government troops met heavy resistance when advancing into the Vendée in April 1793. Resistance was orchestrated by emerging leaders like François Athanase Charette de la Contrie, Jean-Nicholas Stofflet, Maurice d'Elbée, and Henri de la Rochejaquelein. However, the rebels, estimated at 60,000-strong, had no sense of a wider aim beyond driving the Republicans from the Vendée and were deficient in both organization and coordination, although they did choose a former church sexton, Jacques Cathelineau, as their supreme commander after taking Saumur in June 1793. However, a subsequent advance on Nantes failed, and Cathelineau was killed. In turn, republican commanders were greatly impeded by the interference of politicians in Paris, but 12,000 experienced regulars were dispatched to the west under Gen. Jean-Baptiste Kléber in August 1793 and threw back the Vendéans from Cholet in October. By December, the rebel armies had disintegrated.

Garrisons were established throughout the region, crops and livestock seized, suspects shot out of hand, other inhabitants deported, and *colonnes infernales* (infernal columns) unleashed to systematically comb the region. De Rochejaquelein and d'Elbée were both killed in January 1794. However, it was recognized by the republican authorities that the methods being employed were counterproductive, and a more moderate policy was adopted in the summer of 1794 by Gen. Lazare Hoche. Indeed, Charette signed an armistice in February 1795, although he was really buying time and resumed operations in June 1795 to coincide with a British and royalist émigré landing at Quiberon in Brittany. However, the landing was repulsed by Hoche, who now concentrated anew on the surviving Vendéan bands. Stofflet was captured and executed in February 1796, Charette the following month.

There were brief revivals of insurrection in the Vendée in 1799–1800, 1815, and 1831–1833. The French theorist C. M. Roguet wrote a classic study of the Vendée in 1833 largely in response to the last of the uprisings, recommending the opening of "strategic routes" for troops into the countryside as a means of dealing with future disturbances. Roguet also drew lessons on the importance of a coordinated hearts-and-minds approach in countering insurgency. However, the revolt was generally neglected outside France, although the Prussian military theorist Carl von Clausewitz did apparently prepare a manuscript on the revolt that has since been lost.

See also: Clausewitz, Carl von; French army; Roguet, Gen. C. M.
Further Reading: Paret, Peter, *Internal War and Pacification* (Princeton, 1961).

Venezuela

Venezuela witnessed an early example of urban-based insurgency between 1963 and 1965. However, like other urban guerrilla groups that emerged in Latin America later in the 1960s, Fuerzas Armadas de Liberación Nacional (FALN) miscalculated, overstepping the line between public sympathy and public opposition by attacking innocent civilians. FALN originated in January 1963 from a fusion of dissident military officers and an earlier revolutionary group, Movimiento de Izquierda Revolucionaria (MIR), or the Movement of the Revolutionary Left. MIR had failed in its attempt

to emulate the success of Fidel Castro on Cuba by creating a rural *foco* group along the lines recommended by Che Guevara. As a result, FALN turned to urban guerrilla warfare in the capital, Caracas.

Pres. Rómulo Betancourt proved equal to the challenge by keeping his armed forces in check and demonstrating an exaggerated respect for normal legal processes. Thus, he could preserve democracy *and* resist the attempts by FALN to provoke an extreme reaction that would alienate the population. Betancourt believed in minimum use of force but within the context of maximum display of force, troops dominating the rooftops and crossroads of Caracas. When FALN attacked an excursion train in September 1963, Betancourt felt able to introduce emergency legislation with public support. He also held the scheduled elections in December 1963, and more than 90 percent of those eligible voted despite FALN's attempts to encourage a boycott. FALN fragmented soon afterward, and Betancourt oversaw an orderly transfer of power to his successor in 1964.

See also: Betancourt, Rómulo; *Foco;* Fuerzas Armadas de Liberación Nacional (FALN); Guevara, Ernesto Che; Urban guerrilla warfare
Further Reading: Kohl, J., and J. Litt, *Urban Guerrilla Warfare in Latin America* (Cambridge, MA, 1974).

Vietcong (VC)

The communist Vietcong (VC) was the guerrilla organization fighting against the government of South Vietnam from 1960 until 1975, although after the heavy losses suffered by the VC during the Tet offensive in 1968, the burden of the communist war effort fell to the North Vietnamese army (NVA). Military and political subversion of South Vietnam began as early as August 1957 but at a relatively low level, and the North Vietnamese leadership resolved to escalate the level of conflict in January 1959 only as a result of the growing unpopularity of Pres. Ngo dinh Diem of South Vietnam as well as the damage that Diem was doing to party cadres through an enhanced anticommunist campaign in the south. Ostensibly, the Mat Tran Dan Toc Giai Phong Mien Nam Viet Nam (National Front for the Liberation of South Vietnam) was founded on 20 December 1960 as a coalition of opposition groups dedicated to the overthrow of Diem. Its president, Nguyen Huo Tho, was a noncommunist; religious sects as well as ethnic minorities were all represented. In reality, the National Front for the Liberation of South Vietnam was a front for the communists, and the effective nucleus of the People's Liberation Armed Forces (PLAF) was the 10,000 or so former members of the Vietminh who had remained in the south upon partition of Vietnam in 1954. Soon popularly known as the Vietcong (VC), PLAF was swelled by further infiltration from North Vietnam and by local recruitment. Indeed, VC membership is estimated to have doubled between 1960 and mid-1961, doubled again by late 1961, and doubled once more by early 1962 to about 300,000.

The VC was organized according to the revolutionary guerrilla warfare principles of Mao Tse-tung and the Vietnamese variations of Maoist theory as espoused by Vo Nguyen Giap and Truong Chinh. The Central Committee (COSVN) usually operated from Laos or, occasionally, from the Tay Ninh Province in South Vietnam. The VC's aim was to undermine Diem by political and military means. Thus, a network of three interzonal and seven zonal headquarters, 30 provincial committees, and numerous district, town, and village committees strove to promote other communist front organizations to spread propaganda and to establish "liberated zones." More than 11,000 South Vietnamese were abducted or murdered in 1964 alone as the VC struck at the rural administration in the south. NVA personnel were also involved in the south but, at this stage, primarily as technical experts such as those in Group 559, which began organizing supplies for the VC along the Ho Chi Minh Trail through Laos in May 1959.

The VC's military organization comprised the regular Quan Doi Chu Luc (main force units), who were trained and equipped to meet the South Vietnamese army (ARVN), albeit on terms of its own choosing; full-time guerrillas, who could cooperate with the main force units if necessary; and part-time militiamen, who largely remained at the village level. The primary VC strategy was to consolidate control of rural areas and to encourage urban unrest. Consequently, the adoption of the strategic hamlets program by the Diem government in early 1962 struck at the VC's core support in the villages, and thus strategic hamlets became a priority target for attack.

It became increasingly clear to the North Vietnamese leadership, however, that despite the overthrow of the Diem government in November 1963 U.S. support for South Vietnam would necessitate the commitment of the NVA. It was resolved in December 1963, therefore, to escalate the level of conflict yet again. However, the increasing communist pressure in the south triggered the involvement of U.S. ground forces in March 1965. Technically, the American forces saw their role as countering the NVA and VC main force units in the "main force war"; it was left to the ARVN to continue to wage the "other war" of pacification in the villages. In fact, U.S. reliance on attrition meant little to a Hanoi leadership quite prepared to accept whatever casualties were necessary to achieve the ultimate subjugation of the south. The Tet Offensive of January 1968 was a case in point. In launching largely conventional assaults on the major urban centers of South Vietnam, the VC lost most of the estimated 45,000 communist casualties and was all but destroyed as an effective combatant force. It is reasoned that Hanoi had taken the opportunity to neutralize any possible future rival to its own leadership in the south.

Reduced to perhaps 200,000 by 1971 through the greater coordination of American and South Vietnamese counterinsurgency efforts by the Civil Operations and Rural Development Support (CORDS) organization, the VC took little part in the NVA's major offensive across the demilitarized zone (DMZ) in early 1972. The southern-based Provisional Revolutionary Government (PRG) had been formed in 1969, but it was only nominally in the forefront of the negotiations between the U.S. and Hanoi in Paris. It ceased to exist altogether when the NVA finally seized the south in 1975.

See also: Civil Operations and Rural Development Support (CORDS); Ho Chi Minh Trail; Strategic hamlets; Vietminh; Vietnam War

Further Reading: Duiker, W. J., *The Communist Road to Power in Vietnam* (Boulder, 1981); Pike, Douglas, *Viet Cong* (Cambridge, MA, 1966).

Vietminh

The Vietminh was the communist-dominated nationalist movement that defeated the French in Indochina between 1946 and 1954. It originated in May 1941 as the Viet Nam Doc Lap Dong Minh (Vietnam Independence League). Ostensibly, it was a broad-based coalition of groups fighting the Japanese domination of French Indochina. In reality, it was founded by the leader of the Indochinese Communist Party (ICP), Ho Chi Minh.

Soon taking the abbreviated name Vietminh, the movement received support from the Western Allies, particularly the U.S. Office of Strategic Services (OSS), in return for assisting Allied airmen shot down over Indochina. However, the communist leadership was committed to an armed struggle to overthrow the French colonial authorities as soon as a favorable moment presented itself. That struggle would be conducted along the rural revolutionary principles of Mao Tse-tung. Mao's concepts were espoused in the Vietnamese context by the ICP secretary-general, Truong Chinh, and Vo Nguyen Giap, but it appears to have been Ho himself who resolved to wage a rural guerrilla war. The nucleus for the future Vietminh regular forces (Chu

Luc), officially formed by Giap in December 1944, was found in the party's surviving units from the abortive Bac Son Uprising against the Vichy French authorities in September 1940. Ho himself was detained in China by the nationalist Kuomintang (KMT) in 1942 and did not return to Vietnam until August 1944. Ho vetoed plans made in his absence for another attempted rising because he did not feel the situation was yet favorable.

However, in March 1945 the Japanese seized complete control of French Indochina, eliminated most of the French administration, and set up a puppet government under the titular emperor of Annam, Bao Dai. The Japanese coup d'état enabled Ho to appeal once more to a wider patriotism. Since the Japanese showed little interest in holding anything beyond the major urban centers and principal routes, it was decided to establish a "liberated zone" in the Viet Bac region of northeastern Vietnam. With the dropping of the atomic bombs on Hiroshima and Nagasaki that August, it became clear the Japanese would surrender, thereby immediately opening a power vacuum in Indochina. As a result, Ho's forces seized Hanoi on 19 August and began consolidating control over the rest of the country. Bao Dai abdicated in favor of Ho's provisional government, and on the day of the formal Japanese surrender, 2 September 1945, Ho proclaimed the establishment of the Democratic Republic of Vietnam.

There was no Allied presence in Vietnam until British troops arrived in Saigon on 11 September, and French forces would not reach Indochina in strength until May 1946. The British rearmed some Japanese troops and were able to restore French authority in Saigon. In the north, KMT forces were intended to disarm the Japanese and reestablish French control, but Ho played on his nationalist credentials in order to cultivate a working relationship with the KMT. As a result, the KMT did not seriously hamper the Vietminh administration.

There ensued several months of negotiation. Ho accepted an agreement with the French in March 1946 for limited autonomy within an Indochinese federation to be incorporated into a new French union. However, confidence on both sides steadily eroded, and in November and December 1946 a series of clashes in Hanoi and Haiphong raised tensions to the breaking point despite efforts by Ho and senior French officials to calm the situation. The Vietminh resolved to fight on 18 December 1946; fighting broke out that day.

The French occupied Hanoi, and the Vietminh withdrew again to the Viet Bac. However, the French operated primarily on the defensive, believing they had defeated the communists. In 1949 the French withdrew outlying garrisons north of Hanoi and concentrated on the defense of the vital rice-growing area of the Red River delta in the hope of denying the Vietminh supplies. The Vietminh had been consolidating its support but launched a series of local offensives in late 1949 and early 1950 as the French withdrew. These ultimately led to the fall of most of Tonkin to the Vietminh and a major victory by ejecting the French garrison at Cao Bang on the Chinese frontier.

However, Giap then made the error of launching a full-scale assault between January and June 1951 on the fortified zone established by Gen. Jean de Lattre de Tassigny around the Red River delta. De Lattre established a new French presence at Hao Binh outside the fortified zone, but his successor, Raoul Salan, was compelled to abandon it in early 1952. Another French attempt to advance beyond the delta failed in October 1952, and the focus now shifted to Laos after Giap committed forces there to link with the communist Pathet Lao. The French built up a new fortified position on the Plain of Jars and tried to induce the Vietminh into open battle again, hence Gen. Henri Navarre's plan to seize Dien Bien Phu astride Giap's infiltration route into Laos in November 1953. Giap was able to bring heavy artillery and antiaircraft guns over the mountains to surround Dien Bien Phu, and the French garrison was finally overwhelmed by costly human-wave assaults on 7 May 1954.

An international peace conference convened at Geneva the day after the fall of Dien Bien Phu, and the Vietminh was able to exploit the demoralization of the French and the unpopularity of the war in France itself to achieve a favorable peace settlement. On 21 July 1954 agreement was reached for French withdrawal from Indochina. Whereas Cambodia and Laos became independent, Vietnam would be partitioned along the 17th parallel pending future elections to unite north and south. Technically, the Vietnamese Independence League itself had been dissolved in 1951 and replaced by the broader Lien Viet Front while the ICP separated into three parties for Laos, Cambodia, and Vietnam.

See also: de Lattre de Tassigny, Jean-Marie-Gabriel; Dien Bien Phu, Battle of; French army; French Indochina; Giap, Vo Nguyen; Ho Chi Minh; Kuomintang (KMT); Laos; Mao Tse-tung; Navarre, Gen. Henri-Eugène; Office of Strategic Services (OSS); Pathet Lao; Salan, Gen. Raoul; Truong Chinh; Vietnam War

Further Reading: Duiker, W. J., *The Communist Road to Power in Vietnam* (Boulder, 1981); Pike, Douglas, *A History of Vietnamese Communism* (Stanford, 1978).

Vietnam War (1965–1975)

The Vietnam War was the central drama on the Southeast Asian stage for ten years and held the attention of a global audience. As the North Vietnamese attempted to unify the country under communist control, the United States became increasingly involved. However, whereas the communist leadership in Hanoi was prepared to use all its resources to achieve the subjugation of the south, the United States grew increasingly concerned at the cost of involvement and the failure of its military power to blunt the communist challenge. Disillusioned and facing domestic opposition to the war, the United States withdrew its ground forces from South Vietnam in 1973. Two years later, South Vietnam fell to the communists.

Following the French fall at Dien Bien Phu and the subsequent agreement reached in Geneva in July 1954 that partitioned North and South Vietnam on the 17th parallel, elections were due to be held to reunite the country in 1956. In the event, the elections were never held amid mutual recriminations on the likelihood of a "free and fair" outcome. The new Republic of South Vietnam under Pres. Ngo dinh Diem was supported by the United States as a bulwark against communism. However, Diem ruled a fragmented society divided by religious and ethnic differences. He also faced escalating insurgency by the communist Vietcong (VC), which was supported and orchestrated by Ho Chin Minh's government in Hanoi. Diem came under increasing pressure, and the Kennedy administration, worried by communist successes in the countryside, increased the number of American advisers in South Vietnam.

The U.S. Special Forces, or Green Berets, began organizing the Civilian Irregular Defense Group (CIDG) in December 1961. In February 1962 Military Assistance Command–Vietnam (MAC–V) was established in succession to the Military Assistance Advisory Group (MAAG). In 1963 Buddhist hostility toward Diem resulted in widespread rioting; the U.S. administration even encouraged a coup by the South Vietnamese army (ARVN), whereby Diem was murdered, in November 1963. However, military governments succeeded each other rapidly until the end of 1964, when Air Vice Marshal Nguyen Cao Ky and Gen. Nguyen Van Thieu brought a degree of political stability. It was clear, however, that the VC was increasing its hold over the countryside.

On 2 August 1964 the USS *Maddox* was apparently attacked by North Vietnamese patrol boats, and Pres. Lyndon B. Johnson ordered bombing attacks against North Vietnam. Five days later, the Gulf of Tonkin Resolution in the U.S. Congress empowered Johnson to conduct the war without further congressional approval. Immediate U.S. reaction was confined to air raids, which were stepped up in February 1965 in response to a VC attack on U.S. barracks at Pleiku. The bombing of targets in North Vietnam, codenamed "Operation Rolling Thunder," was launched on 2 March 1965 and continued until 31 October 1968. On 8 March 1965 U.S. Marines landed at Da Nang, ostensibly to guard U.S. airfields. Initially, an "enclave" strategy was considered, whereby U.S. troops would protect only their own bases. However, the head of MAC–V, Gen. William C. Westmoreland, believed that only U.S. forces could take on the VC main force units and the North Vietnamese army (NVA) units that were increasingly infiltrating South Vietnam via the Ho Chi Minh Trail through neutral Laos and Cambodia. Thus, the ARVN was left with the task of pacification. U.S. troop strength reached 184,000 by the end of 1965.

It was assumed that bombing North Vietnam would force Hanoi into negotiations, but in reality it gifted the North Vietnamese a propaganda victory, projecting the image of a small country assailed by a superpower war machine. In any case, the effectiveness of "Rolling Thunder" was limited by the Americans' self-imposed restrictions, and the bombs never stopped the flow of men and supplies down the Ho Chi Minh Trail. Similarly, the U.S. army believed that it could dictate the ground war and inflict such heavy casualties on the NVA and VC that Hanoi would give up the struggle. Yet the communists were prepared to pay any price until the Americans lost resolve.

Failure to translate undoubted military success into political victory increased the pressure on the Johnson administration. In April 1967 Westmoreland was told he could not have more than the "minimum" 550,000 men he demanded to secure victory. Even then the army was ill-prepared for the guerrilla tactics (sometimes utilized by the regular NVA itself). U.S. commanders favored inappropriate, large-scale search-and-destroy operations utilizing large numbers of helicopters and relied on firepower to substitute for permanent occupation of the ground. Moreover, less than 10 percent of American resources were devoted to pacification efforts, and those were often offset by damage to the civilian population through forcible resettlement to strategic hamlets or, even worse, by the internal refugees that resulted from the military operations.

The South Vietnamese government was undeniably tinged with corruption, and even though the population had little love for communism there was little commitment to Saigon, either. Ironically, the massive military defeat of the VC during the Tet Offensive in January 1968 proved the turning point in American resolve. The communists failed to provoke the popular rising they had intended and took huge losses. North Vietnam's military leader, Vo Nguyen Giap, had repeated his error against the French in 1951 by launching a premature conventional offensive that exposed the communists to the full weight of the opponent's firepower. However, images of the VC breaking into the U.S. embassy in Saigon made a profound impact on American audiences, which had believed the war was being won.

As casualties increased, many young Americans resisted conscription, and opposition to the war developed. Johnson decided not to run for reelection and announced a pause in the bombing campaign on 31 October 1968 to allow peace talks to begin in Paris. Richard Nixon was elected president in November 1968 on the promise of finding "peace with honor." Nixon also wanted a "Vietnamization" of the war, with the ARVN gradually assuming responsibility for all operations. It involved a dual strategy of negotiation coupled with maintaining military effort; Nixon sought to put additional pressure on Hanoi by a major incursion into Cambodia to cut the Ho Chi Minh Trail in April 1970. As a result, Congress reasserted its authority and repealed the Gulf of Tonkin Resolution. However, there was a similar incursion by

ARVN forces into Laos in February 1971. In fact, the losses sustained by the VC in 1968 and the new coordination of counterinsurgency efforts achieved by the establishment of Robert Komer's Civil Operations and Rural Development Support (CORDS) organization in May 1967 was damaging the communist infrastructure. Although controversial, the *chieu hoi* (open arms) amnesty program and the neutralization of VC cadres in the Phoenix program did have an impact, but arguably it was too late. Moreover, the pacification effort did not succeed in converting the population's grudging preference for Saigon into wholehearted support.

U.S. troop strength had declined to some 239,000 by 1971, with a concomitant decline in morale and effectiveness. Yet another conventional offensive launched by Giap in March 1972 was destroyed by American airpower, and in April Nixon resumed the bombing of North Vietnam. Each time the continuing negotiations in Paris became bogged down, Nixon increased the pressure. The second "Linebacker" air offensive (between 19 and 30 December 1972) persuaded the North Vietnamese to sign a cease-fire agreement on 9 January 1973. However, Nixon's only real aim was to withdraw U.S. troops, and little was done to ensure the future security of South Vietnam. Though Nixon promised to use airpower again if the North Vietnamese attacked, he resigned from office over Watergate in August 1974.

In South Vietnam, Thieu's government was becoming more unpopular. There had never been a real cease-fire in many areas, and the NVA had continued to consolidate its strength. In early 1975 a new communist offensive took the ARVN by surprise, and it rapidly crumbled. Saigon fell on 30 April 1975. The cost of the Vietnam War was an estimated 3 million lives, including 46,397 American servicemen killed in action and 10,340 more dying from other causes.

See also: Airpower; Cambodia; Civil Operations and Rural Development Support (CORDS); Civilian Irregular

Defense Group (CIDG); Giap, Vo Nguyen; Green Berets; Hamlet Evaluation System (HES); Hearts and minds; Helicopters; Ho Chi Minh Trail; Ho Chi Minh; Komer, Robert William; Laos; McNamara Line; Media; Phoenix program; Rheault affair; Strategic hamlets; Tet Offensive; United States Army; United States Marine Corps (USMC); Vietcong; Westmoreland, Gen. William Childs

Further Reading: Bergerud, Eric, *The Dynamics of Defeat* (Boulder, 1991); Cable, Larry, *Conflict of Myths* (New York, 1986); Cable, Larry, *Unholy Grail* (London, 1991); Cincinnatus [C. B. Currey], *Self-Destruction* (New York, 1981); Herring, George, *America's Longest War* (2d ed., New York, 1986); Hunt, R. A., *Pacification* (Boulder, 1995); Karnow, Stanley, *Vietnam: A History* (New York, 1983); Krepinevich, Andrew, *The Army and Vietnam* (Baltimore, 1986); Palmer, Bruce, *The Twenty-Five-Year War* (New York, 1990); Shafer, D. M., *Deadly Paradigms* (Leicester, 1990).

Walker, Gen. Sir Walter Colyear (1912–)

Walker was the British army's director of operations during the Indonesian/Malaysian Confrontation in Borneo (1962–1966). The son of an Assam tea planter, Walker was educated at Blundell's School and the Royal Military College, Sandhurst. Commissioned into the Brigade of Gurkhas, Walker served in Waziristan on India's North-West Frontier from 1939 to 1941. He served for the remainder of World War II in Burma and was instrumental in creating the improvised jungle patrolling units known as Ferret Force at the beginning of the Malayan Emergency (1948–1960). Walker was also the author of the manual *The Conduct of Anti-Terrorist Operations in Malaya* (1952) and ran a jungle warfare school in Johore.

Appointed director of operations in Borneo in December 1962, Walker realized that he could not prevent infiltration into Malaysian territory. As a result, he sought to concentrate his forces at strategic points and to rely heavily on helicopters to strike at those Indonesian groups that were detected. Drawing on his Malayan experience, Walker also drew up a five-point directive requiring unity of effort through the establishment of a joint headquarters; the coordination of intelligence; speed, mobility, and flexibility; security of British base areas; and domination of the jungle. Walker also moved to win the hearts and minds of the population. Many of the indigenous aborigi-

nals were already well disposed toward the British, and soldiers and police were sent into villages and settlements to protect and advise. Medical and agricultural help was offered, and Special Air Service (SAS) teams worked alongside the villagers. Walker's strategy made it increasingly difficult for the Indonesians to find food, shelter, and information. A permanent presence was established in contested areas; the struggle was then taken into Indonesia proper in the form of the clandestine Claret operations, in which the SAS was often led by Iban native trackers.

The conflict was virtually won by the time Walker handed over operations to his successor, Maj. Gen. George Lea, in March 1965. Walker had ruffled many feathers among his superiors, not least in terms of a vigorous campaign to save the Gurkhas from reduction. As a result, he was earmarked for retirement in 1967 but used his friendship with the senior Labour minister, Denis Healey, who had been minister of defence during the confrontation, to get the Army Board's decision reversed. As a result, Walker was promoted to lieutenant general and became deputy chief of staff to NATO forces in central Europe. Knighted in 1968 and made full general in 1969, Walker became commander in chief of NATO forces in North Europe from 1969 to 1972. However, his alarmist views of the Soviet threat to NATO in northern Europe caused considerable problems.

After retirement, Walker gained further notoriety during the 1970s for his strident anticommunism and attempted sponsorship of a private army. He published *The Bear at the Door* in 1978 and *The Next Domino?* in 1980.

See also: British army; Confrontation, Indonesian/Malaysian; Hearts and minds; Helicopters; Malayan Emergency; Manuals; Special Air Service (SAS)
Further Reading: Mockaitis, Thomas, *British Counter-insurgency in the Post-imperial Era* (Manchester, 1995); Pocock, Tom, *Fighting General* (London, 1973).

Walls, Lt. Gen. Peter (1926–)

"Tommy" Walls was Rhodesia's commander of combined operations from 1977 to 1980. He had previously served in both the British and Southern Rhodesian forces, establishing his reputation by commanding "C" (Rhodesian) Squadron of the Special Air Service (SAS) in the Malayan Emergency (1948–1960). Malaya taught Walls the value of long range penetration operations and the use of helicopters. He put this experience into practice in Rhodesia against Zimbabwe African People's Union (ZAPU) and Zimbabwe African National Union (ZANU) insurgents when he encouraged the formation of the Selous Scouts as a pseudoforce and the fire-force concept. However, Walls became so immersed in day-to-day operations that he failed to balance military with political considerations. Nonetheless, Walls subsequently proved a key figure in negotiations that led to the cease-fire in December 1979, and he declined to countenance a preemptive coup against the guerrillas. Walls briefly headed the new Zimbabwe Joint High Command but was dismissed in September 1980, retiring to South Africa.

See also: Fire force; Pseudoforces; Rhodesia; Selous Scouts; Zimbabwe African National Union (ZANU); Zimbabwe African People's Union (ZAPU)
Further Reading: Cilliers, J. K., *Counter-insurgency in Rhodesia* (London, 1985); Godwin, Peter, and Ian Hancock, *Rhodesians Never Die* (Oxford, 1993).

Western Sahara

The former Spanish Sahara was bitterly contested after Spanish withdrawal in 1975 by Morocco and the Popular Front for the Liberation of Saguiet el Hamra and Rio de Oro (POLISARIO). Saguiet el Hamra is the northern part of the territory, Rio de Oro the southern part. The two were separately designated by the Spanish in 1934 but then united as Spanish Sahara in 1958. Originally, the territory was claimed by Morocco and Mauritania and was partitioned between them in December 1975.

POLISARIO, which was supported by Algeria and Libya, proclaimed the existence of the Sahrawi Arab Democratic Republic in February 1976. Economic difficulties persuaded Mauritania to renounce its claim in July 1979, but fighting between the Moroccans and POLISARIO continued. Indeed, POLISARIO was recognized by the Organization of African Unity (OAU) in February 1982. A UN-sponsored cease-fire was brokered in 1989 and revived in September 1991, pending a referendum on self-determination. However, the referendum has not yet been held.

See also: Morocco; Popular Front for the Liberation of Saguiet el Hamra and Rio de Oro (POLISARIO)
Further Reading: Hodges, Tony, *Western Sahara: The Roots of a Desert War* (Westport, 1983).

Westmoreland, Gen. William Childs (1914–)

Westmoreland headed U.S. Military Assistance Command–Vietnam (MAC-V) from June 1964 to June 1968 and was the architect of the unsuccessful attritional strategy followed by the United States in the Vietnam War. The son of a textile-factory manager, Westmoreland was born in South Carolina and educated at The Citadel (Charleston's military college) and the U.S. Military Academy at West Point. Commissioned in the artillery in 1936, Westmoreland served in North Africa, Sicily, and northwest Europe during World War II, ending the war as a colonel and chief of staff of the Ninth U.S. Division. He commanded an airborne combat team during the Korean War (1950–1953), then held a

General William Westmoreland aims one of the over 600 weapons captured from the Vietcong during a search-and-destroy mission near Thai Thien in South Vietnam, 10 October 1967. (UPI/Corbis-Bettmann)

number of staff appointments before commanding the 101st Airborne Division from 1958 to 1960. Westmoreland was superintendent at West Point from 1960 to 1963 and briefly commanded XVIII Airborne Corps before going to Saigon in January 1964 as deputy to the head of MAC–V, Gen. Paul Harkins.

In taking over for Harkins, Westmoreland presided over the introduction of U.S. ground forces into South Vietnam in March 1965. There were undoubted difficulties in Westmoreland's position because of the lack of effective coordination in command arrangements. Westmoreland was responsible to both naval and military commanders in chief in the Pacific as well as the U.S. ambassador in Saigon; for its part, Washington would constantly interfere in the conduct of the war at all levels. Moreover, Westmoreland's authority did not extend to the U.S. Marine Corps, which had its own area of responsibility in South Vietnam, and he had no control over air operations conducted outside South Vietnam proper. In addition, he was unable to establish a joint U.S.-Vietnamese command due to South Vietnamese reluctance and a fear of creating the impression that the South Vietnamese administration was little more than an American puppet. U.S. civilian agencies also took an independent hand in the war. Westmoreland was not permitted to widen the conflict by taking the war into Laos and Cambodia as he wished.

Nonetheless, Westmoreland was responsible for the transformation of U.S. strategy shortly after the arrival of ground forces in March 1965. Originally, U.S. forces were to adopt an "enclave" strategy and merely protect the airfields from which the air offensive—"Operation Rolling Thunder"—was being conducted against North Vietnam. However, in May 1965 Westmoreland argued vigorously for a more active role in taking on the Vietcong (VC) main force units and those North Vietnamese army (NVA) units increasingly being detected in the south. The South Vietnamese army (ARVN), which was trained only for conventional operations, would be left to concentrate on pacification in the countryside. Such a wider role would allow U.S. firepower to be brought to bear on the "main force," or "big unit," war fought along the frontiers of South Vietnam. Indeed, Westmoreland remarked that "the answer to insurgency is firepower." It was also implicit that the Americans would wage an attritional strategy in the expectation that losses to the VC and NVA would be

so severe that communist leaders in Hanoi would give up the struggle. The new strategy assumed that Hanoi would not be prepared to bear whatever losses were required in order to subjugate the south and that superior technology and firepower could be made to count. Westmoreland's request for 275,000 men was approved on 28 July 1965.

By April 1967 Westmoreland was requesting a minimum of 550,000 men in order to finish the war within five years, or an optimum force of 670,000 to achieve victory within three years. The Johnson administration balked at providing more than 525,000 men; U.S. strength eventually reached 542,000 in January 1969. Losses were being inflicted on the communists, but infiltration continued unabated, and the VC and NVA continued to elude American efforts to "find, fix, and destroy" them. The large-scale communist Tet Offensive in January 1968 proved a significant military defeat for the VC and NVA, for it exposed them to the full force of American firepower. However, the image of a VC squad breaking into the U.S. embassy in Saigon shocked American audiences, whom Westmoreland had told the war was being won. Thus, his request for incremental troop increases totaling 206,000 was turned down, with an internal administration task force headed by a new secretary of defense, Clark Clifford, questioning whether the war could be won even with the additional forces.

Westmoreland had been notified in November 1967 that he was a likely candidate for army chief of staff, and his appointment was announced in March 1968, inevitably leading to the belief he was being "kicked upstairs" following the shocks of Tet. Westmoreland took up his new post in July 1968, retiring in 1972. Westmoreland remained highly defensive about his strategy, even suing the CBS broadcasting company over a disputed television documentary on the war shown in 1982.

See also: Tet Offensive; United States Army; Vietnam War
Further Reading: Westmoreland, William C., *A Soldier Reports* (2d ed., New York, 1989); Krepinevich, Andrew,

The Army and Vietnam (Baltimore, 1986); Benjamin, B., *Fair Play: CBS, General Westmoreland, and How a Television Documentary Went Wrong* (New York, 1988); Zaffiri, S., *Westmoreland* (New York, 1994).

Weyler, Gen. Valeriano, Marqués de Tenerife (1838–1930)

"Butcher" Weyler earned his nickname as the Spanish captain-general of Cuba between November 1896 and October 1897. Of German descent, Weyler had previously been captain-general of the Canary Islands (1878–1883), the Balearic Islands (1883), and the Philippines (1888) before succeeding Martinez Campos on Cuba. Weyler's solution to the Cuban insurrection was to revive a concept previously used on the island in the 1870s, constructing successive fortified lines (*trochas*) from west to east across the island. It was largely a defensive strategy, since a large proportion of Weyler's 196,000 men were always on the sick list, and his subordinates were inefficient. Indeed, Weyler rarely had more than 40,000 men available for field operations and therefore deployed small, mobile columns to comb the areas behind the lines.

Weyler also had to cope with large numbers of sick. At the same time, Weyler imposed resettlement on the population as well as a range of brutal control measures. Weyler was removed in October 1897 as a result of U.S. opposition to his policies. Ultimately, of course, the Americans intervened in Cuba during the Spanish-American War (1898). Weyler himself was Spanish minister of war from 1901 to 1905 and again in 1907, captain-general of Catalonia in 1909, and president of the Supreme War Council in 1910.

See also: Cuba; Resettlement; Spanish army
Further Reading: Payne, Stanley, *Politics and the Military in Modern Spain* (London, 1967).

Wingate, Maj. Gen. Orde Charles (1903–1944)

Wingate was a highly unconventional British officer who helped organize the Special Night Squads (SNS) during the Arab Revolt (1936–1939) in Palestine, then led the Chindits in deep-penetration raids behind Japanese lines in Burma during World War II.

The son of an army officer, Wingate was born in India and educated at Charterhouse and the Royal Military Academy at Woolwich. He was commissioned in the Royal Artillery in 1923 and served in the Sudan Defence Force from 1928 to 1933. As a captain, Wingate was sent to Palestine in 1936 and conceived the Special Night Squads (SNS) in 1938 as a means of protecting vital oil pipelines. Wingate had become a convinced Zionist, and the SNSs recruited from the Jewish population were the forerunners of the Jewish Agency's Palmach (Shock Companies). Promoted to major in 1940, Wingate next organized the so-called Gideon Force to harass the Italians in Ethiopia but suffered a nervous breakdown and even attempted suicide in July 1941.

Wingate's talents had been promoted in Palestine and Ethiopia by Gen. Sir Archibald Wavell, who saw to it that Wingate was made a colonel then brought to Burma in March 1942 to run a bush warfare school at Maymyo. Wingate conceived the concept of long-range penetration operations supplied from the air, and after the British were driven from Burma he was given command of the 77th Indian Infantry Brigade in July 1942 to put the idea into action. The 77th Brigade was committed to an attack on the Mandalay-to-Myitkyina railway line in February 1943. Of the 2,200 Chindits sent into Burma, more than 50 percent became casualties, but the raid was widely publicized, with a newspaper coining the name "Chindits" for Wingate's men after the lion statues outside Burmese temples.

Wingate had also caught the imagination of Prime Minister Winston Churchill. He received the temporary rank of major general in September 1943 and was given five brigades in order to carry out an even larger raid on Myitkyina in February 1944. Immense difficulties were encountered in flying the force into the jungle by gliders, and Wingate's expectation that his columns could hold jungle airstrips and operate for long periods almost as a conventional force proved erroneous. More than 3,600 men became casualties in the second Chindit expedition; Wingate himself was killed in an air crash on 24 March 1944. Wingate had proven that British forces could operate in jungle conditions.

See also: British army; Burma; Palestine; Palmach; Special Forces
Further Reading: Tulloch, D., *Wingate in Peace and War* (London, 1972); Keegan, John (ed.), *Churchill's Generals* (London, 1991).

Wintringham, Thomas Henry (1898–1949)

Tom Wintringham commanded the British battalion of the XV International Brigade fighting for the Republican cause during the Spanish Civil War (1936–1939), then wrote on guerrilla warfare techniques as a means of preparing the British Home Guard for resistance to possible German invasion during World War II.

A solicitor's son, Wintringham was educated at Gresham's School and Balliol College, Oxford. He served with the Royal Flying Corps and Royal Air Force during World War I. The Spanish Civil War was largely a conventional conflict, and the reputation and contribution of the International Brigades has been greatly exaggerated (although there is little doubt they routinely suffered heavy casualties). Nevertheless, Wintringham, who was employed as a military correspondent for *Picture Post* in 1939, had a good grasp of the fundamentals of guerrilla warfare. In May 1940 he made an instant connection between the Spanish militias and the British Local Defence Volunteers (later the Home Guard) and set up an unofficial training school in "ungentlemanly warfare" at Osterley Park, Middlesex. The essence of his course of instruction was published as *New Ways of Warfare*

(1940). Alarmed at the involvement of Wintringham and other Spanish Civil War veterans, the War Office took over Osterley Park in September 1940.

Finding himself sidelined, Wintringham resigned from Osterley Park in May 1941. However, his book remained on the Home Guard's official reading lists. Apart from *New Ways of Warfare*, Wintringham also wrote *Armies of Frogmen* (1940), *Politics of Victory* (1941), *People's War* (1942), *Weapons and Tactics* (1943), and *Your MP* (1945). A memoir of his Spanish experiences, *English Captain,* had appeared in 1939.

See also: Spanish Civil War
Further Reading: MacKenzie, S. P., *Revolutionary Armies in the Modern Era* (London, 1997); MacKenzie, S. P., *The Home Guard* (Oxford, 1995).

Wolseley, Field Marshal Viscount (Garnet Joseph) (1833–1913)

Wolseley was arguably the greatest British exponent of colonial warfare during the late nineteenth century. Indeed, his fame prompted Gilbert and Sullivan to celebrate him as the "very model of a modern major general" in their operetta *Pirates of Penzance;* the popular phrase "All Sir Garnet" signified that all was well.

The son of an impoverished army officer, the young Wolseley made his way in the army, at a time when most commissions were purchased, by dint of his courage in the Second Burma War (1852–1853), Crimean War (1854–1856), Indian Mutiny (1857), and Third China War (1860). Indeed, he was severely wounded twice, losing sight in his left eye in the Crimea. After only eight years' service, Wolseley received the brevet rank of lieutenant colonel. Serving in Canada, Wolseley observed the American Civil War (1861–1865), wrote *The Soldier's Pocket Book* (1869), and commanded the successful Red River Expedition (1870). His reputation was made through masterful conduct of the Second

Ashanti War (1873–1874), for which Wolseley also prepared the army's first real pamphlet on jungle tactics. He also gathered a group of loyal subordinates who became known as the Wolseley "ring," although his continued employment of the same officers aroused jealousy.

In 1875 Wolseley undertook a diplomatic mission to Natal, South Africa, and then led the occupation of Cyprus in 1878. In 1879 he was sent back to Natal to complete the Zulu War after early British failures. In 1880 he became quartermaster-general at the War Office, and in 1882 he became adjutant-general, although he was then sent to command the forces occupying Egypt. Wolseley's victory over the Egyptians at Tel-el-Kebir brought him a peerage and promotion to full general. He returned to Egypt in 1884 to rescue his old friend, Charles Gordon, besieged in Khartoum in the Sudan; Wolseley failed to reach Khartoum in time and never again commanded in the field. Raised in the peerage to a viscount in 1885, Wolseley became commander in chief in Ireland in 1890, then commander in chief of the British army in 1895 (Wolseley had been promoted to field marshal in 1894). Unfortunately, he was now suffering from ill health and found himself powerless to effect the reforms he had once advocated. His tenure was overshadowed by the early reverses suffered by the British in the Second Boer War (1899–1902), and he was succeeded as commander in chief in 1900 by his rival, Lord Roberts.

See also: Ashanti Wars; Boer War; British army; Burma; Colonial warfare; Cyprus; Manuals; Roberts, Field Marshal Earl (Frederick Sleigh)

Further Reading: Lehmann, Joseph, *The Model Major-General* (Boston, 1964).

Yugoslavia

The events in Yugoslavia during World War II are usually regarded as a classic example of partisan warfare. The Germans invaded Yugoslavia in April 1941 largely as an attempt to pacify the country and secure the flank of the forthcoming German invasion of the Soviet Union. However, Yugoslavia had some economic significance as a source of raw materials for the German war effort. Many Croats had welcomed the German invasion, and the fascist Ustashi regime was installed in Croatia. As German allies, Hungary and Bulgaria received parts of Yugoslavia, and the Italians occupied the Dalmatian Coast and Montenegro. Germany extended its own frontier (Austria having become part of Germany) and placed Serbia under military control.

However, resistance came from the royalist and Serbian nationalist Draza Mihailovic and the Yugoslavian Communist Party (CPY) of Josip Broz Tito. Ultimately, Mihailovic reached a tacit agreement with the Germans and Italians, for he regarded communism as the greater threat to Yugoslavia's future. The communist partisans therefore became the principal target for German and, to a lesser extent, Italian military actions. Indeed, there were seven major German offensives against Tito between November 1941 and May 1944. On occasions, the Germans came close to eliminating Tito despite the Germans' lack of equipment and the poor quality of many troops. They also largely succeeded in keeping Tito's forces out of Serbia until a joint offensive by Tito and the Soviet army took Belgrade in October 1944. The Germans' success came despite the loss of the Italians, whose surrender to the Western Allies in September 1943 had suddenly compelled the Germans to occupy much new territory. In fact, the Germans were not seriously inconvenienced in what they regarded as a secondary theater of operations.

See also: German army; Partisans; Tito, Marshal Josip Broz
Further Reading: Beckett, Ian (ed.), *The Roots of Counter-insurgency: Armies and Guerrilla Warfare, 1900–1945* (London, 1988); Kennedy, R. M., *German Antiguerrilla Operations in the Balkans, 1941–1945* (Washington, DC, 1954).

Zimbabwe African National Union (ZANU)

ZANU was one of the two nationalist guerrilla groups fighting for the independence of Rhodesia in the 1960s and 1970s. ZANU was founded in 1963 by the Rev. Ndabaningi Sithole in a split from Joshua Nkomo's Zimbabwe African People's Union (ZAPU). Whereas ZAPU appealed primarily to the minority Ndebele peoples of western Rhodesia, ZANU sought support among the majority Shona of eastern Rhodesia.

ZANU and its military wing, the Zimbabwe National Liberation Army (ZANLA), based itself in Mozambique after the Portuguese withdrawal in 1974. ZAPU remained based in Zambia and Botswana. ZANU also differed from ZAPU in being closer to Mao Tse-tung's principles of rural revolutionary guerrilla warfare, whereas ZAPU preferred to mass its forces for a Soviet-style conventional assault on Rhodesia at the appropriate moment. ZANU became increasingly radical, and Sithole found himself outmaneuvered by Robert Mugabe, who assumed the leadership after being released from detention in 1974. The period was marked by a number of internal upheavals in ZANU. Subsequently, Sithole was one of three African nationalists who participated in an internal settlement with the white government in March 1978. This paved the way for the establishment of the short-lived Zimbabwe-Rhodesia in June 1979, with Bishop Abel Muzorewa as prime minister.

Mugabe had forged the Patriotic Front with Nkomo in 1976, but ZANU posed the greater military threat to the Rhodesians, and ZANU would in fact win the British-supervised elections in February 1980. At the time of the cease-fire in December 1979, most of the 122,500 guerrillas estimated to be inside Rhodesia were from ZANLA, and there were an estimated 16,000 uncommitted ZANLA guerrillas outside Rhodesia. Mugabe has continued to lead Zimbabwe, with ZAPU eventually merging with ZANU in 1988 as a single party known as Zimbabwe African National Union–Patriotic Front (ZANU–PF).

See also: Mao Tse-tung; Mugabe, Robert Gabriel; Nkomo, Joshua; Rhodesia; Zimbabwe African People's Union (ZAPU)
Further Reading: Moorcraft, Paul, and Peter McLaughlin, *Chimurenga* (Marshalltown, 1982).

Zimbabwe African People's Union (ZAPU)

ZAPU was one of two nationalist movements fighting for the independence of Rhodesia in the 1960s and 1970s. ZAPU originated as the African National Congress (ANC), founded by the veteran nationalist Joshua Nkomo in 1957. Banned on a number of occasions, Nkomo's movement reemerged under different titles, becoming the National Democratic Party in 1960 and, finally, ZAPU in 1962. However, ZAPU's appeal was primarily among the minority Ndebele peoples of western Rhodesia, and there would be several splits from the movement. The Rev.

Ndabaningi Sithole broke away to form the Zimbabwe African National Union (ZANU) in 1963, and James Chikerema left to form the Front for the Liberation of Zimbabwe (FROLIZI) in 1972.

Chikerema's defection forced Nkomo to create a joint military command with ZANU, although it did not last for long; the subsequent Patriotic Front forged in 1976 with Robert Mugabe, who had ousted Sithole from the leadership of ZANU two years earlier, was never much more than a paper exercise. Subsequently, Sithole and Chikerema participated in an internal settlement with the white government in March 1978. Although ZANU operated from Mozambique after 1974, ZAPU and its military wing, the Zimbabwe People's Revolutionary Army (ZIPRA), was based in Zambia and Botswana.

Whereas ZANU followed the principles of Mao Tse-tung and waged rural revolutionary guerrilla warfare inside Rhodesia, Nkomo preferred to mass most of his guerrillas in Zambia in order to launch a Soviet-style conventional assault on Rhodesia at the appropriate moment. Thus, virtually all of ZIPRA's 22,000 guerrillas were outside Rhodesia at the time of the cease-fire in December 1979. ZANU won the subsequent British-supervised elections in February 1980. Nkomo served in Mugabe's cabinet but was dismissed in 1982. However, in 1988 ZAPU was merged into ZANU, and Nkomo returned to office as co–vice president in 1990.

See also: Mao Tse-tung; Mugabe, Robert Gabriel; Rhodesia; Zimbabwe African National Union (ZANU)
Further Reading: Moorcraft, Paul, and Peter McLaughlin, *Chimurenga* (Marshalltown, 1982).

Bibliography

Adams, A. E. *Bolsheviks in the Ukraine*. New Haven, 1963.

Akehurst, John. *We Won a War*. Salisbury, 1982.

Alexander, Don W. *Rod of Iron: French Counterinsurgency Policy in Aragon During the Peninsular War*. Wilmington, 1985.

Allen, W. E., and P. Muratoff. *Caucasian Battlefields*. Cambridge, 1953.

Anderson, John Lee. *Che Guevara: A Revolutionary Life*. New York, 1997.

Andrew, Christopher, and David Dilks, eds. *The Missing Dimension*. London, 1984.

Arthur, P., and Jeffery Keith. *Northern Ireland since 1969*. Oxford, 1988.

Asprey, Robert. *War in the Shadows*. London, 1976.

Auty, Phyllis. *Tito*. London, 1970.

Bass, Robert. *Swamp Fox*. New York, 1959.

Bass, Robert. *The Green Dragoon*. London, 1957.

Beckett, Ian. *Johnnie Gough, VC*. London, 1989.

Beckett, Ian, ed. *The Roots of Counter-insurgency: Armies and Guerrilla Warfare, 1900–1945*. London, 1988.

Beckett, Ian, and John Pimlott, eds. *Armed Forces and Modern Counter-insurgency*. London, 1985.

Begin, Menachem. *The Revolt*. London, 1951.

Belich, James. *The New Zealand Wars and the Victorian Interpretation of Racial Conflict*. Auckland, 1986.

Bell, J. Bowyer. *On Revolt*. Harvard, 1976.

Bell, J. Bowyer. *The Irish Troubles: A Generation of Violence, 1969–1992*. New York, 1993.

Bender, G. J. *Angola under the Portuguese*. London, 1978.

Benjamin, B. *Fair Play: CBS, General Westmoreland and How a Television Documentary Went Wrong*. New York, 1988.

Benson, M. *Nelson Mandela: The Man and the Movement*. New York, 1986.

Bergerud, Eric. *The Dynamics of Defeat*. Boulder, 1991.

Berman, Larry. *Planning a Tragedy*. New York, 1982.

Bigeard, Marcel. *Pour une parcelle de gloire*. Paris, 1975.

Blaufarb, D. S. *The Counter-insurgency Era*. New York, 1977.

Bolger, D. P. *Scenes from an Unfinished War*. Leavenworth, 1991.

Bond Brian, ed. *Victorian Military Campaigns*. London, 1967.

Bowden, Tom. *The Breakdown of Public Security*. London, 1977.

Braestrup, Peter. *Big Story*. New Haven, 1983.

Bridgeman, J. M., *The Revolt of the Hereros*. Los Angeles, 1981.

Brown, M., and J. Zasloff. *Apprentice Revolutionaries*. Stanford, 1986.

Budiarjo, C., and L. S. Liong. *The War Against East Timor*. London, 1984.

Butson, T. G. *The Tsar's Lieutenant, the Soviet Marshal*. New York, 1984.

Byrne, Hugh. *El Salvador's Civil War: A Study of Revolution*. Boulder, 1996.

Cable, Larry. *Conflict of Myths*. New York, 1986.

Cable, Larry. *Unholy Grail*. London, 1991.

Cabral, Amílcar. *Revolution in Guinea*. New York, 1969.

Callwell, Charles. *Small Wars: Their Principles and Practice*. London, 1896.

Cann, John. *Counterinsurgency in Africa: The Portuguese Way of War, 1961–1974*. Westport, 1997.

Carr, Raymond. *The Spanish Tragedy*. London, 1993.

Carruthers, Susan. *Winning Hearts and Minds*. London, 1995.

Carver, Michael. *Harding of Petherton*. London, 1978.

Chabal, Patrick. *Amílcar Cabral: Revolutionary Leadership and People's War*. Cambirdge, 1983.

Chandler, David. *Brother Number One*. Boulder, 1992.

Charters, David. *The British Army and Jewish Insurgency in Palestine, 1945–1947*. London, 1989.

Charters, David, and Maurice Tugwell, eds. *Armies in Low-intensity Conflict*. London, 1989.

Chinh, Truong. *Primer for Revolt*. New York, 1963.

Christian, Shirley. *Nicaragua: Revolution in the Family*. New York, 1985.

Cilliers, J. K. *Counter-insurgency in Rhodesia.* London, 1985.

Cincinnatus [C. B. Currey]. *Self-Destruction.* New York, 1981.

Clark, R. W. *Lenin: A Biography.* New York, 1987.

Clarke, T. *By Blood and Fire.* New York, 1981.

Clausewitz, Carl von. *On War.* Trans. Howard, Michael and Peter Paret. Princeton, 1976.

Clayton, Anthony. *Counter-insurgency in Kenya.* Manhattan, 1984.

Clayton, Anthony. *France, Soldiers and Africa.* London, 1988.

Clayton, Anthony. *The French Wars of Decolonisation.* London, 1994.

Cloake, John. *Templer: Tiger of Malaya.* London, 1985.

Clodfelter, Mark, *The Limits of Air Power: The American Bombing of North Vietnam.* New York, 1989.

Close, David H., *The Greek Civil War.* New York, 1993.

Clutterbuck, Richard. *Guerrillas and Terrorists.* London, 1977.

Clutterbuck, Richard. *Protest and the Urban Guerrilla.* London, 1973.

Clutterbuck, Richard. *The Long Long War.* London, 1966.

Coates, John. *Suppressing Insurgency.* Boulder, 1992.

Cobban, H. *The PLO.* Cambridge, 1984.

Coogan, Tim Pat. *The IRA: A History.* 11th ed., London, 1998.

Corbett Robin, ed. *Guerrilla Warfare.* London, 1986.

Corpus, Victor. *Silent War.* Manila, 1989.

Costeloe, M. P. *Response to Revolution: Imperial Spain and the Spanish American Revolutions, 1810–1840.* Cambridge, 1986.

Crawshaw, Nancy. *The Cyprus Revolt.* London, 1978.

Crowder, Michael. *West African Resistance.* London, 1971.

Cuneo, John. *Robert Rogers of the Rangers.* 2d ed., Ticonderoga, 1988.

Currey, C. B. *Edward Lansdale: The Unquiet American.* Boston, 1988.

Currey, C. B. *Victory at Any Cost.* New York, 1997.

Dalloz, Jacques. *The War in Indochina.* New York, 1990.

Davidson, Basil. *The People's Cause.* London, 1981.

Davidson, Phillip. *Vietnam at War.* Oxford, 1988.

Davis, Burke. *Marine!* Boston, 1966.

de Arriaga, Kaulza. *The Portuguese Answer.* London, 1973.

de Moor, J. A., and H. L. Wesseling, eds. *Imperialism and War: Essays on Colonial War in Asia and Africa.* Leiden, 1989.

de Spinola, Antonio, *Portugal and the Future.* Johannesburg, 1974.

Debray, Régis. *Revolution in the Revolution.* Harmondsworth, 1972.

Debray, Régis. *Strategy for Revolution.* Harmondsworth, 1973.

Dederer, J. M. *Making Bricks Without Straw: Nathanael Greene's Southern Campaign and Mao Tse-tung's Mobile War.* Manhatten, 1983.

Dewar, Michael. *Brush Fire Wars.* London, 1984.

Dewar, Michael. *The British Army in Northern Ireland.* London, 1985.

Dine, Philip. *Images of the Algerian War.* Oxford, 1994.

Duffy, Christopher. *The Military Experience in the Age of Reason.* London, 1987.

Duiker, W. J. *The Communist Road to Power in Vietnam.* Boulder, 1981.

Dunkerley, James. *The Long War: Dictatorship and Revolution in El Salvador.* London, 1982.

Dunn, Peter. *The First Vietnam War.* London, 1985.

Dupuy, R. E., and W. H. Baumer. *The Little Wars of the United States.* New York, 1968.

Eddy, Paul, Hugo Sabogal, and Sara Walden. *The Cocaine Wars.* London, 1988.

Edgerton, Robert. *Mau Mau: An African Crucible.* London, 1990.

Elliott, J. G. *The Frontier, 1839–1947.* London, 1968.

Ellis, John. *A Short History of Guerrilla Warfare.* London, 1975.

Ellis, John. *From the Barrel of a Gun.* Mechanicsburg, 1995.

Ellis, Stephen. *The Rising of the Red Shawls.* Cambridge, 1985.

Eyck, F. G. *Loyal Rebels: Andreas Hofer and the Tyrolean Uprising of 1809.* New York, 1986.

Fairbairn, Geoffrey. *Revolutionary Guerrilla Warfare: The Countryside Version.* Harmondsworth, 1974.

Fall, Bernard, *Hell in a Very Small Place.* London, 1966.

Fellman, Michael. *Inside War: The Guerrilla Conflict in Missouri during the American Civil War.* New York, 1989.

Finlay, M. *The Most Monstrous of Wars.* Charleston, 1994.

Foley, Christopher. *Island in Revolt.* London, 1962.

Foley, Christopher, ed. *The Memoirs of General Grivas.* London, 1964.

Foot, M. R. D. *Resistance.* London, 1976.

Foot, M. R. D. *SOE in France.* London, 1966.

Foot, M. R. D., ed. *War and Society.* London, 1973.

Ford, R. E. *Tet 1968: Understanding the Surprise.* London, 1995.

Fuller, S. M., and W. H. Cosmas. *Marines in the Dominican Republic, 1916–1924.* Washington, 1974.

Furedi, Frank. *The Mau Mau War in Perspective.* London, 1989.

Gall, Carlotta, and Thomas de Waal. *Chechnya: Calamity in the Caucasus.* New York, 1998.

Galula, David. *Counter-insurgency Warfare.* New York, 1964.

Gann, L. H. *The Guerrilla in History.* Stanford, 1971.

Gann, L. H., and T. H. Henriksken. *The Struggle for Zimbabwe.* New York, 1981.

Gardner, Brian. *German East.* London, 1963.

Gates, David. *The Spanish Ulcer.* London, 1986.

Gates, J. M. *Schoolbooks and Krags.* Westport, 1973.

George, Bruce. *The Burma Wars, 1824–1886.* London, 1973.

George, T. J. S. *Revolt in Mindanao: The Rise of Islam in Philippines Politics.* Singapore, 1980.

Geraghty, Tony, *Who Dares Wins: The Story of the Special Air Service.* London, 1980.

Gerassi, John, ed. *Venceremos!: The Speeches and Writings of Che Guevara.* London, 1968.

Geyer, Dietrich. *Russian Imperialism.* New Haven, 1987.

Giap, Vo Nguyen. *People's War, People's Army.* New York, 1962.

Gillespie, R. *Soldiers of Peron.* Oxford, 1982.

Girling, J. L. S. *People's War.* London, 1969.

Godwin, Peter, and Ian Hancock. *Rhodesians Never Die.* Oxford, 1993.

Gooch, John. *Army, State, and Society in Italy, 1870–1915.* London, 1989.

Gott, Richard. *Rural Guerrillas in Latin America.* 2d ed. Harmondsworth, 1973.

Gravel, Senator. *The Pentagon Papers.* Boston, 1971.

Greenberg, L. M. *The Hukbalahap Insurrection.* Washington, DC, 1987.

Griffith, Paddy. *Military Thought in the French Army, 1815–1851.* Manchester, 1989.

Griffith, Samuel, ed. *Mao Tse-tung on Guerrilla War.* New York, 1978.

Griffith, Samuel, ed. *Sun Tzu's Art of War.* Oxford, 1972.

Grivas, George. *Guerrilla Warfare.* London, 1964.

Guevara, Che. *Reminiscences of the Cuban Revolutionary War.* London, 1968.

Gwynn, Charles. *Imperial Policing.* London, 1934.

Hallin, Daniel. *The Uncensored War.* Oxford, 1986.

Hamill, Desmond. *Pig in the Middle.* London, 1985.

Hamilton, Donald. *The Art of Insurgency.* Westport, 1998.

Handel, Michael. *Masters of War.* London, 1992.

Harper, Stephen. *Last Sunset.* London, 1978.

Harris-Smith, R. *OSS.* Los Angeles, 1972.

Hastings, Max. *The Korean War.* London, 1987.

Haycock Ronald, ed. *Regular Armies and Insurgency.* London, 1979.

Heathcote, Tony. *The Afghan Wars, 1839–1919.* London, 1980.

Heggoy, A. A. *Insurgency and Counterinsurgency in Algeria.* Bloomington, 1972.

Heilbron, Otto. *Partisan Warfare.* London, 1962.

Heinl, R. D. *Soldiers of the Sea.* Baltimore, 1991.

Henderson, W. O. *The German Colonial Empire, 1884–1919.* London, 1993.

Henissart, Paul. *Wolves in the City.* London, 1970.

Henriksen, T. H. *Mozambique: A History.* London, 1978.

Henriksen, T. H. *Revolution and Counter-revolution: Mozambique's War for Independence, 1964–1974.* Westport, 1983.

Herring, George. *America's Longest War.* 2d ed. New York, 1986.

Hilsman, Roger. *American Guerrilla: My War Behind Japanese Lines.* New York, 1990.

Hilsman, Roger. *To Move a Nation.* New York, 1967.

Hodges, Tony. *Western Sahara: The Roots of a Desert War.* Westport, 1983.

Hoffman, Bruce. *The Failure of British Military Strategy in Palestine, 1939–1947.* Tel Aviv, 1983.

Hoffman, R., Thad Tate, and Peter Albert. *An Uncivil War.* Charlottesville, 1985.

Holland, Robert, ed. *Emergencies and Disorder in the European Empires after 1945.* London, 1994.

Holmes, Richard. *The Road to Sedan.* London, 1984.

Horne, Alistair. *A Savage War of Peace.* London, 1977.

Hossington, W. A. *Lyautey and the French Conquest of Morocco.* London, 1996.

Howard, Michael. *Clausewitz.* Oxford, 1983.

Howard, Michael. *The Franco-Prussian War.* London, 1961.

Hoyt, E. P. *Guerrilla.* New York, 1981.

Hughes, D. C., ed. *The Philosophy of the Urban Guerrilla: The Revolutionary Writings of Abraham Guillén.* New York, 1973.

Hunt, R. A. *Pacification.* Boulder, 1995.

Hutton, Paul. *Phil Sheridan and His Army.* Lincoln, 1985.

Hutton, Paul, ed. *The Custer Reader.* Lincoln, 1992.

Isby, David, *War in a Distant Country, Afghanistan: Invasion and Resistance.* London, 1989.

Jackson, K. D., ed. *Cambodia, 1975–1978: Rendezvous with Death.* Princeton, 1989.

Jacobs, W. D. *Frunze: The Soviet Clausewitz.* The Hague, 1969.

James, D., ed. *The Complete Bolivian Diaries of Che Guevara and Other Captured Documents.* London, 1968.

James, David. *The Life of Lord Roberts.* London, 1954.

James, H., and D. Sheil-Small. *The Undeclared War: The Story of the Indonesian Confrontation, 1962–1966.* London, 1971.

Jeapes, Tony. *SAS Secret War.* London, 1996.

Jeffery, Keith. *The British Army and the Crisis of Empire, 1918–1922.* Manchester, 1984.

Jones, V. C. *Grey Ghosts and Rebel Raiders.* New York, 1956.

Karnow, Stanley, *Vietnam: A History.* New York, 1983.

Katz, S. M. *Israeli Special Forces.* Osceola, 1993.

Keegan, John, ed. *Churchill's Generals.* London, 1991.

Kelly, G. A. *Lost Soldiers*. Cambridge, MA, 1965.

Kenez, P. *Civil War in South Russia*. Berkeley, 1971 and 1977), 2 vols.

Kennedy, R. M. *German Anti-guerrilla Operations in the Balkans, 1941–1945*. Washington, DC, 1954.

Kerkvliet, B. J. *The Huk Rebellion*. Berkeley, 1977.

Kessler, R. J. *Rebellion and Repression in the Philippines*. New Haven, 1989.

Kiernan, Ben. *How Pol Pot Came to Power*. New York, 1985.

Kiernan, Ben. *The Pol Pot Regime*. New Haven, 1996.

Killingray, David, and David Anderson, eds. *Policing and Decolonisation: Nationalism, Politics, and the Police, 1917–1965*. Manchester, 1992.

Kitson, Frank. *Bunch of Five*. London, 1977.

Kitson, Frank. *Gangs and Counter-gangs*. London, 1960.

Kitson, Frank. *Low Intensity Operations*. London, 1971.

Klare M. T., and P. Kornbluh, eds. *Low Intensity Warfare*. New York, 1988.

Kohl, J., and J. Litt. *Urban Guerrilla Warfare in Latin America*. Cambridge, MA, 1974.

Komer, Robert. *Bureaucracy at War*. Boulder, 1986.

Korngold, Ralph. *Citizen Toussaint*. 2d ed., Westport, 1979.

Krepinevich, Andrew. *The Army and Vietnam*. Baltimore, 1986.

Lacoutre, Jean. *Ho Chi Minh*. New York, 1968.

Langley, L. D. *The Banana Wars*. Lexington, 1985.

Lansdale, Edward. *In the Midst of Wars*. New York, 1972.

Laqueur, Walter. *Guerrilla: A Historical and Critical Study*. London, 1977.

Laqueur, Walter. *Terrorism*. London, 1977.

Laqueur, Walter. *The Age of Terrorism*. London, 1987.

Laqueur, Walter. *The Guerrilla Reader*. London, 1978.

Ledger, David. *Shifting Sands: The British in South Arabia*. London, 1983.

Lee, C. S. *Counterinsurgency in Manchuria: The Japanese Experience*. Santa Monica, 1967.

Lehmann, Joseph. *The Model Major-General*. Boston, 1964.

Levine, S. I. *Anvil of Victory: The Communist Revolution in Manchuria, 1945–1948*. New York, 1987.

Lewy, Gunther. *America in Vietnam*. New York, 1978.

Li, L. *The Japanese Army in North China, 1937–1941*. Tokyo, 1975.

Lincoln, W. Bruce. *Red Victory*. New York, 1989.

Linn, B. M. *Guardians of Empire: The U.S. Army and the Pacific, 1902–1940*. Chapel Hill, 1997.

Lloyd, Alan. *The Drums of Kumasi*. London, 1964.

Long, David. *The Anatomy of Terrorism*. New York, 1990.

Luttichau, C. P. von. *Guerrilla and Counter-guerrilla Warfare in Russia During World War II*. Washington, DC, 1963.

Macaulay, N. *The Sandino Affair*. Durham, 1985.

Mackay, James. *Michael Collins: A Life*. Edinburgh, 1996.

MacKenzie, S. P. *Revolutionary Armies in the Modern Era*. London, 1997.

MacKenzie, S. P. *The Home Guard*. Oxford, 1995.

Mackie, J. *Kronfrontasi*. Oxford, 1974.

Maclean, Fitzroy. *Tito*. London, 1980.

Maclear, Michael. *The Ten Thousand Day War*. London, 1981.

Magnus, Philip. *Kitchener: Portrait of an Imperialist*. London, 1958.

Mahon, John K. *The History of the Second Seminole War, 1835–1842*. Gainesville, 1967.

Majdalany, Fred. *State of Emergency: The Full Story of Mau Mau*. London, 1962.

Malet, M. *Nestor Makhno in the Russian Civil War*. London, 1982.

Manwaring Max, ed. *Uncomfortable Wars*. Boulder, 1991.

Mao Tse-tung. *Selected Military Writings*. Peking, 1967.

Marcum, John A., *The Angolan Revolution*. Cambridge, MA, 1969 and 1978), 2 vols.

Marighela, Carlos. *For the Liberation of Brazil*. Harmondsworth, 1971.

Marks, Tom. *Maoist Insurgency since Vietnam*. London, 1996.

Martin, M. L. *Warriors and Managers*. Durham, 1981.

Massu, Jacques. *La Vraie Bataille d'Alger*. Paris, 1971.

May, Glenn A. *Battle for Batangas*. New Haven, 1991.

McCuen, John J. *The Art of Counter-revolutionary War*. London, 1966.

McCulloch, J. *In the Twilight of the Revolution: The Political Theory of Amílcar Cabral*. London, 1983.

Meyer, M. C., and W. L. Sherman. *The Course of Mexican History*. Oxford, 1987.

Miller, S. C. *Benevolent Assimilation*. New Haven, 1982.

Milton, John. *The Edges of War: A History of Frontier Warfare, 1702–1878*. Cape Town, 1983.

Mitchell, Colin. *Having Been a Soldier*. London, 1969.

Mockaitis, Thomas. *British Counter-insurgency, 1919–1960*. London, 1990.

Mockaitis, Thomas. *British Counter-insurgency in the Post-imperial Era*. Manchester, 1995.

Mohan, Ram. *Sri Lanka: The Fractured Island*. Harmondsworth, 1989.

Mondlane, Eduardo. *The Struggle for Mozambique*. Harmondsworth, 1969.

Moorcraft, Paul, and Peter McLaughlin. *Chimurenga*. Marshalltown, 1982.

Moss, Robert. *Urban Guerrilla Warfare*. London, 1971.

Moss, Robert. *Urban Guerrillas*. London, 1972.

Moyar, Mark. *Phoenix and the Birds of Prey.* Annapolis, 1997.

Mugabe, Robert. *Our War of Liberation.* Gweru, 1983.

Munslow, B., ed. *Samora Machel, An African Revolutionary: Selected Speeches and Writings.* London, 1985.

Nalty, B. C. *The U.S. Marines in Nicaragua.* Washington, 1961.

Nasution, Abdul Haris. *Fundamentals of Guerrilla Warfare.* London, 1965.

Nevill, H. L. *North-West Frontier.* 2d ed. London, 1992.

Newitt, Marlyn. *A History of Mozambique.* London, 1995.

Newitt, Marlyn. *Portugal in Africa.* London, 1981.

O'Ballance, Edgar. *The Kurdish Revolt, 1961–1970.* London, 1973.

O'Neill, Bard. *Armed Struggle in Palestine.* Boulder, 1978.

O'Neill, Bard, W. R. Heaton, and D. J. Alberts, eds. *Insurgency in the Modern World.* Boulder, 1980.

O'Neill, Robert. *General Giap: Politician and Strategist.* New York, 1969.

Omissi, David. *Air Power and Colonial Control.* Manchester, 1990.

Oquist, Paul. *Violence, Conflict, and Politics in Colombia.* Berkeley, 1978.

Osterling, Jorge. *Democracy in Colombia: Clientelist Politics and Guerrilla Warfare.* New Brunswick, 1989.

Paddock, A. H. *U.S. Army Special Warfare: Irs Origins.* Washington, 1982.

Paget, Julian. *Counter-insurgency Campaigning.* London, 1967.

Paget, Julian. *Last Post: Aden, 1964–1967.* London, 1969.

Pakenham, Thomas. *The Boer War.* London, 1979.

Palmer, Bruce. *The Twenty-Five-Year War.* New York, 1990.

Palmer, David Scott, ed. *The Shining Path of Peru.* London, 1992.

Pardo-Maurer, R. *The Contras, 1980–1989: A Special Kind of Politics.* New York, 1990.

Paret, Peter. *French Revolutionary Warfare from Indochina to Algeria.* London, 1964.

Paret, Peter. *Internal War and Pacification.* Princeton, 1961.

Paret, Peter, ed. *Makers of Modern Strategy.* Princeton, 1986.

Payne, Stanley. *Politics and the Military in Modern Spain.* London, 1967.

Pike, Douglas. *A History of Vietnamese Communism.* Stanford, 1978.

Pike, Douglas. *Viet Cong.* Cambridge, MA, 1966.

Pimlott, John, ed. *British Military Operations, 1945–1984.* London, 1984.

Pimlott, John, ed. *Guerrilla Warfare.* London, 1985.

Pimlott, John, ed. *The Middle East Conflicts.* London, 1983.

Pocock, Tom. *Fighting General.* London, 1973.

Ponchaud, Francois. *Cambodia Year Zero.* New York 1978.

Pool, D. *Eritrea: Africa's Longest War.* London, 1982.

Porch, Douglas. *The Conquest of Morocco.* London, 1982.

Porch, Douglas. *The Conquest of the Sahara.* Oxford, 1986.

Porch, Douglas. *The French Foreign Legion.* New York, 1991.

Porch, Douglas. *The Portuguese Armed Forces and the Revolution.* London, 1977.

Porzecanski, A. C. *Uruguay's Tupamaros: The Urban Guerrilla.* New York, 1973.

Preston, Paul. *Franco: A Biography.* London, 1994.

Preston, Paul, ed. *Revolution and War in Spain, 1931–1939.* London, 1984.

Prucha, Francis. *The Sword of the Republic.* Toronto, 1969.

Pushtay, John. *Counterinsurgency Warfare.* New York, 1965.

Radkey, O. H. *The Unknown Civil War in Soviet Russia.* Stanford, 1976.

Reddaway, John. *Burdened with Cyprus.* London, 1986.

Reid-Daly, Ron, and Peter Stiff. *Selous Scouts: Top Secret War.* Cape Town, 1982.

Rich, Paul, and Richard Stubbs, eds. *The Counterinsurgent State.* London, 1997.

Ridley, Jasper, *Garibaldi.* New York, 1976.

Robinson, William, and Kent Norsworthy. *David and Goliath: Washington's War against Nicaragua.* London, 1987.

Roy, Jules. *The Battle of Dien Bien Phu.* London, 1965.

Roy, O. *Islam and Resistance in Afghanistan.* Cambridge, 1986.

Ryan, Tim, and Bill Parham. *The Colonial New Zealand Wars.* Wellington, 1986.

Sarkesian, Sam C. *America's Forgotten Wars.* Westport, 1984.

Sarkesian, Sam C. *Unconventional Conflicts in a New Security Era.* Westport, 1993.

Sarkesian, Sam C., ed. *Revolutionary Guerrilla Warfare.* Chicago, 1975.

Schaffer Ronald, ed. *The Small Wars Manual.* Reprint of 1940 ed. Manhattan, 1989.

Schmidt, H. R. *The U.S. Occupation of Haiti, 1915–1934.* Rutgers, 1971.

Schmitt, M. F., ed. *General George Crook: His Autobiography.* Norman, 1946.

Selser, G. *Sandino.* New York, 1981.

Shafer, D. M. *Deadly Paradigms.* Leicester, 1990.

Sherman, Richard. *Eritrea: The Unfinished Revolution.* New York, 1980.

Short, Anthony. *The Communist Insurrection in Malaya, 1948–1960.* London, 1975.

Shy, John. *A People Numerous and Armed.* 2d ed. Ann Arbor, 1990.

Simson, H. J. *British Rule and Rebellion.* London, 1937.

Smith, B. F. *The Shadow Warriors.* New York, 1983.

Smith, Martin. *Burma: Insurgency and the Politics of Ethnicity.* London, 1991.

Smithers, A. J. *The Kaffir Wars, 1779–1877.* London, 1973.

Smythe, D. *Guerrilla Warrior.* New York, 1973.

Soggot, D. *Namibia: The Violent Heritage.* New York, 1986.

Spies, S. B. *Methods of Barbarism?* Cape Town, 1977.

Steele, Ian. *Warpaths: Invasions of North America.* New York, 1994.

Stewart, A. T. Q. *The Pagoda War.* London, 1972.

Stubbs, Richard. *Hearts and Minds in Guerrilla Warfare.* Oxford, 1989.

Sullivan, A. T. *Thomas-Robert Bugeaud.* Hamden, 1983.

Sun Tzu. *The Art of War.* Oxford, 1963.

Swinson, Arthur. *North-West Frontier.* London, 1967.

Szuk, Tad. *Fidel: A Critical Portrait.* New York, 1986.

Taber, Robert. *The War of the Flea.* London, 1970.

Talbott, John. *The War Without a Name.* New York, 1980.

Tanham, George. *Communist Revolutionary Warfare.* Santa Monica, 1961.

Taruc, Luis. *He Who Rides the Tiger.* New York, 1967.

Taylor, Diana. *Disappearing Acts.* Durham, 1997.

Taylor, Peter. *Provos.* London, 1997.

Taylor, Rex. *Michael Collins.* London, 1970.

Thomas, Hugh. *The Cuban Revolution.* London, 1971.

Thompson, Robert. *Defeating Communist Insurgency.* London, 1966.

Thompson, Robert. *Make for the Hills: Memories of Far Eastern Wars.* London, 1989.

Thompson, Robert. *No Exit from Vietnam.* London, 1969.

Thompson, Robert. *Revolutionary War in World Strategy.* London, 1970.

Throup, David. *Economic and Social Origins of Mau Mau, 1945–1953.* London, 1987.

Thwaites, Peter. *Muscat Command.* London, 1995.

Tone, John L. *The Fatal Knot: The Guerrilla War in Navarre and the Defeat of Napoleon.* Chapel Hill, 1994.

Tønnesson, Stein. *The Vietnamese Revolution of 1945.* Oslo, 1991.

Towle, Philip. *Pilots and Rebels.* London, 1989.

Townshend, Charles. *Political Violence in Ireland: Government and Resistance since 1848.* Oxford, 1983.

Townshend, Charles. *Britain's Civil Wars.* London, 1986.

Townshend, Charles. *The British Campaign in Ireland, 1919–1921.* Oxford, 1975.

Toye, Hugo. *Laos: Buffer State or Battleground.* Oxford, 1968.

Trinquier, Roger. *Modern Warfare: A French View of Counterinsurgency.* New York, 1963.

Tulloch, D. *Wingate in Peace and War.* London, 1972.

Urban, Mark. *Big Boys' Rules.* London, 1992.

Utley, Robert. *Frontier Regulars.* 2d ed. Bloomington, 1977.

Utley, Robert. *The Indian Frontier of the American West, 1846–1890.* Albuquerque, 1984.

Valentine, D. *The Phoenix Program.* New York, 1990.

Valeriano, N. D., and C. T. R. Bohannan. *Counterguerrilla Operations: The Philippines Experience.* New York, 1962.

Vandiver, Frank. *Black Jack.* College Station, 1973, 2 vols.

Walton, George. *Fearless and Free.* Indianapolis, 1977.

Warwick, Peter, ed. *The South African War.* London, 1980.

Weber, H. *Nicaragua: The Sandinista Revolution.* London, 1981.

Weigley, Russell. *The Partisan War.* Columbia, 1970.

Westmoreland, William C. *A Soldier Reports.* 2d ed., New York, 1989.

Whittam, John. *The Politics of the Italian Army.* Hamden, 1977.

Wilkinson, Paul. *Terrorism and the Liberal State.* London, 1986.

Wilson, Dick. *China's Revolutionary War.* New York, 1991.

Wilson, Jeremy. *Lawrence of Arabia: The Authorised Biography.* London, 1989.

Windrich, Elaine. *The Cold War Guerrilla.* Westport, 1992.

Wintle, Justin. *The Vietnam Wars.* London, 1991.

Wirtz, J. T. *The Tet Offensive.* New York, 1991.

Woolman, David. *Rebels in the Rif.* London, 1969.

Young, Crawford, and Thomas Turner. *The Rise and Decline of the Zairean State.* Madison, 1986.

Young, Kenneth Ray. *The General's General.* Boulder, 1996.

Young, Peter, ed. *Defence and the Media in Time of Limited War.* London, 1991.

Zadka, Saul. *Blood in Zion.* London, 1995.

Zaffiri, S. *Westmoreland.* New York, 1994.

Chronology

1755   *May* Defeat of Braddock by the French and Native Americans on the Mononghela

1759   *October* Robert Rogers raids the St. Francis native village

1775   *April:* Start of the American War of Independence

1781   *January* Battle of Cowpens
October The British surrender at Yorktown

1783   *September* End of the American War of Independence

1791   *November* Defeat of St. Clair by Miamis on the Wabash

1793   *February* Start of the Vendéan Revolt in France

1792   *December* Start of the French Revolutionary and Napoleonic Wars

1794   *August* Defeat of the Miamis in Battle of Fallen Timbers

1796   *July* End of the Vendéan Revolt in France

1808   *May* French occupation of Spain

1809   *April* Start of the Tyrolean Revolt led by Andreas Hofer against the French

1810   *February* Execution of Andreas Hofer by French

1814   *February* The French are expelled from Spain

1815   *June* Final defeat of French Emperor Napoleon

1823   *September* Start of the First Burma War

1824   *January* First Ashanti War

1826   *February* End of the First Burma War

1830   *June* Start of the French conquest of Algeria

1835   *December* Start of the Second Seminole War

1838   *December* Start of the First Afghan War
August End of the Second Seminole War

1842   *December* End of the First Afghan War

1844   *August* Abd el-Kader is defeated by the French at Isly, Algeria

1845   *May* Start of the First Maori War

1846   *January* End of the First Maori War

1847   *December* Abd el-Kader surrenders to the French in Algeria

1852   *April* Start of the Second Burma War

1853   *January* End of the Second Burma War

1854   *August* First clash between U.S. troops and Lakota Sioux

1855   *December* Start of the Third Seminole War

1858   *May* End of the Third Seminole War

1860   *March* Start of the Second Maori War
November End of the Second Maori War

1861   *April* Start of the American Civil War

1863   *April* French Foreign Legion in action at Camerone in Mexico
Start of the Third Maori War

1865   *April* End of the American Civil War

1866   *December* The Fetterman Massacre

1870   *January* Massacre of Piegan village on Marias River by Eugene Baker

1872   *May* End of the Third Maori War

1873   *June* Start of the Second Ashanti War

1874   End of the Second Ashanti War

1876   *June* Custer's Last Stand on the Little Big Horn

1878   *November* Start of the Second Afghan War

1880   *December* Start of First Boer War

1881   *April* End of the Second Afghan War
August End of the First Boer War

1885   *October* Start of the Third Burma War

1889   *November* End of the Third Burma War

1890   *December* Last engagement of the American Indian Wars at Wounded Knee

1894   *December* Start of the French conquest of Madagascar

1895   *December* Start of the Third Ashanti War

1896   *January* End of the Third Ashanti War
February Appointment of Valeriano Weyler as captain-general of Cuba
March Defeat of Italians at Battle of Adowa in Abyssinia
April Red Shawls Revolt on Madagascar
August Filipinos revolt against Spain
October Removal of Weyler from Cuba

1898   *April* Start of the Spanish-American War

1899   *February* Start of the insurgency against U.S. forces in the Philippines
October Start of the Second Boer War

1902   *May* End of the Second Boer War

May End of the insurgency in the Philippines
October Revolt of the "Mad Mullah" against the British in Somaliland

1903   *August* Attempted Internal Macedonian Revolutionary Organization insurrection against Turkey in Macedonia

1904   *January* Start of the Herero Revolt in German South-west Africa

1905   *July* Start of the Maji Maji Rising in German East Africa

1906   *December* End of the Herero Revolt

1907   *January* End of the Maji Maji Rising

1912   *March* The French establish a protectorate over Morocco

1914   *August* Start of the First World War

1915   *July* U.S. Marines intervene in Haiti

1916   *March* Pancho Villa raids Columbus, New Mexico
June Start of the Arab Revolt against Turkey in Palestine
November U.S. Marines intervene in the Dominican Republic

1917   *November* Start of the Russian Civil War

1918   *January* Start of the Basmachi Revolt against Bolsheviks in Turkestan
November End of the First World War

1919   *January* Start of the Anglo-Irish War
May Third Afghan War

1920   *January* Defeat of the "Mad Mullah" in Somaliland
June Start of the Iraq Revolt against the British
August Start of the Antonov Revolt against Bolsheviks in Tambov
October End of the Iraq Revolt

1921   *June* End of the Anglo-Irish War
July Defeat of the Spanish by the Rifs at the Battle of Anual in Spanish Morocco
August Nestor Makhno flees from the Bolsheviks in the Ukraine
August Start of the Moplah Rebellion in India

1922   *February* End of the Moplah Rebellion in India
June Death of Antonov in the Tambov
August Michael Collins killed in an ambush during the Irish Civil War

1924   *September* U.S. Marines withdrawn from the Dominican Republic

1926   *May* Rif leader Abd el-Krim surrenders to the French

1927   *April* Start of the Chinese Civil War
July Start of Sandino's campaign against U.S. Marines in Nicaragua

1931   *September* Japanese invasion of Manchuria

1933   *January* Withdrawal of U.S. Marines from Nicaragua
October End of the Basmachi Revolt

1934   *February* Execution of Sandino in Nicaragua
August U.S. Marines withdrawn from Haiti

October Start of the Chinese communists' "Long March"

1936   *June* Start of the Arab Revolt against the British in Palestine
July Start of the Spanish Civil War

1937   *July* Start of the Japanese attempt to conquer China

1939   *March* End of the Spanish Civil War
September Start of the Second World War

1940   *July* Formation of the Special Operations Executive
August Communists' "Campaign of a Hundred Regiments" against the Japanese in China

1941   *April* German invasion of Yugoslavia
May Establishment of the Vietminh in Vietnam
June German invasion of Russia
December Japanese attack on Pearl Harbor
December The First Partisan Brigade formed by Tito in Yugoslavia

1942   *March* Establishment of the Hukbalahap in the Philippines
June Creation of the Office of Strategic Services
October Appointment of Bach-Zelewski as German chief of anti-bandit warfare in Russia

1943   *February* Start of the first "Chindit" operation against the Japanese in Burma

1944   *March* Start of second "Chindit" operation in Burma

1944   *October* Tito enters Belgrade in Yugoslavia
December Creation of the first Vietminh military units

1945   *April* Surrender of Germany
May The Sétif Uprising against the French in Algeria
September Surrender of Japan
Ho Chi Minh proclaims the Democratic Republic of Vietnam
October Start of the Jewish campaign against the British in Palestine

1946   *May* Start of the Huk insurgency in the Philippines
July Bombing of the King David Hotel in Jerusalem by Irgun
November Start of the First Vietnam War against the French
December Start of the Greek Civil War

1947   *March* Start of the Malagasy Revolt on Madagascar
June Start of the Dutch "police action" on Java in the Dutch East Indies

1948   *May* Independence of Israel
June Start of the Malayan Emergency

1949   *January* Start of the Karen Revolt in Burma
February End of the Malagasy Revolt on Madagascar
October Proclamation of the Chinese People's Republic by Mao Tse-tung
Cease-fire in the Greek Civil War
December Independence for Indonesia

1950 *April* Appointment of Harold Briggs as director of operations in Malaya
June Start of the Korean War
September Magsaysay becomes secretary of national defense in the Philippines
1952 *February* Sir Gerald Templer appointed high commissioner in Malaya
June Revival of the U.S. Special Forces (Green Berets)
October Start of the emergency in Kenya
1953 *June* Armistice in Korea
November The French seize Dien Bien Phu
1954 *May* Surrender of the French at Dien Bien Phu
End of the First Vietnam War
Surrender of the Huk leader Luis Taruc in the Philippines
July Agreement in Geneva for French withdrawal from Indochina
November Start of the Algerian War
1955 *November* Start of the emergency on Cyprus
1956 *December* Start of Castro's campaign on Cuba
1957 *January* Start of the Battle of Algiers
August Independence of Malaya
September End of the Battle of Algiers
September Completion of the Morice Line in Algeria
1958 *December* EOKA cease-fire on Cyprus
1959 *January* Castro's victory on Cuba
1960 *January* End of the emergency in Kenya
July End of the emergency in Malaya
December Creation of the Vietcong
1961 *January* Start of the war in Angola
April Attempted French army coup in Algiers
July Formation of the Sandinistas in Nicaragua
September Start of the Kurdish Revolt in Iraq
The British Advisory Mission arrives in South Vietnam
December Establishment of the first CIDG in South Vietnam
1962 *March* First strategic hamlets are constructed in South Vietnam
July Independence of Algeria
November Ethiopian annexation of Eritrea
December Start of the Indonesian/Malaysian Confrontation
1963 *January* Start of the FALN campaign in Venezuela
Start of the PAIGC campaign in Portuguese Guinea
December Beginning of the emergency in Aden
1964 *August* The Gulf of Tonkin incident
September Start of FRELIMO campaign in Mozambique
1965 *February* Start of U.S. bombing of North Vietnam
March Withdrawal of British Advisory Mission from South Vietnam

March U.S. ground forces arrive in South Vietnam
June Start of the insurgency in Dhofar Province of Oman
August Start of communist insurgency in Thailand
November Rhodesia unilaterally declares independence from Britain
1966 *August* End of the Indonesian/Malaysian Confrontation
August Start of the SWAPO campaign in Namibia
November Arrival of Che Guevara in Bolivia
December First armed clash between police and Tupamaros in Uruguay
1967 *April* Construction of McNamara Line starts in South Vietnam
May Establishment of CORDS in South Vietnam
June Start of the Phoenix program in South Vietnam
October Che Guevera killed in Bolivia
November British withdrawal from Aden
1968 *January* Start of communists' Tet Offensive in South Vietnam
October Cessation of U.S. bombing of North Vietnam
1969 *January* South Vietnam peace talks open in Paris
February Assassination of Eduardo Mondlane of FRELIMO
August Start of "the Troubles" in Northern Ireland
September Death of Ho Chi Minh
November Death of Carlos Marighela in a gun battle in Brazil
1970 *April* U.S. incursion into Cambodia
July Sultan Qaboos seizes power in Oman
1971 *August* Introduction of internment in Northern Ireland
1972 *March* Imposition of British direct rule in Northern Ireland
April U.S. resumes bombing of North Vietnam
September Imposition of martial law in the Philippines
December ZANU opens a new "front" in Rhodesia
1973 *January* Assassination of Amílcar Cabral of PAIGC
Cease-fire in South Vietnam
March U.S. forces leave South Vietnam
November Selous Scouts raised in Rhodesia
1974 *April* Military coup in Portugal
September Independence of Guinea-Bissau
1975 *April* Fall of Phnom Penh in Cambodia to the Khmer Rouge
April Fall of Saigon in South Vietnam to North Vietnamese
June Independence of Mozambique
June Fall of Vientiane in Laos to Pathet Lao
November Independence of Angola
November Indonesian invasion of East Timor
December End of the Dhofar campaign
December Partition of Western Sahara by Morocco and Mauritania

1976 *February* POLISARIO proclaims a republic in Western Sahara
March South African withdrawal from Angola
March Start of the dirty war in Argentina
April Founding of M-19 in Colombia
1978 *March* Internal settlement in Rhodesia
December Vietnamese invasion of Kampuchea
1979 *July* Overthrow of the Somoza dynasty by the Sandinistas in Nicaragua
December Soviet intervention in Afghanistan
December Cease-fire in Rhodesia
1980 *April* Independence for Zimbabwe
May Surrender of the Karen leader Mahn Ba Zan in Burma
1986 *October* Samora Machel of FRELIMO killed in an aircrash
1987 *August* Indian intervention in Sri Lanka
1989 *February* Soviet withdrawal from Afghanistan
Vietnamese withdrawal from Kampuchea
December Surrender of the Malayan communist leader Chin Peng
1990 *February* Electoral defeat of the Sandinistas in Nicaragua
March Independence for Namibia

March Indian withdrawal from Sri Lanka
March M-19 signs peace accord in Colombia
September Supreme National Council formed in Cambodia
1991 *May* Tamil Tigers assassinate Rajiv Gandhi, former Indian prime minister
September Cease-fire in Western Sahara
November Chechnya declares independence from Russian federation
1992 *January* Elections cancelled in Algeria
September Arrest of Abimael Guzmán of the Shining Path in Peru
1993 *May* Independence for Eritrea
1996 *August* Peace agreement in Chechnya
September The Taleban takes Kabul in Afghanistan
1997 *April* Government of National Unity and Reconciliation formed in Angola
May Laurent Kabila comes to power in Zaire
July Military coup in Cambodia
July Pol Pot is sentenced to life imprisonment by the Khmer Rouge
Provisional IRA cease-fire in Northern Ireland
1998 *April* Agreement in Northern Ireland
April Pol Pot dies in Cambodia

Index